CHOICE OVER TIME

CHOICE OVER TIME

·

Edited by

GEORGE LOEWENSTEIN AND JON ELSTER

RUSSELL SAGE FOUNDATION   NEW YORK

The Russell Sage Foundation

The Russell Sage Foundation, one of the oldest of America's general purpose foundations, was established in 1907 by Mrs. Margaret Olivia Sage for "the improvement of social and living conditions in the United States." The Foundation seeks to fulfill this mandate by fostering the development and dissemination of knowledge about the political, social, and economic problems of America.

The Board of Trustees is responsible for oversight and the general policies of the Foundation, while administrative direction of the program and staff is vested in the President, assisted by the officers and staff. The President bears final responsibility for the decision to publish a manuscript as a Russell Sage Foundation book. In reaching a judgment on the competence, accuracy, and objectivity of each study, the President is advised by the staff and selected expert readers. The conclusions and interpretations in Russell Sage Foundation publications are those of the authors and not of the Foundation, its Trustees, or its staff. Publication by the Foundation, therefore, does not imply endorsement of the contents of the study.

Library of Congress Cataloging-in-Publication Data

Choice over time/[edited by] George Loewenstein, Jon Elster.
   p. cm.
   Includes bibliographical references and index.
   ISBN 0-87154-558-6
   1. Choice (Psychology) 2. Utility theory. 3. Self-control.
  4. Time—Psychological aspects. I. Loewenstein, George.
II. Elster, Jon, 1940–
BF611.C48 1992
153.8'3—dc20   91-42816
                                                  CIP

The paper used in this publication meets the minimum requirements of American National Standard for Information Sciences—Permanence of Paper for Printed Library Materials, ANSI Z39.48-1984.

RUSSELL SAGE FOUNDATION
112 East 64th Street, New York, New York 10021

10 9 8 7 6 5 4 3 2 1

Contents

Contributors

George Ainslie Psychologist, Veterans Administration Medical Center and Thomas Jefferson Medical College, Coatesville, PA

Gary S. Becker Professor of Economics and Sociology, University of Chicago

Jon Elster Professor of Political Science, University of Chicago

Robert H. Frank Professor of Economics, Ethics, and Public Policy, Cornell University

Michael Grossman Professor of Political Science, Towson State University

Nick Haslam Graduate Student, University of Pennsylvania

Richard J. Herrnstein Professor of Psychology, Harvard University

George Loewenstein Professor of Economics, Carnegie-Mellon University

Walter Mischel Professor of Psychology, Columbia University

Kevin M. Murphy Professor of Economics, University of Chicago

Drazen Prelec Professor of Management Sciences, MIT

Howard Rachlin Professor of Psychology, State University of New York, Stony Brook

Andres Raineri Graduate Student, State University of New York, Stony Brook

Monica L. Rodriguez   Professor of Psychology, State University of New York, Albany

Thomas Schelling   Professor of Political Economy, John F. Kennedy School of Government, Harvard University

Hersh M. Shefrin   Professor of Economics, Santa Clara University

Yuichi Shoda   Associate Research Scientist, Columbia University

Richard H. Thaler   Professor of Economics, Johnson Graduate School of Management, Cornell University

Preface

Daily life requires frequent trade-offs between costs and benefits that occur at different points in time. To sleep late or rise early, munch snacks or eat a healthy lunch, buy the snazzy sports car or the reliable sedan, get a job or go to college, risk pregnancy or use a contraceptive—these and many other decisions require us to weigh consequences that are distributed over time. How they are resolved is the central focus of this book. In it, we explore the psychological processes underlying intertemporal choice, propose formal models of these processes, and apply the models to various social problems.

Choice Over Time is the product of a group that met annually for four years to discuss intertemporal choice. Brought together under the auspices of the Russell Sage Foundation's program on behavioral economics, scholars from diverse disciplines presented their own perspectives, listened skeptically as others did the same, discussed empirical findings, and debated interpretations of those findings. Because these discussions revolved around the axis of behavioral economics, much of the book that emerged from them is devoted to a critique of the current economic approach to modeling intertemporal choice. The dominant model of intertemporal choice employed by economists—the discounted utility model (DU)—provides an implicit (and sometimes explicit) benchmark against which many of the authors contrast their contributions. The reader who is unfamiliar with DU will find a brief description of the model in Chapter 1, and an in-depth analysis of its assumptions and implications in Chapter 5.

Despite their extensive use of DU, economists do not have a strong intellectual commitment to the model. This ambivalence stems from two sources. First, few economists versed in the details of intertemporal choice are comfortable with DU's behavioral assumptions. Indeed, Samuelson, who first proposed the model in 1938, commented that several features of the model were "completely arbitrary" (see Chapter 1). Koopmans (1960) who proposed a set of axioms consistent with the model, enumerated serious objections to all of the important ones. Thus, DU is flawed both as a descriptive and normative model.

Second, and perhaps more importantly, the conventional discounting model does a very poor job of predicting or explaining behavior. When scrutinized through the lens of DU, intertemporal choices observed in practice appear hopelessly inconsistent. Examples of behavior at the extremes of high, low, and even negative time discounting are easy to identify, not only across different persons (which the model can accommodate), but also in the behavior of a single person. For example, when purchasing energy-consuming appliances or insulating their houses, people display extreme temporal myopia, underinvesting in efficiency to a degree that implies discount rates in the hundreds of percents. At the same time, however, many of these people visit the dentist regularly, eat nutritious but bland breakfast foods, and manage to finance comfortable retirements. These behaviors are difficult to reconcile with an economic perspective which assumes that each person has a single discount rate representing his or her attitude toward the future.

The same apparent inconsistency can be observed at a societal level. We construct shoddy highways, refuse to switch to the metric system, even type on a keyboard that was designed to slow the typist down to a rate that 19th-century typewriters could accommodate. But we also invest in basic research whose payoff is remote and eschew nuclear waste disposal sites because they may cause problems centuries hence. While the mechanisms that drive discounting behavior at the individual and societal levels are different, both domains display great variance in apparent concern for the future.

The elegance of the economic approach inheres in its simplicity; its main drawback is its low congruence with reality. The psychological perspectives presented here, on the other hand, offer not one, but several models, each of which captures a critical dimension of real human behavior. It is our hope that bringing these contributions together in one volume will help to spawn a synthesis that incorporates the advantages of each approach.

The book consists of five parts. The first examines historical perspectives on intertemporal choice, focusing specifically on the causes of time discounting and the relationship between social organization and individual time discounting. The second part offers a variety of contemporary perspectives on intertemporal choice by authors who span a broad spectrum of disciplines and subdisciplines: psychiatry, behavioral psychology, social psychology, and behavioral decision theory. The third part examines several multiple-self models that apply game-theoretic reasoning to the analysis of intrapersonal conflict and self-control. The fourth part focuses on internalities in intertemporal choice—situations in which actions at one point in time affect utility or tastes at other points. The fifth part applies insights from the previous parts to a variety of real world problems: savings behavior, addiction, and wage-setting practices.

Part One: Historical Overview

In Part One, two chapters provide historical overviews of different aspects of intertemporal choice. Chapter 1, "The Fall and Rise of Psychological Explanations in the Economics of Intertemporal Choice" by Loewenstein, examines the evolution of economists' answers to the fundamental question of why people discount the future.

One can draw a parallel between 17th century speculation over man's natural state—his nature in the "state of nature"—and the ruminations of 19th-century economists about man's baseline or "natural" time discounting. One school of thought, exemplified by the contributions of W.S. Jevons, insisted that the natural human tendency is to ignore the future. The other, first propounded by N.W. Senior, assumed that equal treatment of present and future was natural. These contrary assumptions led to two very different explanations of time discounting.

To explain why people took account of the future at all, the "myopia" school pointed to the existence of emotions experienced in the present but associated with the anticipation of future pleasures and pains. Such emotions were thought to give the future an immediate impact, overcoming what would otherwise be a total preoccupation with the present. In this view, discounting occurred due to the relative weakness of such emotions and from an inability to imagine the future in vivid and accurate detail. Those 19th-century economists who assumed that human beings weighted present and future equally, on the other hand, argued that the temptation of immediate consumption distorted people's natural inclinations toward such a balanced treatment of the present and future.

Far from being just of antiquarian interest, the question of whether time discounting derives from the temptations of the moment, or from the inadequate motivational force of the future, continues to guide current investigations. In considering emotions associated with anticipation, several contributions in Part Four of this book revive the "myopic" perspective. Contributions in Part Two, in contrast, continue the effort to show how the lure of immediate consumption can produce extremes of shortsightedness. Part Three, on self-control, considers the tactics that people use to resist such temptations.

In "Intertemporal Choice and Political Thought," Elster positions intertemporal choice in the social arena. Anticipating the discussion of self-control tactics contained in the third part of the book, Elster shows that provisions which make it difficult for democracies to amend their constitutions act as a political self-control device. In the same way that individuals learn rules such as "count to ten before responding," such measures protect legislatures from overreacting to momentary passions. Elster also provides an introduction to the contributions of Tocqueville on the question of how civic culture and individual time preference influence one another. He identifies two mechanisms through which political institutions influence individual time discounting. The "spill-over" effect refers to situations in which farsighted public institutions exert a demonstrational or learning effect, inducing a comparable perspective at the individual level. The "displacement effect," on the other hand, refers to situations in which the government fulfills needs relating to the future, leaving individuals free to pursue more short-term goals. De Tocqueville's view was not, however, a simple one in which government influenced individual time preferences. Instead, as Elster documents, he envisioned a complex interaction between the civic, religious, and familial spheres of activity.

Part Two: General Perspectives

In Part Two, four contributions offer an overview of contemporary psychological research on intertemporal choice. The first two of these focus specifically on the shape of the discount function, which specifies the relationship between the time at which an object will be received, and its present subjective value. Both "Hyperbolic Discounting" by Ainslie and Haslam, and "Irrationality, Impulsiveness, and Selfishness as Discount Reversal Effects," by Rachlin and Raineri examine the evidence for and implications of the observation that time discounting tends to follow a hyperbolic rather than exponential form. However, as discussed below, their perspectives differ on several critical points.

The discounted utility model assumes exponential discounting at a constant rate. This implies that a given time delay leads to the same degree of time discounting regardless of when it occurs. Under exponential discounting, a one-day delay has the same significance if it means deferring an outcome from today until tomorrow, or from one year from today to a year and a day from today. Thus, for example, a person who is indifferent to the choice between one apple today and two apples tomorrow should be indifferent to the choice between one apple in one year and two apples in a year and a day.[1]

As first noted by the economist Strotz (1955), exponential discount functions have the desirable property of implying that behavior will be consistent over time. For example, an exponential discounter who prefers an expensive French dinner in twelve months to a nice Chinese dinner in eleven, should also prefer the French dinner after six months have passed (and the Chinese dinner is five months away and the French dinner six), and should continue to prefer the French dinner even when the actual date for the Chinese dinner arrives. Nonexponential discounters, in contrast, are subject to a phenomenon Strotz called "time inconsistency"; their preferences change systematically with the passage of time.

The hyperbolic discount curves discussed in chapters 3 through 5 produce a particular form of time inconsistency. When faced with a choice between an inferior early option and a superior later option, hyperbolic discounters will tend to prefer the later, superior, option when both are remote, but switch to a preference for the earlier, inferior, option as both approach in time. A hyperbolic discounter who preferred the French restaurant over the Chinese when the former was delayed by six months and the latter by five, would be likely to opt for the Chinese dinner when it became immediately available; under hyperbolic discounting, the Chinese dinner becomes disproportionately tempting when it is imminent but the French dinner is still a long month away.

Time inconsistent behavior is different from a high rate of time discounting per se. High time discounting signifies that outcomes experienced earlier are much more highly valued than outcomes experienced later. Time inconsistency, on the other hand, refers to changes in time discounting as a function of delay. A high rate of

[1] Example from Thaler (1981).

time discounting is possible without inconsistency, and vice versa. Indeed, as Elster and Loewenstein show in Chapter 9, examples of time inconsistency associated with negative time discounting are not uncommon—as illustrated by the behavior of misers who plan to splurge in the future, but inevitably fail to carry out the plan when the appointed time arrives.

Given the frequency with which hyperbolic discounting arises, it may be worthwhile to provide some historical background on the evolution of the idea. In the early 19th century, before the discounted utility model established exponential discounting as the hallmark of rationality, the notion of exponential discounting had no special status, and its significance for the consistency of behavior was not appreciated. Nonetheless, many 19th-century economists displayed an awareness of the nonconstancy of discounting. Jevons, for example, noted that:

> An event which is to happen a year hence affects us on the average about as much one day as another; but an event of importance, which is to take place three days hence will probably affect us on each of the intervening days more acutely than the last. (1871:34)

Böhm-Bawerk commented that:

> It is not true that the individual who undervalues a future utility that will mature in *one* year by 5% will necessarily undervalue one due in *two* years by 10% and one that is only three *months* off by exactly 1.25%. . . . We [may] look for a very marked difference in valuation as between momentary and nonmomentary satisfactions, but on the other hand very little or no difference at all as between moderately distant and remotely distant gratifications. (1889:272)

In fact, much earlier, Spinoza remarked on this phenomenon:

> We can only distinctly imagine distance of time, like that of space, up to a certain limit, that is just as those things which are beyond two hundred paces from us, or, whose distance from the place where we are exceeds that which we can distinctly imagine, we are wont to imagine equally distant from us and as if they were in the same plane, so also those objects whose time of existing we imagine to be distant from the present by a longer interval than that which we are accustomed to imagine, we imagine all to be equally distant from the present, and refer them all as it were to one moment of time. (1677:145)

The first empirical studies to demonstrate nonexponential discounting were conducted with animals, beginning with a study by

Chung and Herrnstein (1964). In Chung and Herrnstein's procedure, pigeons pecked two buttons, each of which occasionally produced food according to a prearranged schedule. A "successful" peck did not produce food immediately, but only after a brief delay, lasting on the order of several seconds. Chung and Herrnstein found that pigeons divided their choices between the two keys in inverse proportion to the ratio of delays imposed by the keys. In other words, if the delay on one key was twice as long as the delay on the other, the pigeon would peck twice as much on the latter alternative, all other things being equal. On the basis of this result, they concluded that the subjective value of a delayed reward is inversely related to the duration of the delay. The "biological" discount function, in other words, is the simple reciprocal function: $f(t) = 1/t$.

More recent animal studies, notably Mazur (1987) have slightly qualified this finding. Mazur presented pigeons with two delayed rewards of different magnitudes, and explored the combination of delay durations that made the animals indifferent between the two alternatives. Exponential discounting predicts that these matching delays should differ by a constant amount, while reciprocal discounting predicts that the delays should be in constant proportion. Mazur found that the relationship between the two delays was linear and located in between the two extremes of constant proportionality and constant difference. Such a relationship is consistent with the hyperbolic discount function, $f(t) = 1/(1 + kt)$, which had already been suggested by Herrnstein (1981). Indeed the most general discount function consistent with the observed linear indifference relations between delays for small and large rewards is the power hyperbola, $f(t) = (1 + at)^{-b/a}$ (see Chapter 5).

Richard Thaler (1981) was the first to document the effect with data from human subjects. His study also produced the first evidence of other choice patterns incompatible with DU, including higher discounting of gains than losses and higher discounting of small outcomes than large. Subsequently, many experiments (e.g., Benzion, Rapoport, and Yagil, 1989), including some using real money outcomes (e.g., Holcomb and Nelson, 1989), have replicated the finding of nonexponential time discounting in humans. (For a review of these findings see Chapter 5.)

Ainslie and Haslam, in the first chapter of this section, use hyperbolic discounting to explain a broad range of human behaviors—from the mundane (e.g., semi-voluntary scratching an itch) to the momentous (e.g., addictions). In their view, the hyperbolic discounting and the reversals of preference which it produces (e.g., from the French to the Chinese dinner) are a powerful motive force underlying human behavior. They believe that the lure of immediate self-gratification at every moment establishes competing interests within the individual that struggle between themselves for dominance (see also their Chapter 8). Most controversially, they argue that pain can be explained in terms of hyperbolic discounting—that the experience of pain results from a surrender to a momentary temptation.

Rachlin and Raineri, while also endorsing hyperbolic discounting, disagree with Ainslie and Haslam on several fundamental issues. First, hyperbolic discounting assumes far less prominence in their overall view of human behavior. They see time discounting as only one of a broad class of subjective phenomena that follow a hyperbolic pattern. These other phenomena include the discounting of uncertain rewards according to the probability of receiving them, which tends to overweight certain outcomes relative to uncertain outcomes in the same way that hyperbolic discounting overweights immediate outcomes. Forgetting also tends to assume a hyperbolic form—a regularity known as Jost's law in which recently assimilated information is more likely to be forgotten than information assimilated in the distant past. Similarly, the loudness of a sound, intensity of a light source, size of an object, and other stimulus dimensions vary hyperbolically as a function of the distance between the observer and the source. All of these phenomena can produce reversals similar to the preferential reversals observed in intertemporal choice. For example, when far away from a city, one can generally gauge accurately the relative heights of buildings. But when in its midst, buildings that are near tend to look taller than those which are far.

Rachlin and Raineri view hyperbolic discounting not only as only one of many related phenomena, but also see the reversals of preferences it implies as relatively rare. As a supportive analogy they point to the phenomenon of size constancy in perception. Even though the image formed on the retina of the eye grows hyperbolically as an object approaches, given appropriate visual cues, we are usually able to compensate and estimate the object's size without bias. In the same way, they argue, people can naturally overcome the effect of hyperbolic discounting and behave in a time-consistent manner.

Taking the analogy one step further, they contend, just as size constancy can be made to appear or disappear through appropriate provision of cues, seemingly minor situational variations can lead the decision-maker either to extreme myopia or farsightedness. Mischel, Shoda, and Rodriguez, for example, show that simply having someone wait in the presence of the immediate and deferred objects can significantly affect willingness to delay (see Chapter 6).

Ainslie and Haslam disagree on all of these points. They view time discounting as quite distinct from other subjective phenomena assuming a hyperbolic shape. And they disagree that human beings have the same effortless ability to overcome time inconsistency that they have in compensating for source distance when judging size, loudness, or intensity. Indeed, for these authors the *lack* of such an ability is a key feature, which distinguishes time discounting from these other effects.

The difference between Ainslie and Haslam, on the one hand, and Rachlin and Raineri, on the other, recalls the dispute among 19th-century economists about whether complete myopia or equal treatment of present and future was the norm, deviations from which needed to be explained. Ainslie and Haslam view time inconsistency as a pervasive problem only to be overcome through intricate and energetic efforts at self-control. For Rachlin and Raineri, however, it is an aberrant behavior that people display only when normal cues are absent. The specifics have changed, but debate continues to revolve around the question of the natural form of time discounting.

Chapter 5, "Anomalies in Intertemporal Choice: Evidence and an Interpretation," by Loewenstein and Prelec, criticizes the discounted utility model. They enumerate a series of intertemporal choice anomalies—common patterns of behavior that are inconsistent with DU—that are analogous to the well-known expected utility anomalies in decision-making under uncertainty. The intertemporal choice anomalies include nonconstant discounting, as discussed in the prior two chapters, and a variety of other phenomena such as the fact that losses tend to be devalued less rapidly than gains, that large losses and gains are devalued less rapidly than small ones, and that people display asymmetric preferences for speed-up and delay of consumption. To account for these anomalies, Loewenstein and Prelec develop a mathematical model of intertemporal choice which, like the contributions in the prior two chapters, incorporates hyperbolic discounting, but which also makes a variety of assumptions about the form of the utility function.

The last chapter in this section, "Delay of Gratification in Children," by Mischel, Shoda, and Rodriguez, reviews three decades of research on delay of gratification by Mischel and his colleagues. Mischel's research has gone through several transitions during this period. His earliest work focused on delay-choice—that is on children's initial choices between rewards to be obtained at different points in time. In the mid-1960s, however, Mischel became interested in a different aspect of intertemporal choice, namely the implementation of the initial choice, which he termed "delay of gratification." The initial decision to eschew an immediate reward in favor of a greater reward in the future exposes the individual to the temptation of bailing out and opting for the inferior immediate reward during the waiting period. Mischel and his co-authors examine a variety of situational and cognitive factors that influence the likelihood of such a bail-out occurring.

The finding that subtle changes in situational variables can produce striking changes in modal behavior led Mischel to reevaluate the significance of situation as a determinant of behavior. In his 1968 book *Personality and Assessment*, he argued that situation shapes behavior more than personality does—or at least more than was commonly believed. However, Mischel's most recent work takes a slightly different perspective. Drawing on recent research with troubled children at a summer camp, Mischel now contends that individuals differ in terms of measurable and fairly stable competencies that interact with situational variables to produce behavior. In a follow-up of the subjects from his early delay of gratification experiments, he has discovered strong correlations between delay of gratification in preschoolers and their adult characteristics and achievements. However, these correlations occur only within specific experimental conditions—when the rewards children waited for were exposed. This evidence, of temporal consistency in certain situations but not in others, support his current interactionist perspective.

Part Three: Self-Control

The hyperbolic discounting models presented in this book imply that behavior will be inconsistent over time in the absence of efforts at self-control. Similarly, the difficulties of executing a decision to delay (as documented by Mischel), particularly when the delayed reward is exposed to view, induce a form of time inconsistency—subjects who initially chose to wait for a delayed reward bail out during the waiting period.

In daily life, however, consistency appears to be the rule and inconsistency the exception. How is such consistency achieved? Rachlin and Raineri suggest that consistency is learned through day-to-day experience much in the same way that we learn to compensate for distance when judging the size of a remote object. Mischel and his co-authors point to a wide range of cognitive tactics, such as distraction and cognitive restructuring, that people employ to avoid time-inconsistent bail-outs. Elster and Loewenstein in Chapter 9 show that pleasure and pain derived from memory and anticipation can mitigate myopia, in some cases actually leading to negative time discounting—e.g., deferring desired outcomes or getting unpleasant outcomes over with quickly. Herrnstein and Prelec, in Chapter 13, argue that social norms (e.g., eat only three meals a day; don't drink in the morning) provide additional defenses against the lure of temptation. Shefrin and Thaler, in Chapter 12, examine a wide range of individual and social mechanisms that promote self-control.

The most influential explanation for time-consistency in the presence of myopic discount curves, however, relies on the notion of multiple selves, and conflicts between those selves. Such multiple-self models give expression to the introspective experience of internal conflict ("the devil made me do it") that philosophers and writers of all historical periods have commented upon. Whereas the theoretical models reviewed in the second section have their intellectual roots in neoclassical economics, the multiple choice models presented in this section have a closer affinity to game theory.

Schelling, whose chapter "Self-Command: A New Discipline" opens this section, applies insights from his well-known work on interpersonal bargaining to bargaining within the self. In his view, self-control can be seen as an intimate struggle between two selves, one farsighted, the other shortsighted. Schelling depicts the strategies and tactics employed by the farsighted self to constrain the behavior of the myopic self. These are very similar to those that might be used by one individual in bargaining with another. In the same way that a union leader might commit himself to attaining a particular wage demand by staking his reputation on achieving that wage, individuals can stake their reputations or, through side-bets with other people, stake material possessions on their own avoidance of temptation.

Ainslie and Haslam's Chapter 8 "Self-Control," building on a framework first articulated in a highly influential earlier paper (Ainslie, 1975), models self-regulation as a repeated two-person prisoners' dilemma, with one person representing the long-term, and the other the short-term, perspective. The authors point out that conflicts are rarely one-shot; internal struggles such as those involved in dieting or waking up in the morning tend to repeat themselves over time. And, just as early interactions between two individuals can influence later ones by creating precedents and establishing reputations, the same is true in the intrapersonal context. Any lapse by the self can undermine the individual's belief that future temptations can be avoided. Both the reluctance to destroy reputational capital, and the tendency to perceive a breach as only the first of a long string of lapses (bunching), promote the long-term perspective. Ainslie and Haslam's perspective differs from Schelling's mainly in that the latter focuses predominantly on tactics that involve third parties (e.g., giving one's car keys to the party's host), while the former are more centrally interested in "intrapsychic" tactics in which the self plays the policing role.

Stimulated by these authors' work, many other multiple-self models have been proposed to deal with the subjective experience of internal conflict. In the "planner-doer" model, presented by Shefrin and Thaler in Chapter 12, intrapersonal conflict results from the interaction of a single farsighted superego-like planner with a series of id-like myopic doers. The planner represents the notion that at all times an individual has some sense of his or her long-term best interest; the doers reflect the temptations of the immediate moment that inevitably conflict with the individual's long-term interests. The planner-doer model, however, is tied more closely to principal-agent theory in economics than to game theory, as are the two contributions just discussed.

Part Four: Internalities

Choice at any one time has consequences for other points in time. Just as empathy causes people to share another person's pleasure or pain, anticipation and memory extend the hedonic impact of an episode across time. The authors in this section examine a variety of behavioral implications that are rooted in these simple observations.

In "Utility from Memory and Anticipation," Elster and Loewenstein enumerate the various ways that emotions arising from memory and anticipation influence utility, and discuss the implication of such effects for behavior. They distinguish between two types of emotional influences that can operate either through memory or anticipation: that is, consumption effects, whereby utility experienced in the past or future positively influences current utility, and contrast effects in which the relationship is negative. For example, a delicious dinner at a four-star restaurant last weekend could enhance current well-being by providing pleasurable memories (a consumption effect), or detract by providing an unfavorable contrast to tonight's fast-food repast. An individual who includes such effects in his or her calculations of utility, even if a discounted utility maximizer, will display anomalous patterns of preference, such as preferring wage profiles that improve over time over declining profiles of comparable undiscounted value (see Chapter 15).

In "Melioration," Herrnstein and Prelec examine suboptimal patterns of choice that occur when tastes result from a long series of choices, each of which has a small individual impact. In these situations, the choices of an optimizing decision-maker would take into account the incremental effect of current choice on satisfaction from subsequent choices. But the authors present experimental results showing that, in a conceptually simple situation, people ignore indirect effects and, as a result, fail to maximize their well-being. They argue that the failure to take account of taste internalities underlies a large number of suboptimalities commonly observed in choice. Among these are underinvestment in skill-intensive consumption activities (such as music appreciation), and overconsumption of activities, such as eating, which have negative indirect effects. Their later chapter, in the following section, develops these insights into a theoretical model of addiction.

Although the arguments of Elster and Loewenstein, on the one hand, and Herrnstein and Prelec, on the other, might appear contradictory, the conflict is largely illusory. Herrnstein and Prelec focus on the impact of the present on the future, arguing that this impact is routinely ignored or severely underweighted in decision-making. Elster and Loewenstein focus primarily on the impact of the future on the present, arguing that this influence is quite profound.

In Chapter 11, "The Role of Moral Sentiments in the Theory of Intertemporal Choice," Robert Frank examines the social function that emotions play in overcoming social dilemmas. In his book *Passions Within Reason*, Frank argues that emotions such as anger and gratitude benefit society by causing people to reciprocate defection and cooperation in situations in which narrow self-interest would suggest the opposite course. Anticipation of retaliation and reciprocal cooperation alters the prisoners' dilemma in a manner that promotes cooperation. According to Frank, emotions can affect cooperation while other mechanisms cannot because emotions are experienced as immediately as the temptation to defect. In contrast to, for example, the contemplation of the potential future benefits of cooperation, emotions circumvent the steep discounting of even slightly delayed rewards, as implied by hyperbolic discounting.

Part Five: Applications and Extensions

The final section offers a small sampling of how theoretical insights into intertemporal choice can illuminate real world phenomena. Shefrin and Thaler's chapter "Mental Accounting, Saving, and Self-

Control" applies a self-control perspective to savings behavior. In much the same way that Chapter 5 challenged the validity of the discounted utility model, this chapter criticizes the life-cycle model that dominates contemporary economic analysis of savings behavior. Using a model based on Thaler's influential work on mental accounting, the authors show that the central predictions of the life-cycle model are refuted, and that actual behavior typically deviates from the predictions of the life-cycle model in a manner predicted by their behavioral life-cycle model.

The next two chapters take radically different approaches to the problem of addiction. Herrnstein and Prelec in Chapter 13, "A Theory of Addiction," present a theory of addiction based on the concept of the "primrose path"—the idea that addiction is a trap that people enter slowly and unknowingly and then find it difficult to extricate themselves. They dismiss the notion that people can predict and respond optimally to the changes in taste which accompany addiction, a perspective they dismissively label "rational self-medication." Such a model is precisely what Becker, Grossman, and Murphy offer in their chapter "Rational Addiction and the Effect of Price on Consumption." In their model, addiction has a long-term negative impact on well-being, but overall, the addict is better off than he or she would have been in the absence of the addiction.

Given the major difference in starting assumptions between the two chapters, their theoretical frameworks are remarkably similar. This affinity is most strikingly evident in the resemblance between Becker et al.'s Figure 1, and Herrnstein and Prelec's Figure 2, each of which contains two stable and one unstable equilibrium point located at approximately equivalent positions.

In the final chapter of the book, "Frames of Reference and the Intertemporal Wage Profile," Robert Frank applies the idea that past consumption sets a standard against which current consumption is evaluated (the contrast effect from Chapter 9) to the analysis of wage profiles. As already noted, the contrast effect can induce a preference for sequences of utility that improve over time, even among those who discount the future. If people found it easy to implement saving plans, the creation of such an improving living standard would simply be a matter of optimal saving. But, as Thaler and Shefrin note in Chapter 12, saving is anything but effortless. As a result, such a pattern of improving consumption, while desired in the abstract, may be difficult to achieve. Frank argues that institutions that satisfy the desire for improvement have evolved over time—that is, seniority-pegged wage increases which exceed the rates of increase explicable on purely economic grounds.

Concluding Comments

With ever greater insistence, American social scientists are being called upon to explain and offer remedies for a broad range of societal problems that seem to reflect suboptimal time discounting. These include paradigmatic economic variables that must appear on the debit side of the U.S. balance sheet: a low savings rate, low rates of corporate investment, and ballooning private and public debt. They also encompass social ills such as abysmal educational attainments, AIDS, environmental degradation, high rates of infant mortality, crime, and teenage pregnancy. Whether in the role of consumer, manager, voter, student, criminal, or parent, many Americans exhibit behavior that reflects a heavy weighting of the present relative to the future.

The economic approach to intertemporal choice provides few useful insights into these problems. It assumes that each individual has a rate of time discounting that he or she applies to all domains of behavior, economic and otherwise. But the research reviewed in this book suggests a much more complicated picture. While individual discount rates, to the extent that they exist, may be high, humans possess remarkable capabilities to overcome these rates. Social and political organizations, elaborate strategies and tactics of self-control, social norms, and emotions arising from memory and anticipation all mitigate the otherwise pernicious effects of hyperbolic discounting.

Simplistic solutions that ignore psychology will inevitably founder. Successful policy must be based on a more nuanced understanding of the psychological mechanisms underlying time preference. We hope that *Choice Over Time* will provide a significant step in the development of such an understanding.

References

Ainslie, G. "Specious Reward: A Behavioral Theory of Impulsiveness and Impulse Control," *Psychological Bulletin,* 82 (1975): 463–509.

Benzion, U., A. Rapoport, and J. Yagil. "Discount Rates Inferred from Decisions: An Experimental Study." *Management Science,* 35 (March, 1989): 270–284.

Böhm-Bawerk, E.v. *Capital and Interest.* South Holland, IL: Libertarian Press (1889), 1970.

Jevons, W.S. *Theory of Political Economy.* London: Macmillan, 1871.

Koopmans, T.C. "Stationary Ordinal Utility and Impatience," *Econometrica,* 28 (1960): 287–309.

Mazur, J.E. "An Adjustment Procedure for Studying Delayed Reinforcement," Chap. 2 in M.L. Commons, J.E. Mazur, J.A. Nevins, and H. Rachlin (eds.). *Quantitative Analysis of Behavior: The Effect of Delay and of Intervening Events on Reinforcement Value.* Hillsdale, NJ: Erlbaum, 1987.

Mischel, W. *Personality and Assessment.* New York: Wiley, 1968.

Rae, J. *The Sociological Theory of Capital* (reprint of original 1834 edition). London: Macmillan, 1905.

Samuelson, P. "A Note on Measurement of Utility," *Review of Economic Studies* 4 (1937): pp. 155–161.

Senior, N.W. *An Outline of the Science of Political Economy.* London: Clowes and Sons, 1836.

Spinoza, *Ethics.* London: J.M. Dent & Sons Ltd., 1989.

Thaler, R., "Some Empirical Evidence on Dynamic Inconsistency." *Economics Letters,* 8 (1981): 201–207.

PART ONE

·

Historical Overview

· 1 ·

The Fall and Rise
of Psychological Explanations
in the Economics
of Intertemporal Choice

GEORGE LOEWENSTEIN

IN RECENT years, despite lingering skepticism, the influence of psychology on economics has steadily expanded. Challenged by the discovery of individual and market level phenomena that contradict fundamental economic assumptions, and impressed by theoretical and methodological advances, economists have begun to import insights from psychology into their work on diverse topics. This influence has been most pronounced in the area of decision making under uncertainty, but recently it has extended to the cognate topic of intertemporal choice.

Economists have joined psychologists in using experimental methods to address fundamental questions about time preference. Moving beyond the usual attempts to measure discount rates, this research seeks to test critically the predictions and assumptions of the discounted utility model (DU), the most widely employed model of intertemporal choice. These studies have generally not affirmed the descriptive validity of DU; observed patterns of choice violate virtually every one of the model's basic assumptions and, therefore, its implications.

The exchange between psychology and economics has also occurred at a theoretical level. The descriptive inadequacies of DU have led economists and other social scientists to develop alternative theoretical models that incorporate psychological insights. Some of these retain DU's multiplicative formulation, introducing specialized discount or utility functions. But others adopt radically different frameworks, modeling intertemporal choice as a collective action or principal-agent problem between temporally situated "selves."

Although commonly credited to psychology, many of the insights currently enriching the economics of intertemporal choice were prefigured in the work of nineteenth- and early twentieth-century economists. In a period when the border between psychology and economics was less sharply defined, economists like Rae, Senior, Jevons, and Böhm-Bawerk addressed such fundamental questions as "Why do people discount the future?" In some cases their answers reveal a sophisticated grasp of psychology.

It is possible to discern four basic historical stages in the evolution of the economics of intertemporal choice. In the first stage, nineteenth-century economists such as Senior and Jevons explained time discounting in terms of what psychologists now label *motivational effects;* these refer to emotional and/or hedonic influences on behavior. Both Senior and Jevons believed that willingness to defer gratification depended on immediate emotions experienced by decision makers.

In the second stage, which was dominated by contributions from Böhm-Bawerk and Fisher at the turn of the century, intertemporal choice was viewed in cognitive terms, as a tradeoff between present and future satisfactions. Discounting was attributed mainly to inadequacies in the decision maker's ability to imagine the future.

The third stage entailed an attempt to eliminate psychological content from the economics of intertemporal choice. In the first decades of the twentieth century, a distaste for psychology became widespread among economists. In part because of their dismay over new developments in psychology that did not seem amenable to interpretation as utility maximization (e.g., Freud's theory of unconscious motivations), economists sought to stake out the independence of their profession.[1] The psychological richness that characterized early discussions of intertemporal choice was supplanted by mathematical and graphical analyses that seemed to render psychology superfluous. Psychological concepts reflecting motivational and cognitive influences—*willpower* and *imagination*—gave way to nonevocative terms such as *time preference* that were deliberately agnostic about underlying causes.

Finally, in the last few decades, a fourth stage has emerged characterized by a renewed interest in psychology by economists interested

---

[1]See, for example, Davenport (1901).

in intertemporal choice. The shift in perspective has benefited from research by contemporary psychologists. Much of this work is represented in the chapters of this book.

This chapter follows the economics of intertemporal choice from its infancy to the present. The first section discusses the nineteenth-century contributions of Rae, Senior, and Jevons. The second examines the pivotal work of Böhm-Bawerk and Fisher at the turn of the century. Section 3 examines the ordinal utility revolution and its consequences for intertemporal choice.

Rae, Senior, and Jevons: Three Early Perspectives

John Rae, an obscure and tragic economist of Scottish descent,[2] provided the first in-depth treatment of intertemporal choice. Rae's interest in the topic, like that of other economists of the period, arose from his desire to understand changes in the standard of living over time and differences across countries. Earlier economists such as Smith had argued that such discrepancies derived from differences in the accumulation of capital. They believed that such differences depended on the proportion of the surplus product of labor devoted to production of *capital* as opposed to *consumption* goods. Rae recognized that such accounts, although not inaccurate, were incomplete. If capital accumulation depended on the allocation of surplus product between consumption and production, on what did that allocation depend?

Rae argued in the 1834 volume, *Statement of Some New Principles on the Subject of Political Economy*,[3] that the allocation of the surplus prod-

---

[2]The exceptionally creative Rae was repeatedly undermined by a chain of misfortunes. At 20 he dropped out of Edinburgh University, where he was studying medicine, disappointed with his professors' response to his thesis topic, and convinced (correctly, as it turned out) that it was ahead of its time. Five years later, disillusioned, impoverished by his father's bankruptcy, and ostracized for marrying the daughter of a shepherd, he emigrated to Quebec, where he taught school and established himself in Montreal's Scottish expatriate community. During this period he published his magnum opus, *Statement of Some New Principles on the Subject of Political Economy*. His book was initially poorly received, in large part because of its vitriolic attacks on the inviolable Adam Smith. Having failed to establish his intellectual credentials, he was forced to take a job as headmaster in Hamilton, Ontario, at that time a rural outpost. Later dismissed in a power struggle, he drifted to California, where he took part in the 1848 gold rush, and then to Hawaii. In the last year of this life, he moved to Staten Island, New York, to live with a former student from Hamilton. He appears to have died unaware that his work was already widely cited and praised by the major economists of his time. For a superb account of Rae's life and works, see James (1965).

[3]Later renamed *Sociological Theory of Capital*.

uct depended on the public's willingness to defer gratification—on the "effective desire of accumulation." If this desire for accumulation were high, then people would be willing to allocate the surplus product to capital rather than consumption. Rae identified four major determinants of the effective desire of accumulation, the first two limiting the desire for accumulation, and the second two promoting it. First, he cited the brevity and uncertainty of human life:

> Were life to endure for ever, were the capacity to enjoy in perfection all its goods, both mental and corporeal, to be prolonged with it, and were we guided solely by the dictates of reason, there could be no limit to the formation of means of future gratification, till our utmost wishes were satisfied. A pleasure to be enjoyed, or a pain to be endured, fifty or a hundred years hence would be considered deserving the same attention as if it were to befall us fifty or a hundred minutes hence. (1834, p. 119)

In support of this argument, he cited numerous examples:

> When engaged in safe occupations, and living in healthy countries, men are much more apt to be frugal, than in unhealthy, or hazardous occupations, and in climates pernicious to human life. Sailors and soldiers are prodigals. In the West Indies, New Orleans, the East Indies, the expenditure of the inhabitants is profuse. The same people, coming to reside in the healthy parts of Europe, and not getting into the vortex of extravagant fashion, live economically. Wars and pestilence, have always waste and luxury, among the other evils that follow in their train. (1834, p. 57)

Rae's second factor limiting the effective desire for accumulation was the psychological discomfort of deferring gratification—what Senior was to call *abstinence:*

> Such pleasures as may now be enjoyed generally awaken a passion strongly prompting to the partaking of them. The actual presence of the immediate object of desire in the mind by exciting the attention, seems to rouse all the faculties, as it were to fix their view on it, and leads them to a very lively conception of the enjoyments which it offers to their instant possession. The prospects of future good, which future years may hold out to us, seem at such a moment dull and dubious, and are apt to be slighted, for objects on which the daylight is falling strongly, and showing us in all their freshness just within our grasp. . . . Everywhere we see, that to spend is easy, to spare, hard. (1834, p. 120)

Counterpoised against the brevity of life and the psychological discomfort of deferral were two factors contributing to the effective desire of accumulation: "the prevalence throughout the society of the social and benevolent affections" (in contemporary parlance, the "bequest motive"), and "the extent of the intellectual powers, and the consequent prevalence of habits of reflection, and prudence, in the minds of the members of society" (1834, p. 58). It was to this last factor that Rae devoted most of his book. Perhaps because of his personal experience with different cultures, Rae saw culture as the critical determinant of differences in the effective desire of accumulation: "The mass of the individuals composing any society, being operated on by the same causes, and having similar manners, habits, and to a great extent feelings also, must approximate to each other, in the strength of their effective desires of accumulation" (1834, p. 198). As a result, much of his book is devoted to anecdotes about different countries, social classes, and historical epochs, all illustrating a simple point: that in early times, more primitive societies, and "lower" orders of society, intellectual powers, habits of reflection, prudence, and, hence, the effective desire of accumulation were less well developed.

Although cited cursorily by Senior, Rae first gained prominence in 1848 with the publication of J.S. Mill's *Principles of Political Economy*.[4] Mill devoted an entire chapter titled "Of the Law of the Increase of Capital" to Rae's work, in the process citing vast passages verbatim. Indeed his coverage of Rae was so extensive that it may have discouraged people from examining the original work; later commentators tended to cite the passages that were presented in Mill's book. This is unfortunate because Mill focused almost exclusively on Rae's sensational sociological observations—in the process neglecting to credit him for his fundamental insights into the determinants of time preference.

Senior

Two years after Rae published his book, the English economist N.W. Senior came out with his influential *Outline of the Science of Political Economy*, in which he expounded a new theory of capital that, like Rae's, emphasized the psychological element. Senior's analysis of intertemporal choice (like much recent work) was motivated by a paradox: Why should interest be paid on a capital sum? As expressed

---

[4]Mill credited Senior for having brought Rae to his attention.

by Smart (1891, p. 675):

> The striking aspect which interest presents when one's critical attention is first drawn to it is, that it is an income got apparently from simple possession of wealth. There seems some reason why *rent* should be paid:—is it not the price of the original and indestructible powers of the soil, from whence must come all food and raw material? There is even stronger ground for paying wage:—does not labor involve sacrifice of time, brain, and body, and is there not a visible return to the labor of every man who can put a spade into the earth? But [why should] the owner of wealth, whose tangible property, perhaps, consists in a few securities locked away in a safe, be able for all time to draw income without work and, practically, without risk?

Early treatments of capital had skirted this problem by noting that most loans went to capital creation and that capital generally provided a positive rate of return; it seemed natural that those who provided funds for the capital would earn a return. However, as Senior recognized, this perspective did not explain why the rate of interest was positive. Why didn't investors continue to invest in increasingly low-yield investments until the rate of return fell to zero?

Senior was the first to provide a psychological explanation for interest. In Senior's "abstinence theory," interest was viewed as compensation to the holder of capital for enduring the pain of abstaining from consumption, which he viewed as "among the most painful exertions of the human will" (1836, p. 60).[5] In this view new investment ceased when, at the margin, its return could no longer compensate for the pain of deferring consumption.

However, Senior went further, when perhaps he should have quit while he was ahead; he actually defined abstinence as an input into production rather than a determinant of the supply of loanable funds: "By the word Abstinence, we wish to express that agent, distinct from labor and the agency of nature, the concurrence of which is necessary to the existence of Capital" (1836, p. 49).

The notion of abstinence as a factor of production later came under blistering attack from Irving Fisher and Böhm-Bawerk, both of whom were inclined to separate the production side of capital from the

---

[5]This view of the agonies of deferral was attacked by socialists such as Lassalle, who noted the evident absurdity of the notion that wealthy investors suffer great privation while they forestall from consuming their entire income at once. But, as Cassel (1903) later rebutted, this criticism fails to draw the appropriate distinction between total and marginal privation. In fact, the wealthy are prone to abstention precisely because they suffer, on average, little privation in doing so.

psychological side. Senior's inclusion of abstinence as a factor of production was distasteful to them because it assimilated the psychological element into the production perspective.

Senior's abstinence perspective remained popular during the remainder of the century, but there were few efforts to develop further his scant psychology. Besides the observation that the pain of abstinence is inversely related to wealth, debate among subscribers to the abstinence view was confined to an often tedious back and forth about whether *abstinence* was the best term for the concept it represented. Cairnes (1874) suggested the term *postponement*, Macvane (1887) proposed *waiting*, while others insisted on the superiority of expressions such as *forbearance* and *frugality*.

Jevons

Thirty years after Senior proposed his abstinence theory, Jevons advanced a characterization of intertemporal choice that turned Senior's perspective on its head. Whereas Senior had viewed equal treatment of present and future as the baseline and asked why people commonly deviated from that baseline, Jevons implicitly asked a more fundamental question: Why do people take the future into account at all?

Jevons' answer can be understood only in the context of a paradox bequeathed him by Bentham. Benthamite man, as interpreted by later commentators such as James Mill, was highly self-centered with respect to other individuals and centered in the present with respect to himself at other points in time. This characteristic presented Jevons, a Benthamite who sought to develop a theoretical account of intertemporal choice, with a problem: Why should such a myopic decision maker ever defer consumption into the future? His solution was to identify specific presently felt pleasures and pains that resulted from contemplating future consumption:

> Bentham has stated, that one of the main elements in estimating the force of a pleasure or pain is its *propinquity* or *remoteness*. It is certain that a large part of what we experience in life depends not on the actual circumstances of the moment so much as on the anticipation of future events. As Mr. Bain says, "the foretaste of pleasure is pleasure begun." (1871, p. 40)

Pleasures and pains associated with the future, but realized in the present rescued the Benthamite decision maker from total myopia. In Jevons' view, the decision maker who deferred consumption did not defer pleasure but substituted pleasure from anticipation—what Bentham had referred to as "pleasures of expectation"—for pleasure from current consumption.

Jevons was convinced that his theory was not qualitatively different from Senior's, and argued that Senior's abstinence was simply the inverse of his pleasures of expectation. And the two perspectives do indeed share important commonalities. Unlike later perspectives, which were to view intertemporal choice as a tradeoff between utility at different points in time, Senior and Jevons saw decision makers as highly anchored in present and influenced by immediately experienced emotions. The theories are, however, strikingly different in the way that they characterize these emotions; Senior focused exclusively on the immediate pain of deferral, Jevons on the immediate pleasure of deferral.

Jevons, like Senior, viewed equal treatment of present and future as a norm of behavior, and wanted to understand why human behavior deviated from the norm. But, whereas Senior's explanation for discounting centered on the pain of abstinence, Jevons' hinged on imperfections in the translation of future events into present utility. In his framework, the ideal would only be realized if "all future pleasures or pains should act upon us with the same force as if they were present" (1871, p. 76). But he recognized that "no human mind is constituted in this perfect way."

Jevons went to great lengths to describe the mechanics of pleasure and pain from anticipation. For example, he noted that rate of devaluation of the future relative to the present would likely be greater for short time delays than for long ones,[6] an insight taken up a century later by Strotz (1955) and Ainslie (1975): "The intensity of present feeling must, to use a mathematical expression, be some function of the future feeling, and it must increase as we approach the moment of realization. The change, again, must be less rapid the further we are from the moment, and more rapid as we come nearer to it" (1871, p. 41).

Although Jevons' conceptualization of intertemporal choice was rapidly displaced by newer contributions, elements of his perspective can be discerned in the work of later economists. For example, although Marshall's views on intertemporal choice were very close to those of Böhm-Bawerk, his writings contain passages that sound distinctly Jevonian. In a chapter of his *Principles* titled "Choices Between

[6]This does not mean that the distant future is devalued less than the immediate future, but rather that the amount of devaluation *per unit of time delay* is smaller.

Different Uses of the Same Thing: Immediate and Deferred Uses," he states, somewhat ambiguously, "When a person postpones a pleasure-giving event he does not postpone the pleasure; but he gives up a present pleasure and takes in its place another, or an expectation of another at a future date" (1898, p. 121). In this passage it is unclear whether the tradeoff is between present utility from present consumption and present utility from future consumption (as Jevons saw it), or between present utility from present consumption and future utility from future consumption (Böhm-Bawerk's perspective, which is discussed in the next section). The first part of the statement—that deferral of consumption does not involve postponement of pleasure—is clearly Jevonian; the second part, where it is acknowledged that the substitute pleasure could occur at another date is more in line with Böhm-Bawerk.

Noting this inconsistency, Böhm-Bawerk, in a late edition of *Capital and Interest*, classified Marshall as an "eclectic" who, "unable to make one of his own [theories], or equally unable or unwilling to align himself completely with one of the available theories, selected from two or three or even a greater number of heterogeneous theories such features as appealed to him, and wove them together into a whole that was for the most part lacking in unity" (1914, p. 322).

Pareto, too, in spite of his central role in the depsychologizing of the utility concept, evinced a Jevonian perspective in his discussion of intertemporal choice. For example, in considering the problem of why seldom used goods may nevertheless fetch high prices, Pareto noted:

> If a woman has ten dresses, she need not wear them all at once; also it is not customary to wear all the gowns one possesses. . . . But granted that, the meaning of the quantities regarding goods which enter into the formulas of pure economics changes somewhat. They are no longer quantities consumed, but quantities which are at the individual's disposal. . . . For the sensation of present consumption we substitute, as the cause of the actions of the individual, the *present sensation of the future consumption* of the goods which are at his disposal (italics added). (1909, p. 181)

Finally, the contemporary economist Shackle adopts a pure neo-Jevonian perspective in his book *Time in Economics*. In a section titled "Enjoyment by Imaginative Anticipation," he writes, "The enjoyment or satisfaction which the decision-maker seeks to maximize by his choice of one action-scheme rather than others is a pleasure of the imagination" (1958, p. 41).

Böhm-Bawerk, Fisher, and the Discounted Utility Model

The second stage in the evolution of the economics of intertemporal choice witnessed an Indian summer of psychological insight. Böhm-Bawerk and Fisher's accounts of intertemporal choice were profoundly psychological and illustrate the potential for fruitful interaction between economics and psychology. Böhm-Bawerk introduced a radically new, cognitively based theory of intertemporal choice, while at the same time assimilating the psychological observations of his predecessors.

Nevertheless, specific features of their contributions—Böhm-Bawerk's view of intertemporal choice as essentially comparable to atemporal choice, and Fisher's indifference curve analysis—paved the way for the subsequent stripping away of psychology. Böhm-Bawerk and Fisher, therefore, occupied pivotal positions in the history of the economics of intertemporal choice.

Böhm-Bawerk

Until Böhm-Bawerk turned his attention to the problem, all treatments of intertemporal choice were subsidiary to discussions of capital and interest. This tie hindered progress on intertemporal choice because the psychological determinants of time preference were always discussed in connection with the productivity of capital. Böhm-Bawerk eliminated this connection by observing, in *Capital and Interest*, that the interest rate could be viewed entirely independent of capital—as the relative price of current as compared with future consumption. It followed logically that this single price could play the role of equilibrating the demand for capital (determined by willingness to delay gratification) and its supply (determined by technical factors). Böhm-Bawerk assailed Senior and others who had attempted to incorporate the psychological factor into the supply side:[7] "Nothing is further from my thoughts than to follow the example of Senior

---

[7] Böhm-Bawerk was a victim of his own personality; he lacked the willpower to resist denigrating all previous intellectual contributions. This enraged his contemporaries and inspired countless efforts to demonstrate that *his* views were derivative. The most common charge was that Böhm-Bawerk had gleaned most of his insights from Rae, whose work he denigrated in the later editions of *Capital and Interest*. Böhm-Bawerk took pains to note, in later editions, that "when the first edition of Capital and Interest appeared, his [Rae's] book was completely unknown to me" (1889, p. 209).

and attempt to claim that saving constitutes a third factor of production arrayed beside nature and labor. It does not stand beside them, but in the background behind them . . . saving does not belong among the *means* of production but among the *motives* which determine the direction that production shall take (1889, p. 117).

Böhm-Bawerk's second major contribution was to provide a new account of intertemporal choice based on what would now be considered a "cognitive" perspective. Like Senior and Jevons, Böhm-Bawerk believed that interest resulted from a difference in the evaluation of present and future consumption. However, his psychological analysis was radically different. Senior's and Jevons' decision makers were intrinsically oriented to the present; their deficient evaluation of the future resulted from presently experienced emotions—in the one case deprivation, in the other, the insufficient potency of immediate utility from anticipation. Böhm-Bawerk envisioned a much more evenhanded choice between present and future. Instead of maximizing immediate well-being, his decision makers traded off satisfactions at different points in time. He attacked the Jevonian notion that intertemporal choice actually involved a maximization of current utility: "It can hardly be maintained, as some of our older economists and psychologists used to be fond of assuming, that we possess the gift of literally *feeling in advance* the emotions we shall experience in the future" (1889, p. 260).

In Böhm-Bawerk's writings, the distinction between utility from immediate sensation and from anticipation disappears; rather, gratifications stemming from all points in time are thought to be comparable because placed on a cognitive plane: "*These imagined future emotions are comparable*. Indeed, they are comparable not only with present emotions experienced at the moment, but also with each other; and that comparability, furthermore, obtains irrespective of whether they belong to the same or different future periods of time" (1889, p. 261).

Böhm-Bawerk, like Senior and Jevons, viewed equal treatment of present and future as an ideal: "What is going to happen to us in a week or in a year is no less something touching *us*, than what happens to us today. It is therefore equally entitled to be considered in our own economy, for the object of that economy is to provide for *our well-being*" (1889, p. 262). But, like his predecessors, he acknowledged, "Whether this equality of rights as a matter of principle is matched by a full equality of rights as a matter of practice is another question" (1889, p. 262).

Böhm-Bawerk provided a list of the determinants of time preference, which he divided into two categories. The first was "the relation of supply and demand as it exists at one point in time and that relation as it exists at another point in time" (1889, p. 266). This is simply the impact of the temporal distribution of consumption on marginal utility at different points in time. Because people tend to become wealthier over time, Böhm-Bawerk believed that the marginal utility of wealth would be lower in the future than in the present, leading to a disproportionate valuation of current wealth. He saw this factor as one that would decrease effective impatience. This factor is, however, in some ways uninteresting, because the distribution of consumption over time is largely a matter of choice—of individual decisions to borrow and save. The argument that time preference depends on the marginal utility of consumption, which in turn depends on the outcome of a decision that depends on time preference, has a certain circularity.

Far more interesting was Böhm-Bawerk's second set of causes, which encompassed several distinct psychological determinants including those mentioned by Rae, Senior, and Jevons, plus one of his own.

Böhm-Bawerk's original contribution was a "systematic tendency to underestimate future wants" based on a rather sophisticated cognitive psychology similar to modern concepts such as "availability" (Tversky and Kahneman, 1973):

> We feel less concerned about future sensations of joy and sorrow simply because they do lie in the future, and lessening of concern is in proportion to the remoteness of that future. Consequently we accord to goods which are intended to serve future ends a value which falls short of the true intensity of their future marginal utility. *We systematically undervalue our future wants and also the means which serve to satisfy them.* . . . It may be that we possess inadequate power to imagine and to abstract, or that we are not willing to put forth the necessary effort, but in any event we limn a more or less incomplete picture of our future wants and especially of the remotely distant ones. And then there are all those wants that never come to mind at all. (1889, pp. 268–269)

A final cause of discounting was a failure of willpower, in effect the obverse of Rae's "reflection and prudence":

> It occurs frequently, I believe, that a person is faced with a choice between a present and a future satisfaction or dissatisfaction and that he decides in favor of lesser present pleasure even though he knows perfectly well, and is even explicitly aware at the moment he makes his choice, that the future disadvantage is the greater and that therefore

his well-being, on the whole, suffers by reason of his choice . . . how often does each of us "give in to weakness" and allow himself to be swept along into acquiescence or action which he knows immediately he is going to regret on the morrow.

In introducing willpower—a psychological element that implies that deferring gratification requires effort—Böhm-Bawerk clearly deviated from his intention to depict intertemporal choice in purely cognitive terms. If time preference arose solely from a tendency to undervalue future satisfactions, there would be no need for willpower because discounting would reflect what appeared to be a rational tradeoff. If they mobilize willpower ("moral effort") to defer consumption, people must want, at some level, to delay consumption but find it difficult to implement that preference. Inclusion of the willpower element implicitly acknowledges that intertemporal choice does involve an emotional element.

Later writers have sometimes mistakenly attributed to Böhm-Bawerk the belief that people tend to view time itself in distorted terms. This view, in fact, comes from Pigou. In a frequently cited passage in his *Economics of Welfare*, Pigou referred to time discounting as a perspective phenomenon analogous to an optical illusion: "Our telescopic faculty is defective, and . . . we, therefore, see future pleasures, as it were, on a diminished scale." The difference between this and Böhm-Bawerk's failure of imagination can be seen by analogy between time perspective and a driver's view of objects on the road. On the one hand, analogous to Böhm-Bawerk's failure of imagination, objects in the distance may seem blurry, or not be visible at all. On the other hand, and in line with Pigou, we may actually misestimate the distance of remote objects; objects may appear to be more distant than they actually are.

Fisher

Irving Fisher's main contribution was to clarify and formalize Böhm-Bawerk's analysis. Fisher was the first to apply the indifference curve apparatus to intertemporal choice and to express Böhm-Bawerk's theory in mathematical terms. Figure 1.1 reproduces a temporal indifference diagram of the type first presented by Fisher in *The Theory of Interest*. Consumption in the current year is represented on the abscissa, and consumption in the following year is represented on the ordinate. A series of indifference curves or "willingness lines" (as Fisher called them) for a single person are depicted in the figure.

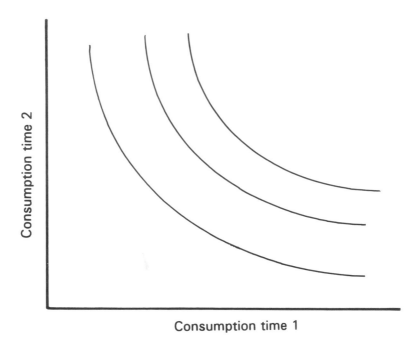

Figure 1.1.

Each curve represents different levels of current and future consumption that the individual is indifferent between. Lines lying to the northeast are preferable to those to the southwest.

The slope of the tangent to any indifference curve corresponds to time-preference or "impatience";[8] it represents the individual's willingness to give up current consumption in exchange for future consumption. The steeper the curve, the less the willingness to sacrifice current for future consumption and, hence, the greater the rate of time preference.

The lines become steeper toward the northwest because time preference becomes more pronounced, the greater is consumption in the future relative to consumption in the present. This curvature reflects

---

[8]Fisher used "impatience" interchangeably with "time preference," an unfortunate practice that continues to the present. This definition of impatience created semantic problems when he discussed the various determinants of impatience. Fisher wished to state that self-control is one factor that determines time preference. However, because of his equating of impatience with time preference, he was forced to speak of self-control as a determinant of impatience rather than, as is conventional, the act of resisting impatience.

Böhm-Bawerk's first cause of time discounting. The slope of the tangent at points intersecting the 45° line emanating from the origin represents the individual's rate of time preference when consumption is equal in the present and future. This can be seen as a proxy for the "pure rate of time preference" and corresponds to Böhm-Bawerk's second set of causes.

Fisher's exposition then introduced "investment opportunity" lines into the graphical analysis. These lines represented the economy's ability to transform consumption physically in one period into consumption in the other. The forces of supply and demand would then equate the average of individuals' marginal tradeoffs between current and future consumption to the economy's ability to transform one type of consumption into the other at the margin.

Expressing intertemporal choice in terms of indifference curves had two consequences. First, it suggested that intertemporal choice was not qualitatively different from atemporal choice, because the graphical representations of choice in the two domains were virtually indistinguishable before one labeled the axes. Second, Fisher's analytical separation of "willingness" (time preference) and "investment opportunity" lines made crystal-clear the separation of the supply and demand for capital and the role of interest in equilibrating supply and demand. Fisher denounced those who persisted in emphasizing one at the expense of the other:

> Any attempt to solve the problem of the rate of interest exclusively as one of productivity or exclusively as one of psychology is necessarily futile. The fact that there are still two schools, the productivity school and the psychological school, constantly crossing swords on this subject is a scandal in economic science and a reflection on the inadequate methods employed by these would-be destroyers of each other. (1930, p. 312)

Fisher's writings included extensive discussions of the determinants of time preference. Like Böhm-Bawerk he divided his list of determinants into two major categories: objective factors, and psychological determinants that he called "the personal factor." Objective factors included the time path of income, which he acknowledged to be identical to Böhm-Bawerk's "first cause," and the influence of risk, a factor not discussed by Böhm-Bawerk. Fisher's view was that

> "the risk of losing the income in a particular period of time operates, in the eyes of most people, as a virtual impoverishment of the income

in that period, and hence increases the estimation in which a unit of certain income in that particular period is held. If that period is a remote one, the risk to which it is subject makes for a high regard for remote income; if it is the present (immediate future), the risk makes for a high regard for immediate income" (1930, pp. 78–79).

The impact of risk on time preference, therefore, could not be determined a priori, because it depended on its incidence over time. However, Fisher believed that in general, the future tends to be riskier than the present and the distant future riskier than the near future. As a result, he thought, the overall impact of risk would be to increase appreciation for the future and therefore to reduce time preference.

Fisher's list of "personal" determinants of time preference included foresight (the inverse of Böhm-Bawerk's "systematic tendency to underestimate future wants"), and four factors first mentioned by Rae: (1) self-control, (2) habit, (3) life expectancy, and (4) concern for the lives of other persons. Fisher's new contribution was what he called *fashion*, which he believed to be "of vast importance to a community, in its influence both on the rate of interest and on the distribution of wealth itself" (1930, p. 88):

> The most fitful of the causes at work is probably fashion. This at the present time acts, on the one hand, to stimulate men to save and become millionaires, and, on the other hand, to stimulate millionaires to live in an ostentatious manner. . . . In whatever direction the leaders of fashion first chance to move, the crowd will follow in mad pursuit until almost the whole social body will be moving in that direction. (1930, p. 87)

Despite evident similarities, Fisher's view of psychological factors differs in one important respect from those of Rae and Böhm-Bawerk. They had viewed culture, social class, and racial differences as the most important determinants of the psychological factors responsible for time preference. Fisher, in contrast, paid much greater heed to situational factors. For example, whereas Rae and Böhm-Bawerk saw poverty mainly as the *product* of high time preference,[9] Fisher recognized that causality might run in the opposite direction. While "poverty bears down heavily on all portions of a man's expected life," Fisher wrote, "it increases the want for immediate income *even more*

---

[9]In one of many passages to this effect, Rae commented that "all members of any society, whose accumulative principle is lower than the average, are gradually reduced to poverty" (1834, p. 199).

than it increases the want for future income" (1930, p. 72). To illustrate the lack of class-based inborn impatience, Fisher cited the example of the English poor, who had been widely viewed as spendthrifts, but who had rapidly developed the habit of saving following the introduction of postal savings banks. And he wryly commented that the English upper class could be induced to display extremes of self-denial or profligacy, depending on the vicissitudes of fashion. He also attacked Rae's imputation of Chinese improvidence based on the flimsiness of their housing, noting the "large accumulations of capital made by Chinese living abroad where they are freed from the exactions of arbitrary governors and from the tyranny of the clan-family system" (1930, p. 378).

Despite the sophistication of his psychological reflections, Fisher had difficulty integrating the psychology with his analytical and graphical analysis. The value of the psychological insights are not dependent on the validity of the analytics, and the implication of the psychology for his equations or graphs is unclear. The two contributions are segregated into separate chapters in his book with little cross-referencing.

This bifurcation turned out to be convenient in the next phase in the development of the economics of intertemporal choice, with its antagonism toward psychology. Fisher's analytical contributions were adopted and further developed in the decades following the publication of *Theory of Interest*, but his psychological insights were all but forgotten.

The Discounted Utility Model and the Ordinal Utility Revolution

The next critical step in the economics of intertemporal choice was the formulation of the discounted utility model by Samuelson in 1937. In its most restrictive form, the discounted utility model states that consumption sequence $(c_1, c_2, \ldots c_n)$ is preferred to sequence $(d_1, d_2, \ldots d_n)$ if and only if,

$$\sum U(c_t) \delta^t > \sum U(d_t) \delta^t,$$

where U is a "ratio scale" utility function with positive first and negative second derivative, and δ^t is the discount function with $0 < \delta < 1$. The discounted utility model, in effect, partitions Böhm-

Bawerk's first and second causes of time discounting. His first cause—variations in marginal utility arising from differences in level of consumption at different points in time—is captured in the utility function. His second set of causes leading to a systematic tendency to undervalue the future are captured in the discount function, which is independent of consumption plans. The discount rate is sometimes referred to as the "pure rate of time preference," indicating that it is invariant with respect to a person's immediate wealth or consumption plans.

Samuelson was very cautious in presenting his new model, pointing to potential problems at every step of his exposition, and stressing the arbitrariness of the underlying assumptions: "It is completely arbitrary to assume that the individual behaves so as to maximize an integral of the form envisaged in [DU]. This involves the assumption that at every instant in time the individual's satisfaction depends only upon consumption at that time, and that furthermore, the individual tries to maximize the sum of instantaneous satisfactions reduced to some comparable base by time discount" (1937, p. 159). But despite its arbitrariness, the simplicity and elegance of his apparatus were irresistible. The discounted utility model was rapidly established as the framework of choice for analyzing decisions with a temporal component.

Almost as soon as it was proposed, however, DU confronted a serious challenge to its scientific status. The concept of utility maximization in economics had undergone a transformation during the past half century, which culminated in the so-called ordinal utility revolution that swept the field of economics in the early 1940s. DU relies on a strongly cardinal (ratio-scale) form of utility of a type inimical to the ordinal perspective.[10] The ordinalists proposed replacing DU with the more general assumption that decision makers maximize some arbitrary function of current and future consumption—$U(c_1, \ldots . c_n)$—which was a generalization of Fisher's two-period indifference curve formulation. However, this formulation proved insufficiently restrictive in practice, and has enjoyed little popularity outside of advanced microeconomic textbooks.

[10] The ordinal utility revolution reflected the belief that motivational concepts could be dispensed with to explain individual behavior. In the ordinalists' view it was only necessary to know an agent's preference ranking of alternative consumption bundles in order to explain her behavior. Ordinal utility constituted a repudiation of theories of behavior based on psychological concepts such as maximization of well-being or satisfaction of desires. Ironically, Samuelson, whose discounted utility model was thrown into scientific limbo by ordinal utility, was one of the triumvirate who initiated the revolution.

The work of Koopmans (1960) can be viewed, in part, as an attempt to restore DU to its former stature. Following von Neumann and Morgenstern's (1949) similar efforts in decision making under uncertainty, Koopmans formulated a set of axioms governing the manner in which people rank temporal sequences of consumption that, taken together, are logically equivalent to the DU model. Restricted in this manner, the DU framework can be shown to be compatible with the ordinal approach. The rehabilitation of DU, however, was not completely successful. As both Samuelson and Koopmans recognized, DU and its axioms are deficient either as normative standards or positive descriptions of choice.

At the core of the discounted utility model are two basic assumptions—a strong form of preferential independence, and a property called *stationarity*.[11] The independence property states that if two temporal prospects, $X \equiv (x_1, \ldots x_n)$ and $Y \equiv (y_1, \ldots y_n)$, share a common outcome at a given point in time, then preference between them is determined solely by the remaining $(n - 1)$ outcomes. In combination with a series of technical axioms collectively referred to as "completeness," outcome separability implies that preferences can be represented by the *general additively separable* (GAS) formula:

$$U(X) = \sum u_t(x_t).$$

The stationarity condition states that if the first outcome in both X and Y is the same, $x_1 = y_1$, then preference between X and Y will be preserved by dropping the first outcome and shifting the remaining outcomes by one period.

Stationarity and intertemporal independence (along with the technical axioms) imply that any representation of preferences over temporal prospects can be monotonically transformed into a discounted-utility representation.

At a normative level, DU has many appealing features. Stationarity, which implies logarithmic discounting at a constant rate, is attractive in the sense that it implies a neutral attitude toward time delay; a given time delay has the same impact on preferences, regardless of when it occurs. The additive separable form implied by independence has, from a normative perspective, one desirable and one undesirable consequence. The desirable consequence is that it implies that different outcomes are discounted at the same rate; time preference is independent of atemporal preference. To see why this is desir-

---

[11] This discussion is adapted from an early draft of Prelec and Loewenstein (1990).

able, imagine the intertemporal allocation problem of an individual for whom this is not the case. Imagine a person who must allocate a fixed bundle of apples and oranges between present and future. Suppose she prefers apples to oranges in the present and in the future, but prefers oranges in the present to oranges in the future and apples in the future to apples in the present. The person's time preferences would lead her to delay apple consumption and speed up orange consumption, which would conflict with atemporal preference for apples.

The undesirable consequence of preferential independence is the implication that consumption in one period has no effect on preferences in other periods. It is easy to construct counter-examples that are normatively compelling. For example, consider a gastronome who is indifferent between chicken and beef. Independence implies that such a person would be indifferent between beef today, beef tomorrow, and beef the day after, on the one hand, and beef today, chicken the day after, and beef on the third day. There is no good reason, besides analytical simplicity, to assume that such indifference would hold.

At a descriptive level, DU's problems are far more striking. Numerous behavioral tendencies have been observed that are incompatible with DU. There is a common tendency to bite the bullet, to get unpleasant outcomes over with quickly rather than to defer them as predicted by DU (Loewenstein, 1987) (see Chapter 9). Losses are generally discounted at a lower rate than gains (Thaler, 1981). People have asymmetric preferences for the speedup and delay of consumption (Loewenstein, 1988) when, according to DU, these preferences should be symmetrical. A list of discounted utility "anomalies" has been enumerated, including these and a variety of other phenomena (Loewenstein and Thaler, 1989; Prelec and Loewenstein, 1991; Loewenstein and Prelec, Chapter 5 and 1991). Recognition of these anomalies has been one of the factors stimulating the reintroduction of psychology into the economics of intertemporal choice.

New Evidence for Old Theories

Although the psychological analyses of nineteenth- and early twentieth-century economists were derived from introspection or casual empiricism, many of the insights of these economists have been confirmed in recent research. Psychologists since the early 1960s and, more recently, economists, have conducted empirical research addressing basic issues of time preference. Most of the speculations of Rae, Senior, Jevons, Böhm-Bawerk, and Fisher have been evaluated empirically.

Rae and Senior

All four of the determinants of time preference cited by Rae—the brevity and uncertainty of life, the bequest motive, the painfulness of deferring gratification, and the impact of socioeconomic and cultural factors—have been examined in empirical research.

It is difficult to test for the effect of life expectancy on time preference cross-sectionally, because people who differ in life expectancy often differ in other respects that may be associated with attitude toward the future. However, one empirical analysis has avoided this pitfall by employing a time-series approach. Slemrod (1984, 1986) found a small but systematic relationship between changes in the threat of nuclear war as measured by the setting of the "doomsday" clock published monthly in the *Bulletin of the Atomic Scientists* and changes in the national savings rate—a proxy for time perspective; the savings rate tends to drop when the clock setting approaches zero. He has also found an inverse relationship, cross-sectionally, between saving rates in different countries and fear of nuclear war. Although only suggestive, these results are consistent with the notion that life expectancy influences time preference.

Evidence concerning the bequest motive is mixed. Some economists have argued that bequests play a key role in saving behavior (Kotlikoff and Summers, 1981), at least among those at the upper levels of income (Moore, 1978). The bequest motive has been used to explain why the elderly continue to save after retirement rather than dissaving as predicted by a stripped-down life-cycle model (Danziger, v.d. Gaag, Smolensky, and Taussig, 1982). But others have argued that observed dissaving is illusory (Diamond and Hausman, 1984), and one empirical study that compared savings by those with and without living children found no difference (Hurd, 1987). Although Rae's assertion that the benevolent affections influence time preference seems intuitively plausible, the effect is remarkably difficult to demonstrate.

Numerous articles in the 1960s and early 1970s examined the relationship between some of the socioeconomic characteristics discussed by Rae—social class, wealth, and ethnicity—and time discounting. However, most of these analyses were severely flawed methodologically and suffered from what modern cognitive psychologists term *confirmation bias*. Studies correlating time perspective with demographic characteristics almost disappeared from mainstream journals after Mischel (1968) demonstrated that differences in situations have a greater effect on willingness to delay gratification than differences between persons. However, Mischel's more recent work—mainly his finding of strong continuity in delay of gratification over a person's lifetime (Mischel, Shoda, and Peake, 1988)—once again highlights the importance of individual differences.

Whether there are strong socioeconomic correlates of time preference, and the cause of such differences if they exist, has not been addressed satisfactorily. Hausman (1979) did find a striking negative relationship between income and discounting, as measured by the tradeoff between immediate purchase price of air conditioners and delayed energy payments. But his results could plausibly be explained by liquidity constraints at low income levels or simple ignorance of the tradeoff rather than discounting per se.

Finally, Rae's notion that people find it painful to defer consumption, which also underlay Senior's abstinence perspective, has received considerable support. Social psychologist Mischel and his colleagues view delay of consumption in much the same way as Senior did: as a cause of frustration. Their aim is to understand the conditions that intensify or attenuate that frustration. In Mischel's two-stage theory of intertemporal choice (or "delay of gratification"), the first step is reminiscent of Böhm-Bawerk, the second of Senior. The first stage consists of the decision to defer, and depends on a relatively dispassionate assessment of costs and benefits. The second stage entails the implementation of the decision to defer during which the decision maker must actually endure the pain of abstinence.

In a series of experiments using children as subjects, Mischel (1974) focused on the implementation stage. In a typical experiment, a child is placed in a room and learns that he or she can summon the experimenter by ringing a bell. The experimenter then shows the child an inferior and a superior object and explains that the child will receive the superior object if he or she can wait for the experimenter to return, but that he or she can obtain the inferior object at any time by ringing the bell. The dependent variable in these experiments is the length of time the child is able to wait, limited by a fixed interval (typically 15 minutes) after which the experimenter returns with the promised reward.[12]

---

[12] In earlier experiments subjects were not informed of the exact duration of the delay period. Recently, however, Mischel has run several experiments in which chil-

In his early work, Mischel examined the effect of the visible presence or absence of the immediate and deferred rewards on waiting times. These experiments demonstrated that children wait less in the physical presence of either reward than when the rewards are absent. In later experiments, children were instructed to distract themselves while waiting or to transform the rewards cognitively (e.g., to think of marshmallows as little white clouds or chocolate bars as logs). Mischel found that both distraction and cognitive transformation lengthened waiting times.

These results can be easily assimilated into the abstinence perspective. Factors that increase privation during waiting, such as the presence of the reward, appear to decrease the ability to wait. However, when subjects are distracted from the privation of waiting, or when privation is reduced by denigration of the reward, ability to delay is enhanced.

Jevons

Perhaps even more than the abstinence perspective, the Jevonian view has many connections to current theories and observations. To the modern economist, Jevons' views on intertemporal choice seem rather extreme. Clearly, we often defer consumption without immediate compensation in the form of pleasure from anticipation. Our conception of self extends forward in time so that we do not perceive deferral as a sacrifice to an alien other, and do not require immediate compensation (in the form of pleasure from anticipation) for such deferral. Nevertheless, there is considerable truth in Jevons' perspective. Much of our pleasure and pain in life *does* stem from expectations of the future as Bentham and Jevons argued, and these pleasures and pains have profound implications for behavior.

One of the most persuasive modern arguments in favor of the Jevonian perspective is presented by Cottle and Klineberg (1974) in *The Present of Things Future*. They argue that the ability to imagine the future is not sufficient for voluntary deferral and that, as Jevons argued, deferral will only occur if such imagery is associated with immediately experienced emotions. They cite evidence ranging from animal behavior to the myopic behavior of people who have had frontal lobotomies in support of their claim.

The so-called immediacy effect (Prelec and Loewenstein, 1991)—

---

dren are informed of the delay period, and has not observed any substantial differences in behavior under the two conditions.

the finding that people give far greater weight to current consumption than to consumption delayed for any length of time—is also congruent with Jevonian perspective. While emphasizing the importance of pleasure and pain from anticipation, Jevons keenly recognized the greater power of immediate experience over anticipation of the future. The former is immediate and highly salient; the latter is hypothetical. This difference is analogous to that between actual and "statistical" accident victims. It has been observed that people are willing to expend large amounts to save the life of an identifiable accident victim, such as a child who has fallen into a well, but resist expending resources on preventive measures that benefit statistical victims.

Substantial evidence bolsters the notion of an immediacy effect.[13] Consumption items that are immediately available seem to exert a disproportionate pull; similarly, it is very difficult to impose pain on oneself, even when it is known that the pain will be short-lived and the beneficial consequences prolonged. Witness, for example, the difficulty of plunging into a swimming pool even when other swimmers can be seen paddling about with no apparent discomfort. In a study that illustrates this point, Christensen-Szalanski (1984) elicited expectant mothers' preferences for anesthesia during childbirth. When asked at various intervals leading up to labor, a sizable majority stated a preference for childbirth without medication. However, preferences shifted abruptly following the onset of labor. Christensen-Szalanski explained these reversals by the tendency for discounting to increase as time delay diminishes (Ainslie, 1975). However, a simpler explanation follows from the distinction between pleasure and pain from anticipation and that arising from current sensation.[14]

---

[13] A similar point has been made by Phelps and Pollak (1968) in an intergenerational context. In their intergenerational welfare analysis, they use two distinct discount factors to balance the competing utility of successive generations: the first a conventional discount rate that simply refers to a generation's distance from the present, and a second that overweights the utility of the current generation relative to all other generations. The latter, which suggests that the current generation does not put the consumption of hypothetical future generations on an equal footing with its own immediate consumption, is analogous to the notion that people are unable to treat their own immediate and hypothetical future consumption as perfectly commensurable. This analogy between the intergenerational and intraindividual cases was proposed by Elster (1985).

[14] The preference shift does not appear to be due to the decrease in time delay prior to labor per se, as suggested by the standard account of time inconsistency but rather to the actual experience of pain. If the declining discounting explanation was correct, we would expect to observe some women reversing their preference at intermediate

This same logic also provides a simpler explanation for various other examples of time inconsistency. For example, Schelling notes the difficulty of responding to the alarm clock, cavalierly set to an early hour the night before. When set, the pain of waking and the benefits of early rising were both on the same cognitive plane. But when the alarm drones, the pain of waking is immediate and real, while the benefits of early rising remain abstract and in the future.

A second phenomenon that resists interpretation by DU, while easily explicable in Jevons' terms, concerns time preferences for undesirable outcomes (Loewenstein, 1987). DU, with positive discounting, predicts that people should always prefer to defer undesirable outcomes, because doing so moves the negative impact on utility to a time that is less heavily weighted. However, considerable evidence suggests that the opposite—a preference for getting losses over with quickly—is a common, perhaps even typical, pattern of preference. For example, Thaler (1981) found that an unexpectedly high proportion of respondents to a hypothetical choice questionnaire preferred to pay parking tickets immediately rather than defer payment, despite considerations of interest. Carlsmith (1962) and others (Barnes and Barnes, 1964; Knapp, Krause, and Perkins, 1959; Mischel and Grusec, 1967) discovered that subjects, given a choice, prefer to experience aversive stimuli, such as an unavoidable electric shock, sooner rather than later. The usual explanation for such behavior is that waiting for unpleasant outcomes induces anxiety that can be avoided by getting the outcomes over with quickly. Such an explanation is consistent with a Jevonian tradeoff between reduced pain from anticipation and increased immediate pain.

Recent advertising, in which "peace of mind" allegedly flows from the purchases of automobile maintenance contracts,[15] universal life

---

points prior to the onset of labor. But as noted, virtually all shifts occurred only after labor had begun. It also can't be argued that the preference reversal observed by Christensen-Szalanski was caused by unfamiliarity with and, thus, an underestimation of future pain. The effect was observed equally often in women giving birth for a second or subsequent time, when women should be familiar with the pain and when, in fact, labor is typically less painful than initial childbirth.

[15] For example, a recent advertisement for an automobile maintenance contract read, "Backed by GM and honored at GM dealerships throughout the US and Canada, the protection plan gives you added convenience and peace of mind." GM's competitor in this area, USAA, advertised, "Only you can decide if a service contract is worth the price to you, but if peace of mind is what you need, an extended warranty is a wise investment." A variant of this is the slogan of the French insurance conglomerate GAN on cartoon posters that juxtapose the potential chaos of an accident with the smug satisfaction of a man who has anticipated it: "Un homme assuré est un homme tranquille."

insurance, and other current expenditures, also attests to the significance of pain deriving from anticipation. Similarly, lottery ticket purchases may be viewed not simply as uncertain investments yielding high potential payoffs, but as a certain investment—in pleasurable anticipation. As M. Landau, the former director of the Israeli lottery, commented, "In spite of the great unlikelihood of winning the desirable sum of money, an individual may still be willing to pay a relatively high price for a lottery ticket because of the satisfaction he is deriving from the thrill of anticipation" (1968, p. 36). The common "buy a dream" sales pitch reinforces such nonpecuniary motivations for buying lottery tickets.

Böhm-Bawerk and Fisher

The psychology underlying the second phase of the economics of intertemporal choice, epitomized by Böhm-Bawerk and Fisher, was predominantly cognitive. Although there was lingering discussion of motivational elements such as willpower, Böhm-Bawerk and Fisher believed that cognitive limitations were predominantly responsible for time discounting. Such a perspective is well represented in modern work on intertemporal choice and in the various chapters of this book.

Mischel, Ebbesen, and Zeiss (1972) found that, while actual presence of a desired reward decreased waiting time, viewing a photograph of the reward actually enhanced deferral of gratification. Apparently the photograph increases the reality of the reward for delaying without increasing frustration to the same extent as the sight (and perhaps smell) of the actual object.

Research on intertemporal framing (Loewenstein, 1988) also corroborates the cognitive perspective in the sense of demonstrating that how a person internally represents (frames) a choice can have a major impact on willingness to delay. For example, people dislike delaying scheduled consumption but are relatively indifferent to speedup. As a result, when deciding between an inferior immediate and superior delayed consumption objects, they may select the immediate object if the alternative is expressed as delayed, but later object if the immediate object is described as having been sped up. The theory of melioration (Herrnstein and Prelec, Chapter 13) is also reminiscent of Böhm-Bawerk's perspective in its assertion that people tend to ignore (or at least underweigh) information about the future consequences of decisions.

Although difficult to evaluate empirically, the concept of willpower, which appeared in Böhm-Bawerk and Fisher's work, and the idea that deferral of gratification involves as Schelling (1984) expresses it, an "internal struggle for self-command," has received empirical support. For example, Sjöberg and Johnson (1978) repeatedly interviewed smokers who attempted to quit (see, also, Sjöberg, 1980). They found that subjects who resumed smoking often were aware of "cognitive distortions of reality"—rationalizations—that occurred prior to the resumption of smoking. According to Sjöberg and Johnson, the stress engendered by quitting smoking "may leave the door open for a corrupt, twisted, and shortsighted reasoning which generates excuses for changing the initial decision" (1978, p. 151). Rook and Hoch (1985), in interviewing consumers who purchase on impulse, obtained numerous testaments to inner conflict: "The pants were shrieking 'buy me,' so I knew right then that I better walk away and get something else done." "It gnaws at me until I buy it. If I want to get it I keep thinking about it. It won't get out of my mind until I buy it." Ainslie (1987) elicited college students' and prisoners' endorsement of various types of self-control tactics. These included extrapsychic devices (e.g., taking pills to change appetite), attention control (distraction), emotional control, and private rules (e.g., a rigid diet). He found that all four of the self-control devices were approximately equally endorsed, but that the types of strategies endorsed by a particular individual correlated in an intuitively sensible way, with measured personality traits.

There is also some evidence supporting Pigou's notion that people view time in a distorted fashion. Ekman and Lundberg (1971) asked people to rate the "subjective temporal distance" of a range of different objective time delays and to also rate their emotional involvement with different periods. From both of these judgments they estimated psychophysical time functions that were not linear, but conformed closely to a power function of the form $t_s = t_o^\alpha$, with $0 < \alpha < 1$, where the subscripts s and o stand for "subjective" and "objective."

The Ordinalists

Even the third stage in the economics of intertemporal choice, despite its antagonism toward psychology, makes connections to modern psychology. Among contemporary psychologists, there are those who adhere to a perspective that is closely analogous to the ordinal approach. Behavioral psychologists such as Herrnstein and Rachlin (in their earlier work) and, more recently, Mazur (1987), Logue (1987), and many others, eschew cognitive and motivational psychology, restricting themselves to encoding behavior mathematically. These psychologists have sought to estimate mathematical functions representing the desirability of rewards as a function of time delay. The research has generally involved animals instead of humans, presumably with the goal of avoiding the idiosyncratic concerns that inevitably come into play with human subjects. Interestingly, even the animal work has tended to reinforce some of the observations made by early economists. For example, in line with Jevons' observations, neither animals nor people discount the future at a constant rate; most species are disproportionately sensitive to short as opposed to long time delays. As Strotz (1955) demonstrated, such a discount function implies time inconsistent behavior; we always plan to be more farsighted in our future behavior than we are in the present. In confronting the problem of how people deal with the problem posed by time consistency, behavioral psychologists have fallen into the same trap as Böhm-Bawerk in his attempt to reduce intertemporal choice to a cognitive plane. Concepts such as "self-control" (Rachlin and Green, 1972) are not easily reduced to equation form.

Concluding Remarks

In his essays on the history of economic thought, Stigler (1965) argues that, to take root, an economic theory must meet the triple criteria of generality, manageability, and congruence with reality. Because, in his view, ideas compete with one another in the intellectual marketplace, the most general, manageable, and realistic must inevitably triumph. The case of intertemporal choice chronicled here points to a more cyclical pattern of scientific progress.

The early history of intertemporal choice demonstrates a relatively unself-conscious cooperation between psychology and economics, which was followed by a century of work that attempted—never with full success—to expunge the psychological content from the economics. In recent decades, however, economists have begun to reawaken to the possibility that the discarded psychology was not quite as superfluous as had been supposed.

Rather than an evenhanded balancing of Stigler's three criteria, the economics of intertemporal choice has bounced between the three extreme points on the triangle. In the first critical transition, from the psychological perspectives of Senior, Jevons, and Böhm-Bawerk to the formulation of DU by Samuelson, realism was sacrificed for manageability; in the second, albeit only partially successful transition from DU to the ordinal approach, manageability was sacrificed for generality. Thus, the economics of intertemporal choice has not evolved toward Stigler's ideal.

Until recently, economists who sought a descriptive theory of intertemporal choice were caught in an uncomfortable dilemma. On the one hand, they could plead ignorance of the intricacies of intertemporal choice and treat time simply as an additional dimension of choice over which preferences are defined, an approach compatible with the ordinalist perspective. The problem is that the ordinalist alternative suffers from excessive generality and ignores what is known about the economics and psychology of intertemporal choice. As Samuelson notes, "functions that allow unlimited interrelationships become so general as to be almost vacuous" (1937, p. 155). Another problem is its intractability, which probably explains the infrequent appearance of the generalized formulation in economic modeling.

Alternatively, economists could rely on the discounted utility framework. However, DU's psychology is dubious: Few people are willing to accept the axioms of Koopmans either as descriptions of, or as prescriptions for, intertemporal choice behavior. DU is not an explanatory theory; it cannot explain why objects lose or gain in value when delayed. It is simply a way of summarizing and encoding intertemporal preference. But as a method of encoding preferences, it is also deficient. Its behavioral implications are contradicted by empirical research and common experience.

The new borrowings from psychology offer the possibility to transcend the conflict between tractability and realism. Economists need a more refined model of intertemporal choice than that offered by the ordinalist approach. But they want a restrictive model that is realistic. This is where modern psychology can play a constructive role. The speculations of Freud and LeBon have been largely displaced by a contemporary academic psychology that is much closer to economics, both theoretically, and in terms of research methods. During much of the time that economics was purging itself of psychological content, these psychologists have been studying empirically, and in many cases validating, the very insights discarded by economists.

In order to formulate a more realistic theory of intertemporal choice, economists must grapple with the problems confronted by their predecessors and by modern psychologists. Why do individuals take account of the future? How is utility from future consumption experienced in the present? What are the determinants of pleasure from anticipation and privation? They must become aware of the distinction between cognitive and motivational determinants of time preference and of their implications for intertemporal choice.

This book provides a sample of work from a group of psychologists and economists who have met annually to discuss issues relating to intertemporal choice. It is one example of the growing number of exchanges between the two disciplines (see, e.g., Hogarth and Reder, 1987). If the exchange, so far, has tended to be unidirectional, economists can take comfort in the observation that, in borrowing from psychology, they are, in effect, rediscovering their own past.

•

I thank Nora Bartlett, John Campbell, Donna Harsch, Steve Hoch, Joshua Klayman, Marilyn Quadrel, George Stigler, and especially James Thompson for invaluable comments and suggestions. The Russell Sage Foundation and the Alfred P. Sloan Foundation provided support for this research.

References

Ainslie, G. "Specious Reward: A Behavioral Theory of Impulsiveness and Impulse Control." *Psychological Bulletin* 82 (1975): 463–509.
——. "Self-reported Tactics of Impulse Control." *International Journal of Addictions* 22 (1987): 167–179.
Barnes, O., and L.W. Barnes. "Choice of Delay of Inevitable Shock." *Journal of Abnormal Social Psychology* 68 (1964): 669–672.
Böhm-Bawerk, E.v. *Capital and Interest.* South Holland, IL: Libertarian Press (1889), 1970.
——. *History and Critique of Interest Theories.* South Holland, IL: Libertarian Press (1914), 1970.
Cairnes, J.H. *Some Leading Principles of Political Economy Newly Expounded.* New York: Harper, 1874.
Carlsmith, J.M. *Strength of Expectancy: Its Determinants and Effects.* Unpublished doctoral dissertation, Harvard University, 1962.
Cassel, G. *The Nature and Necessity of Interest.* New York: Macmillan, 1903.
Christensen, Szalanski, and J.J. Jay. "Discount Functions and the Measurement of Patients' Values: Women's Decisions During Childbirth." *Medical Decision Making* 4 (1984): 47–58.
Cottle, T.J., and S.L. Klineberg. *The Present of Things Future: Explorations of Time in Human Experience.* New York: Free Press, 1974.
Danziger, S., J.v.d. Gaag, E. Smolensky, and M.K. Taussig. "The Life-Cycle Hypothesis and the Consumption Behavior of the Elderly." *Journal of Post-Keynesian Economics* 5 (1982): 208–227.
Davenport, H.S. "Proposed Modifications in Austrian Theory and Terminology." *Quarterly Journal of Economics* 16 (1901): 355–383.
Diamond, P., and J. Hausman. "Individual Retirement and Savings Behavior." *Journal of Public Economics* 23 (1984): 81–114.

Ekman, G., and U. Lundberg. "Emotional Reaction to Past and Future Events as a Function of Temporal Distance." *Acta Psychologica* 35 (1971): 430–441.

Elster, J. "Weakness of Will and the Free-Rider Problem." *Economics and Philosophy* 1 (1985): 231–265.

Fisher, I. *The Theory of Interest.* New York: Macmillan, 1930.

Hausman, J. "Individual Discount Rates and the Purchase and Utilization of Energy-Using Durables." *Bell Journal of Economics* 10 (1979): 33–54.

Hogarth, R.M., and M.W. Reder. *Rationale Choice: The Contrast Between Economics and Psychology.* Chicago: University of Chicago Press, 1987.

Hurd, M.D. "Savings of the Elderly and Desired Bequests." *American Economic Review* 77 (1987): 298–312.

James, R.W. *John Rae, Political Economist.* Toronto: University of Toronto Press, 1965.

Jevons, W.S. *Theory of Political Economy.* London: Macmillan, 1871.

Knapp, R.K., R.H. Kause, and C.C. Perkins. "Immediate versus Delayed Shock in T-Maze Performance." *Journal of Experimental Psychology* 58 (1959): 357–362.

Koopmans, T.C. "Stationary Ordinal Utility and Impatience." *Econometrica* 28 (1960): 287–309.

Kotlikoff, L.J., and L.H. Summers. "The Role of Intergenerational Transfers in Aggregate Capital Accumulation." *Journal of Political Economy* 89 (1981): 706–732.

Landau, M. *A Manual on Lotteries.* Israel: Massada Publishing, 1968.

Loewenstein, G. "Anticipation and the Valuation of Delayed Consumption." *Economic Journal* 97 (1987): 666–684.

———. "Frames of Mind in Intertemporal Choice." *Management Science* 34 (1988): 200–214.

———, and D. Prelec. "Negative Time Preference." *American Economic Review* 81 (1991): 347–352.

———, and R. Thaler. "Anomalies: Intertemporal Choice." *Journal of Economic Perspectives* 3 (1989): 181–193.

Macvane, S.M. "Analysis of Cost of Production." *Quarterly Journal of Economics* 1 (1887): 481–487.

Marshall, A. *Principles of Economics.* London: Macmillan, 1898.

Mazur, J.E. "An Adjustment Procedure for Studying Delayed Reinforcement," Chap. 2 in M.L. Commons, J.E. Mazur, J.A. Nevins, and H. Rachlin (eds.). *Quantitative Analysis of Behavior: The Effect of Delay and of Intervening Events on Reinforcement Value.* Hillsdale, NJ: Erlbaum, 1987.

Mill, J.S. *Principles of Political Economy,* 5th ed. New York: D. Appleton, 1864.

Mischel, W. *Personality and Assessment.* New York: Wiley, 1968.

———. "Processes in Delay of Gratification," in D. Berkowitz (ed.). *Advances in Experimental Social Psychology,* vol. 7. 1974, pp. 249–292.

———, E.B. Ebbesen, and A. Zeis. "Cognitive and Attentional Mechanisms in Delay of Gratification." *Journal of Personality and Social Psychology* 21 (1972): 204–218.

———, and J. Grusec. "Waiting for Rewards and Punishments: Effects of Time and Probability on Choice." *Journal of Personality and Social Psychology* 5 (1967): 24–31.

———, Y. Shoda, and P.K. Peake. "The Nature of Adolescent Competencies Predicted by Preschool Delay of Gratification." *Journal of Personality and Social Psychology* 54 (1988): 687–696.

Moore, B.J. "Life-cycle Saving and Bequest Behavior." *Journal of Post Keynesian Economics* 1 (1978): 79–99.

Pareto, V. *Manuel D'Économie politique* (Alfred Bonnet trans.). Paris: Giard & Briétr, 1909.

Phelps, E.S., and R.A. Pollak. "On Second-best National Saving and Game-theoretic Equilibrium Growth." *Review of Economic Studies* 35 (1968): 185–199.

Pigou, A.C. *The Economics of Welfare.* London: Macmillan, 1920.

Prelec, D., and G. Loewenstein. "Decision Making over Time and Under Uncertainty: A Common Approach." *Management Science* 37 (1991): 770–76.

Rachlin, H., and L. Green. "Commitment, Choice and Self-Control." *Journal of the Experimental Analysis of Behavior* 17 (1972): 15–22.

Rae, J. *The Sociological Theory of Capital* (reprint of original 1834 edition) London: Macmillan, 1905.

Rook, D., and S. Hoch. "Consuming Impulses." In E.C. Hirschman and M.B. Holbrook (eds.). *Advances in Consumer Research,* vol. 12, Provo, UT: Association for Consumer Research, 1985, pp. 23–27.

Samuelson, P. "A Note on Measurement of Utility." *Review of Economic Studies* 4 (1937): 155–161.

Senior, N.W. *An Outline of the Science of Political Economy.* London: Clowes and Sons, 1836.

Shackle, G.L.S. *Time in Economics.* Amsterdam: North Holland, 1958.

Sjöberg, L. "Volitional Problems in Carrying Through a Difficult Decision." *Acta Psychologica* 45 (1980): 123–132.

———, and T. Johnson. "Trying to Give up Smoking: A Study of Volitional Breakdowns." *Addictive Behaviors* 3 (1978): 149–164.

Slemrod, J. "The Economic Impact of Nuclear Fear." *Bulletin of the Atomic Scientists* 40 (1984): 42–43.

Slemrod, J. "Saving and the Fear of Nuclear War." *Journal of Conflict Resolution* 30 (1986): 403–419.

Smart, W. "The New Theory of Interest." *Economic Journal* (1891): 675–687.

Stigler, G. "The Development of Utility Theory," Chap. 5. *Essays in the History of Economics.* Chicago: University of Chicago Press, 1965.

Strotz, R.H. "Myopia and Inconsistency in Dynamic Utility Maximization." *Review of Economic Studies* 23 (1955): 165–180.

Thaler, R. "Some Empirical Evidence on Dynamic Inconsistency." *Economic Letters* 8 (1981): 201–207.

Tversky, A., and D. Kahneman. "Availability: A Heuristic for Judging Frequency and Probability." *Cognitive Psychology* 5 (1973): 207–232.

von Neumann, J., and O. Morgenstern. *Theory of Games and Economic Behavior.* Princeton: Princeton University Press, 1949.

· 2 ·

Intertemporal Choice
and Political Thought

JON ELSTER

Mʘᴏsᴛ ᴡᴏʀᴋ on intertemporal choice has been done within philosophy, psychology, and economics. Much of it is surveyed elsewhere in this book. In this chapter I discuss how issues of myopia, deferred gratification, and self-control have been discussed within political theory. I first consider political constitutions as examples of imperfect rationality, that is, as devices of precommitment against future weakness of will. To the extent that constitutions are considered as devices that bind later generations, we may inquire into the optimal tightness of the bounds as well as the optimal difficulty of untying them. Next I survey at some length the views of Alexis de Tocqueville—of all political theorists probably the one who attached most importance to problems of intertemporal choice. He discussed how political institutions affect the general ability of the citizens to defer gratification, and—probably the most original aspect of this thinking—how the ability to defer gratification in one part of life affects the ability to do so in others.

Constitutional Self-binding

Most Western democracies have written constitutions. (Great Britain and Israel are the main exceptions.[1]) Their task is to set up the ma-

---

[1] For a survey, see V. Bogdanov, *Constitutions in Democratic Politics*, Aldershot: Gower, 1988. Yet both the British and the Israeli political systems have quasi-

chinery of government and to protect basic rights and freedoms. Constitutional clauses differ from ordinary laws in two ways. First, they are supposed to deal with more basic or fundamental issues.[2] If this were the only difference between the constitution and other laws, there would not seem to be much point in having one. In virtually all cases, however, constitutions also differ in being more difficult to change. Whereas ordinary legislation usually requires no more than a single majority vote, constitutional changes have to pass more difficult hurdles. Qualified majorities, ranging from 60 percent to 75 percent, are very common.[3] In federal systems, a qualified majority of the states may have to give their consent. Often, constitutions impose delays that prevent changes from being made on short notice. The new clause may have to be passed by several successive parliaments or, as in Norway, be proposed during one parliament and passed by the following one. Some constitutions (such as the Norwegian one) impose both qualified majorities and delays; others (such as the Swedish one) requires only delays[4]; still others (such as the West German and U.S. ones), only qualified majorities; while New Zealand appears to be unique in that here "only ordinary legislative efforts are required to supplement, modify or repeal the Constitution."[5]

---

constitutional elements. For Britain, see, for instance, the practice described in footnote 3. In Israel, many basic laws contain entrenchment clauses similar to constitutional amendment clauses.

[2]Obviously, the distinction between basic and nonbasic is anything but hard and fast. In the Fifth French Republic, for instance, the electoral system is not mentioned in the constitution. In consequence, parliament is free to stipulate proportional representation and single-member districts according to the interests of the current majority.

[3]In the Independence Constitution of Kenya, the majority required to change certain parts of the document was set at nine tenths of the vote in the Senate (J. Jaconelli, "Majority Rule and Special Majorities." *Public Law*, 1989, pp. 587–616, at p. 600). As observed by Alexander Hamilton (*The Federalist*, no. 75), similarly difficult hurdles may be created by requiring a qualified majority of the total composition of the body, irrespective of how many are actually present to vote. When turnout is traditionally low, even a simple majority of the electorate may prove difficult to obtain.

[4]A similar practice obtains in Great Britain: "Under the Parliament Act 1911, as amended by the Parliament Act 1949, a non-money bill can be passed into law over the opposition of the House of Lords if it has been passed by simple majority in two consecutive sessions of the House of Commons and one year has elapsed between the second reading of the Bill in the Commons in the first sessions its third reading in the Commons in the second session." (Jaconelli, "Majority Rule and Special Majorities," p. 597.)

[5]J.N Eule, "Temporal Limits on the Legislative Mandate," *American Bar Journal Foundation*, 1987, pp. 379–459, at p. 394). Eule goes on to say, however, that "even in such a system . . . there remain moral and political restraints on the legislative alteration of constitutional doctrine."

It is commonly asserted that these hurdles are a form of *self-binding*. The term, although convenient, is multiply misleading. First, the constitution, even if followed religiously, rarely binds in an absolute sense, because it is usually possible to unbind oneself by going through the required procedure.[6] Second, there is no certainty that the constitution will be followed, religiously or even approximately. Extraconstitutional action is a permanent possibility. An individual may bind himself through court-enforceable promises, but the World Court cannot ensure that societies stick to the constitutions they have given themselves. Third, a constitution usually binds more than "oneself," because it is almost invariably intended to last beyond the current generation.[7] It is only by the dubious device of construing the nation over time as a single entity that constitutions can be viewed as acts of *self*-binding.[8] In all these respects, constitutional self-binding differs from individual acts of precommitment such as voluntary and irreversible commitment to mental institutions.[9]

The constitution binds, and only the constitution can bind. In particular, a legislature cannot bind its successors. Blackstone's dictum, that "Acts of Parliament derogatory from the power of subsequent parliaments bind not," seems to apply to all parliamentary systems.[10] In political systems without a constitution, there is no way in which the actions of future majorities can be restricted: The majority can neither bind nor be bound.[11] In constitutional systems, simple majori-

[6]This statement requires two qualifications. First, some constitutions contain clauses that cannot be undone by the usual amendment procedure or indeed in any other way. Thus, the constitution of West Germany makes it impossible to undo the federal nature of the system. Similarly (although slightly more weakly), Article V of the Constitution of the United States stipulates that "no state, without its consent, shall be deprived of its equal suffrage in the senate." In Canada, there are a number of matters that can be amended only by unanimous provincial agreement (including an amendment of the amendment procedure). Second, the fact that a clause can be changed may be totally irrelevant if, as is often the case, the amendment procedure is time-consuming and the need for change is urgent.

[7]An exception is found in another part of Article V in the U.S. Constitution: "no amendment which may be made prior to the year one thousand eight hundred and eight, shall in any manner affect the first and fourth clauses [related to slavery] of the first article."

[8]Also, a majority may use the constitution to bind the minority. Suppose that the constitution requires three fifths majority for a change. A majority of 61 percent that fears that one day it might find itself in a minority of 49 percent might then implement its partisan interests through the constitution rather than through ordinary legislation.

[9]On this issue, see J. Elster, *Ulysses and the Sirens*, rev. ed., Cambridge University Press, 1984, p. 38 and, for a much more extensive treatment, R. Dresser, "Ulysses and the Psychologists," *Harvard Civil Rights-Civil Liberties Review* 16 (1982): 777–854.

[10]Eule, ibid.

[11]One might argue, however, that this fact in itself constitutes a minimal unwritten constitution. Cp. also the following note.

ties can be bound but not bind.[12] Although the people can bind its representatives through the constitution, the representatives cannot bind the people by limiting the freedom of action of future representatives.

This is not to say that legislative attempts to bind future legislatures are unheard of. In a survey of the problem, Julian Eule mentions as one example Rule 32 (2) of the Standing Rules of the American Senate: "The rules of the Senate shall continue from one Congress to the next Congress unless they are changed *as provided in these rules.*"[13] According to Eule, there is little doubt that the rule is unconstitutional. The Balanced Budget and Emergency Deficit Control Act (the Gramm-Rudman Act) enacted by the American Congress in 1985 intended to curb the spending of Congress by establishing "maximum fiscal deficits" for each of the next 6 fiscal years. Eule argues that the Act, although leaving future Congresses free to repeal the enactment by simple majority, represented an unconstitutional attempt to bind the future by setting the form by which prior legislation can be altered.[14] Under the Constitution, he argues, a later Congress could just ignore the Act: Explicit repeal is not necessary. The Congress that enacted Gramm-Rudman bound its successors *de facto* if not *de jure,* by exploiting the fact that explicit repeal would create greater political risks for the legislators than overspending by itself would do.

The purpose of entrenched clauses (i.e., those that cannot be changed by a simple majority vote) is to ensure a reasonable degree of stability in the political system and to protect minority rights. By "reasonable," I mean that there should neither be too much nor too little stability. If all decisions were made by simple majority vote, small changes in the electorate and their representatives could create drastic changes on major issues.[15] Even without any changes in the representatives and their preferences, the problem of cyclical majorities (the Condorcet paradox) would leave collective decisions dangerously vulnerable to agenda manipulation.[16] Conversely, the current

[12] Eule, op. cit., p. 405 argues persuasively that the inability of one Congress to bind its successors follows from the constitution itself.

[13] Cited after Eule, op. cit., p. 408; italics added.

[14] Op. cit., note 16 and note 215.

[15] An extreme case of such instability is provided by fourteenth-century Florentine politics. See J. Najemy, *Corporatism and Consensus in Florentine Electoral Politics, 1280–1400.* Chapel Hill: University of North Carolina Press, 1982.

[16] For a survey of this and similar problems, see W. Riker, *Liberalism against Populism,* San Francisco: Freeman, 1982. Strictly speaking, qualified majorities do not eliminate the problem of cycling. If one imposes certain weak constraints on the admissible

majority could reshape electoral arrangements so as to reduce the chances of the opposition of ever getting into power.[17] Unchanging rules facilitate the change of majorities, without which democracy has little substance.

None of these arguments for collective self-binding has an analogue at the individual level. Yet in other cases we can find a parallel. When an individual tries to bind himself in advance to a certain course of action, it is usually for one of two reasons. First, as Thomas Schelling has shown us, by throwing away some of his options, an individual may gain a strategic advantage in his dealings with others.[18] Second, if the individual is subject to weakness of will, he may follow the example of Ulysses and bind himself to the mast.[19] Of these, the first reason is rarely present as an argument for constitutional self-binding.[20] The second, however, is massively important. The remainder of this survey will be devoted to a discussion of collective analogies to individual weakness of will and to self-binding as a remedy (and a problem).[21]

In the heat of passion or under the influence of some immediate temptation, an individual can deviate from prudent plans formed in advance or do things that he will later regret. Groups of individuals,

---

combinations of individual preferences, one can show, however, that qualified majorities prevent cycles from arising. See, for instance, A. Caplin and B. Nalebuff, "On 64% Majority Rule," *Econometrica* 56 (1988): 787–814.

[17] Thus, the French socialist party recently used their majority in parliament to replace the single-member district elections with proportional representation, to improve their electoral prospects. Electoral redistricting in the United States provided many examples of similar strategies, until the landmark 1962 decision of the Supreme Court in Baker v. Carr (369 U.S. 186).

[18] T.C. Schelling, *The Strategy of Conflict,* chap. 5, Cambridge, MA: Harvard University Press, 1960.

[19] For an analysis of weakness of will in terms of nonexponential time discounting, see the contributions of George Ainslie to this volume.

[20] In the recent Gulf crisis, Germany was prevented by its constitution from sending forces to the Middle East, thus sparing it the necessity of doing its fair share in a common task. The relevant constitutional clause was, of course, set up with quite different eventualities in mind. Another possible exception to the statement in the text (suggested to me by Aanund Hylland) arises from constitutional clauses stipulating the indivisibility of the national territory. It is likely that a federal system with a constitutional right to secession might be more vulnerable to divide and conquer tactics by other nations. On this issue, see also C. Sunstein, "Constitutionalism and Secession," *University of Chicago Law Review* 58 (1991): 633–670.

[21] Individual self-binding for the purpose of curbing impulsive behavior may also be advantageous in one's dealings with others, who are more likely to trust an individual who has precommitted himself to make backsliding impossible. A political example (discussed later) is that a nation may find it easier to get credit from other nations through a constitutional clause forbidding the printing of paper money.

such as voters or members of a political assembly, are no less prone to such irrational behavior. Sometimes, aggregate irrationality is simply the sum of irrational individual responses to the same external situation; at other times, passionate factions may form by interaction effects and crowd psychology. Whatever their origin, collective fits of passion can be extremely destructive in their effects. Inflamed majorities have violated the rights of minorities, spent money they did not have, and declared war for no good reason.

Although a qualified majority is less likely than a simple majority to yield to irrational impulses, it is by no means immune against such temptations. Hence, a constitutional requirement of a qualified majority does not by itself provide much of a protection against the people's propensity to collective weakness of will. As explained earlier, the purpose of such clauses is rather to make the system less vulnerable to random fluctuations and manipulation. To alleviate the problem of collective passions, other procedures are necessary. In the Athenian assembly, for instance, new legislation was made by the *nomothetai*, a group of individuals chosen by lot and summoned by the assembly with the task of debating and then approving or rejecting laws proposed in the assembly. They met only for a single day, presumably to make them immune to factionalism and corruption. Another institution with a similar purpose was the *graphe paranomon*, whereby an individual might be punished for having made an illegal proposal in the assembly, even if it had already been passed.[22] These quasi-constitutional procedures served to protect democracy against itself.

In modern constitutions different devices are adopted to protect the people against itself or—on an alternative interpretation—to reduce the power of the people. Some of these are constitutional constraints on ordinary legislation. Executive veto is one example.[23] Another is to adopt a bicameral system, with one chamber representing the parts of the electorate who can be expected to hold the more conservative views.[24] Other devices include constitutional constraints

[22] For details, see D.M. MacDowell, *The Law in Classical Athens*, Ithaca, NY: Cornell University Press, 1978, chap. III; M.H. Hansen, *The Sovereignty of the People's Court in Athens in the Fourth Century B.C. and the Public Action against Unconstitutional Proposals*, Odense: Odense University Press, 1974; M.H. Hansen, *The Athenian Assembly*, Oxford, UK: Blackwell, 1987.

[23] The French constituent assembly of 1789–1791 adopted a suspensive veto for the king, that is, essentially a cooling or delaying device. The presidential veto adopted by the Federal Convention does not serve this purpose, as the veto can be overridden by a two-thirds majority in Congress.

[24] The "saucer anecdote" told about George Washington illustrates the point. Some time after the Federal Convention, Thomas Jefferson asked Washington why it had

on constitutional change, notably through clauses that ensure some delay between the time a proposal to change the constitution is first made and when it is finally adopted. This is the main case in which the self-binding interpretation is compelling. Executive veto and bicameralism may just as plausibly, and sometimes more plausibly, be viewed as devices for controlling the people, quite independently of the more or less well considered nature of the popular will.

A classic argument for the need for constitutional self-binding was made by Madison at the Federal Convention in Philadelphia.

> In order to judge of the form to be given to [the Senate], it will be proper to take a view of the ends to be served by it. These were first to protect the people agst. their rulers: secondly to protect the people agst. the transient impressions into which they themselves might be led. A people deliberating in a temperate moment, and with the experience of other nations before them, on the plan of Govt. most likely to secure their happiness, would first be aware, that those chargd. with the public happiness, might betray their trust. An obvious precaution agst. this danger wd. be to divide the trust between different bodies of men, who might watch & check each other. . . . It would next occur to such a people, that they themselves were liable to temporary errors, thro' want of information as to their true interest, and that men chosen for a short term, & employed but a small portion of that in public affairs, might err from the same cause. . . . Another reflection equally becoming a people on such an occasion, wd. be that they themselves, as well as a numerous body of Representatives, were liable to err also, from fickleness and passion. A necessary fence agst. this danger would be to select a portion of enlightened citizens, whose limited number, and firmness might seasonably interpose agst. impetuous counsels. It ought finally to occur to a people deliberating on a Govt. for themselves, that as different interests necessarily result from the liberty meant to be secured, the major interests might under sudden impulses be tempted to commit injustice on the minority.[25]

Although the argument is not free of ambiguities, one strand is reasonably clear. The people, "deliberating in a temperate moment," would want to protect themselves against its predictable tendency to

---

established a Senate. "Why," Washington responded, "do you pour coffee into your saucer?" "To cool it," Jefferson replied. "Even so," Washington said. "We pour legislation into the Senatorial saucer to cool it." (M. Farrand, ed., *Records of the Federal Convention*, vol. III, Yale University Press, 1966, p. 359). For a discussion of the relation between qualified majorities and bicameralism, see Jaconelli, "Majority Rule and Special Majorities," p. 611 ff.

[25] Farrand (ed.), *Records of the Federal Convention*, vol. I, p. 421. See also *The Federalist*, no. 62.

"err from fickleness and passion" and to act on "sudden impulses." At this point, the analogy to individual precommitment becomes very close.

The analogy may be pursued further. Individual self-binding can be a risky business. The money that I have saved but cannot touch may be needed for an important operation. Unless I am let out of the drug clinic for a few days, my firm may go bankrupt. Ulysses might regret being bound to the mast if his ship comes into dangerous waters that his men cannot navigate on their own. Ideally, Ulysses and his successors would like to be *loosely bound* to the mast—with ties strong enough to keep them from acting against their own interest, but not so strong as to prevent him from intervening in an emergency. Usually, one cannot have it both ways. One cannot anticipate all legitimate exceptions to self-binding contracts, and among the unanticipated exceptions, it is often impossible for the enforcing party to distinguish between the genuine ones and those that were the raison d'être for the contract in the first place. What was intended as a safeguard against impulsivity may turn into a prison.[26]

Political precommitment, similarly, can lead to dangerous rigidities. There are, in fact, several reasons why the constitution should not be immutable en bloc. First, the normative views of the citizens may change. If a large majority of the citizens adopted libertarian views, they ought not to be prevented from writing a ban on income taxes into the constitution. Second, their factual beliefs about institutional means to political ends may be modified as they learn more about the effects of the system. If it turns out that the reeligibility of the president has bad incentive effects, it ought to be possible to limit his tenure to one term. Third, changes in external factors such as technology or international relations may force rethinking about constitutional matters. If Norwegian entry into the Common Market comes to be seen as imperative by a large majority, the constitution ought not to be an absolute obstacle (and it isn't).

Monetary policy offers many examples of the attractions and dangers of constitutions.[27] Governments are often tempted to print money, devalue the currency, and expand credit, to the detriment of

---

[26] At the level of individual self-binding, this problem can arise in two ways (see Ainslie's Chap. 8 in this volume). In addition to the dangers of precommitment, there are the dangers of *bunching*—of coming to see each act of backsliding as a predictor of total moral collapse. Although efficient in preventing backsliding, the bunching strategy can be crippling to emotional life by the excessive rigidities it imposes in the individual. Here again, *loose* bunching is the ideal.

[27] See, for instance, the essays in L.B. Yeager (ed.), *In Search of a Monetary Constitution*, Cambridge, MA: Harvard University Press, 1962.

the long-run performance of the economy. A constitution that prevents them from doing so may be a salutary yoke—or, in times of crisis, a dangerous impediment. At the Federal Convention, James Wilson argued that "it will have a most salutary influence on the credit of the U. States to remove the possibility of paper money."[28] Against this view—which eventually prevailed—George Mason asserted, "Though he had a mortal hatred to paper money, yet as he could not foresee all emergences, he was unwilling to tie the hands of the Legislature. He observed that the late war could not have been carried on, had such a prohibition existed."[29] Two centuries later, William Nordhaus pointed to a similar dilemma. To prevent "political business cycles" one might, he observes,

> entrust economic policy to persons that will not be tempted by the Sirens of partisan politics. This procedure is typical for monetary policy, which for historical reasons is lodged in the central bank (as in the independent Federal Reserve System in the US or the Bank of England). A similar possibility is to turn fiscal policy over to a Treasury dominated by civil servants. It may be objected, however, that delegating responsibility to an agency that is not politically responsive to legitimate needs is even more dangerous than a few cycles. This danger is frequently alleged regarding central banks which pay more attention to the "soundness of the dollar" or the latest monetarist craze than to fundamental policy problems.[30]

The argument that a constitutional remedy may be worse than the democratic disease has also been made in the context of Israeli politics. While some have "stressed the stabilising effect of a constitution, which is particularly necessary in a dynamic and volatile population",[31] others have "stressed the dangers of a rigid constitution . . . , especially in a dynamic society."[32] Does a changing society need a stable constitution as a flywheel—or a flexible constitution that can adjust to the changing environment? Because both arguments have obvious merits, one needs to find an optimal balance between stability and rigidity. Here "rigidity" may refer to the obstacles created by the constitution to the passage of ordinary laws, or to the obstacles

---

[28] Farrand (ed.), *Records of the Federal Convention*, vol. II, p. 310.

[29] Ibid., p. 309.

[30] W. Nordhaus, "The Political Business Cycle," *Review of Economic Studies* 42 (1975): 169–190, at p. 188.

[31] E. Gutmann, "Israel: Democracy Without a Constitution," in V. Bogdanov (ed.), *Constitutions in Democratic Politics*, pp. 290–308, at p. 292.

[32] Ibid., p. 295.

it creates to amending its own clauses. As to the former, Madison observed that in deciding on the majority needed to overrule the veto of the president "we must compare the danger from the weakness of ⅔ with the danger from the strength of ¾."[33] As to the latter, Lally-Tollendal remarked in the French Assemblée Constituante of 1789–1791 that "In a given space of time the Constitution may be destroyed by lack of change just as much as by too many changes. It must be neither easy nor impossible to modify it."[34]

There may be limits to what can be achieved by piecemeal constitutional revision, especially if some clauses are so entrenched as to be virtually immutable. Many have argued, therefore, the need for periodically occurring constitutional conventions, for instance at 20 or 30 years' intervals, so that each generation could have a chance of fixing its own constitution rather than being under the domination of earlier ones. The issue was not debated at the Federal Convention, although Jefferson (who was not at the Convention) later expressed strong views to the effect that "the dead have no rights."[35] At the Assemblée Constituante, many speakers urged the need for periodical conventions that were to have a free hand in drawing up a new constitution.[36] Generally speaking, the proposal is open to two objections, each of which is sufficient to destroy it. First, as the time for revision approaches, political life will be inflamed to a high degree, so that at the convention "the *passions*, not the *reason*, of the public would sit in judgment."[37] Far from being "the people deliberating in a temperate moment," the convention would be a struggle of factions. Second, the ground rules for the periodical conventions—notably the electoral and voting procedures—would have to be laid down by the existing constitution and to that extent just constitute another instance of the dead exercising their sway over the living. If, for instance, the new convention were to discuss the extension of the suffrage to new groups, ought not these groups to be represented?

I have tried to highlight the features that are common to constitutional self-binding and individual precommitment. In both cases, pre-

---

[33] Farrand (ed.), *Records of the Federal Convention,* vol. II, p. 587.

[34] Speech of August 31, 1789, in F. Furet and R. Halévi (eds.), *Les orateurs de la révolution française. Vol. I: Les Constituants,* éd. de la Pléiade, Paris: Gallimard, 1989, pp. 364–388, at p. 372.

[35] For a discussion of Jefferson's and related views, see S. Holmes, "Precommitment and the Paradox of Democracy," in J. Elster and R. Slagstad (eds.), *Constitutionalism and Democracy,* Cambridge, UK: Cambridge University Press, 1988, pp. 195–240, at p. 202 ff.

[36] See the *Archives Parlémentaires,* vol. XXX, pp. 35 ff.

[37] *The Federalist,* no. 49 (Madison).

dictable weakness of will is a major reason for restricting future opportunities for action. In both cases, the pervasive uncertainty surrounding human affairs is a major reason for taking great caution before imposing heavy constraints. Although the weakness may be predictable, many other aspects of the situation are not. I have also stressed some differences between the two cases. Some of the reasons for constitutional self-binding derive from specifically political matters, such as fluctuating majorities or procedural manipulations, that have no analogue at the individual level. Conversely, some of the "solutions" to individual weakness of will have no analogue at the collective level. An individual may overcome his tendency toward backsliding through the mental bookkeeping device of "bunching" together a series of future decisions, thus raising the stakes so high that he or she is able to resist temptation. To summarize: The problem of weakness of will and the use of precommitment techniques for solving it are found both at the individual and the political levels. The individual problem, however, can be solved in a different way; and the political solution can be a response to a different problem.

Tocqueville and the Problem of Myopia

Alexis de Tocqueville was only marginally concerned with the issues discussed so far. Although he does refer to the control of the Bank of the United States over the money supply as a "salutary control" (DA 389[38]) which the provincial banks and the "blind democratic instincts of the country" (ibid.) have great difficulties in accepting, he nowhere suggests that this is a constraint the people has imposed on itself. In fact, the only reference in his writings to any kind of self-control is a heavily ironical one, which tends to dismiss the idea that individuals or communities might try to protect themselves against their own passions. It occurs in a chapter from *Democracy in America* entitled "Some Observations on the Theater Among Democratic Peoples," where the following argument (in fact an obvious petitio principii) purports to "show that the stage is not very popular in America":

> The Americans, whose laws allow the utmost freedom, and even
> license, of language in other respects, nevertheless subject the drama
> to a sort of censorship. Plays can only be performed by permission

[38] Page references to *Democracy in America*, New York: Anchor Books, 1969.

of municipal authorities. This illustrates how like communities are to individuals: without a thought they give way to their chief passions, and then take great care not to be carried away by tastes they do not possess. (DA 493)

By contrast, Tocqueville was passionately interested in the causes and consequences of what today we would call myopia, the tendency of individuals to act in light of their short-term self-interest instead of extending their horizon to their life as a whole. To understand his analysis, some preliminary remarks on his psychological conceptions are needed.[39]

In *Democracy in America*, Tocqueville is constantly concerned with explaining the formation of preferences and desires. Sometimes he appeals to the extrapsychic environment, as when he explains preference formation in terms of conformism to other people or in terms of adaptation to the inevitable. At other times he invokes various intrapsychic mechanisms by which one desire can favor or, on the contrary, block the emergence of another.

Consider first what we might call the *spillover effect:* Habits and dispositions that have been formed in one sphere of life spill over into other arenas. Here are some examples:

> In Europe almost all the disorders of society are born around the domestic hearth and not far from the nuptial bed. It is there that men come to feel scorn for natural ties and legitimate pleasures and develop a taste for disorder, restlessness of spirit, and instability of desires. Shaken by the tumultuous passions which have often troubled his own house, the European finds it hard to submit to the authority of the state's legislators . . . [By contrast], the American derives from his home that love of order which he carries over into affairs of state. (DA 291–292)

> The passions that stir the Americans most deeply are commercial and not political ones, or rather they carry a trader's habit over into the business of politics. (DA 285)

> In civil life each man can, at a stretch, imagine that he is in a position to look after himself. In politics, he could never fancy that. So when a people has a political life, the idea of associations and eagerness to form them are part of everybody's everyday life. Whatever natural

[39] For a fuller exposition, see Chapters III and IV of J. Elster, *Psychologie Politique*, Paris: Editions de Minuit, 1990 (English translation forthcoming).

distaste men may have for working in common, they are always ready to do so for the sake of a party. In this way politics spreads a general habit and taste for association. (DA 521)

> That constantly renewed agitation introduced by democratic government into political life passes . . . into civil society. Perhaps, taking everything into account, that is the greatest advantage of democratic government, and I praise it much more on account of what it causes to be done than for what it does. (DA 243)

The spillover effect operates to the extent that people have an integrated personality, in which the same habits and behavioral dispositions regulate all parts of their life. Walter Mischel argued in a classic study that such intraindividual consistency is much weaker than is often supposed. Mischel added, however, that the cross-situational correlations, although weak, are often statistically significant. "Statistically significant relationships of this magnitude are sufficient to justify personality research on individual and group differences. It is equally plain that their value for making statements about an individual are severely limited."[40] Although Tocqueville seems to assume that the correlations are very strong, this assumption may not really be necessary for his sociological purposes. Later I discuss an alternative interpretation of Mischel's finding.

The second mechanism is that of a *compensation effect:* Desires or needs that are not satisfied in one arena seek an outlet in others. Tocqueville assumes that people have certain basic needs, which seek satisfaction one way or another. Here are two examples, both of which invoke the compensation effect to explain the emergence of religion in, respectively, aristocratic and democratic societies. The first explanation is of the "opium of the people" variety, whereas the second belongs to the "fear of freedom" category.

> In nations where an aristocracy dominates . . . the imagination of the poor turns to the next world; it is closed in by the wretchedness of the actual world but escapes therefrom and seeks for joys beyond. (DA p. 531)

> For my part, I doubt whether man can support complete religious independence and entire political liberty at the same. I am led to think that if he has no faith, he must obey, and if he is free he must believe. (DA p. 444)

[40] W. Mischel, *Personality and Assessment,* New York: Wiley, 1968, p. 38.

The compensation effect is related to what is sometimes called the *hydraulic model* of the working of the mind. Although the model can produce absurd results, the idea that people eschew uniformity of behavior across arenas is not necessarily absurd. I return to that question below. Here I want to observe that 20 years after the publication of *Democracy in America*, Tocqueville himself expressed his dissatisfaction with hydraulic reasoning, in a remarkable passage from the notes for the second volume of *The Old Regime:*

> It would seem that civilized people, when restrained from political action, should turn with that much more interest to the literary pleasures. Yet nothing of the sort happens. Literature remains as insensitive and fruitless as politics. Those who believe that by making people withdraw from greater objects they will devote more energy to those activities that are still allowed to them treat the human mind along false and mechanical laws. In a steam engine or a hydraulic machine smaller wheels will turn smoother and quicker as power to them is diverted from the larger wheels. But such mechanical rules do not apply to the human spirit.[41]

I now proceed to Tocqueville's analysis of intertemporal choice. Tocqueville observes, somewhat tritely, that men always and everywhere tend to be selfish and myopic (DA 264). More interesting is the claim that the "democratic social state," characterized by economic and social equality and especially by high rates of mobility, tends to create a short time horizon:

> When everyone is constantly striving to change his position, when an immense field of competition is open to all, when wealth is amassed or dissipated in the shortest possible space of time in the turmoil of democracy, men think in terms of sudden and easy fortunes, of great possessions easily won and lost, and chance in every shape and form. Social instability favors the natural instability of desires. Amid all these perpetual fluctuations of fate the present looms large and hides the future, so that men do not want to think beyond tomorrow. (DA 548)

Elsewhere Tocqueville explains that individuals have a short time horizon because they are able to *recognize* that their desires tend to change constantly. The observation occurs in a brief chapter on "How democratic institutions and mores tend to raise rent and shorten the

---

[41] From the notes to the second volume to the Old Regime, translated in A. de Tocqueville, *"The European Revolution" and Correspondence with Gobineau*, edited by J. Lucas, Gloucester, MA: Peter Smith, 1968, p. 168.

terms of leases":

> In such a mental climate landlord and tenant too feel a sort of instinctive terror of long-term obligations; they are afraid that one day they will be hampered by the agreement which at the moment profits them. They are vaguely conscious of the possibility of a sudden and unexpected change in their condition. They are afraid of themselves, dreading that, their taste having changed, they will come to regret not being able to drop what once formed the object of their lust. (DA 582)[42]

The causal chain, in other words, goes from (1) unstable social conditions through (2) unstable desires to (3) the recognition of their instability and (4) the subsequent shortening of the time horizon. Among the effects of this tendency, Tocqueville cites not only the shortening of the term of leases, but also the U.S. predilection for general ideas:

> One of the characteristics of democratic times is that all men have a taste for easy successes and immediate pleasures. This is true of intellectual pursuits as well as of all others. Most men who live in times of equality are full of lively yet indolent ambition. They want great success at once, but they want to do without great efforts. These contrary instincts lead them straight to looking for generalizations, by means of which they flatter themselves that they can paint vast canvases very cheaply and attract public attention without trouble. (DA 440)

Matters are, however, more complicated, because democratic societies also tend to produce antidotes against myopia. One such antidote is religion. We have seen how democracies produce religion, through the compensation effect. The following passage explains how religion then counteracts myopia, through the spillover effect:

> In ages of faith the final aim of life is placed beyond life. The men of those ages therefore naturally and almost involuntarily grow accustomed to fix their eyes for years together on some static object toward which their progress is ever directed, and they learn by imperceptible degrees to repress a crowd of petty passing desires in order ultimately best to satisfy the one great permanent longing which obsesses them.

---

[42]Cp. also DA p. 453: "I once met an American sailor and asked him why his country's ships are made so that they will not last long. He answered offhand that the art of navigation was making such quick progress that even the best of boats would be almost useless if it lasted more than a few years."

When these same men engage in worldly conduct, such habits influence their conduct. They gladly fix some general and definite aim as the object of their actions here below and direct all their efforts toward it. They do not shift from day to day, chasing some new object of desire, but have settled designs which they never tire of pursuing. . . . Religions instill a general habit of behaving with the future in mind. In this respect they work as much in favor of happiness in this world as of felicity in the next. (DA 547)

This type of argument occurs frequently in Tocqueville: The ills of democracy are cured by democracy itself.[43] Here, religion—itself an endogenous outcome of free democratic institutions—is praised for extending the time horizon of the citizens. Elsewhere, it is praised for restricting their desires: "while the law allows the American people to do everything, there are things which religion prevents them from imagining and forbids them to dare" (DA 292).

Tocqueville also cites the specifically U.S. habit of acting according to enlightened self-interest (*intérêt bien entendu*). As far as I can understand (Tocqueville never defines the concept), this simply means acting according to long-term interest. In the two chapters Tocqueville devotes to this idea, it is taken as exogenously given, and not itself to be explained in terms of further motives. It is, however, used to explain a number of other phenomena, including religion:

I do not see . . . any plain reason why the doctrine of self-interest properly understood should drive men away from religious beliefs, but rather do I see how to unravel the ways in which it brings them close thereto. Let us start from the assumption that in order to gain happiness in this world a man resists all his instinctive impulses and deliberately calculates every action of his life, that instead of yielding blindly to the first onrush of his passions he has learned the art of fighting them, and that he habitually and effortlessly sacrifices the pleasure of the moment for the lasting interests of his whole life. If such a man believes in the religion that he professes, it will hardly cost him anything to submit to such restrictions as it imposes. Reason itself advises him to do so, and habits already formed make it easy. (DA 529)

Here, the spillover effect works in the opposite direction, from the habit of taking the long-term view in secular matters to the ability to act for the sake of the afterlife.

There are further complications. Although Tocqueville believes that democracies spontaneously generate religion, he also envisages

---

[43] See J. Elster, "Patterns of Causal Analysis," in Tocqueville's *Democracy in America*, *Rationality and Society* 3 (1991): 277–297.

the possibility of having democracy without religion.[44] The effect of skepticism and incredulity is that "once [people] have grown accustomed not to think about what will happen after their life, they easily fall back into a complex and brutish indifference about the future" [DA 548], an effect that is reinforced by democracy, as we saw earlier. Tocqueville concludes that "In such a country where unhappily skepticism and democracy exist together, philosophers and the men in power should always strive to set a distant aim as the object of human efforts" (ibid.). The most important is the advice he gives to the rulers:

> It is at all times important that the rulers of nations should act with the future in view. But this is even more necessary in ages of democracy and skepticism than in any others. By giving such a lead, the chief men in democracies not only bring prosperity in public affairs but also teach individuals by their example to conduct their affairs properly. They must especially strive to banish chance, as much as possible, from the world of politics. The sudden and undeserved promotion of a courtier in aristocratic country causes no more than an ephemeral impression, because the whole complex of institutions and beliefs forces men to progress slowly along paths they cannot leave. But such events give the worst possible example to a democratic people, for they urge it on down in the direction whither all its emotions are anyhow leading it. So it is chiefly in times of skepticism and equality that particular precautions are required to prevent the favor of prince or people, which comes and goes at random. One must hope that all promotion will be seen as the reward of effort, so that no high position should be too easily required and men of ambition should be obliged to plan well ahead before they reach their goal. (DA 584-49)

The idea is that of a spillover effect from politics to other secular matters. (This might in fact provide an explanation of the tendency to behave according to enlightened self-interest.) Tocqueville then completes the circle by suggesting a further spillover to religion:

> Once men have become accustomed to foresee from afar what is likely to befall them in this world and to feed upon hopes, they can hardly keep their thoughts always confined within the precise limits of this life and will always be ready to break out through these limits and consider what is beyond. I have therefore no doubt that, in accus-

[44] In some contexts, he even suggests that democracies tend to drive people away from religion, by installing in them "an almost invincible distaste for the supernatural" (DA 430). As I show at some length in Chapter III of *Psychologie Politique*, such contradictions occur very frequently in Tocqueville's writings.

toming the citizens to think of the future in this world, they will gradually be led without noticing it themselves towards religious belief. Thus
the same means that, up to a certain point, enable men to manage
without religion are perhaps after all the only means we will possess
for bringing mankind back, by a long and roundabout path, to a state
of faith. (DA 549)

Initially, politics is the functional equivalent of religion. We may
think of this as a social analogue of the compensation effect, on the
condition that we keep in mind the nonexplanatory nature of "social
needs." An *individual* who finds himself without religion, may, for
that very reason, form a desire for an authoritarian ruler. This is the
compensation effect proper, based on the need for authority and the
fear of limitless freedom. If a *society* finds itself without religion, there
is no mechanism that tends to ensure that politics will be organized
so as to perform the same function of counteracting natural myopia.
Indeed, if the loss of faith leads to the desire for an authoritarian
ruler and ultimately to the advent of such a ruler, he will probably
be less predictable and more arbitrary than rulers who are guided by
institutional constraints. Nevertheless, if a predictable political system does emerge as the functional equivalent of religion, it may itself,
by the spillover effect, resurrect the lost faith.

Let me try to summarize this argument. Democracy as a *social*
state, characterized by high rates of social mobility, tends to exacer-
bate men's spontaneous and natural tendency to seek immediate
gratification. By the psychological mechanism I have referred to as
the compensation effect, democracy as a *political* system also tends
to create an antidote to this tendency. Because people need some
kind of authority in their lives, political democracy spontaneously
generates religion, which in turn counteracts myopia. If, however,
an irreligious democracy should emerge, an alternative antidote to
myopia would be to make the political system as predictable and as
responsive to individual effort as possible.

Tocqueville's argument raises some more general questions. Is it
in fact true that, for a given individual, rates of time discounting tend
to be the same across different arenas? Do those who save out of
their income for their old age also stand out with respect to other
activities that require the ability to defer gratification, such as physical
exercise, dieting, and abstention from drug abuse? There are several
conceivable mechanisms that might support this hypothesis. The exercise of willpower is partly a question of skill and techniques, which
can be carried over from one arena to others. Also, Ainslie's argument about "bunching" is relevant here. People might come to use

failure in one arena (e.g., violating the private rule of never having a drink before dinner) as a predictor for failure in other arenas (e.g., failing to get up at 6 A.M. to do one's regular exercise). The benefit of this strategy is that it raises the stakes so high that conformity with the rules is facilitated. The drawback is that it tends to create rigid, compulsive individuals who are never able to give themselves a break.

The spillover effect suggests a positive correlation between intertemporal choice behavior in different arenas. The compensation effect would suggest a negative correlation: The more people defer gratification in one arena, the less they do so in others. Having achieved a success in one domain, they might reward themselves by lax behavior in another.[45] The need for some kind of oral stimulus may prevent overweight smokers from giving up both of their bad habits. Judging from myself and my acquaintances, I would conjecture that the spillover effect dominates in some individuals, whereas the compensation effect is the more prominent in others. This observation, if more generally valid, suggests a different perspective on Mischel's finding of a weak positive correlation across arenas.[46] Might it not be the case that the population is heterogeneous, consisting of some for whom there is a strong positive correlation and others for whom there is a somewhat weaker negative correlation?[47]

[45]For findings to this effect, see M. Nisan, "Limited Morality," in M.W. Berkowitz and F. Oser (eds.), *Moral Education: Theory and Practice*, Hillsdale, NJ: Erlbaum, 1985, pp. 403–420.

[46]Studies of intraindividual consistency have moved a long way since Mischel's 1968 study. Recent research tends to emphasize the nature of the situations that trigger responses of various kind, so that one person might be consistently capable of delaying gratification in one type of setting, for example, one that requires ability to wait, and consistently incapable of doing so in another setting, for example, one that requires ability to resist temptation (W. Mischel, Y. Shoda, and P. Peake, "The Nature of Adolescent Competencies Predicted by Preschool Delay of Gratification," *Journal of Personality and Social Psychology* 54 (1988): 687–696). Unless situations and settings are defined so as to render the consistency hypothesis true by definition, one might still ask, however, whether intrasetting relations are governed by the spillover effect or the compensation effect.

[47]Similarly, the definition of targets of *envy* can be governed by either of the two mechanisms, both of which are mentioned by Plutarch. On the one hand, there is a spillover effect: Once the habit of envying enemies is established, "it sticks; then from habit we start hating and envying friends." On the other hand, there is a zero-sum effect: If envy is denied one outlet, it will seek another. "Envy is a fact of life, unload it on enemies, who will render you pleasanter to your friends in their prosperity by draining your potential for envy." (For references, see P. Walcot, *Envy and the Greeks*, Warminster, UK: Aris and Phillips, 1978, p. 36.)

PART TWO

·

General
Perspectives

· 3 ·

Hyperbolic Discounting

GEORGE AINSLIE AND NICK HASLAM

7/8/96

O F THE MANY striking psychiatric syndromes known to man, the most dramatic is the multiple, or *split,* personality. Unrelated to coincidentally named schizophrenia, the *ego-splitting* of multiple-personality disorder confronts its sufferers with sudden shifts of values, plans, behaviors, ideas, and, indeed, everything that forms the human character (Putnam, 1989). Where some of these values and plans are incompatible with others, one set is apt to disappear from the patient's ken while he is under the influence of the incompatible set; alternatively, the patient seems to go about while under the influence of one set destroying the other—giving away valuable possessions, offending friends, even getting arrested—just so as to defeat the alternative plans.

At one time this condition was looked upon as exotic, and the report of a case guaranteed a book, and often a movie, about the patient. However, we are gradually becoming aware that multiple personality, while uncommon, is not rare (Bernstein and Putnam, 1986; Braun, 1986) and, furthermore, that lesser forms of ego splitting abound in the form of amnestic episodes (*blackouts* in the alcoholic, *flashbacks* in the posttraumatic stress patient, *fugues* in many people under stress) and binge disorders (bulimia, exhibitionism, some patterns of alcoholism, and similar episodes occurring sometimes in all of the dozens of addictions that have so far been described—Ainslie,

1992, Chapter 2). More important, there is growing evidence of self-defeating behavior traits in ordinary citizens, habits that make it seem as though the person at one time forgets or disregards earlier personal plans. "Bad habits" like nail biting, staying up too late, procrastinating, and failing to stick to a budget have long been familiar, but systematic research has recently revealed that people evaluate choices inconsistently even in dispassionate discussion of them (Benzion et al., 1989; Loewenstein, 1988, Thaler; 1987–1992; Tversky and Kahneman, 1981). Often this inconsistency is such that their conscious, deliberate preference is to choose the larger and later of two alternative cash prizes when both are distant, but to change to the smaller, earlier one as they draw nearer (Ainslie and Haendel, 1983). Such reversals of preference occur despite the constancy of environmental factors and the person's thorough familiarity with them.

The pervasiveness and robustness of such observations suggests that the problem may not come from some extraordinary condition that impairs the normal operation of intentionality, but rather from the process by which all people, perhaps all organisms, evaluate future goals. That is, the split ego may not be a freak of nature but the condition of nature itself, uncorrected, in these cases, by the learning process that comes to compensate for it at least partially in most people. There is now evidence that the basic temporal discount function of man and lower animals is such that elementary splits—reversals of preference between successive motivational states—can be expected to arise regularly in the absence of some influence to the contrary. The derivable consequences for an intelligent organism like man resemble many of the conflicting structures that have been proposed by Freud and other students of self-defeating behavior. But they also differ in that they can be parsimoniously integrated with existing motivational science. At least that is our argument in this chapter.

We briefly review how people have been described to devalue the future, then argue that such devaluation must occur in a curve that is more deeply bowed than economists' familiar exponential curve if it is to explain self-defeating behavior. We show that a well-documented discount function, Herrnstein's matching law, has the necessary shape. The matching law predicts temporary preferences for poorer, earlier alternatives when they are imminently available, a phenomenon that has been directly observed in both animals and man, and which provides a paradigm for self-defeating behavior. We deal with the counter-intuitive quality of such a model, then point out some of the long-standing puzzles it can explain, a task that will continue in Chapter 8 of this book. In this chapter, we show that regularly recurring preferences interact somewhat like the interests in a legislature, and that depending on their duration, they may induce a variety of ambivalently valued activities such as (1) addictions; (2) briefer itchlike urges that include some psychiatric symptoms; (3) subjectively involuntary experiences, including pain and fear; and (4) at the other end of this scale of durations, more stable but still undesirable activities that are often ascribed to character flaws.

The Pervasive Devaluation of the Future

Major theories of self-defeating behavior include an extra choice-making center that is unconscious or otherwise autonomous, the classical conditioning of motives, and cognitive errors such as superstition, misinterpretation, and faulty logic. These theories, critically reviewed in Ainslie (1992, Chapter 2), can be shown to be inadequate explanations of self-defeating behavior because of faults in their internal logic and/or in their empirical foundations. That review also presents the conclusion of behavioral researchers that all bodily responses depend on differential reward or on events that are its functional equivalent. Such a conclusion does not imply that all behavior is deliberate, voluntary, or even conscious, but it does require that even self-defeating behavior be explained according to strict utilitarian logic. Freud's "economic" model attempted such an explanation, but no modern theorist has produced one.

It is significant that many diverse theorists have mentioned the incidental implication that their mechanism causes subjects to devalue the future: Freud's *Project for a Scientific Psychology* (1895) quite explicitly contends that repression defers the obligatory passage of painful stimuli through consciousness, thus trading an immediate discomfort for a later one; later Freud proposed that the pleasure principle (1911), which became the id (1920), is marked by the pursuit of "momentary pleasure" at the cost of better "pleasure at a later time" (1911, p. 223). The behaviorists' conditioned motives are, by their nature, the near-immediate consequences of the supposed conditioned stimulus and, thus, must differ from ordinary goal-directed motives, which can arise from distant expectations. Cognitive theories of self-defeating behavior propose that people fail to picture delayed consequences adequately (Mischel and Staub, 1965), underestimate the control exerted over later outcomes by their present behavior (Bialer, 1961; Strickland, 1972; Walls and Smith, 1970), or find waiting aversive (Mischel and Staub, 1965). Whatever their mechanism, these assorted hypotheses all imply a devaluation of delayed events relative to more imminent ones.

However, these theorists have usually stopped short of saying that the human tendency to devalue future goods is fundamental. Although they often mention relative unresponsiveness to future contingencies as part of the problem, they portray it as exceptional and ascribe it to a more basic cause within their preferred theories, be it repression, conditioning, or illogical thinking. This is natural enough. We are used to thinking of ourselves as consistent, and we are often right. People do not radically devalue the future for most purposes, but preserve their interests over the years and save their money.

It is just as supportable, however, to say that living mostly for the present moment is our natural mode of functioning, and that consistent behavior is sometimes acquired, to a greater or lesser extent, as a skill. Both a general tendency to discount future events and a valuable but elusive trait countervailing this tendency have long been recognized. John Stuart Mill spoke of the conflict as commonplace:

> Many who are capable of the higher pleasures, occasionally, under the influence of temptation, postpone them to the lower. But this is quite compatible with a full appreciation of the intrinsic superiority of the higher. Men often, from infirmity of character, make their election for the nearer good, though they know it to be the less valuable; and this no less when the choice is between two bodily pleasures than when it is between bodily and mental. They pursue sensual indulgences to the injury of health, though perfectly aware that health is the greater good. (1871, p. 19)

The Victorian economist, Jevons, described the conflict similarly:

> To secure a maximum of benefit in life, all future events, all future pleasures or pains, should act upon us with the same force as if they were present, allowance being made for their uncertainty. The factor expressing the effect of remoteness should, in short, always be unity, so that time should have no influence. But no human mind is constituted in this perfect way: a future feeling is always less influential than a present one. (1871/1911, pp. 72–73)

In this century, Pigou perceived the same split between rationality and human nature:

People distribute their resources between the present, the near future and the remote future on the basis of a wholly irrational preference. When they have a choice between two satisfactions, they will not necessarily choose the larger of the two, but will often devote themselves to producing or obtaining a small one now in preference to a much larger one some years hence. (1920, p. 25)

Systematic research on the discounting of delayed goals began with Thorndike's animal analogs of human choice situations. He found that "increasing the interval between the response and the satisfaction or discomfort . . . diminishes the rate of learning" (1911; quoted in Benjamin and Perloff, 1983). An army of subsequent investigators have found that even short delays cause profound declines in reward effectiveness, even when subjects are signaled immediately that the reward is sure to come (Ainslie, 1975; Kimble, 1961; Renner, 1964).

Empirical research on human devaluation of the future rewards has not been done until recently; perhaps the question of devaluation seemed adequately answered by economic statistics on how the delay of a good decreases its value in the free market. However, when the notion that market discount rates reflect spontaneous preference is tested systematically, it does not hold true, even in the realm of consumer economics. For instance, one study of actual air conditioner purchases showed that, in accepting higher operating costs in return for lower purchase prices, consumers devalued the future at annual rates as high as 89 percent (Hausman, 1979). Similar studies have sometimes found rates in the hundreds of percent (Gately, 1980; Ruderman, Levine, and McMahon, 1986).

The objection that economic realities may have compelled choices contrary to subjects' objective preferences in such research has been refuted in four studies where people were asked how they would trade off amount and delay of extra income that were hypothetical (Ainslie and Haendel, 1983; Benzion, Rapoport, and Yagil, 1989; Kurz, Spiegelman, and West, 1973; Lea, 1979). In the Ainslie and Haendel study, for instance, employees and patients in a substance abuse treatment unit were asked to imagine that they had won a certified check for $1,000 that could be cashed in a week, but that they had the option of getting a $2,000 certified check that could only be cashed after a greater delay. They were then asked to name the delay at which they would be indifferent between this check and the $1,000 one-week check. They were told to assume that the checks were entirely sound and that they could be sure of getting the money at the stated time. The geometric mean time that patients would wait for the $2,000 was 31 days; the employees' answers were not significantly longer at 43 days. These groups were reporting that they would have to get annual interest rates on the order of 30,000–300,000 percent to make it worth leaving their prize money invested.

It might be objected that this was hypothetical money and that the subjects were more careless with it than they would have been with real money. To some extent this was probably true, although there is no reason to suppose the subjects were not frankly reporting what they felt. If they had wanted to impress the interviewer with how good their judgment was, they should have reported less discounting than they spontaneously performed, not more. In fact, given a situation where the patients could "invest" real money earned as subjects (from $2 to $10) for 3 days and collect 25 percent more, a third of them always chose not to do so, and another third sometimes chose not to. These patients were rejecting an annual interest rate of about one billion percent, even though they generally had little spending money, and their earnings were significant to them (Ainslie and Haendel, 1983).

Such a finding should not lead us to believe that these subjects never put money in the bank at 6 percent, or even that they do so less than most people. Rather, it supports the common observation that they are not *always* motivated to do so.

Crossing Curves Needed for Ambivalence

For some theorists, the simple discounting of delayed events explains all behaviors that are apparently imprudent or irrational. Logue (1988) suggests that organisms change their preferences over time because of a limited awareness of the future, or *time window*. Similarly, those of Cross and Guyer's (1980) *social traps* that are based on discounting are *time delay traps* attributed to simple discounting of the future. Economists Becker and Murphy (1988) invoke the same mechanism to assert that all addiction is rational, in that it must at every moment maximize the person's expected utility: They express the current utility of an alternative as the integral from the present moment through the person's expectable lifespan of $e^{\sigma t}$ times the momentary utility of that alternative at each delay, where σ is "a constant rate of time preference," and t is delay (their Formula 3). Because σ represents the steepness of exponential discounting, theirs is another time window hypothesis; ultimately they hold a person to be impulsive because he simply discounts the future too much. The trouble with such theories is not that time windows are nonexistent—a *time horizon* has been noted in the plans of even economically sophisticated people (Friedman, 1963)—but that these theories cannot deal with the common case where a subject knows he will change preference in the future and is still at pains to prevent this.

The hypothesis that the "true" or innate discount rate for future events is extremely steep accounts for disregard of the future, but by itself it does not explain the persistently unresolved conflict between "higher" and "lower" behaviors that clinicians call ambivalence. A steep discounting rate per se should simply enfranchise Freud's pleasure principle. The person might intellectually appreciate that his preferences were costly in overall reward, but it is still not clear how such knowledge alone could weigh against the person's short-sighted motives. A high discount rate would mean by definition that the person does not care about this cost. Such carelessness might threaten the individual's survival as an organism, and an observer might wonder how this trait was ever selected for in evolution; but it cannot generate motivational conflict.

For a discount function to produce motivational conflict between alternatives, it must generate curves that either lie so close together as to prevent one from dominating the other, or that cross one another as time elapses. The former situation must indeed arise from time to time, but in any important choice, the value of reaching a resolution should add weight to an alternative that gets even a slight, temporary edge, permitting arbitrary choice.[1]

As for the latter situation, discount curves that cross as a function of time alone do not arise from the conventional, exponential form of discounting. Exponential curves decline by a constant proportion of the remaining balance per unit of time elapsed. Unless different events are discounted at different rates, this kind of curve will never predict vacillations in their relative values, much less a discrete period of temporary preference for an alternative that is otherwise less valued.

Of course, there is no reason that different kinds of events, for instance, drinking alcohol and eating, could not be discounted at different rates. Thus, if a person valued drinking alcohol more than

---

[1]Sometimes people hesitate long over what is simply a close choice, perhaps to learn more information, perhaps to change or escape the choice situation itself (e.g., which person to marry, or "Sophie's choice" of which child to save from the Nazis). Where this hesitation is not self-destructive per se, it need not be conflictual in any way that cannot be accounted for by conventional motivational theory.

eating when both were imminently available but discounted alcohol more steeply than food, we would expect him to prefer alcohol only temporarily, when it was available in the near future. This example seems true to life as far as it goes. It could be that rewards that are commonly the subject of impulses—addictive substances, "thrills," and escape from pain, for instance—are discounted in the familiar exponential curves, but more steeply than other rewards. However, many impulses seek the same rewards that are at stake in the long run, only on a schedule that delivers a smaller amount of them at a shorter delay. Thus, a person may temporarily prefer immediate but transitory social approval, sexual gratification, or relief of pain at the expense of greater long-term occurrence of the very same

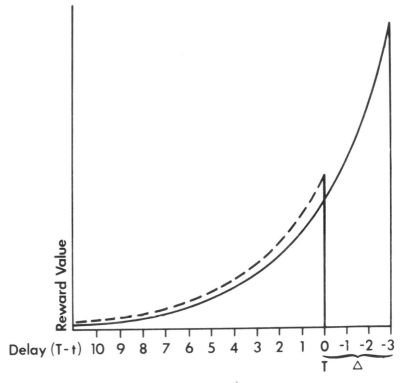

Figure 3.1. Exponential curves of the value of a reward expected at time T and an alternative that is objectively twice as great, expected 3 units of time later, as a function of decreasing delay ($D = T - t$) before they become available. Note that the X-axis in all figures is simple time, elapsing from left to right.

events. A person may be avaricious or not, but exponential curves give no reason why short-sighted avarice should conflict with far-sighted avarice.

Figure 3.1 shows two alternative amounts of the same good available at different times. The exponential curves drawn from them to show their discounted value at all times before they are due may decline sharply, but they remain proportional to one another. The only discount functions that can create conflicts between immediate and delayed consumption of the same good differ from conventional discount functions, not just in steepness but in their basic shape.

Herrnstein's Matching Law

For temporary preferences to form between rewards of the same type as a function of time, their discount curve must be more bowed than an exponential function. That is, it must decline steeply over small delays but level out into a long tail (Figure 3.2) that is higher at long delays than the tail of an exponential curve. In fact, a seemingly universal discount function that has just such a form has been observed in both people and animals.

Three decades ago, Herrnstein described a simple principle predicting subjects' relative valuation (V), as measured by frequence of choice, for each of two options in concurrent reward schedules, where behavior to obtain each option is rewarded unpredictably but at a set average rate (R) (Herrnstein, 1961), in a set amount (A) (Neuringer, 1967), and at a set average delay after the successful behavior $(T - t$, where T is the time each reward is due, and t the time of the behavior that obtains it) (Chung and Herrnstein, 1967). This principle, adapted from Killeen (1972), is as follows:

$$\frac{V}{V'} = \frac{R}{R'} \cdot \frac{A}{A'} \cdot \frac{T' - t}{T - t} \tag{1}$$

was parsimonious in the extreme, containing no empirical constants. It described preference as simply proportional to reward rate and amount, and inversely proportional to delay. Shortly afterwards, Ainslie (1974) pointed out its relevance to the problem of ambivalence, because the simple proportions that comprise it become hyperbolic curves when they are shown as graphs; hyperbolas have the

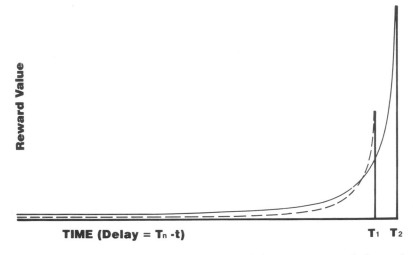

Figure 3.2. Hyperbolic curves of the value of the same expected alternative rewards as in Figure 3.1, drawn according to Equation (3).

curvature required to cross as a function of time, thus predicting temporary preferences in many cases.

Many subsequent experiments suggested small changes in the matching law's specific shape. Most significant for our present purposes was the finding that delay is not measured truly in concurrent variable interval schedules, and requires a more arduous discrete-trial "adjusting procedure" for literal accuracy (Mazur, 1987). The resulting formula for discounting the value of a single pair of rewards is:

$$\frac{V}{V'} = \frac{A}{A'} \cdot \frac{Z + \Gamma (T' - t)}{Z + \Gamma (T - t)} \tag{2}$$

where Z is an empirical constant that limits maximum value at zero delay, and Γ determines the delay gradient, that is, the subject's sensitivity to delay. The discounted value of a single reward, taken as its ability to compete with alternatives, can be expressed as:

$$V = \frac{A}{Z + \Gamma (T - t)} \tag{3}$$

We shall use this formula hereafter—setting Z and Γ at 1.0, following Mazur, because data about their proper value at long delays are not available. Although derived empirically, this modification of the original matching formula has fortunate theoretical properties: Reward values are proportional to the size of the reward at long delays, rise sharply as delay approaches zero and yet never become infinite.

Consider two alternative rewards, one of which, A, will be available at time T, and a greater one, A', will be available at time $T + \Delta$. Equation (2) says that subjects will prefer them equally when:

$$\frac{V}{V'} = \frac{A}{A'} \cdot \frac{1 + (T + \Delta) - t}{1 + T - t} = 1$$

where t is the time the choice is made, and the "rates" of reward drop out because they are equal. Solving for t,

$$t_{\text{indifference}} = \frac{A\,(1 + T + \Delta) - A'\,(1 + T)}{A - A'} \tag{4}$$

If A' were twice as great as A and Δ were 3 units of time, then $t_{\text{indifference}} = T - 2$; the delay at which the subject will be indifferent, $T - t_{\text{indifference}}$, is 2. At all choice points before $T - 2$ units, the alternative rewards should be preferred in the order of their amounts, which is to say that later, larger alternative rewards should be preferred. (At $t = T - 5$ units, e.g., the later reward should be preferred by $\frac{2}{9}$ to $\frac{1}{6}$, or 1.33). However, at all choice points after $T - 2$ units, the smaller alternative should be preferred over the larger one (e.g., at $t = T - 1$ units, by $\frac{1}{2}$ to $\frac{2}{5}$, or 1.25).

Direct Observations of Temporary Preference

The crucial aspect of any discount curve that is meant to explain impulsiveness is the degree to which it is bowed—whether rewards delayed by different times lose value in proportional curves or else in more concave curves that can cross, creating a conflict between present and future motives (Figure 3.2). Conventional concepts of motivation have assumed that the discount curve is exponential, probably *because* a more concave function produces intertemporal conflict and, hence, apparent irrationality.

Maximization of aggregate reward over time, discounted only in a shallow exponential curve, is still the basic valuation process in the eyes of most economists, even those dealing with individual irrationality (e.g., Stigler and Becker, 1977). In fact, demonstration of any intrinsic discounting of future events (a "positive time preference") is still problematic for some (reviewed in Olson and Bailey, 1981). Even those economists who have dealt with cases like addiction, where a person seems to discount his or her future massively, regard the person's discount function as exponential (Becker and Murphy, 1988). Only recently have some economists begun to follow Strotz' (1956) suggestion that choice naturally changes over time, and to catalog behaviors that are paradoxical from the viewpoint of overall utility maximization (Loewenstein, 1988; Thaler, 1980, 1987–1992; Winston, 1980).

The ecological counterpart of economics, foraging theory, has assumed a choice principle that maximizes aggregate net energy gain as a necessary outcome of evolution (Krebs, 1978; Maynard Smith, 1978); accordingly it has not examined the discounting process until recently. When investigators have done so, they have found that animals will regularly choose poorer, imminently available prey over better, delayed alternatives to the detriment of overall foraging efficiency (Lea, 1979; Snyderman, 1983).

In behavioral psychology itself, theories that assume consistent maximization of reward or "molar maximization" are still advocated (Kagel, Battalio, and Green, 1983; Rachlin, 1983; Rachlin, Green, Kagel, and Battalio, 1976, 1981; Staddon and Motheral, 1978). However, behaviorists have been able to use the very property that makes molar maximization intuitively attractive to test it decisively: As we have seen, molar maximization implies an exponential discount curve and, thus, stable choice over time once an organism is familiar with the contingencies of reward (Figure 3.1). Conversely, the highly bowed curve generated by matching predicts that there will be some pairs of alternative rewards such that a larger, later reward is preferred when the choice is seen from a distance, but the smaller, earlier reward is preferred as it becomes imminent (Figure 3.2). Rather than waiting for the shape of the discount curve to be quantified precisely, some researchers have bypassed this question. Temporary change of preference is an empirical phenomenon in its own right and has been accessible to study.

The experimental paradigm to elicit temporary change of preference follows Equation (3): A reward is made available at time T, and a larger, alternative reward at time $T + \Delta$. The subject is offered the choice at some earlier time t. With Δ held constant, the delay ($T - t$) at which the choice is made is varied parametrically. A switch of choice from the larger, later to the smaller, earlier reward as t approaches T represents a temporary change of preference.

A number of experiments have shown preference for the smaller-earlier reward when the delay $T - t$ is short, and for the larger-later reward when this delay is long. Such a switch has been obtained in animals choosing between two amounts of food at different delays (Ainslie and Herrnstein, 1981; Green, Fisher, Perlow, and Sherman, 1981; Navarick and Fantino, 1976; Rachlin and Green, 1972), in undergraduates choosing between longer or shorter periods of access to a video game (Millar and Navarick, 1984) or relief from noxious noise (Navarick, 1982; Solnick, Kannenberg, Eckerman, and Waller, 1980), in women deciding whether or not to have anesthesia for childbirth (Christensen-Szalanski, 1984), in substance-abuse patients choosing between different amounts of real money (Ainslie and Haendel, 1983), and even in the conscious self-reports of various human subjects choosing between hypothetical amounts of money (Ainslie and Haendel, 1983; Thaler, 1981). For instance, a majority of people say they would prefer to have a prize of a $100 certified check available immediately over a $200 certified check that could not be cashed for 2 years; the same people do not prefer a $100 certified check that could be cashed in 6 years to a $200 certified check that could be cashed in 8 years, even though this is the same choice seen at 6 years' greater delay $(T - t)$. They generally do not notice that these choices differ only in the time they are made, and cannot give an economically consistent explanation of their reported intention to change their choice when this is pointed out to them.

These experiments provide evidence that a discount curve more deeply bowed than an exponential one governs the subjects' choices in the situations tested. Such findings do not establish a precise shape, and they do not rule out a curve that is deeply concave but not hyperboloid (e.g., that suggested by Logan, 1965). However, the differences among deeply bowed curves are not important for the model of motivational conflict proposed here. It is temporary preference per se that explains persistent self-defeating behavior.

Aside from the theoretical expectation that the matching law's hyperbolic discount curves would be maladaptive as the basic mechanism of choice, the main arguments against it have come from certain experimental findings: Human subjects often come to maximize aggregate reward, especially when they know the nature of reward schedule, and even lower animals sometimes move in the direction of maximization of reward after long experience. It has been proposed that the acknowledged examples of matching be relegated to the status of special cases, either as derivable from maximization theory (Rachlin, Green, Kagel, and Battalio, 1976; Staddon and Motherall, 1978) or as one end of an evolutionary spectrum of sensitivity to "postreinforcer delay," with maximization at the other end (Logue, 1988).

However, the ability of adult humans to maximize income is not a surprise. People are known to be capable of great feats of gratification deferral. An organism that can spare next year's seed by rationing food over long periods of scarcity, and is known for resisting torture, is unlikely to be coerced by immediate reward in a laboratory experiment. The question is not whether people's choice pattern is limited to matching, but whether matching is the underlying mechanism of choice. If it is, it should remain detectable as a factor in decision making even after the person has largely achieved "rationality." How the person can achieve rationality within the constraints of the matching law will then be a large topic, somewhat overlapping the existing area of ego psychology.

To observe human matching directly, we have to observe situations where the subject is not challenged to exercise self-control and where the delays studied end in primary rewards or punishments, not tokens or warnings that these will come in the relatively distant future. Matching would not be expected in a procedure like that reported by Logue, Pena-Correal, Rodriguez, and Kabela (1986), where undergraduates chose between schedules of accumulating points that would later be converted to cash: Keeping cumulative scores challenges a subject to maximize these scores as a game in its own right, that is, as a rational task that "should" override current feelings of comfort or discomfort; differences in such feelings are minimized by rewarding with tokens exchangeable for money, which is in turn only a token exchangeable for still more delayed rewards. In the experiments just described where human subjects showed temporary preference, there was nothing inducing them to play a maximizing game; the rewards were either primary experiences, or money delayed by periods much longer than the time it would take to buy such experiences.

The human subjects in the latter experiments have undoubtedly shown better self-control at other times in their lives. However, in the experimental situations, they expressed a spontaneous preference for impulsive alternatives. We shall argue in Chapter 8 that a moderately small, one-time windfall like a prize or earnings as an experimental subject is exactly the situation where people do not apply their self-control. Here it is enough to note that people do not seem to outgrow in any general sense their tendency to form temporary preferences, but rather selectively apply the impulse-avoiding skills that they have acquired.

As for the experiments showing an apparent shift toward maximizing in animals, some pigeons have learned to be slightly less impulsive than they were at first after long experience in an amount versus delay choice situation; but their gratification-delaying behavior is easily disrupted (Logue and Mazur, 1981) and never arrives at a pattern consistent with noncrossing discount curves (Todorov, de Oliveira Castro, Hanna, de Sa, and de Queiroz Barreto, 1983).

The universal report of temporary preference when it is looked for in animals, together with human subjects' similar behavior when expressing spontaneous preference, strongly suggests that deeply bowed discount functions and consequent temporary preferences for imminent rewards are fundamental properties of motivation.

The Counterintuitive Nature of Hyperbolic Discounting

The wisdom of the ages has held that future events should not be discounted (while recognizing a proneness to do so in the sin of usury). Pigou (1920) said

> Generally speaking, everybody prefers present pleasures or satisfactions of given magnitude to future pleasures or satisfactions of equal magnitude, even when the latter are perfectly certain to occur. But this preference for present pleasures does not—the idea is self-contradictory—imply that a present pleasure of given magnitude is any greater than a future pleasure of the same magnitude. It implies only that our telescopic faculty is defective. (pp. 24–25)

We have just seen modern theories in both economics and psychology that allow for steep discounting, but even they have mostly stuck to the conventional exponential discount curve that leaves temporary preference unexplained. Yet hyperbolic functions are commonplace in the perception of quantities that do not involve delay. According to a principle known since the nineteenth century, the Weber-Fechner law, a change in a physical stimulus is perceived not proportionately to its absolute amount but as a ratio of the change to the prior amount (Boring, 1950, p. 280). For the perception of value specifically, recognition that it is based on a ratio dates back to Bernouilli: "Any increase in wealth, no matter how insignificant, will always result in an increase in utility which is inversely proportionate to the quantity of goods already possessed" (1738/1954, p. 25). Accordingly, Gibbon (1977) has suggested that the ratios described by the matching law simply represent the Weber-Fechner law as applied to the perception of delay. As applied to discounting, this law predicts that a delay from tomorrow to the day after tomorrow should be spontaneously perceived as 30 times as great as the delay from next month to next month plus a day.

But something seems wrong with this analysis. If we have reason to do so, we can correct for our human distortion of brightness, or loudness, or length, the dimension to which we analogize time (Benjamin, 1966; Kummel, 1966). The photographer can train his eye to estimate true light levels at least roughly, and a child soon learns to perceive automatically that the telephone pole down the street is as tall as the one nearby. Where an educated eye does not suffice, we easily believe the data of the light meter or tape measure. It becomes second nature to abstract a "real" object from our changing sensory impressions (Piaget, 1954). That is, we adjust our sensory impressions to agree with our best information, and we do so without the feeling that we are wrestling with some inner resistance.

Our norms call for the same adjustment when we are evaluating goods at various delays, but despite data from clock and calendar, such adjustment seems to occur irregularly, sometimes not at all. It typically takes some kind of effort, like "will power," to evaluate a present good as less desirable than a greater one in the future. This is where the analogy of delay to length breaks down: A person may move through time toward a goal just as he moves through space toward a building. The matching law formula describing the person's spontaneous valuation of a goal [Equation (2)] is close to the formula for the retinal height of the building ($Y = 1/X$, where Y is the magnitude in question, and X is the distance to the building or goal). The building does not seem to get larger as it gets closer, but the goal often seems to get more valuable. Insofar as the person fails to make the analogous correction, poorer goals that are close can loom larger than better, distant goals.

This is the heart of the temporary preference hypothesis. The original evaluation of delayed goods takes place in the same way as the perception of other magnitudes, but a person cannot learn to correct it as well, just as Pigou said. A larger image on the retina does not of itself motivate a person one way or another and, thus, does not resist transformation by abstraction. *Satisfaction,* on the other hand, is the fundamental selective force of choice, and however the person perceives or categorizes it with his *telescopic faculty,* he is still acted upon by its direct influence. That is to say, there is a raw process of reward that constitutes the active determinant of value. While value can be perceived abstractly, it does not motivate differently because of this abstraction.[2] Abstraction occurs downstream, as it were, from where motivation occurs.

The inconstant valuation of events that results from this property of motivation causes preferences to change between a given pair of alternatives as time elapses. In ordinary speech, the process of establishing a stable preference, when acknowledged as an activity in its own right, is called *making* a decision. The term implies that this process is indeed not as automatic as the correction for retinal size, for it requires deliberate action from time to time. Still, once we have "made" a decision in a particular direction, we expect it to continue in that direction over time unless acted upon by new events, almost as if it obeyed Newton's first law of motion. Not to make decisions, that is, to undergo vacillation, is called weak, impulsive, or otherwise pathological, an extraordinary situation that needs explanation.

Because people sometimes stick to their original decisions and sometimes do not, it might seem arbitrary to say that sticking to them, rather than abandoning them, is what requires special explanation. But this could also have been said of the first law of motion: The objects of everyday experience tend to come to rest; why not see this behavior as the norm?

The answer is obvious. When Aristotelian philosophers looked for propellants rather than retardants, they actually found none and had to account for momentum with ad hoc constructs that lacked predictive power, such as streams of air doubling back from the front of a thrown stone to push it from behind (Andrade, 1954). When we have looked for factors that change preferences rather than maintain them, we seem to have been equally misled; existing theories of "irrational" or ambivalent behavior are a hodgepodge. Given experimen-

---

[2]Of course a person's expectations of his goals can be manipulated by intellectual processes, but the person's valuation of these expectations is strictly constrained by this application of the Weber-Fechner law. The person may, for instance, convince himself that giving in to a disproportionate urge this time will bode doing the same to similar future urges that he now sees in their true proportions and, thus, come to have additional motivation against the current urge (see Chapter 8). However, although the person may thus be able to find extra incentives, he cannot make any incentive bigger or smaller by force of intellect.

tal evidence that preference intrinsically tends to change as a function of time, it makes sense to look instead for what factors produce constancy.

Deeply bowed discount functions tell us that the shift of preferences in the absence of new incentives is not an exceptional event that attacks some naturally linear perspective on value through the intervention of repression conditioned motivation, or cognitive lapses. Rather, they predict that preference tends to be dominated by skewed momentary perspectives. Other things being equal, it will shift as our perspectives shift, even if we have experienced these same shifts until they are thoroughly familiar. It says in effect that what Eve did in the Garden of Eden was not to eat the fruit of knowledge but to swing on the universal discount curve from delayed rewards, bending it permanently from a shape that had always generated simple preferences to a shape that generates persistent motivational conflicts.

The Formation of Intrapsychic Interests

The conflicts created by highly bowed discount curves are unresolvable because each alternative is dominant at a different time. At most points in time, the person prefers a "rational" behavior, but when an opportunity to lapse is imminent, he changes to an equally sincere preference for its alternative. Objectively, the rewards for rationality are greater, but the highly bowed discount curve should make these rewards ineffective from some perspectives. People often report just such frank reversals of preference, but usually only in some areas of their lives, where they experience their wills as weak. It remains to be seen whether the matching law, which would seem to make the reversals the norm, can account for the controls that make impulses exceptional (see Chapter 8). It must be remembered that matching only describes the behavior to which a particular set of rewards will move an organism in the absence of additional motives, not what it will inevitably choose.

Given repeated choice of a temporarily preferred imminent reward, the person's motivation to seek a delayed, larger alternative will die away, because the person will have learned that he never actually waits for it. However, behaviors that include committing devices to forestall the change of preference (or its consequent behaviors) will result in delivery of the larger, later reward, and will be valued according to the original curve from the larger reward. If this value has not been discounted too much at the time that these committing behaviors are available, they will be adopted; but if the person discovers a behavior that can evade this commitment at a time when the curve from the smaller reward is uppermost, the person will adopt this behavior in turn. The value of the committing behaviors will then decline, because they no longer guarantee the reward on which they are based. Thus, the effect created by successively dominant rewards is not simple turn taking, but a struggle for survival by the set of behaviors that tend to produce one reward against those that tend to produce its alternative. The turnings of this struggle can generate the whole range of behaviors that are seen in motivational conflict and that often seem paradoxical. The parties to the struggle are best described as "interests."

In political economy, an interest is an identified motive that acts on a group of people or would act on them if they were thoroughly familiar with the situation (e.g., "they have an interest in outcome X"). At the same time, it refers to the group that is defined by this motivation (e.g., "the votes of the X interest"). We propose that regularly recurring rewards create internal interests in the same way that economic opportunities create businesses to exploit them.

The reader may object to the idea of internal interests. They may seem to be another set of homunculi within the person, like the superego and id, or angels and devils. Such pairs of personifications of higher and lower motives have reemerged so often that they probably refer in some way to actual observation, but they have been defined only vaguely and have tended to deteriorate into allegory. However, the problem with such constructs has not been their personlike qualities, but the lack of a principle that could relate them to the whole person on one hand, and to the known elements of motivation on the other. We propose to supply such principles.

Interests are separated when the goods on which they are based are mutually incompatible. They may coalesce or divide over time, because they need not have an institutional life of their own. If I want to drink coffee, although it keeps me awake and I need sleep for an early appointment tomorrow, I have competing interests based on the rewards of coffee and sleep. If my appointment is changed so that I may sleep late tomorrow, they cease to support discrete interests. Thus, the term is one of convenience and implies nothing profound.

Furthermore, the concept of internal interests is convenient only because contradictory goals that are preferred at different times are not weighed against each other to produce a single, unambivalent purpose, but rather tend to produce conflicting sets of processes that persist as long as they sometimes obtain their respective goals. When conflicts are not based upon the opposition of shorter- and longer-range goals, unambivalent and stable choices will result, and there is no more point in talking of interests.

Examples of the alternation of power between interests may be trivial. Take, for instance, a person who stays up too late at night, not particularly concerned about what he will feel in the morning when it is time to get up. The person's interest in staying up could be said to win out over his interest in feeling good in the morning. When the alarm rings in the morning, he regrets having stayed up so late and perhaps plans how to avoid staying up as late the following night—the balance of power between these interests has shifted. Now we also see an interest in going back to sleep, which may win out over one to get up and go to school or work; if the former interest prevails, the person will regret it in turn later on, when the latter regains its dominance. This alternation may be discerned on many successive nights and mornings, even though at each of those times, his motives will be different in some respects from each other time.

Thus, the case that is important for the problem of ambivalence entails a short-range interest based on the upward spike of the discount curve when the smaller reward is imminent, and a long-range interest based on the "objective" valuations described by the tail of the curve from a more delayed alternative reward. The long-range interest is based on heavily discounted motivation but has the advantage of foresight—it can take steps to forestall the temporary change of preference toward the poorer alternative, like the frequently cited example of Ulysses tying himself to the mast to nullify the influence of the Sirens (Elster, 1979). The short-range interest is powerfully motivated by the proximity of its reward and can be expected to prevail if it has not been previously forestalled.

Interests must be based strictly on increases in aggregate expectable discounted reward. A person has no interest in modifying future self-motives except when such modification will increase his present discounted expectation of reward. An interest based on getting chocolate ice cream for dessert does not increase expectable reward by forestalling an interest based on getting lemon meringue pie, even if the two rewards are alternative to one another. Neither interest includes a motive to interfere with the person's free choice between them. But an interest based on not gaining weight may increase overall discounted reward by adopting committing devices against a dessert interest.

The point of the temporary preference theory we are presenting is that there are many incompatible interests that will not reach a stable resolution in which one of them simply wins, because they take turns being dominant. Any behavior in this situation must allow for the fact that the interest upon which it is based may not be dominant long enough to obtain the goal. Just as a currently dominant interest in a mature democracy must plan for the fate of its programs when a party that favors an opposing interest takes power, the person, in his present frame of mind, must take into account the tendency of currently unpreferred goals to become preferred at a later time if he is ever to see his current long-range plans realized.

We restate this theory: A person's motivation in general is divided into interests by the operation of the matching law. These interests are limited in their duration of dominance, but not necessarily in their access to any of the functions that comprise the *self* in any of its definitions. Like parties vying to rule a country, internal interests gain access to most of the person's resources when they prevail. The person who wants to stay up late at night, and the person who wants to rest in the morning, are indeed entire personalities, in the sense that they have the person's whole psychic apparatus at their disposal; yet they are clearly in conflict with one another. When an intelligent person is acting in his long-range interest not to smoke, he may use that intelligence to devise better stratagems to commit future behavior; but when he acts in his short-range interest to have a cigarette, that same intelligence can be marshaled to evade these devices.

The Effects of Temporary Preference Duration

Interests are apt to have a characteristic period of dominance, the length of time when their discount curves rise above those of competitors. This period depends on the kinds of rewards the interests have arisen to exploit, and on the intrinsic limitations of their particular modes of exploitation. It has in turn a major effect on what behaviors particular interests typically support. Duration of dominance affects not only how they defeat and are defeated by other interests, but also the affective quality of their motivation and whether behaviors based on them feel voluntary or not.

For example, conflictual sexual behaviors are temporarily preferred over various durations: Most obviously ambivalent are recurrent sexual rituals like exhibitionism, which are strongly preferred for the period in which they are executed (usually a matter of hours) but disowned at other times. Other preferences are longer lasting: Driven, rather hollow behaviors such as satyriasis (the Don Juan syndrome) or nymphomania may be dominant for months or years at a time in someone who nevertheless believes the trait is harmful and sometimes tries to end it. Conversely, some preferences are brief, such as the surrender to a premature urge for ejaculation, which the person is motivated to avoid even a second before he gives in to it. Other processes like performance fears are experienced as lacking a preferred period altogether; yet they must compete with other emotions for dominance, which suggests, as we shall argue shortly, some form of preferability.

Differences in affective quality and perceived voluntariness serve to define five rough zones of preference duration, four of which are temporary (see Table 3.1). The fifth zone contains activities for which one never regularly changes preference.

Table 3.1   Zones of Temporary Preference Duration

Descriptor	Distinguishing Feature	Duration of Cycle	Time Until Recognized as a Problem	Examples
Optimal	Never aversive	No cycle	Never	Conflict-free satisfactions, "To love and to work"
Sellouts	Ambiguous feeling of aversion	Months to years	Decades	Constrictions of personality; seven deadly sins
Addictions	Clear periods of pleasure and aversion	Hours to days	Years	Substance abuse, destructive emotions
Itches	Ambiguous pleasurable phase but conscious participation	Seconds	Minutes	Physical itches, obsessions, tics, mannerisms, hypochondria
Pains	Never pleasurable, no sense of participation	Fractions of second	Fractions of second	Physical pain, panic

Addictions

The behaviors that best seem to fit the description "temporarily preferred" are often called addictions. They have a clear phase of conscious preference, plainly tied to the proximity of the addictive reward, followed by an equally clear period of regret. Many of these activities involve the consumption of drugs that produce physiological habituation as they are consumed and aversive withdrawal states when consumption is discontinued. But this is not true of thrill-seeking behaviors like pathological gambling, courting fights, runnings risks with the law, the ritualized sexual offenses (e.g., exhibitionism, voyeurism), or kleptomania. Some addictions do not involve a thrill but rather short-sighted relief from chronic unhappiness. For some people, that is the value of drugs, especially the opiates; it is also the basis for social withdrawal in schizophrenic, schizoid, and simply shy people (Baumeister and Scher, 1988), for self-laceration in some borderline characters (Asch, 1971; Bach-y-Rita, 1974; Pao, 1969), and the avoidance of stimulation in patients with chronic pain (Philips and Jahanshahi, 1985). Many addictive activities are seen as ordinary habits: bad habits, perhaps, but not badges of psychopathology. The "type A" person who tries to reform finds an overwhelming temptation to drive the car competitively, step on others' sentences, and otherwise indulge in impatience (Friedman and Rosenman, 1974). People may find themselves unable to give up a habitual stance in relationships or, more subtly, the "games" in Berne's perceptive taxonomy (1964), and there are many eating and sexual habits that people say they want to give up. Perhaps the most elementary addiction is procrastination—simply postponing the relatively unrewarding parts of an activity (Lachenicht, 1989).

Sellouts

Many behaviors are indulged in for years at a time despite the person's sense that they impair richer, still longer-term activities. Complaints based on this kind of conflict are the hardest to understand because they arise in an apparently healthy lifestyle: The person is successful at the job but undergoes a crisis because he is not getting the satisfaction that was expected; he is successful in romance but loses interest in his partners, and so on. Often these conflicts are seen in philosophical or religious rather than clinical terms. For instance, the seven deadly sins described in medieval times (lust, wrath, avarice, pride, envy, sloth, and gluttony) include activities that can be highly stable and may never be renounced or even questioned but tend to become empty in the long run. These are major strategies for reward seeking, which often become stabilized as character traits—the Don Juan, the Narcissus, the embittered loser, the miser, etc. More complex but equally confining patterns are described in Berne's "scripts" (1972). Such strategies tend to be more narrow or concrete than other possible activities, and only some of their habitués come to identify them as unsatisfactory; for the others, of course, they are not conflictual but represent, however erroneously, their best guesses about how to obtain long-range satisfaction. Individuals may or may not ultimately reject them. The process of rejection is apt to involve long periods of reform alternating with surrender to the trait in question, during which the trait's character as a long but temporary preference is apparent. However, sometimes rejection comes decisively in a sudden "conversion" with no further changes of preference, and often the person expects to regret the trait years before he ever rejects it, making this category somewhat idiosyncratic among the temporary preferences. There is no accepted generic term for these slowly changing preferences with a clear-cut attractive phase and an ambiguous or variably experienced aversive phase, but they are sometimes called *sellouts,* and we shall adopt that term. We do not mean it to include those behaviors that an observer calls a sellout but that the subject himself does not expect to regret, for instance, the substitution of monetary gain for art as the goal of one's writing.

Itches

Some temporary preferences are briefer than the addictions. Unlike sellouts, which the person has at one time taken to heart and which may seem to be part of the self, preferences that are briefer than addictions are apt to seem external to the person. The individual is able to report participating in or "going along with" such activities but describes his motive not as pleasure but as an urge. The prototype of such activities is an itch, which the person wants to be rid of and which will abate if ignored, but which he usually maintains because of brief preference for the sensation of scratching. Many pathological forms of thought and behavior seem to follow this pattern, including hypochondria, persistent self-consciousness, obsessional doubts or worries, compulsive rituals, and the brief outbursts of social offensiveness called Tourette's syndrome, all of which are perceived by the person as undesirable, and all of which get worse with repetition, but which nevertheless seem to be hard to give up. In everyday life, mannerisms of speech and behavior like teeth grinding, lip smacking, nail biting, hair pulling, psychogenic coughing, the use of "um," fidgeting, etc., are all patterns that produce some relief or satisfaction but that the person generally wants to be rid of (e.g., Azrin, Nunn, and Frantz-Renshaw, 1982; Gay, Blager, Bartsch, Emery, Rosenstiel-Gross, and Spears, 1987). Unlike literal itches, most of these activities lack a physiologically stereotyped need state and cannot be dismissed as pain avoidance.

Pains

As periods of preference get shorter, the motivation to participate in the activity is increasingly experienced as ego-alien. This relationship suggests that there is a fourth zone of temporary preference on the brief end of the scale that has the basic properties of pain: aversiveness combined with a great tendency to attract some kind of participation, a participation that is related to but not, as we shall see, identical with paying attention to the painful stimulus.

Like many of the implications of highly bowed discount curves, this concept of pain is counterintuitive. It has been developed at length elsewhere (Ainslie, 1987, 1992) but can be summarized as follows:

Aversive events—variously called punishments, pains, annoyers, or unpleasant stimuli—superficially appear to be the simple opposite of rewards. They were conceived in that way by philosophers of behavior until this century. Experimental psychology continued in this tradition. Rewards were held to simply deepen the pathway that led to them, while aversive events were thought to obliterate these pathways (e.g., Thorndike, 1935).

It has never been clear, however, what obliges the organism to pay attention to the aversive stimulus itself (Erdelyi, 1974; Smith, 1954). It may seem only common sense that pain is peremptory and has to be attended to. However, there is convincing evidence that pain is not an arbitrary reflex in an otherwise free market of behaviors but instead must compete for expression like any other alternative. Evidence from hypnosis research (Hilgard and Hilgard, 1975; Spiegel and Spiegel, 1978), neurophysiology (Melzack and Casey, 1970; Wall, 1977), and neurosurgery (Mark, Erwin, and Yakovlev, 1963) suggests that a motivational-affective, or aversive, aspect of pain can be separated from a sensory-discriminative, or informational, aspect, perhaps with the former representing a response to the latter (Sternbach,

1968). Aversive stimuli must compete, sometimes unsuccessfully, for the organism's attention and beyond that for its active generation of the emotion of aversion. They must then have a common dimension with behavioral rewards along which this competition can take place.

The subjective term that best captures the nature of this dimension is *urge*. An urge is clearly a motive and can be resisted, but it expresses an instinctive, demanding quality that a term like *temptation* does not. There is an urge to attend to aversive stimuli, or, more precisely, to generate motivational-affective pain or other negative emotions in response to aversive stimuli; but it probably does not differ in kind from the urge for one to shiver when cold, scratch what itches, or drink alcohol when tense.

An aversive stimulus cannot be simply rewarding, or it would not deter motor behavior; it cannot be simply nonrewarding, or it would fail to support attention and the motivational-affective pain response. However, the matching law predicts that a pattern of intense but brief reward followed by a longer inhibition of reward will be temporarily preferred during the time when it is imminently available. A brief spike of reward that undermines the effectiveness of other rewards for a relatively long time after it occurs will produce temporary preference for the event over ongoing alternative rewards during the period when it is imminently available, but nonpreference at all other times (Figure 3.3). If this aversive process produces rapidly regenerating reward spikes, it can reward a motivational-affective or attention-directing response, but it will punish motor behaviors. If these cycles occur rapidly enough, they may be experienced as a blend of aversion and attraction, just as a person who watches a spinning placard sees both sides of the placard superimposed on each other. For the whole pattern to appear as pain, the obligatory fall in reward will have to be long enough so that the aggregate, discounted value of this brief spike of reward is less than that of the ongoing alternative reward at all times except just before the spike is available.

The hypothesis that unpleasant stimuli lure us rather than attack us should not be hard to accept. There are many familiar behaviors that we find unpleasant and can withhold, but only with the greatest effort: biting a canker sore, reliving a bygone humiliation, or reacting with arousal when we hear a dripping faucet while trying to go to sleep. Indeed, the combination of attention-drawing and behavior-deterring characteristic of physical pain is shared by a number of other aversive processes. These hinge on behaviors as brief as the person's very notice. Phobias are the most important category; their participatory nature is shown by their responsiveness to behavior therapies that give patients practice in resisting the urge to panic

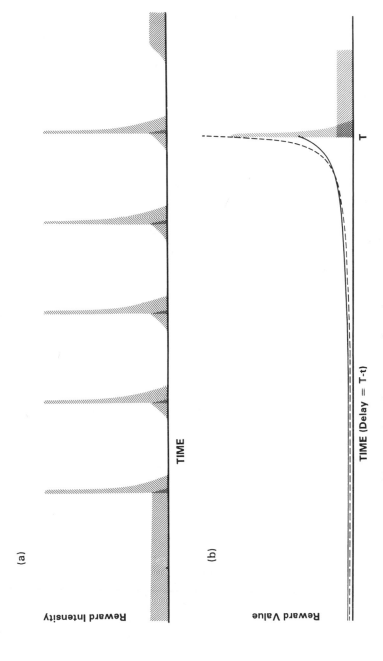

Figure 3.3. Amounts and hyperbolic value curves from five expected spikes of pain (Figures 3.3a) and from a small, constant reward that is alternative to a single spike (Figure 3.3b).

83

(reviewed in Clum, 1989). Tinnitus (ringing in the ears) seems to be another example of a perception that can be reduced by training in structuring attention (Ince, Greene, Alba, and Zaretsky, 1984). There are many other feelings that are experienced as "happening to" the person but that can be cultivated or, conversely, starved out by some kind of practice. If the person experiences them as happening without his participation and avoids them from their first appearance, they should be regarded as temporary preferences in the pain range of duration.

The Interaction of Interests

Deeply bowed discount functions suggest there should be a radical change in our traditional binary perception of motivation. As we have just seen, the sharpest division of incentives is not between pleasures and pains but between those rewards that are temporarily preferred and those that are preferred without conflict. Simple nonreward is probably neutral rather than aversive, a barren contingency that is avoided routinely and without much notice as a byproduct of the quest for reward. Aversive stimuli are at one end of the continuum of temporarily preferred incentives; they are not experienced as having a rewarding component because their duration of reward is so short. We must infer the rewarding aspect of aversive stimuli from their ability to reward attention. Activities preferred temporarily, but longer than pains, tend to be the subject of conscious ambivalence, which is felt differently depending largely on the duration of this preference. The classification of temporary preference for a given kind of activity according to the rough experiential benchmarks described earlier (Table 3.1) will often change from one situation to the next. For instance, the feelings called pain and fear are usually aversive throughout their duration. However, when the person seeks pain to prove virtue or bravery, or as an adjuvant to sexual pleasure, he may prefer it temporarily in the addiction or sell-out range (as in masochism) or may prefer it unambivalently. Similarly, a person may wholeheartedly cultivate an appetite for frightening movies, but when a child repeatedly seeks to watch them and suffers nightmares after each one, he is preferring them in the addiction range; if he experiences an unpleasant urge to rehearse scenes from them during the day, this activity (as opposed to the activity of going to these movies per se) will be an itch. The same person may be subject to related fears that never feel like he is bringing them on; these are pains in the sense described earlier.

Some feelings have no characteristic zone of preference but play different roles depending on their use for the individual and the particular occasions that evoke them. Anger, for instance, may be felt unambivalently, or may be cultivated in the sellout range as self-righteous hatred, perhaps as one of the many cult hatreds (Ku Klux Klan, anarchism, etc.) in a person who "knows better." Explosive personalities who lose their tempers and feel remorse over a cycle of hours to days could be said to be addicted to anger, while for the obsessional patient, angry thoughts may be an itch, and for some schizophrenic or terribly inhibited patients, anger may be a pain that breaks through their consistent attempts to avoid it.

To complicate classification further, a given reward-getting process may have separable components that are preferred over different time courses. An exhibitionist is apt to prefer this sexual behavior for periods of time in the addiction range (a few hours at a time), but he also prefers generating fantasies about it in the itch range (seconds to minutes before suppressing them). An alcoholic not only prefers drinking in the addiction range but is apt to entertain cravings for alcohol in the itch range and also emit motivational-affective withdrawal symptoms in the pain range. Those vegetarians who classify the eating of meat as an addictive behavior may or may not suffer cravings for meat in the itch range. Where a behavior is not preferred temporarily, the appetite is not apt to be subject to ambivalence, either.

"Higher" Interests

There are many activities that are preferred consistently over time, that is, they are never regularly avoided or regretted. These may be trivial, routine tasks: a manner of walking, a particular job, combing one's hair. However, they also include the subtle "higher purposes" of life that tend to be spoken of rather mystically, in such terms as harmony with God or nature, self-actualization (Maslow, 1968), or ego autonomy (Loevinger, 1976).

The model proposed here differs from the many other hierarchies of maturity or ego function that have been proposed (reviewed in Loevinger, 1976) in that those hierarchies are nonconflictual; they depict the person as simply advancing upwards as he learns more about life, abandoning leaner activities as richer ones are discovered. The interests just described also form a hierarchy (Table 3.1), but the lower activities persist as temptations that threaten higher ones, and what is learned as the person matures are behaviors that can potentially join any of these interests in its competition with any other.

The other models predict that the person who has learned self-actualization should give up nail biting and overeating. In the model proposed here, the highest or richest activities stay in competitive equilibrium with bad habits, forestalling them when the person both knows how and is so motivated, succumbing to them when he knows how to evade such prior forestalling and is so motivated. In this model, too, many itches and pains that are usually counted as involuntary are brought into the hierarchy. If people are supposed to outgrow lower behaviors, reaction to a painful stimulus with pain behavior would be evidence of immaturity; but in a model that includes robust temporary preferences, there is no such implication.

Impulses as a Chain of Predation

While attaching a longer-range interest, a short-range interest must also guard against attacks by still shorter-range interests. This possibility makes sense of Jon Elster's paradoxical predicament: "I wish that I didn't wish that I didn't wish to eat cream cake. I wish to eat cream cake because I like it. I wish that I didn't like it, because, as a moderately vain person, I think it is more important to remain slim. But I wish I was less vain" (1989, p. 37 note).

His long-range wish is not to be vain, which defines vanity as a temporary preference in the sellout range. His vanity is in turn threatened by an appetite for cream cake, a temporary preference in the addiction range. Note that, given only what the example tells us, we would not call the appetite for cream cake a temporary preference if the vanity were not present.

In theory, there could be any number of different activities, each with slightly more immediate goals than the next and incompatible with it, which form something like a chain of predation within the person's repertoire of choices. However, it is hard to think of examples with more conflicting elements then there are in Table 3.1, that is, about five. An example with just that many elements might be a person with bulimia nervosa. This person's longest-range interest is to eat normally, that is, so that he is pleased when looking both forward and backward over periods of years. However, he derives shorter (sellout) range satisfaction from mortifying his appetite to the extent that no evidence of fat remains on his body—a preoccupying asceticism, called anorexia nervosa when pursued consistently, which interferes with richer satisfactions and which the person probably knows he will ultimately regret. This person does not pursue it consistently, but episodically has a food binge and then tries to undo the damage by inducing vomiting. His preferences for a binge last a matter of an hour or two and, thus, are in the addiction range. Now say that he has read of injuries caused by self-induced vomiting, and develops a hypochondriacal preoccupation with having damaged his throat. When he is on a binge he repeatedly feels compelled to examine his swallowing sensations for evidence of damage, an urge in the itch range that interferes with the reward of eating. Finally, if he confronts evidence of injury, he may surrender to a panic that undermines even his ability to worry; this is experienced as happening without his participation and, thus, falls in the pain range.

Conflicts among interests in more than two ranges—that is, among short-, long-, and midrange interests—may underlie the pathological side effects of some kinds of impulse-controlling measures. This possibility will be described in Chapter 8.

Conclusion

The matching law and its hyperboloid discount function have broad ✕ implications. Without the nonexponential relation of motivational value to delay, we are at a loss to explain the inconsistency of preferences, the temporary dominance of inferior choices, and the apparent evidence of competing interests within the individual that have been widely reported. With the assumption of nonexponentiality, amply supported by behavioral research, we can account for "unwanted" behaviors ranging from character flaws to addictions to mannerisms to pain itself, the victim's participation in which has become increasingly evident in recent research. Although much previous writing on self-defeating behavior has contained intimations of a discounting theory, only a strict motivational accounting using these curves promises a comprehensive understanding of human irrationality.

References

Ainslie, G. "Impulse Control in Pigeons." *Journal of the Experimental Analysis of Behavior* 21 (1974): 485–489.

———. "Specious Reward: A Behavioral Theory of Impulsiveness and Impulse Control." *Psychological Bulletin* 82 (1975): 463–496.

———. "Aversion with only One Factor." in M. Commons, J. Mazur, A. Nevin, and H. Rachlin (eds.). *Quantitative Analysis of Behavior: The Effect of*

Delay and of Intervening Events on Reinforcement Value, Hillsdale, NJ: Erlbaum, 1987.

―――. *Picoeconomics: The Strategic Interaction of Successive Motivational States within the Person.* Cambridge, UK: Cambridge University Press, 1992.

―――, and V. Haendel. "The Motives of the Will." in E. Gottheil, K. Druley, T. Skodola, H. Waxman (eds.). *Etiology Aspects of Alcohol and Drug Abuse,* Springfield, IL: Charles C. Thomas, 1983.

―――, and Herrnstein, R. "Preference Reversal and Delayed Reinforcement." *Animal Learning and Behavior* 9 (1981): 476–482.

Andrade, C. *Sir Isaac Newton.* New York: Doubleday & Company, 1954.

Asch, S.S. "Wrist Scratching as a Symptom of Anhedonia: A Predepressive State." *Psychoanalytic Quarterly* 40 (1971): 603–617.

Azrin, N.H., R. Nunn, and S. Frantz-Renshaw. "Habit Reversal vs. Negative Practice of Self-Destructive Oral Habit (Biting, Chewing, or Licking of Lips, Cheeks, Tongue, or Palate)." *Journal of Behavior Therapy and Experimental Psychiatry* 13 (1982): 49–54.

Bach-y-Rita, G. "Habitual Violence and Self-Mutilation." *American Journal of Psychiatry* 131 (1974): 1018–1020.

Baumeister, R.F., and S.J. Scher. "Self-Defeating Behavior Patterns Among Normal Individuals: Review and Analysis of Common Self-Destructive Tendencies." *Psychological Bulletin* 104 (1989): 3–22.

Becker, G., and K. Murphy. "A Theory of Rational Addiction." *Journal of Political Economy* 96 (1988): 675–700.

Benjamin, A.C. "Ideas of Time in the History of Philosophy." in J.T. Fraser (ed.). *The Voices of Time.* New York: George Braziller, 1966.

Benjamin, L.T., and R. Perloff. "E.L. Thorndike and the Immediacy of Reinforcement." *American Psychologist* 38 (1983): 126.

Benzion, U., A. Rapoport, and J. Yagil. "Discount Rates Inferred from Decisions: An Experimental Study. *Management Science* (1989): 35: 270–284.

Berne, E. *Games People Play.* New York: Grove Press, 1964.

―――. *What Do You Say After You Say Hello?* New York: Grove Press, 1972.

Bernoulli, D. "Exposition of a New Theory on the Measurement of Risk." *Econometrica* 22 (1954): 23–26.

Bernstein, E., and F.W. Putnam. "Development, Reliability and Validity of a Dissociation Scale." *Journal of Nervous and Mental Disease* 174 (1986): 727–735.

Bialer, I. "Conceptualization of Success and Failure in Mentally Retarded and Normal Children." *Journal of Personality* 29 (1961): 303–320.

Boring, E.G. *A History of Experimental Psychology.* New York: Appleton-Century-Crofts, 1950.

Braun, B.G. "Issues in the Psychotherapy of Multiple Personality." in B.G. Braun (ed.). *The Treatment of Multiple Personality Disorder.* Washington, DC: American Psychiatric Press, 1986.

Christensen-Szalanski, J.J. "Discount Functions and the Measurement of Patients' Values." *Medical Decision Making* 4 (1984): 47–58.

Chung, S., and R.J. Herrnstein. "Choice and Delay of Reinforcement." *Journal of the Experimental Analysis of Behavior* 10 (1967): 67–74.

Clum, G.A. "Psychological Interventions vs. Drugs in the Treatment of Panic." *Behavior Therapy* 20 (1989): 429–457.

Cross, J.G., and M.J. Guyer. *Social Traps*, Ann Arbor, MI: University of Michigan Press, 1980.

Dweyer, P., and E. Renner. "Self-Punitive Behavior: Masochism or Confusion?" *Psychological Review* 78 (1971): 333–337.

Elster, J. *Ulysses and the Sirens: Studies in Rationality and Irrationality*. Cambridge, UK: Cambridge University Press, 1979.

———. *Nuts & Bolts for the Social Sciences*. Cambridge, UK: Cambridge University Press, 1989.

Erdelyi, M.H. "A New Look at the New Look: Perceptual Defense and Vigilance." *Psychological Review* 81 (1974): 1–25.

Freud, S. *The Complete Psychological Works of Sigmund Freud*, vol. 2. (J. Strachey and A. Freud, eds.). London: Hogarth (1895), 1956.

———. *Ibid.*, vol. 12, 1911.

———. *Ibid.*, vol. 18, 1920.

Friedman, M. "The Concept of Horizon in the Permanent Income Hypothesis." in C.F. Christ et al. (eds.). *Measurement in Economics: Studies in Mathematical Economics and Econometrics*. Stanford, CA: Stanford University Press, 1963.

Friedman, M., and R. Rosenman. *Type A Behavior and Your Heart*. New York: Knopf, 1974.

Gately, D. "Individual Discount Rates and the Purchase and Utilization of Energy-Using Durables: Comment." *Bell Journal of Economics* 11 (1980): 373–374.

Gay, M., F. Blager, L. Bartsch, C., Emery, A. Rosenstiel-Gross, and J. Spears. "Psychogenic Habit Cough: Review and Case Reports." *Journal of Clinical Psychiatry* 48 (1987): 483–486.

Gibbon, J. "Scalar Expectancy Theory and Weber's Law in Animal Timing." *Psychological Review* 84 (1977): 279–325.

Green, L., E.B., Fisher, Jr., S. Perlow, and L. Sherman. "Preference Reversal and Self-Control: Choice as a Function of Reward Amount and Delay." *Behaviour Analysis Letters* 1 (1981): 43–51.

Hausman, J.A. "Individual Discount Rates and the Purchase and Utilization of Energy-Using Durables." *Bell Journal of Economics* 10 (1979): 33–54.

Herrnstein, R. "Relative and Absolute Strengths of Response as a Function of Frequency of Reinforcement." *Journal of the Experimental Analysis of Behavior* 4 (1961): 267–272.

Hilgard, E.R., and J.R. Hilgard. *Hypnosis in the Relief of Pain*. Los Altos, CA: William Kaufman, 1975.

Ince, L. P., R.Y. Greene, A. Alba, and H.H. Zaretsky. "Learned Self-Control of Tinnitus Through a Matching-to-Sample Technique: A Clinical Investigation." *Journal of Behavioral Medicine* 7 (1984): 355–365.

Jevons, W.S. *The Theory of Political Economy*. London: Macmillan (1871), 1911.

Kagel, J.H., R.C. Battalio, and L. Green. "Matching versus Maximizing: Comments on Prelec's Paper." *Psychological Review* 90 (1983): 380–384.

Killeen, P. "The Matching Law." *Journal of the Experimental Analysis of Behavior* 17 (1972): 489–495.

Kimble, G. *Hilgard and Marquis' Conditioning and Learning.* New York: Appleton-Century-Crofts, 1961.

Krebs, J.R. "Optimal Foraging: Decision Rules for Predators." in J.R. Krebs and N.B. Davies (eds.). *Behavioral Ecology.* Sunderland, MA: Sinauer, 1978, pp. 23–63.

Kummel, F. "Time as Succession and the Problem of Duration." in J.T. Fraser (ed.). *The Voices of Time.* New York: George Braziller, 1966.

Kurz, M., R. Spiegelman, and R. West. "The Experimental Horizon and the Rate of Time Preference for the Seattle and Denver Income Maintenance Experiments: A Preliminary Study." *SRI International Research Memorandum* No. 21 (Nov. 1973).

Lachenicht, L. "Powers to Do: Commands, Conflict, Moral Orders and Indirect Rationality in the Analysis of Procrastination." Paper given at "Knowledge and Method Conference," Pretoria, HSRC, South Africa, January 1989.

Lea, S.E.G. "Foraging and Reinforcement Schedules in the Pigeon." *Animal Behavior* 27 (1979): 875–886.

Loevinger, J. *Ego Development.* San Francisco, CA: Jossey Bass, 1976.

Loewenstein, G. "The Weighting of Waiting: Response Mode Effects in Intertemporal Choice." Unpublished manuscript, 1988.

Logan, F.A. "Decision-Making by Rats: Delay Versus Amount of Reward." *Journal of Comparative and Physiological Psychology* 59 (1965): 1–12.

Logue, A.W. "Research on Self-Control: An Integrating Framework." *Behavioral and Brain Sciences* 11 (1988): 665–709.

———, and J.E. Mazur. "Maintenance of Self-Control Acquired Through a Fading Process: Follow Up on Mazur and Logue (1978)." *Behaviour Analysis Letters* 1 (1981): 131–137.

———, T.E. Pena-Correal, M.L. Rodriguez, and E. Kabela. "Self-Control in Adult Humans: Variations in Positive Reinforcer Amount and Delay." *Journal of the Experimental Analysis of Behavior* 46 (1986): 113–127.

Mark, V., F. Erwin, and P. Yakovlev. "Stereotactic Thalamotomy." *Archives of Neurology* 8 (1963): 528–538.

Maslow, A. *Toward a Psychology of Being.* New York: Van Nostrand, 1968.

Maynard Smith, J. "Optimization Theory in Evolution." *Annual Review of Ecology and Systematics* 9 (1978): 31–56.

Mazur, J.E. "An Adjusting Procedure for Studying Delayed Reinforcement." in M.L. Commons, J.E. Mazur, J.A. Nevin, and H. Rachlin (eds.). *Quantitative Analyses of Behavior V: The Effect of Delay and of Intervening Events on Reinforcement Value.* Hillsdale, NJ: Erlbaum, 1987.

Melzack, R., and K.L. Casey. "The Affective Dimension of Pain." in M.B. Arnold (ed.). *Feelings and Emotions.* New York: Academic, 1970, pp. 55–68.

Mill, J.S. *Utilitarianism.* London: Routledge, 1871.

Millar, A., and D.J. Navarick. "Self-Control and Choice in Humans: Effects of Video Game Playing as a Positive Reinforcer." *Learning and Motivation* 15 (1984): 203–218.

Mischel, W., and E. Staub. "Effects of Expectancy on Working and Waiting for Longer Rewards." *Journal of Personality and Social Psychology* 2 (1965): 625–633.

Navarick, D.J. "Negative Reinforcement and Choice in Humans." *Learning and Motivation* 13 (1982): 361–377.

———, and E. Fantino. "Self-Control and General Models of Choice." *Journal of Experimental Psychology: Animal Behavior Processes* 2 (1976): 75–87.

Neuringer, A. "Effects of Reinforcement Magnitude on Choice and Rate of Responding." *Journal of the Experimental Analysis of Behavior* 10 (1967): 417–424.

Olson, M., and M.J. Bailey. "Positive Time Preference." *Journal of Political Economy* 89 (1981): 1–25.

Pao, P. "The Syndrome of Delicate Self-Cutting." *British Journal of Medical Psychology* 42 (1969): 195–206.

Phillips, H. and M. Jahanshahi. "Chronic Pain: An Experimental Analysis of the Effects of Exposure." *Behaviour Research and Therapy* 23 (1985): 281–290.

Piaget, J. *Construction of Reality in the Child.* New York: Basic, 1954.

Pigou, A.C. *The Economics of Welfare.* London: Macmillan, 1920.

Putnam, F.W. *Diagnosis and Treatment of Multiple Personality Disorder.* New York: Guilford, 1989.

Rachlin, H. "How to Decide Between Matching and Maximizing: A Reply to Prelec." *Psychological Review* 90 (1983): 376–379.

———, and L. Green. "Commitment, Choice, and Self-Control." *Journal of the Experimental Analysis of Behavior* 17 (1972): 15–22.

———, L. Green, J.H. Kagel, and R.C. Battalio. "Economic Demand and Psychological Studies of Choice." in G. Bower (ed.). *The Psychology of Learning and Motivation,* vol. 10. New York: Academic Press, 1976.

Renner, K.E. "Delay of Reinforcement: A Historical Review. *Psychological Bulletin* 66 (1964): 341–361.

Ruderman, H., M. Levine, and J. McMahon. "Energy-Efficiency Choice in the Purchase of Residential Appliances." in W. Kempton and M. Neiman (eds.). *Energy Efficiency: Perspectives on Individual Behavior.* Washington, DC: American Council for an Energy Efficient Economy, 1986.

Smith, K. "Conditioning as an Artifact." *Psychological Review* (1954): 217–225.

Snyderman, M. "Optimal Prey Selection: Partial Selection, Delay of Reinforcement and Self-Control. *Behavioral Analysis Letters* 3 (1983): 131–147.

Solnick, J., C. Kannenberg, D. Eckerman, and M. Waller. "An Experimental Analysis of Impulsivity and Impulse Control in Humans." *Learning and Motivation* 11 (1980): 61–77.

Spiegel, H., and D. Spiegel. *Trance and Treatment: Clinical Uses of Hypnosis.* New York: Basic Books, 1978.

Staddon, J.E.R. and S. Motheral. "On Matching and Maximizing in Operant Choice Experiments." *Psychological Review* 85 (1978): 436–444.

Sternbach, R.A. *Pain: A Psychological Analysis.* New York: Academic Press, 1968.

Stigler, G., and G. Becker. "De gustibus non est disputandum." *American Economic Review* 67 (1977): 76–90.

Strickland, B.R. "Delay of Gratification as a Function of Race of Experimenter." *Journal of Personality and Social Psychology* 22 (1972): 108–112.

Strotz, R.H. "Myopia and Inconsistency in Dynamic Utility Maximization." *Review of Economic Studies* 23 (1956): 166–180.

Thaler, R. "Toward a Positive Theory of Consumer Choice." *Journal of Economic and Behavior Organization* 1 (1980): 39–60.

———. "Some Empirical Evidence on Dynamic Inconsistency." *Economic Letters* 8 (1981): 201–207.

———. "Anomalies." A quarterly series in *Journal of Economic Perspectives*. 1987–1992.

Thorndike, E.J. *The Psychology Wants, Interests, and Attitudes.* New York: Appleton-Century, 1935.

Todorov, J.C., J. de Oliveira Castro, E.S. Hanna, M.C.N. de Sa, and M. de Queiroz Barreto. "Choice, Experience, and the Generalized Matching Law." *Journal of the Experimental Analysis of Behavior* 40 (1983): 90–111.

Tversky, A., and D. Kahneman. "The Framing of Decisions and the Psychology of Choice." *Science* 211 (1981): 453–458.

Wall, P. "Pain and the Peripheral Neuropathies: Mechanisms and Therapies." in E.S. Goldensohn and S.H. Appel (eds.). *Scientific Approaches to Clinical Neurology,* vol. 2. Philadelphia: Lea and Feibiger, 1977, pp. 1942–1958.

Walls, R.T., and T.S. Smith. "Development of Preference for Delayed Reinforcement in Disadvantaged Children." *Journal of Educational Psychology* 61 (1970): 118–123.

Winston, Gordon C. "Addiction and Backsliding: A Theory of Compulsive Consumption." *Journal of Economic Behavior and Organization* 1 (1980): 295–324.

· 4 ·

Irrationality, Impulsiveness, and Selfishness as Discount Reversal Effects

HOWARD RACHLIN AND ANDRES RAINERI

IMAGINE two rewards, one clearly preferable to the other—for instance, a large candy bar versus a small candy bar—offered to a child. As long as the large and small candy bars are offered at the same time, the child prefers the large one. Imagine that the preferred reward was not available until tomorrow. The child may well prefer the small candy bar now to the large one tomorrow. Imagine that the temporal difference between the rewards is held constant but that both are further delayed—the child is offered a choice between the small candy bar a week from now and the large one a week and a day from now. Preference may reverse; the child may again prefer the large candy bar. The reversal is due to different rates of temporal discounting of the large and small rewards. We call it a *discount reversal effect*.

Consider the following physical experiment: Two sound sources (A and B) are placed together next to a meter that can measure the intensity of the energy from each. The intensity at the sources is adjusted until A is measured to be twice as intense as B. Then source A is moved away from the meter until the intensity at the meter is greater for B than for A. Finally the meter itself is moved in the opposite direction away from both sources. As this is done, a point will be reached where the measured intensity of A and B becomes equal; beyond that point, as the meter is moved further, the intensity of A will again be greater than that of B. The intensity of a radiant energy source such as a sound source decreases as the inverse of the square of the distance between the meter and the source. The reversal would not have occurred if intensity decayed exponentially with distance. Figure 4.1 is a diagram of (a) the reversal with inverse square discounting and (b) the lack of reversal with exponential discounting.

The representation in Figure 4.1 of the discount reversal effect follows Ainslie's (1974) description of corresponding reversals in self-control situations such as that of the child and the candy. To understand why the discount reversal effect occurs in psychological and economic systems, it may be instructive to examine why it occurs in physical systems such as that of the two sound sources and the meter. The two sound sources are assumed to approximate point sources. (With "pure" point sources, discount functions would rise to infinity at the source. The reverse curvature of the two functions of Figure 4.1a at the points labeled A and B reflects the fact that at very small distances, all real sound sources approximate planes rather than points.) When the high-intensity sound is moved back from the meter (arrow 1), its intensity at the meter decays. The reduced intensity of source A as measured by a meter (or by a human perceiver) could be equal to that of a hypothetical point source of lower intensity closer to the meter. However, a point source of sound at a distance is not in every way equivalent to a point source up close even when their intensities are equalized.

Energy from a point source spreads out over the surface of a sphere as its radius (distance from the meter) increases; the meter integrates the energy over a small sector of the sphere's surface. Although the total energy flux may be equal over a fixed area of the surface of a small and a large sphere, the two physical systems are not in every way equivalent. In particular, the energy flux through a fixed area on the small sphere would decay much faster than its equivalent on a large sphere with an equal increase in their radii. If, as in Figure 4.1a, the energy of a low-intensity source happens to be greater than the "discounted" energy from a high-intensity source, its greater rate of decay would eventuate in a reversal as the distance from them to the meter increased by a fixed amount (arrow 2).

Similarly, although we might equalize the value of a large delayed reward and a small immediate reward, the two rewards are not in every way equivalent. In economic terms, they are not completely fungible (Thaler, Chapter 12). If they were completely equivalent, one could be substituted for the other with no effect. But if a delayed reward (e.g., in the form of a bond) were traded for an equivalent-valued but more immediate reward, value would increase faster with

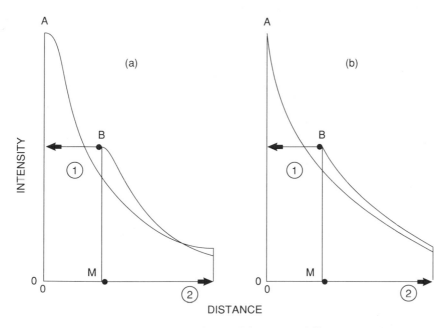

Figure 4.1.   Measured intensity of sound from two different sound sources, A and B: after higher intensity source is moved away from meter at M (arrow 1); after meter is moved away from sound sources (arrow 2). Graph (a) shows discount reversal effect with (actual) inverse square functions. Graph (b) shows lack of reversal with (hypothetical) exponential function.

time than if the delayed reward were retained. The only sort of discount functions that would ensure equal rates of change for equivalent-valued rewards of various amounts and delays are exponential discount functions (see Loewenstein and Prelec, Chapter 5) such as illustrated in Figure 4.1b. Thus, in the world of economics where exponential discounting prevails, a bond is in every way equivalent of its present cash value.[1] This is perhaps why, in economics, exponential discounting is considered normative and rational (Strotz, 1955). But in the real world (where nonexponential discount

[1] It has to be. Otherwise people would profit or lose by taking their money out of one bank and putting it into another even with the same degree of discounting. For instance, a bank that offered a bonus such as an appliance to new depositors would be in effect offering steeper than exponential interest rates. If more than one bank with identical nominal exponential interest rates did this, and if none required a minimum time of deposit, depositors could accumulate appliances at almost any rate they desired by repeatedly switching accounts.

functions are common), it may make a great difference whether or not a bond is cashed in.

Further Examples of Discount Reversal

Perhaps the best known example of discounting in psychology is the decay of memory with time. An early group of studies by Jost (described in Woodworth and Schlosberg, 1954, p. 730) established a set of empirical "laws" of memory that have never been seriously challenged (as empirical facts). Jost's first law states, "If two associations are now of equal strength but of different ages, the older one will lose strength more slowly with the further passage of time." For instance, I remember what I had for breakfast today with about the same vividness as I remember what was served at my bar mitzvah. But as the years pass, my breakfast will have faded to oblivion, while the roast chicken and stuffed derma of my bar mitzvah will still be a dim memory. Figure 4.2a illustrates how the discount reversal implicit in Jost's law is described by the same functions that describe the discount reversal with sound sources and meter.

Another example of discount reversal comes from real-world economics. Perhaps the most notorious example of economic decay is the rapid depreciation of automobiles (beginning the minute the car leaves the lot). Figure 4.2b shows data from *The 1987 Complete Car-Cost Guide* (Intelligent Choice Information Co., San Jose, CA) that illustrate the discount reversal effect.[2] Both memory and automobile value depreciate with time. But the same effect would occur with other modes of depreciation (age or interference in the case of memory, mileage or body rust in the case of automobiles).

The correspondence in decay over time among delayed rewards, memories, and the value of automobiles does not necessarily lie in any common mechanism in the three cases. The mechanism of automobile depreciation (some combination of fashion, friction, and rust as they interact with the economy) undoubtedly differs at many levels from the physiological mechanisms underlying delayed reward and memory decay. The question, *how* do values reverse in these three

---

[2] As people suspect, all of the "irrational" depreciation of car value occurs during the first year. Lincolns, for instance, depreciate about 22 percent during the first year. After that they depreciate about 10 percent (of previous year's price) per year. Thus, after the first year, car prices do depreciate exponentially.

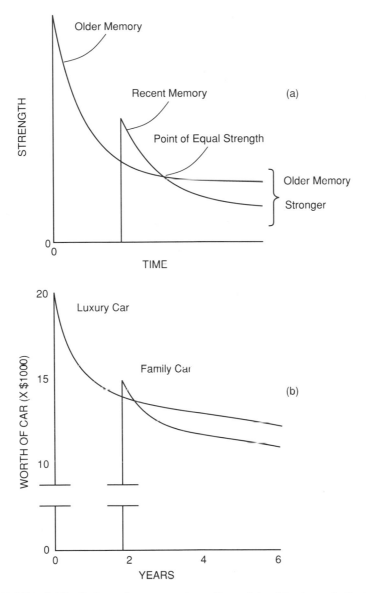

Figure 4.2. (a) Jost's law of memory strength explained by hyperbolic functions. (b) Comparison of used-car values for luxury car and family car bought 2 years later assuming equal depreciation rates.

cases, the question of mechanism, is not addressed by the present research. But the question *why* do values reverse—answered as being due to nonexponential discounting—is common to the three cases and, as will be argued later, may apply to *social* discounting (numbers of people) as well as *temporal* discounting. The remainder of this chapter is concerned with the particular form, the effect of combination and the application, of discount functions.

A General Discount Equation

The following equation has been found by Mazur (1987) to describe pigeons' choices among delayed rewards of various amounts:

$$v = \frac{V}{1 + kd} \tag{1}$$

where v is discounted value of the reward, d is the delay between choice and acquisition of the reward, and V is the undiscounted value of the reward.[3] Here it is considered whether the domain of Equation (1) may be extended to other forms of discounting, particularly probability discounting. In its general form, the variable d of Equation (1) is the magnitude of discounting (delay of reward), and k is a constant determining the degree of discounting.[4] If k is zero $v = V$ for all magnitudes of d and there is no discounting, hence, there is no reversal. For all greater constants (k's), the discount reversal effect is possible.

Figure 4.3 plots indifference contours (loci of constant v) implied by Equation (1) (see Chapter 5 in this book for a more detailed analysis). These contours "fan out" from a point equal to $-1/k$ on the

---

[3]This nomenclature differs from that of Ainslie and Haslam (this volume) by discounting the more general undiscounted value (V) rather than amount (A). In practice both present-volume articles as well as Mazur (1987) assume that the ratio of the undiscounted values of two (completely substitutable) choice alternatives is proportional to the ratio of their amounts.

[4]More general forms of Equation 1 have been suggested in which the entire denominator is exponentiated (Prelec, 1989; Rachlin, 1989) or in which only the delay term is exponentiated (Logue, 1988; Mazur, 1987). These formulations, with an extra parameter, of course explain more of the variance of obtained data than Equation (1) does. However, the simpler form adequately explains the data discussed in the present chapter.

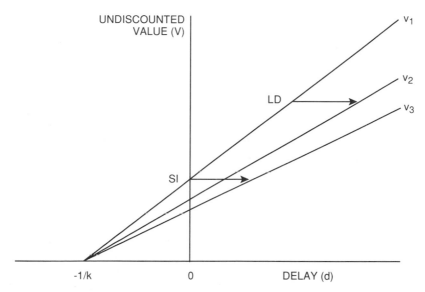

Figure 4.3.   Indifference contours (loci of constant discounted value) based on Equation (1). The ordinate represents undiscounted value of a reward (V). The abscissa represents delay (d). The contours of constant discounted value (v) fan out from a point on the abscissa equal to $-1/k$. The points labeled SI and LD represent small-immediate and large-delayed rewards, and the arrows represent a fixed additional delay discounting both rewards.

abscissa. Their values are in order, $v_1 > v_2 > v_3$. The points labeled *SI* and *LD* represent small immediate and large-delayed rewards of equal value (v). The two equal-length arrows extending to the right from the two points represent a fixed additional delay discounting both rewards. Note that (corresponding to Jost's law of memory) the large-delayed reward is more valuable after the fixed discount (v_2) than is the small-immediate reward (v_3). The fanning out of the indifference contours ensures this effect regardless of the duration of the fixed delay (the size of the equal-length arrows).

If the indifference contours of Figure 4.3 were parallel, equal delays added to *SI* and *LD* would terminate as well as originate on the same contour (would be equally valuable after as well as before discounting). As the constant k of Equation (1) decreases, the point of origin of the fanning lines moves further to the left. The further to the left the point of origin, the more nearly parallel the indifference contours would be at positive delays. Therefore, as k decreases, the discount reversal effect tends to diminish.

Irrationality

As an example of a discount reversal in probabilistic discounting, consider the following results (Rachlin, Castrogiovanni, and Cross, 1988): It can safely be assumed that $4 is universally preferred to $1. But if the $4 is risky, it may be worth less than $1 for sure. For instance, student subjects almost unanimously chose $1 available with (near) certainty in preference to $4 discounted by a probability of 5/18. However, when both the already discounted $4 and the almost certain $1 were both discounted further by 3/18, $4 was chosen. Such a reversal when two alternatives are discounted by the same probability seems irrational and is seen as a paradox (Allais, 1953).

Equation (1) may be applied to probabilities in two steps. First, a probability (p) may be expressed as a waiting time; if you were flipping a coin, throwing a die, or spinning a roulette wheel every t seconds, the average time you could expect to wait before winning equals $t\Theta$ where $\Theta = (1 - p)/p$ = "odds against" winning.[5] Second, the waiting time may be substituted for the delay in the general discount equation:

$$v = \frac{V}{1 + h\Theta} \tag{2}$$

The coefficient (h) incorporates t and determines the degree of discounting. In terms of probabilities:

$$v = \frac{pV}{p + h(1 - p)} \tag{2a}$$

Note that when $h = 1$, $v = pV$ where pV is the "expected value" of the alternative. Just as the hyperbolic delay discount equation [Equation (1)] accounts for the discount reversal effect with delay discounting ("impulsiveness"), so the hyperbolic probability (or "odds

---

[5]This formulation assumes that the die is thrown or the wheel is spun immediately and that the throwing or spinning itself takes no significant time relative to the time between throws or spins. In the more general case, $d = [(t + c)/p] - t$ where c is the time taken for the die to be thrown or the wheel to be spun. The assumption that c is negligible, like the assumption that delay between choice and outcome may be zero, is an idealization. In relating probability to delay this assumption arbitrarily sets the idealization, $d = 0$, as equivalent to the idealization, $p = 1$. In reality, just as nothing is immediate (the time between choice and outcome can never be zero), nothing is certain.

against") discount equation [Equation (2)] accounts for the discount reversal effect with probability discounting ("irrationality").

Impulsiveness and Irrationality Compared

Reversals of preference among delayed rewards implied by Equation (1) are common in the everyday life of human beings and other animals (Ainslie, 1974; Logue, 1988; Rachlin and Green, 1972) and are often labeled *impulsiveness*. There is evidence that the delay discounting that describes impulsiveness is similar in form to the probability discounting that describes irrationality (Benzion, Rapoport, and Yagil, 1989; Mischel and Grusec, 1967; Rachlin, Logue, Gibbon, and Frankel, 1986; Stevenson, 1986).

Rachlin, Raineri, and Cross (1991) attempted to determine this relationship by asking human subjects to indicate their preference between an outcome discounted by a probability and that same outcome discounted by a delay. Probabilities and delays were varied so as to obtain probability-delay pairs between which subjects were indifferent. The following paragraph illustrates the instructions to the subjects:

> Imagine I were to offer you the following chance to win $1,000. I would spin a spinner. (The experimenter points to a circle divided into white and black sectors proportional to probability of a win or a loss.) If it landed on white, I would immediately hand you $1,000. But if the spinner landed on black, you would get nothing. Now suppose, as an alternative, I were to offer you the same $1,000 for sure, without spinning the spinner. However, before you got the money, you would have to wait the amount of time indicated on this card. (The experimenter points to a card with "One Month" written on it.) I would like to know if you prefer to take a chance to spin for the $1,000 right now or to get the money for sure one month from now?

In some conditions, delay was constant, and probability was varied up and down (titrated) in order to find a point of indifference; in other conditions, probability was constant, and delay was titrated. The data described later were obtained by titrating delay. Note that subjects were always asked to choose between two alternatives. They were never asked to make a judgment about a single reward. The distinction is important because results of human choice experiments may differ radically from results of human judgment experiments

(Bostic, Herrnstein, and Luce, 1991; Lichtenstein and Slovic, 1971; Tversky, Sattath, and Slovic, 1988).

The experiment obtained points of indifference between $1,000 discounted by probability and that same amount discounted by delay. Equations (1) and (2) together predict:

$$\frac{V}{1 + kd} = \frac{V}{1 + h\Theta}$$

$$d = \frac{h}{k}\Theta = t\Theta \qquad (3a)$$

$$d = t[(1/p) - 1] \qquad (3b)$$

where t is a constant of proportionality (equal to the interval between trials with probability p, which would yield an average waiting time, d).

The results were in general agreement with Equation (3). Figure 4.4 shows the delays of $1,000 and the probabilities of $1,000 between

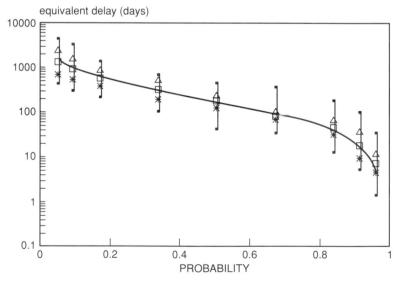

Figure 4.4.   Indifference curve showing delay of (a hypothetical) $1,000 certain reward as a function of the probability of an immediate $1,000 reward. The solid line is Equation (3). The stars are medians of an up-down titration; the triangles, medians of a down-up titration; the squares, overall medians. The vertical lines indicate interquartile ranges.

which subjects were indifferent. Equation 3a describes the data of Figure 4.4 quite well (correlating log d vs. log Θ, $r^2 = .96$, slope of predicted vs. actual data $= .99$.)

Impulsiveness and Irrationality Combined

Unlike Equations (1) and (2) (which are based on previous experiments), Equation (3) (which describes the data of the Rachlin, Raineri, and Cross experiment) is not a discount function. That is, Equation (3) does not relate discounted value to undiscounted value. In order to test the validity of Equations (1) and (2) in the present context and to investigate the way in which probability and delay discounting combine, we obtained discount functions of probabilistic rewards, delayed rewards, and delayed-probabilistic rewards. For one group of subjects (twenty Stony Brook undergraduates), the *present value* of a certain reward was varied (titrated) to find a point of equivalence between it and a future probabilistic reward of $1,000. For another group of subjects (twenty Stony Brook undergraduates), the *future value* of a certain reward was titrated to find a point of equivalence between it and an immediate but probabilistic reward of $1,000. In this experiment probability was expressed as a percent (e.g., ". . . a 70% chance of winning. . . .") rather than an area under a spinner. Otherwise, the procedure corresponded to that of the Rachlin, Raineri, and Cross experiment.

In the zero-delay condition, the first condition to which all subjects in both present-value and future-value groups were exposed, the amount of an immediate-certain reward was titrated against an immediate probabilistic reward of $1,000 available with various probabilities. For the present-value group, in subsequent conditions, the delay of the probabilistic $1,000 reward was increased to 1 month ($d = 31$ days), to 1 year ($d = 365$ days), and to 3 years ($d = 1,095$ days). Thus, for the present value group, points of indifference were obtained between an amount of money (A_1) available with no delay and for certain ($d_1 = 0$; $\Theta_1 = 0$) and $1,000 both delayed and probabilistic ($A_2 = 1,000$; $d_2 > 0$; $\Theta_2 \geq 0$).

For the future-value group, in conditions after the first, the delay of the certain reward was increased to 1 month, to 1 year, and to 3 years. For the future-value group, therefore, points of indifference were obtained between the amount (A_1) of this delayed and certain reward ($d_1 > 0$; $\Theta_1 = 0$) and $1,000 available immediately but with a given probability ($A_2 = 1,000$; $d_2 = 0$; $\Theta_2 \geq 0$).

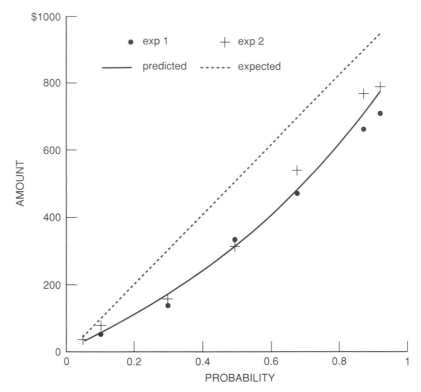

Figure 4.5. Indifference curve showing amount of a certain reward as a function of the probability of winning (a hypothetical) $1,000 reward. The solid line is Equation (2).

In the initial (zero-delay) condition, however, both groups were treated identically. The indifference-points of each group in this condition are shown on the same set of axes in Figure 4.5. The amounts plotted on the vertical axis are the certain equivalents of $1,000 with a probability given on the horizontal axis (both alternatives immediate). The data bear a striking resemblance to a hypothesized function relating stated probability to decision-weight assumed to account for probabilistic choice (Kahneman and Tversky, 1979). Note the discontinuity at $p = 1.0$. People must be indifferent between identical certain $1,000 rewards (the point at $A = 1,000$, $p = 1.0$). But the data reveal strong preference for the certain reward over even slightly uncertain rewards ($p = .95$). Kahneman and Tversky call the discontinuity at the upper part of the function "the certainty effect." The certainty effect can be expressed by assuming that all uncertain rewards are discounted by a fixed fraction (b) in addition to the specific

probability discount. The solid line of Figure 4.5 is a plot of Equation
(2) with the ordinate equal to $v' = bv = .8v$.

Given several parameters and assumptions used in constructing
the solid line of Figure 4.5, it is not surprising that the data are well
described by the line ($r^2 = .99$, slope $= 1.00$). However, the equations and parameters derived from this condition may be applied to
other experimental conditions.

Figure 4.6 plots the obtained indifference points for the present-
value and future-value groups for those conditions where the proba-

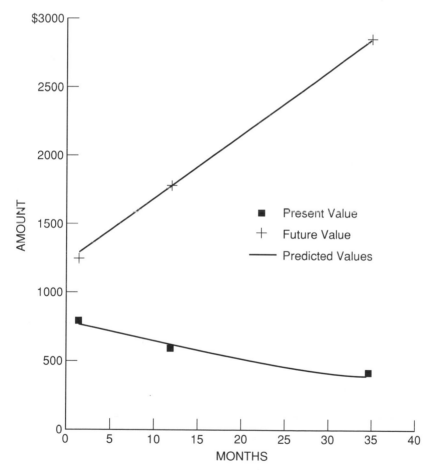

Figure 4.6. The circles show points of indifference between amount (present value) of an immediate reward and delay of (a hypothetical) $1,000 re-
ward. The squares how indifference points between amount (future value)
of a delayed reward and immediate (hypothetical) $1,000 reward. The solid
lines are predicted by Equation (1).

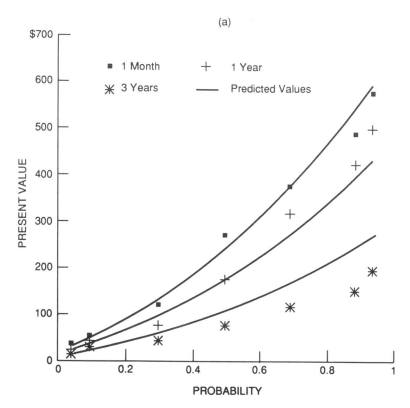

Figure 4.7. Indifference curves showing (a) amount (present value) of a certain-immediate reward as a function of the probability of winning (a hypothetical) $1,000 probabilistic-delayed reward between which and the certain-immediate reward subjects were indifferent. Delays were 1 month, 1 year,

bility of both rewards was 1.0. It seems clear from Figure 4.6 that there exists a discontinuity at $d = 0$ (an "immediacy" effect with delay) corresponding to the certainty effect observed with probability; less-than-immediate rewards (the constant $1,000 reward for the present-value group and the titrated, variable reward for the future-value group) are valued sharply lower than alternative immediate rewards.

The solid lines in Figure 4.6 show the predictions of Equations (1) and (2) with $b = .8$ (from the data of Figure 4.5), and $k = .0011$ for *both* the present value and future value groups. The predicted values fit the obtained points very well (correlating the six predicted and obtained points, $r^2 = .99$, slope $= .98$). The data of Figure 4.6 were fit with only one parameter (k) allowed to vary. The result indicates

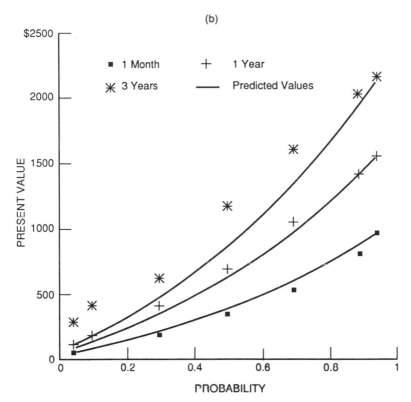

(b)

and 3 years. The solid lines are the products of Equations (1) and (2). Indifference curves showing (b) amount (future value) of a certain-delayed
reward as a function of the probability of winning (a hypothetical) $1,000
probabilistic-immediate reward. The solid lines are predicted values from
Equations (1) and (2).

not only that there exists an immediacy effect corresponding to the
certainty effect but also that the immediacy effect is not constrained
to the present-value procedure—it applies equally well in the future-
value procedure where the adjusted value was delayed, and the fixed
stated value was immediate.

Because there are only three points to the present-value function
of Figure 4.6, it is not possible to test the fit of a hyperbolic function
versus a (normative) exponential function.[6] The future-value func-

---

[6] However, another group of 30 subjects was tested under the present-value conditions with eight delays spread over a wider range. A hyperbolic function described
these data significantly better than did an exponential function. Of course, other un-
tested functions may well provide a better fit for the data of Figures 4.5, 4.6, or

tion provides a more definitive test. Note that Equation (1) predicts a linear relation between undiscounted value (V) and delay (d) as shown in Figure 4.3 and that the points of the future-value function of Figure 4.6 fall nearly on the predicted straight line. Exponential discounting predicts a logarithmic future-value function. The average future-value function in Figure 4.6 deviates considerably from a logarithmic one as do the data of individual subjects. The future-value data, thus, are at least consistent with a hyperbolic discount function and inconsistent with an exponential one.

It is now necessary to account for data with *both* probabilistic and delayed rewards. For each group there were 21 such points (3 non-zero delays times 7 nonzero, nonunity probabilities). These indifference points (not overlapping with either those of Figure 4.5 or 4.6) are plotted in Figure 4.7a (present value group) and Figure 4.7b (future value group).

For the present-value group, the $1,000 fixed reward was both delayed and probabilistic. Perhaps the most straightforward assumption regarding the interaction of probability and delay is that total discount is the product of the individual probability and delay discount functions.

The solid lines in Figure 4.7a represent the product of Equations (1) and (2) all with constants estimated previously from other data. The 21 points of Figure 4.7 were more or less precisely described by Equations (1) and (2) with no free parameters. Despite a tendency for the equations to underestimate the 3-year delays, a correlation of these 21 predicted versus obtained values accounts for 95% of the variance ($r^2 = .95$) and has a slope of 1.01.

Another possible mode of combination of delay and probability discounting, suggested by Rachlin, Logue, Gibbon, and Frankel (1986), supposes that probability and delay are additive in the sense that probability is converted to waiting time and added to delay. However, this mode of combination of probability and delay increases systematic deviations between predicted and obtained values. Therefore, we assume the multiplicative rule represents how delay and probability discounting were combined in this experiment.

Multiplication is consistent with a two-stage discounting process; subjects may have first discounted the $1,000 by either probability or delay, obtained a discounted value, then discounted that value by delay or probability. This suggests that delay structured as X days plus Y days would be discounted more than one structured as Z days

---

4.7. However, the typical *normative* functions, expected-value and exponential, are significantly worse than the hyperbolic as descriptions of the data.

(where $Z = X + Y$). This speculation has yet to be tested with human subjects. However, pigeons choosing between segmented delays of reinforcement (in which the delay period is segmented by a salient stimulus change) and unsegmented delays prefer unsegmented delays (Fantino, 1983; Leung and Winton, 1986); segmentation reduces value. If the pigeons hyperbolically discounted the reinforcement to the stimulus change and then hyperbolically discounted the already discounted (conditioned) reinforcement to the point of choice, the compount-hyperbolic discount would be greater than the single (unsegmented) discount, and the reinforcement delayed by a segmented period would be worth less than the one delayed by an unsegmented period.

For the future value group, probability and delay discounting were not combined. The solid lines in Figure 4.7b represent predicted future values with constants as before. Again, despite a tendency to underestimate the points of equivalence of the longest (3-year) delays, Equations (1) and (2) combined, with no free parameters at all, describe the future-value data well (correlating predicted and obtained values, $r^2 = .96$, slope $= 1.01$).

Avoidance of Reversals

Preference reversals with crossing delay discount functions may be avoided by prior commitment (Ainslie, 1974; Rachlin and Green, 1972). People typically prefer a large to a small reward if both are available at specific distant times in the future even if the larger reward is slightly more delayed. However, as time passes, the smaller reward will eventually be available immediately. If the discount functions cross, the smaller reward will be preferred after that point is reached. Let us call the relatively immediate availability of the smaller reward a *temptation*. Prior to that point, commitment to the larger reward (in the form of a response that cancels the availability of the small reward) avoids temptation and insures that the larger reward will be obtained. Pigeons, children, and adult humans make such commitment responses when they are available (Logue, 1988). More or less rigid commitment devices such as Christmas clubs, health club memberships, enrollment in schools, verbal promises, etc. are commonly available in everyday life. However, people (and other animals as well) often avoid temptations even when no commitment devices are apparently available.

The earlier analysis would attribute avoidance of reversals to a low value of the constant k in a hyperbolic discount function [Equation (1)]. The lower this constant is, the less likely preference is to reverse (see Figure 4.3 and discussion). The lower the value of the constant in their discount functions, the less impulsive or irrational (or, as we will argue later, selfish) people appear to be. Attribution of particular personal characteristics to particular values of constants in a discount equation provides a good description of behavior, and a behaviorist might argue that such attribution should suffice for explanation as well as description. Nevertheless, without hypothesizing about underlying physiological, cognitive, or mentalistic processes, it is possible to speculate about more molecular but still behavioral processes that may underlie differences in discounting.

When do discount functions appear to change? Consider the following experiment in perception. In a completely darkened room, devoid of any cues to distance, a person judges the lengths of two luminous rods. Assume that judgments are made monocularly with a fixed eye and separately so that no parallax or interposition cues are present. As diagrammed in Figure 4.8a, a shorter rod, closer to a person at position 1, may be judged to be longer than an actually longer rod further away. If the person is moved back to position 2, however, the longer rod may be judged longer. The discount reversal effect would be obtained, because by hypothesis retinal size is the

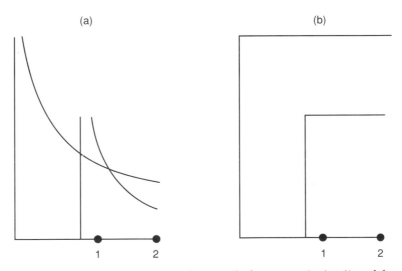

Figure 4.8. Judged relative sizes of two rods from near (point 1) and from further back (point 2) with (a) no cues other than visual angle; (b) with many cues.

only cue to the length of the rod, and retinal size decreases (non-exponentially) with the inverse of the distance between object and eye.

Now suppose that the room lights are turned on, both eyes are used, the subject can move, etc. In other words, distance, illumination, interposition, parallax, and all other cues to size are restored. With all of these cues, subjects can make veridical judgments of size; judgments do not reverse. Figure 4.8b shows the implied new gradients. This perceptual phenomenon is the familiar one of size constancy. In Equation (1), as $k \rightarrow 0$ the discount function becomes flatter and flatter. Under ordinary conditions, size constancy is maintained by means of a highly abstract analysis of a complex and constantly changing total environment (Gibson, 1966). Even color constancy is not an absolute judgment of wavelength but a relationship of properties of a particular stimulus to properties of the whole perceptual field (Land, 1964).

The capacity to perceive abstract qualities of the environment and to place individual instances correctly into those categories is not limited to adult humans. Mazur and Logue (1978) found that with extended experience, pigeons could learn to avoid temptation (a small amount of food available immediately) and wait (without external commitment devices) for a larger reward. Similarly, the child who without external commitment devices turns down a small candy bar today in preference for a larger one tomorrow may be said to be exhibiting "candy bar constancy."

The differences between these various phenomena (some of which are traditionally called perceptual, some cognitive, some motivational) are less significant than what is common among them—an apparently lowered degree of discounting of what is perceived, remembered, thought, or desired.

It has repeatedly been argued that the behavior of animals is sensitive to highly abstract contingencies of reinforcement definable only over temporally extended periods (Baum, 1973; Herrnstein, 1970; Lacey and Rachlin, 1978). The rat that presses the lever ten times for each food pellet may be conceived as "restructuring" its behavior so that the ten presses form a temporary unit susceptible to discounting as such but not susceptible to internal (within-the-unit) discounting. There is some evidence that with practice, such units are indeed formed (Mowrer and Jones, 1943). The rate at which a rat presses a bar to avoid shock depends on the relationship between the rate of bar pressing and the rate of shock (over a period of minutes) rather than that between any individual bar press and any individual shock (Herrnstein, 1969).

Human beings may be no less sensitive to abstract features of the environment. In some circumstances, this is obviously true. We hear as a tone an abstract property of a waveform not the absolute level of air pressure. But as the gestalt psychologists pointed out, we may perceive a melody and not a tone at all. Jost's laws of forgetting [and Ebbinghaus' (1913/1885) hyperbolic forgetting curves] would apply then to the whole melody, not to parts of it. Rachlin (1990) shows how a certain structure of a series of gambles may be responsible for the positive value of gambling for certain individuals.

Little is known about how and when such restructuring takes place. Nevertheless, we know that very small changes in the context of a problem (what Kahneman and Tversky, 1984, call changes in "frame") can have major effects on discounting. Mischel, Shode, and Rodriguez (1989, described in Chapter 6 in this book) found that children waiting for a large reward and tempted by an immediately available pretzel (a smaller reward) were able to wait longer if they were told to think of the pretzel as a log than if they were told to think of it as food. Mischel interprets these results cognitively in terms of the differing effects of "hot" and "cold" internal thoughts on behavior. But instructions to think of a pretzel as a log may generate self-control (lower degrees of discounting) not by increasing *internalization* but by restructuring—embedding the reward in a wider *external* context. A pretzel seen, conceived, or used as a log has (like a rod in a lit room) a context of external objects (such as log cabins), whereas a pretzel seen, conceived, or used as food has (like a rod in a dark room) a purely subjective context. With neutral instructions, children who were able to restructure waiting time (by turning their backs on the reward, closing their eyes, singing a song to themselves, or even falling asleep) also waited longer.

A child's impulsiveness is easily explained (as earlier) in terms of the child's immediate situation. It is necessary to look elsewhere than the immediate situation for the causes of the child's self control. At issue is whether the wider (the nonimmediate) situation or the child's (interior) cognitive state is more usefully conceived as the locus of those causes. At present it is probably best to pursue both avenues.

Small changes in frame can alter probabilistic discounting as well as temporal discounting. Silberberg, Murray, Christensen, and Asano (1988) found (with repeated gambles) that simply indicating to subjects how many trials remained in the session reduced the degree of probabilistic discounting with long intertrial intervals. One explanation of this finding is that the additional cue (like those provided by turning on the lights in a room) restructured the problem in wider terms and thereby reduced discounting.

Social contingencies and behavior patterns often magnify individual contingencies and patterns. Therefore, let us consider how hyperbolic discounting acts in interactions between people and then draw analogies to individual behavior from time to time.

Selfishness

One way of thinking about Equation (1) is to suppose that the discounted value (v) of a delayed reinforcer is equivalent to an effective or a "subjective" reinforcement rate. A reinforcement rate (like a probability) is a fraction; the numerator is the undiscounted total value (V) of all reinforcers delivered over a certain span of time; the denominator is the time span over which the reinforcers are delivered. In the case of a single, delayed reinforcer, the denominator is the delay. Thus, the actual rate of a reinforcer delayed by a minute is one reinforcer per minute. But in a given case, the effective rate of a delayed reinforcer may be greater or less than its actual rate depending on how the subject estimates the time span. The constant (k) of Equation (1) is in a sense a measure of this estimation; the greater is k, the greater is the effective time span over which the reinforcer may be conceived to be spread.

A parallel conception may apply to the discounted value of a reinforcer divided among a group of people. The numerator of the fraction is again the undiscounted value (V) of the reinforcer. The denominator in this case is not a span of time but the number of people among which the reinforcer is to be shared. For instance, the "objective" value to an individual of $100 to be shared with nine other people is $100/10 = $10. So much is third-grade arithmetic. But in many cases of choice, the very act of sharing may alter the subjective value. Simple division implies, for instance, that a person would choose $11 for him- or herself in preference to $100 shared with nine other people. But if those people were family members or close friends, the person might prefer the shared $100 to even $50 to keep alone. On the other hand, if the nine other people were bitter enemies, the person might prefer $5 for him- or herself alone to $100 shared with *them*. As in the case of delayed rewards, the effective value of a shared reward may be expressed by a constant in the denominator.

Equation (4) expresses the value to an individual of a shared commodity:

$$a = \frac{A}{1 + sN}.$$ (4)

where a is the value to an individual, A is the amount of a commodity to be shared, N is the number of other individuals sharing the commodity, and s is a constant representing the degree to which the individual perceives him- or herself as separate from the group among which the commodity is being shared. The more closely knit the group, the lower would be the value of s. Where the commodity is completely used in common, as it might be in a family, s would be zero. The constant, s, therefore measures "selfishness" in the same sense as the constants h and k represent "irrationality" and "impulsiveness" in the previous discussion.[7]

As Ainslie and Haslam point out (Chapter 3 in this book), the behavior of an individual interacts with that of the other members of a community. The process in social consumption corresponding to "turning on the lights" in the illustration of Figure 4.8 is a decrease in the parameter s of Equation (4). The more cues, signals, group interactions, group activities, common enemies, etc.—the more common the culture—the lower will be the measured value of the "selfishness" parameter, s, of Equation (4). Now let us consider social production.

In both social and individual spheres, cooperation may be required in production of commodities—to be consumed jointly in the social case or by an individual over time. In the latter case, following Ainslie and Haslam, an individual at time C is conceived as cooperating or failing to cooperate with him- or herself at times A, B, D, and E. The effective probability of such cooperation ($h\Theta$) must be a factor in determining the behavior of an individual's choice to cooperate (1) with other people or (2) with him- or herself at other times in the achievement of a common goal. In cases where cooperation is necessary in production, and the goods produced are not public goods but must be shared, Equations (4) and (5) might be expected to act multiplicatively, as probability and delay discounting were shown to act in the experiments reported earlier. For production of many commodities cooperation is necessary in both spheres—between individuals and within individuals over time. To build a building, for instance, a group of people would have to cooperate over an extended period of time. The value of activities such as building and using a building would have to be discounted both by odds against social cooperation and by odds against individual cooperation over

[7] Again, correspondence in functional form between various kinds of discounting does not necessarily imply identical or even corresponding internal mechanisms. A person who is impulsive is not necessarily irrational and selfish as well. Correlations between individuals among the constants k, h, and s have yet to be tested.

time. The experiments reported here imply that the various discount functions involved act multiplicatively. Societal constraints and reward systems seem to be designed to reduce as far as possible odds against cooperation in both spheres.

Another case of joint discounting would appear where a commodity is produced by a group and then shared among that same group or produced by an individual over time and then consumed by the same individual over time. An example of the former interaction would be the self-contained medieval manor or monastery where groups shared what they produced. Examples of the latter interaction are much more common in modern society—most of us work over time for a fixed wage that we spend over the same interval. In both cases, the gross value of the goods potentially produced must be discounted both by the odds against cooperation ($h\Theta$) and the degree of psychological separation between the individual person or moment and the group of people or moments (as measured by the constants s or k). Again, such joint discounting may be expected to act multiplicatively.

Summary and Conclusions

The value of a commodity to an individual may be discounted in several ways; its attainment may be made risky, it may be delayed, or it may be shared among several individuals. A discount function is the relation between value and the dimension of discounting. If discount functions were exponential, choices would not reverse with fixed additions of odds against (a measure of riskiness) delay or size of group. Choices in such cases would be seen as consistent. However, actual human and nonhuman discount functions are better described as hyperbolic than exponential. With hyperbolic functions, choices may reverse with fixed additions of odds against, delay, or size of group. The tendency to reverse increases with the steepness of the hyperbolic function. Individual differences in steepness may be expressed by the value of a discount constant: h, k, or s for the discount dimensions, odds against, delay, or size of group. Such reversals are typically seen as irrational, impulsive, or selfish. Tendencies to irrationality, impulsivity, or selfishness, therefore, may be measured in terms of the three hyperbolic discount function constants.

In many everyday-life cases, commodity value is discounted along more than one dimension; for instance, a reward may be both risky and delayed. Experiments in which human discount functions were obtained for hypothetical amounts of money discounted by both probability and delay revealed that overall discounting was the product of the functions of the individual discount dimensions. This magnifies the steepness of the individual functions. Thus, a person who may not appear impulsive or irrational with delayed or probabilistic rewards could appear both impulsive and irrational with delayed *and* probabilistic rewards.

Irrationality, impulsivity, and selfishness may be avoided by commitment devices that constrain behavior to be rational, self-controlled, and unselfish at points prior to reversal. The social and personal rules of conduct established by contingencies of reinforcement embodied in social organization and individual experience provide such constraints. These rules essentially restructure behavior into larger units so as to provide a bridge over points at which reversals would otherwise occur.

However, just as the highest perception requires a balance between concentration and abstraction (perceptual restructuring), so do the highest levels of rationality, unselfishness, and self-control require a balance. Just as perceptual restructuring obeys economic laws (Navon and Gopher, 1979; Sperling, 1984) so behavioral restructuring may be expected to do so. Avoiding reversals completely may involve a cost. There may well be such a thing as a foolish consistency.

•

This chapter was prepared with the aid of a grant from The National Institute of Mental Health and fellowship (H.R.) at the Russell Sage Foundation.

References

Ainslie, G. "Impulse Control in Pigeons." *Journal of the Experimental Analysis of Behavior* 21 (1974): 485–489.

———— and Haslam (Chapter 3 in this book).

Allais, M. "Le comportement de l'homme rationnel devant le risque: Critiques des postulats et axiomes de l'école américaine." *Econometrica* 21 (1953): 503–546.

Baum, W.M. "The Correlation Based Law of Effect." *Journal of the Experimental Analysis of Behavior* 20 (1973): 137–153.

Benzion, V., A. Rapoport, and J. Yagil. "Discount Rates Inferred from Decisions: An Experimental Study." *Management Science* 35 (1989): 270–284.

Bostic, R., R.J. Herrnstein, and R.D. Luce. "The Effect of the Preference-Reversal Phenomenon of Using Choice Indifferences." *Journal of Economic Behavior and Organization* 13 (1991): 193–212.

Ebbinghaus, H. *Memory.* Translated by H.A. Ruger and C. Bussenius. Educational Reprint No. 3. New York: Teachers College, Columbia University (1885), 1913.

Fantino, E. "On the Cause of Preference for Unsegmented over Segmented Reinforcement Schedules." *Behaviour Analysis Letters* 3 (1983): 27–34.

Gibson, J.J. *The Senses Considered as Perceptual Systems.* Boston: Houghton Mifflin, 1966.

Herrnstein, R.J. "Method and Theory in the Study of Avoidance." *Psychological Review* 76 (1969): 49–70.

———. "On the Law of Effect." *Journal of the Experimental Analysis of Behavior* 13 (1970): 243–266.

Kahneman, D., and A. Tversky. "Choices, Values and Frames." *American Psychologist* 39 (1984): 341–350.

Lacey, H.M., and H. Rachlin. "Behavior, Cognition and Theories of Choice." *Behaviorism* 6 (1978): 177–202.

Land, E.H. "The Retinex." *American Scientist* 52 (1964): 247–264.

Leung, J., and A.S.W. Winton. "Preference for Less Segmented Fixed-Time Components in Concurrent-Chain Schedules of Reinforcement." *Journal of The Experimental Analysis of Behavior* 46 (1986): 175–184.

Lichtenstein, S., and P. Slovic. "Reversals of Preference Between Bids and Choices in Gambling Decisons." *Journal of Experimental Psychology* 89 (1971): 46–55.

Loewenstein and Prelec (Chapter 5 in this book).

Logue, A.W. "Research on Self-Control: An Integrating Framework." *The Behavioral and Brain Sciences* 11 (1988): 665–679.

Mazur, J.E. "An Adjusting Procedure for Studying Delayed Reinforcement." in M.L. Commons, J.E. Mazur, J.A. Nevin, and H. Rachlin (eds.). *Quantitative Analyses of Behavior: Vol 5. The Effect of Delay and of Intervening Events on Reinforcement Value.* Hillsdale, NJ: Erlbaum, 1987, pp. 55–73.

———, and A.W. Logue, "Choice in a Self-Control Paradigm: Effects of a Fading Procedure." *Journal of the Experimental Analysis of Behavior* 30 (1978): 11–17.

Mischel, W. (Chapter 6 in this book).

———, and J. Grusec. "Waiting for Rewards and Punishments: Effects of Time and Probability on Choice." *Journal of Personality and Social Psychology* 5 (1967): 24–31.

———, Y. Shode, and M. Rodriguez. "Delay of Gratification in Children." *Science* 244 (1989): 933–938.

Mowrer, O.H., and H.M. Jones. "Extinction and Behavior Variability as Functions of Effortlessness of Task." *Journal of Experimental Psychology* 33 (1943): 369–386.

Navon, D., and D. Gopher. "On the Economy of the Human Processing System." *Psychological Review* 86 (1979): 214–255.

Prelec, D. *Decreasing Impatience: Definition and Consequences.* New York: Russell Sage Foundation, 1989.

Rachlin, H. *Judgment, Decision and Choice,* New York: Freeman, 1989.

———. "Why Do People Gamble and Keep Gambling Despite Repeated Losses?" *Psychological Science* 1 (1990): 294–297.

———, A. Castrogiovanni, and D.V. Cross. "Probability and Delay in Commitment." *Journal of the Experimental Analysis of Behavior* 48 (1987): 347–354.

———, and L. Green. "Commitment, Choice and Self-Control." *Journal of the Experimental Analysis of Behavior* 17 (1972): 15–22.

———, A.W. Logue, J. Gibbon, and M. Frankel. "Cognition and Behavior in Studies of Choice." *Psychological Review* 93 (1986): 33–45.

———, A. Raineri, and D. Cross. "Subjective Probability and Delay." *Journal of the Experimental Analysis of Behavior* 55 (1991): 233–244.

Silberberg, A., P. Murray, J. Christensen, and T. Asano. "Choice in the Repeated Gambles Experiment." *Journal of The Experimental Analysis of Behavior* 50 (1988): 187–197.

Sperling, G. "A Unified Theory of Attention and Signal Detection." In R. Parasuraman and D.R. Davies (eds.). *Varieties of Attention.* New York: Academic Press, 1984.

Stevenson, M.K. "A Discounting Model for Decisions with Delayed Positive or Negative Outcomes." *Journal of Experimental Psychology: General* 115 (1986): 131–154.

Strotz, R.H. "Myopia and Inconsistency in Dynamic Utility Maximization." *Review of Economic Studies* 23 (1955): 165–180.

Thaler, R. (Chapter 12 in this book).

Tversky, A., Sattath, S., and P. Slovic. "Contingent Weighting in Judgment and Choice." *Psychological Review* 95 (1988): 371–384.

Woodworth, R.S., and H. Schlosberg. *Experimental Psychology.* New York: Henry Holt and Company, 1954.

· 5 ·

Anomalies in Intertemporal Choice: Evidence and an Interpretation

GEORGE LOEWENSTEIN AND DRAZEN PRELEC

Research on decision making under uncertainty has been strongly influenced by the documentation of numerous expected utility (EU)
anomalies—behaviors that violate the expected utility axioms. The relative lack of progress on the closely related topic of intertemporal choice
is partly due to the absence of an analogous set of discounted utility
(DU) anomalies. We enumerate a set of DU anomalies analogous to
the EU anomalies and propose a model that accounts for the anomalies,
as well as other intertemporal choice phenomena incompatible with
DU. We discuss implications for savings behavior, estimation of discount rates, and choice framing effects.

SINCE ITS introduction by Samuelson in 1937, the discounted utility model (DU) has dominated economic analyses of intertemporal
choice. In its most restrictive form, the model states that a sequence
of consumption levels, $(c_o,...,c_T)$, will be preferred to sequence
$(c_o',...,c_T')$, if and only if,

$$\sum_{t=0}^{T} \delta^{t}u(c_t) > \sum_{t=0}^{T} \delta^{t}u(c_t'), \tag{1}$$

where $u(c)$ is a concave ratio scale utility function, and δ is the discount factor for one period. DU has been applied to such diverse

119

topics as savings behavior, labor supply, security valuation, education decisions, and crime. It has provided a simple, powerful framework for analyzing a broad range of economic decisions with delayed consequences.

Yet, in spite of its widespread use, the DU moJel has not received substantial scrutiny—in marked contrast to the expected utility model for choice under uncertainty, which has been extensively criticized on empirical grounds, and which has subsequently spawned a great number of variant models (reviewed, e.g., by Weber and Camerer, 1988).

Our first aim in this chapter is to remedy this imbalance by enumerating the anomalous empirical findings on time preference that have been reported so far. Taken together, they present a challenge to normative theory that is at least as serious as that posed by the much more familiar EU anomalies. Unlike the EU violations, which in many cases can only be demonstrated with a clever arrangement of multiple choice problems (e.g., the Allais paradox), the counterexamples to DU are simple, robust, and bear directly on central aspects of economic behavior. Our second aim is to construct (in the third section) a descriptive model of intertemporal choice that predicts the anomalous preference patterns. In formal structure, the model is closely related to Kahneman and Tversky's "prospect theory" (1979), but the interpretation and shape of the component functions are different. The chapter concludes with a discussion of some additional implications of the model for individual behavior and market outcomes.

Four Anomalies

In this section, we present four common preference patterns that create difficulty for the discounted utility model.

The Common Difference Effect

Consider an individual who is indifferent between adding x units to consumption at time t and $y > x$ units at a later time t', given a constant baseline consumption level (c) in all time periods:

$$u(c + x)\delta^t + u(c)\delta^{t'} = u(c)\delta^t + u(c + y)\delta^{t'}. \tag{2}$$

Dividing through by δ^t,

$$u(c + x) - u(c) = (u(c + y) - u(c))\delta^{t'-t}, \tag{3}$$

shows that preference between the two consumption adjustments depends only on the absolute time interval separating them, or $(t' - t)$ in the example above. This is the *stationarity* property, which plays a critical role in axiomatic derivations of the DU model (Fishburn and Rubinstein, 1982; Koopmans, 1960).

In practice, preferences between two delayed outcomes often switch when both delays are incremented by a given constant amount. An example of Thaler (1981) makes the point crisply: A person might prefer one apple today to two apples tomorrow, but at the same time prefer two apples in 51 days to one apple in 50 days. We will refer to this pattern as the *common difference effect*.[1]

The common difference effect gives rise to dynamically inconsistent behavior, as noted first by Strotz (1955), and richly elaborated in the articles of the psychologist Ainslie (1975, 1985). It also implies that discount rates should decrease as a function of the time delay over which they are estimated, which has been observed in a number of studies, including one with real money outcomes (Horowitz, 1988).[2] See Figure 5.6 for the results of Benzion, Rapoport, and Yagil (1989), which are representative.

The Absolute Magnitude Effect

Empirical studies of time preference have also found that large dollar amounts suffer less proportional discounting than do small ones. Thaler (1980), for example, reported that subjects who were on average indifferent between receiving $15 immediately and $60 in a year, were also indifferent between an immediate $250 and $350 in a year, as well as between $3,000 now and $4,000 in a year. Similar results were obtained by Holcomb and Nelson (1989) with real money outcomes.

---

[1] The common difference effect is analogous to the common ratio effect in decision making under uncertainty (Kahneman and Tversky, 1979). For a discussion of similarities and differences between the EU and DU axioms, see Prelec and Loewenstein (1991).

[2] Horowitz (1988) used a second price sealed bid auction to estimated discount rates for $50 "bonds" of varying maturity. Implicit discount rates were a declining function of time to bond maturity.

~ The Gain-Loss Asymmetry

A closely related finding is that losses are discounted at a lower rate than gains. For example, subjects in a study by Loewenstein (1988c) were, on average, indifferent between receiving $10 immediately and receiving $21 in one year, and indifferent between losing $10 immediately and losing $15 in one year. The corresponding figures for $100 were $157 for gains and $133 for losses. Even more dramatic loss/gain asymmetries were obtained by Thaler (1980), who estimated discount rates for gains that were three to ten times greater than those for losses. Several of his subjects actually exhibited negative discounting, in that they preferred an immediate loss over a delayed loss of equal value (see also, Loewenstein, 1987).

The magnitude and gain-loss effects are problematic for DU in two senses. First, the predictions that DU makes are sensitive to the baseline consumption profile, because the baseline level at a given time period directly controls the marginal utility of an extra unit of consumption. Experimental subjects represent a diversity of baseline levels of consumption, yet these choice patterns are consistent over a wide range of income (and hence consumption) levels. This pattern evokes the comments of Markowitz (1952) on the Friedman-Savage explanation for simultaneous gambling and insurance purchases. Friedman and Savage argued that simultaneous gambling and insurance could be explained by a doubly inflected utility function defined over levels of wealth. Markowitz pointed out that no single utility function defined over levels of wealth could explain why people at vastly different levels of wealth engage in both activities; a function that predicted simultaneous gambling and insuring for people at one wealth level would make counterintuitive predictions for people at other wealth levels.

Second, even the determinate predictions that DU yields, on the assumption that the baseline consumption level is constant across time periods, are not entirely consistent with the effects just described. Note first that the present value of a consumption change at time t, from c to $c + x$, can be measured in two ways, either by assessing the *equivalent* present value $q(x,t)$ defined implicitly by:

$$u(c + q) + \delta^t u(c) = u(c) + \delta^t u(c + x), \qquad (4)$$

or by assessing the *compensating* present value $p(x,t)$ that would exactly balance the change at time t:

$$u(c - p) + \delta^t u(c + x) = u(c) + \delta^t u(c). \qquad (5)$$

(These are also referred to as the methods of *equivalent* and *compensating* variation.)

The gain-loss asymmetry is obtained by comparing the equivalent variation ratios (q/x) for positive and negative x; here, the DU model makes the correct qualitative prediction, as the following simple calculation shows:

$$q(x,t) = u^{-1}\{(1 - \delta^t)u(c) + \delta^t u(c + x)\} - c \text{ [solving from Equation (4)]}$$

$$< (1 - \delta^t)c + \delta^t(c + x) - c \text{ (by concavity of } u(x)) \qquad (6)$$

$$= \delta^t x.$$

Consequently the ratio, $q(x,t)/x$, is smaller than δ^t for positive x, and greater than δ^t for negative x, which is consistent with the observed greater relative discounting of gains.

The critical weakness of this explanation lies in the prediction it makes about the size of the gain-loss asymmetry at different absolute magnitudes. The normative explanation is driven by the global concavity of the utility function, which creates a gap (analogous to a risk premium) between time discounting and the pure rate of time preference. Since the utility function is approximately linear for small intervals ($c - x, c + x$), the gain-loss asymmetry should disappear for small x. Indeed, in the limit as x goes to zero (from either side) the predicted devaluation ratio, q/x, will approach the discount factor δ^t, for both gains and losses. In practice, however, we observe the exact opposite, with the gain-loss asymmetry being most pronounced for small outcomes (Thaler, 1980; Benzion, Rapoport, and Yagil, 1989).

With regard to the magnitude effect, the DU predictions hinge partly on the method of elicitation. When present values are assessed by the equivalent variation method, DU contradicts the magnitude effect. For compensating variation, DU predicts the effect when x is negative, but predicts the exact opposite (i.e., smaller discounting of *small* amounts) for positive x. We now derive this last result as an illustration; the argument in the other cases is similar.

Suppose that p is the most one would be willing to pay now in order to receive $x > 0$ at time t, as in Equation (5), and consider what happens as both p and x are increased by a common factor, $\alpha > 1$:

$$\frac{\partial}{\partial \alpha}\Big|_{\alpha=1} \{u(c - \alpha p) + \delta^t u(c + \alpha x) - (u(c) + \delta^t u(c))\} \text{ [from Equation (5)]}$$

$$= -pu'(c - p) + \delta^t u'(c + x) \qquad (7)$$

$$> 0 \text{ (if the magnitude effect holds)}.$$

After we substitute for δ^t from Equation (5), this inequality reduces to:

$$pu'(c - p)(u(c + x) - u(c)) < xu'(c + x)((u(c) - u(c - p)). \qquad (8)$$

But, because $u(c)$ is concave, we have $u(c + x) - u(c) > xu'(c + x)$ and $u(c) - u(c - p) < pu'(c - p)$, which are jointly incompatible with the stated inequality in Equation (8).

The Delay-Speedup Asymmetery

A recent study by Loewenstein (1988a) has documented a fourth anomaly, consisting of an asymmetric preference between speeding up and delaying consumption. In general, the amount required to compensate for delaying a (real) reward by a given interval, from t to $t + s$, was from two to four times greater than the amount subjects were willing to sacrifice to speed consumption up by the same interval, that is, from $t + s$ to t. Because the two pairs of choices are actually different representations of the same underlying pair of options, the results constitute a classic framing effect, which is inconsistent with any normative theory, including DU.

A Behavioral Model of Intertemporal Choice

This section presents a model of intertemporal choice that accounts for the anomalies just enumerated. Our model assumes that intertemporal choice is defined with respect to *deviations* from an anticipated status quo (or "reference") consumption plan; this is in explicit contrast to the DU assumption that people integrate new consumption alternatives with existing plans before making a choice. The objects of choice, then, are sequences of dated adjustments to consumption $\{(x_i, t_i); i = 1, ..., n\}$, which we will refer to as *temporal prospects.*

As in the prospect theory for risky choice, we will represent preference by a doubly separable formula [Equation (9) later], which rests on three qualitative properties (see appendix in Kahneman and Tversky, [1979], for details). The first property, also invoked by DU, is that preferences over prospects are intertemporally separable (Debreu, 1959), and can, therefore, be represented by an additive utility function, $\Sigma_i\ u(x_i, t_i)$. This important assumption is psychologically most questionable when the choice is perceived to be between complete alternative sequences of outcomes, for example, savings plans, or multiyear salary contracts. In these cases, it appears that people care about global sequence properties, most notably whether the sequence improves over time (Loewenstein and Prelec, 1991; Loewenstein and Sicherman, 1991). The present model is primarily concerned with explaining elementary types of intertemporal choices, involving no more than two or three distinct dated outcomes.

In the absence of any strong contrary evidence, we assume that x and t are separable within a single outcome, so that $u(x,t)$ equals $F(v(x)\phi(t))$, where $v(x)$ is a *value function*, $\phi(t)$ a *discount function*, and F an arbitrary monotonically increasing transformation. To eliminate F, one imposes a distributivity condition: (x,t) is indifferent to $(x,t';x,t'')$, implies (y,t) is indifferent to $(y,t';y,t'')$, for any outcome y, which essentially states that the equality: $\phi(t) = \phi(t') + \phi(t'')$, can be established with any one outcome (Kahneman and Tversky, 1979, p. 290). The discount function is then uniquely specified, given the standard normalization $\phi(0) = 1$. The final model represents preference by the formula:

$$U(x_1,t_1;..;x_n,t_n) = \sum_i v(x_i)\phi(t_i). \tag{9}$$

The remainder of this section specifies the properties of the two component functions and shows how the model accounts for the anomalies presented in the second section.

Discount Function

The common difference effect reveals that people are more sensitive to a given time delay if it occurs earlier rather than later. Specifically, if a person is indifferent between receiving $x > 0$ immediately, and $y > x$ at some later time s, then he or she will strictly prefer the better outcome if both outcomes are postponed by a common amount, t:

$$v(x) = v(y)\phi(s), \quad \text{implies: } v(x)\phi(t) < v(y)\phi(t + s). \tag{10}$$

In order to maintain indifference, the later larger outcome would have to be delayed by some interval s' greater than s. To account for this phenomenon, Ainslie (1975) proposed the discount function, $\phi(t) = 1/t$, which had been found to explain a large body of data on animal time discounting. We now derive a more general functional form, by postulating that the delay that compensates for the larger outcome is a linear function of the time to the smaller, earlier outcome (holding fixed the two outcomes x and y):

$$v(x) = v(y)\phi(s), \quad \text{implies: } v(x)\phi(t) = v(y)\phi(kt + s), \tag{11}$$

for some constant k, which, of course depends on x and y. One can think of this as a more general form of stationarity, in which the "clocks" for the two outcomes being compared run at different speeds. In the normative case, the clocks are identical and $k = 1$, which yields the exponential discount function (Fishburn and Rubinstein, 1982). From Equation (11), it follows that:

$$v(x)\phi(t') = v(y)\phi(kt' + s), \tag{12}$$

$$v(x)\phi(\lambda t + (1 - \lambda)t') = v(y)\phi(k(\lambda t + (1 - \lambda)t') + s) \tag{13}$$

$$= v(y)\phi(\lambda(kt + s) + (1 - \lambda)(kt' + s))$$

$$= v(y)\phi(\lambda\phi^{-1}(v(x)\phi(t)/v(y))$$

$$+ (1 - \lambda)\phi^{-1}(v(x)\phi(t')/v(y)),$$

after substituting for $(kt + s)$ and $(kt' + s)$ from Equations (11) and (12). Letting $r = v(x)/v(y)$, $w = \phi(t)$, $z = \phi(t')$, and $u = \phi^{-1}$ produces a functional equation,

$$ru^{-1}(\lambda u(w) + (1 - \lambda)u(z)) = u^{-1}(\lambda u(rw) + (1 - \lambda)u(rz)), \tag{14}$$

whose only solutions are the logarithmic and power functions: $u(t) = c\ln(t) + d$, $u(t) = ct^\tau + d$ [Aczel, 1966; p. 152, Equation (18)]. As $\phi(t) = u^{-1}(t)$, the discount function must be either exponential or hyperbolic:

(D1) The discount function is a generalized hyperbola:

$$\phi(t) = (1 + \alpha t)^{-\beta/\alpha}, \alpha, \beta > 0, \tag{15}$$

The α-coefficient determines how much the function departs from constant discounting; the limiting case, as α goes to zero, is the exponential discount function, $\phi(t) = e^{-\beta t}$. Figure 5.1 displays the hyperbolic function for three different values of α, along with the pure exponential that is the least convex of the four lines. For each level of α, a corresponding β is selected so that the discount function has value .3 at $t = 1$. When α is very large, the hyperbola approximates a step function, with value one at $t = 0$, and value .3 (in this case) at all other times. This would produce dichotomous time preferences, in which the present outcome has unit weight, and all future events are discounted by a common constant.

As noted already, Equation (15) satisfies the empirical "matching law," which integrates a large body of experimental findings per-

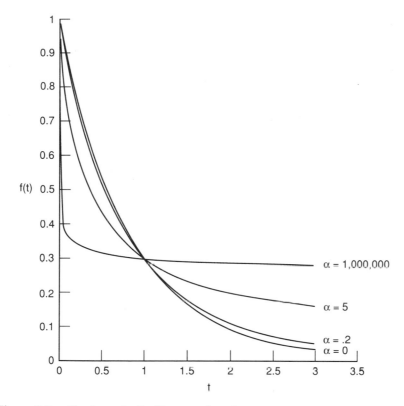

Figure 5.1.   The hyperbolic discount function,

$$\phi(t) = (1 + \alpha t)^{-\beta/\alpha},$$

for the three different levels of α. All β's are adjusted so that curves cross at $\phi(1) = .3$. The most steeply sloped curve represents conventional exponential discounting.

taining to animal time discounting (Chung and Herrnstein, 1967); the special case, $(1 + \alpha t)^{-1}$, was proposed initially by Herrnstein (1981) and further investigated by Mazur (1987); the general hyperbola was defined by Harvey (1968) and given an axiomatic derivation by Prelec (1989) along the lines presented here.

Value Function

A distinguishing feature of the current model is the replacement of the utility function with a value function with a reference point, as

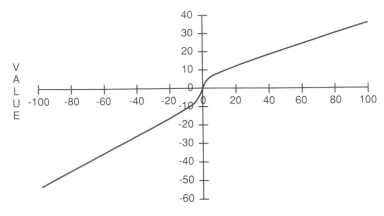

Figure 5.2.   A value function satisfying the three conditions described in the text.

shown in Figure 5.2. The value function is pieced together from two independent segments, one for losses and one for gains, which connect at the reference point. Such functions have previously been applied to decision making under uncertainty (Kahneman and Tversky, 1979), consumer choice (Thaler, 1980), negotiations (Bazerman, 1984), and financial economics (Shefrin and Statman, 1984). The shape and reference point assumption reflect basic psychophysical considerations—extra attention to negative aspects of the environment, decreasing sensitivity to increments in stimuli of increasing magnitude, and cognitive limitations.

It is assumed that the reference level represents the status quo (i.e., the current level of consumption), and that new consumption alternatives are evaluated without consideration of existing plans. In certain cases, however, the reference point may deviate from the status quo to reflect psychological considerations such as social comparison (Duesenberry, 1949), or the effect of past consumption that sets a standard for the present (Ferson and Constantinides, 1988; Pollak, 1970).

The function in Figure 5.2 is representative of a class of functions that is consistent with the behavioral evidence presented earlier in the second section. The first and most elementary assumption built into the figure is *loss aversion* (Tversky and Kahneman, 1990):

(VI) The value function for losses is steeper than the value function for gains:

$$v(x) < - v(-x),$$

which means that the loss in value associated with a given monetary loss exceeds the gain in value produced by a monetary gain of the same absolute size. In this respect, our value function resembles the prospect theory value function (Kahneman and Tversky, 1979), which also places greater weight on losses.

In the context of intertemporal choice, loss aversion specifically penalizes intertemporal exchanges that are framed in compensating variation terms, that is, as the incurring of a loss now in exchange for a future gain, or enjoying a current gain in return for a future loss. For instance, a person who is indifferent between receiving $+q$ now, or $+x$ at some later date, would nevertheless not be willing to pay q now in order to receive $+x$ at the later date, because the value of -9 is greater in absolute magnitude that the value of $+q$.

The remaining two constraints on $v(x)$ are geometrically more subtle, and have not been explicitly discussed in the context of prospect theory. Both constraints pertain to the *elasticity* of $v(x)$,

$$\epsilon_v(x) \equiv \frac{\partial \log(v)}{\partial \log(x)} = \frac{xv'(x)}{v(x)}. \tag{16}$$

Our second assumption about the value function is behaviorally determined by the gain-loss asymmetry.

(V2) The value function for losses is more elastic than the value function for gains:

$$\epsilon_v(x) < \epsilon_v(-x), \quad \text{for } x > 0.$$

Suppose that $+q$ is the equivalent present value of $+x$ at time t, so that, $v(q) = \phi(t)v(x)$. The gain–loss asymmetry then implies that one would prefer to pay $-q$ now instead of $-x$ at time t: $v(-q) > \phi(t)v(-x)$. Equating $\phi(t)$ in both of these expressions shows that:

$$\frac{v(q)}{v(x)} > \frac{v(-q)}{v(-x)}, \quad \text{for all: } 0 < q < x. \tag{17}$$

Consequently, $v(x)$ must "bend over" faster than $v(-x)$, in the precise sense captured by condition V2.[3]

Our third and final assumption about $v(x)$ is dictated by the magnitude effect, in equivalent variation choices. If $+q$ is the equivalent

---

[3] Let $u_1(x) \equiv -ln\{v(x)\}$, and $u_2(x) \equiv -ln\{-v(-x)\}$. Then (17) implies that $u_1(x) - u_1(8) < u_2(x) - u_2(8)$, for all $0 < 8 < x$, or: $u_1'(x) < u_2'(x)$, for all $x > 0$, which is equivalent to Condition V2.

present value for x at time t, $v(q) = \phi(t)v(x)$, then the magnitude effect predicts that a proportional increase in both q and x, to αq and αx, will cause preference to tip in favor of the later positive outcome, $v(\alpha q) < \phi(t)v(\alpha x)$. As in the previous paragraph, by eliminating $\phi(t)$, we have,

$$\frac{v(q)}{v(x)} < \frac{v(\alpha q)}{v(\alpha x)}, \quad \text{for all: } 0 < q < x; \alpha > 1. \tag{18}$$

The value function is *subproportional*, like the probability weighting function in prospect theory. As Kahneman and Tversky remarked (1979, p. 282), such a function is convex in log-log coordinates, which for our model means that the derivative of $\log(v(x))$ with respect to $\log(x)$ is increasing, or that:

(V3) The value function is more elastic for outcomes that are larger in absolute magnitude.

$$\epsilon_v(x) < \epsilon_v(y), \text{ for: } 0 < x < y, \text{ or, } y < x < 0.$$

The implications of this condition can be visually assessed by comparing Figures 5.2 and 5.3. Both figures show the same value function, but plotted over a small (Figure 5.3) or a large range of outcomes (Figure 5.2). For small outcomes, the function is sharply convex, indi-

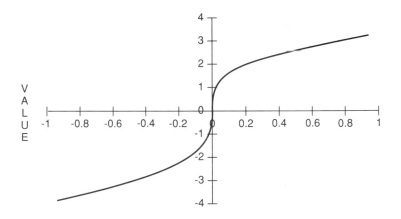

$ CHANGE RELATIVE TO STATUS QUO

Figure 5.3. The same value function as in Figure 5.2, but plotted over a smaller range of outcomes.

cating that there is not much perceived value difference between, say a $1 gain and a $2 gain. This property accounts for the high discount rates that apply to small outcomes (i.e., in a choice between $1 now or $2 in a year). For large outcomes, however, the function straightens out considerably (Figure 5.2), and, as a result, generates much lower discount rates.

Most probably, the elasticity of the value function does not increase indefinitely, but rather attains a maximum at some large dollar amount and then begins to decline. When one is comparing large and unexpected windfalls, it may be reasonable to prefer a million today to several million a few years hence—if drawing on the money in advance was completely prevented. The implausibility of this last requirement makes the interpretation of stated preference over large amounts problematic.

Further Implications of the Model

Aversion to Intertemporal Tradeoffs

It follows from our model that a single individual will reveal not one but several discount factors for future cash outcomes, depending on how the choice is formulated. These discount factors can be geometrically derived, as in Figure 5.4, where we have overlaid the positive and negative branches of the value function, so that positive and negative outcomes can be represented along the positive x axis. Starting with a delayed outcome of absolute magnitude x, and a time interval yielding a discount factor *for utility* of .8, we can generate four distinct "present values" for x, depending on whether x is positive or negative, and whether the elicitation method is equivalent or compensating variation. Each present value, divided by x, then yields a specific discount factor.

From equivalent variation, $v(q) = \phi(t)v(x)$, we get the discount factors for gains (G) and losses (L),

$$\delta_{G,L} = \frac{q}{x} = \frac{v^{-1}\{\phi(t)v(x)\}}{x}, \; (\delta_G \text{ for } x > 0, \delta_L \text{ for } x < 0), \quad (19)$$

while from compensating variation, $(v(p) + \phi(t)v(x) = 0$, we have the *borrowing* (B) and *saving* (S) factors,

$$\delta_{S,B} = \frac{p}{x} = \frac{v^{-1}\{-\phi(t)v(x)\}}{x}, \; (\delta_S \text{ for } x > 0, \delta_B \text{ for } x < 0). \quad (20)$$

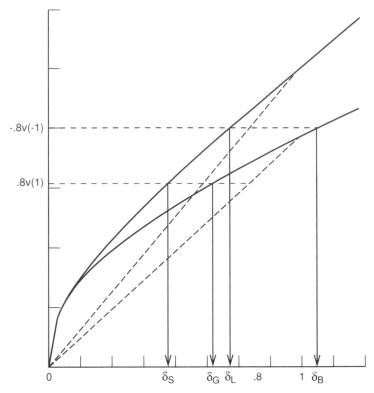

Figure 5.4. Relationship among discount factors for compensating and equivalent variation.

It is apparent from the geometry of the gain and loss value functions in Figure 5.4 that these discount factors are ordered as: $\delta_S < \delta_G < \delta_L < \delta_B$.

A notable aspect of the ranking is the large gap between the savings and borrowing discount factors: A person whose choices are consistent with the value functions in Figure 5.2 would require a much more favorable rate in order to borrow than he or she would to save. The gap between δ_B and δ_S is a measure of how averse a person is to borrowing and savings commitments generally, because it implies a range of risk-free interest rates at which a person will be unwilling to either save or borrow.

The existence of this gap was confirmed by Horowitz (1988), who elicited present and future values for real money payoffs, through a "first-rejected price" auction. According to Horowitz, "The most striking feature of [the] experiment is individuals' apparent aversion to both borrowing and lending." A substantial fraction of subjects revealed discount factors greater than one for borrowing (i.e., they refused zero-interest loans); this, too, is consistent with the model, as we can see from the fact that $\delta_B > 1$ in Figure 5.4.

Framing Effects

As in prospect theory (Kahneman and Tversky, 1979), we assume that the reference level is sensitive to the wording of the questions that elicit the intertemporal tradeoffs. For instance, direct choices between two losses, or two gains, are presumed to be likewise encoded (or "framed") as a pair of positive or negative values. The same would be true of requests for present amounts that create subjective indifference with respect to some future amount of the same sign. In such a context, we would interpret the elicited present value, q, for amount x at time t, according to the equivalent variation formula: $v(q) = \phi(t)v(x)$.

Questions involving delay or speedup of consumption are a clear case where the compenating variation formula is appropriate. A request, for example, for the maximum value that one would be willing to sacrifice in order to speedup some positive amount (x) from time t to the present suggests that the baseline levels are zero now, and $+x$ at the future time. In this frame, the speed-up constitutes a loss of x at time t, and a gain of x minus the speedup cost at time zero. The latter value, p, would then be interpreted according to the compensating variation formula, $v(p) + \phi(t)v(x) = 0$, with $x < 0$ and $p > 0$. The same frame covers delay-of-loss judgments, because in that case, there is again a positive present benefit (avoiding the immediate loss), and a future cost (absorbing the loss at the later date). The two complementary question formats—delaying a gain, and speeding up a loss—would yield present values also consistent with Equation (20) but for a reversal in the sign of p and x, because there is a negative adjustment to current consumption ($p < 0$), and a positive adjustment to future consumption ($x > 0$).

Figure 5.5 compares these predictions with those of the normative model, in which the distinction between a speed-up or delay is not recognized. As indicated in the top half of the figure, the discount rates estimated from expediting and delaying gains should be equal, and higher than the devaluation rates estimated from expediting and delaying losses. In contrast, the reference point model predicts that

Speed-up   Delay

	Speed-up	Delay
Gains	High	High
Losses	Low	Low

Normative Model

	Speed-up	Delay
Gains	High	Low
Losses	Low	High

Reference Point Model

Figure 5.5. Discount rates when expediting and speeding up gains and losses: comparison of DU and reference point model predictions.

common rates will be observed for the diagonal pairs in the matrix, with the delaying gains/speeding-up losses pair producing a higher estimate.

Clear support for the reference point model can be found in the data reported by Benzion, Rapaport, and Yagil (1989). Figure 5.6 displays implicit discount rates calculated from their data for each of the four elicitation methods. As predicted, discount rates are high and virtually identical for expediting a loss (white diamonds) and delaying a gain (black squares), and lower and again virtually identical for expediting a gain (black triangles) and delaying a loss (white squares).

Our second framing example is produced by the discrepancy between discounting of gains and losses. In this study, 85 students in an MBA class on decision making were randomly divided into two groups that each answered one of the following two questions.

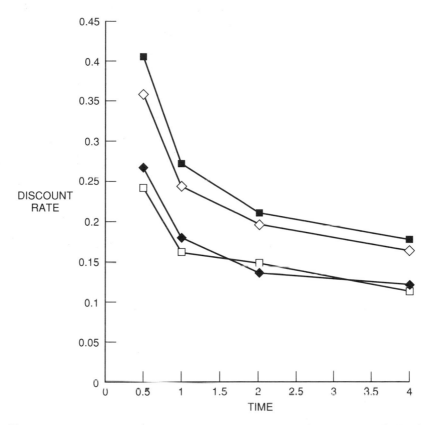

Figure 5.6. Implicit discount rates from Benzion, Rapoport, and Yagil (1989); the rates have been averaged across the four dollar amounts used in their study.

Version 1

Suppose you bought a TV on a special installment plan. The plan calls for two payments; one this week and one in 6 months. You have two options for paying (circle the one that you would choose):

A. An initial payment of $160 and a later payment of $110.
B. An initial payment of $115 and a later payment of $160.

Version 2

Suppose you bought a TV on a special installment plan. The plan calls for two payments of $200; one this week and one in 6 months.

Happily, however, the company has announced a sale that applies retroactively to your purchase. You have two options (circle the one that you would choose):

C.   A rebate of $40 on the initial payment and a rebate of $90 on the later payment.
D.   A rebate of $85 on the initial payment and a rebate of $40 on the later payment.

Because options A and C and options B and D are the same in terms of payoffs and delivery times, DU predicts that there will be no systematic difference in responses to the two versions. Nevertheless, a higher fraction of subjects opted for the lower-discount option (the one involving greater earlier payments) when the question was framed as a loss rather than as a gain. Fifty-four percent of subjects exposed to version 1 stated a preference for A over B. However, a significantly different fraction (33 percent) preferred C over D ($X^2(1)$ = 3.9, $p < .05$). The proposed model explains the observed pattern of responses as follows: In the first frame, the large, negative outcomes suffer less discounting, which causes people to decide on the basis of total payments. In the second frame, however, the outcomes are smaller in absolute magnitude and positive; both of these factors contribute to relatively high discounting of the delayed outcomes, leading to a preference for the second option, which offers a greater initial rebate.

The choice of appropriate frame is not always unambiguous. A savings decision, for example, can be viewed as a simple choice between benefits enjoyed now or later [Equation (19)], or a postponement of present consumption for the future [Equation (20)]. Such changes in frame will, according to our theory, affect the range of interest rates that a person considers acceptable.

Effect of Prior Expectations on Choice

Consider two people waiting for an object (e.g., a computer); one has been told to expect delivery in 2 weeks, the other anticipates delivery in 4 weeks. When 2 weeks pass, both are faced with a new choice: the original computer to be delivered immediately, or a superior computer to be delivered in 2 weeks. Who is more likely to wait? If both parties adapt their reference points to anticipated delivery times, then the reference point model predicts that the person who anticipated delivery in 2 weeks will be more impatient. This person frames the choice as the status quo versus a loss of a computer immediately and a gain of a slightly superior computer in 2 weeks. Loss aversion and discounting both mitigate against choice of the delayed, superior, model. On the other hand, the person who anticipated later delivery would frame the choice as a loss of the later computer and gain of an earlier computer; here, loss aversion discourges the choice of the earlier computer, while discounting has an opposing influence. Thus, we predict that the person anticipating 2-week delivery would be more likely to accept. In effect, people who are psychologically prepared for delay are more willing to wait.

This prediction was tested in a laboratory experiment conducted with 105 suburban Chicago tenth graders (Loewenstein, 1988b). All prizes were in the form of nontransferable gift certificates. As a result of an earlier experiment, half the students expected to obtain a $7 gift certificate at an earlier date, half at a later date. When the earlier date arrived, all subjects were given a new choice between getting the $7 certificate immediately or a larger valued certificate at a later date. As predicted, prior expectations had a significant impact on choice. Twenty-seven out of 47 subjects who anticipated getting the prize at the earlier date opted for the immediate $7; only 17 of the 57 who expected late delivery chose not to wait for the larger prize, a statistically significant difference.

High Discount Rates Estimated from Purchases of Consumer Durables

Several studies have estimated discount rates from purchases of consumer durables (e.g., air conditioners) (Gately, 1980; Hausman, 1979). Such purchases typically involve an up-front charge (the purchase price) and a series of delayed charges (e.g., electricity charges). Because more expensive models are generally more energy efficient, it is possible to calculate the discount rate (or range of discount rates) implicit in a particular purchase. A second source of behavioral estimates of discount rates have been the studies of major economic decisions such as saving (Landsberger, 1971) and intertemporal labor-leisure substitution (Hotz, Kydland and Sedlacek, 1988; Moore and Viscusi, 1988).

The estimates from these two classes of studies have differed sharply. Studies of consumer durable purchases show very high average discount rates (across different income groups), for example, from 25 percent (Hausman, 1979) to 45–300 percent (Gately, 1980). Research on savings behavior or labor supply has almost uniformly found much lower discount rates (typically well below 25 percent). How can these estimates be reconciled? The proposed model predicts that the small delayed electricity charges associated with the consumer durables will be substantially devalued because of the dependence of discounting on outcome magnitude. Thus, consumer durable purchases will be insensitive to electricity charges, and discount rates estimated from those purchases will appear to be high. Discount rates estimated from major economic decisions would not be subject to such small-magnitude effects.

Nonmonotonic Optimal Benefit Plans

Our model makes certain predictions about the shape of the optimal intertemporal allocation of benefits under a constant market present value constraint. If one assumes that consumption at a point in time, $x(t)$, is framed as a positive quantity, the value of the plan, covering the period from 0 to T, is given by the continuous version of the discounted value formula,

$$\int_0^T \phi(t)v(x(t))dt. \tag{21}$$

The optimal plan $x^0(t)$, given a market interest rate r and a present value constraint,

$$\int_0^T e^{-rt}x(t)dt \leq I, \tag{22}$$

can be calculated by standard techniques (Yaari, 1964). Yaari showed that if the optimal plan exists, and if the value function is concave and continuously differentiable, then the rate of change in consumption, for the optimal plan, equals [Equation (21)]:

$$\frac{\partial x^0}{\partial t} = r - \left(-\frac{\phi'(t)}{\phi(t)}\right)\left(-\frac{v'(x^0(t))}{v''(x^0)}\right). \tag{23}$$

As Yaari observed, the direction of local change in consumption rate is controlled by the sign of the difference between the market interest rate and the rate of time preference $(-\phi'/\phi)$. In view of our hyperbolic discounting assumption, this allows for only three qualitatively distinct possibilities: (1) The rate of time preference is always greater than the market rate, in which case consumption is decreasing throughout the interval; (2) the rate of time preference is always lower than the market rate, in which case consumption increases over the interval; and (3) the rate of time preference starts off above the market rate, but eventually drops below it and remains so, in which case consumption will decline to a minimum value (when the two rates equalize) and then increase afterwards.

Relative to normative theory, our model suggests that people may tend to prefer plans that sacrifice the medium-range future for the sake of the short- and the long-term future. There is nothing clearly wrong with this, provided one can commit to an entire plan at the moment of decision; if, however, the optimal plan can be recalculated at later points in time, then the planned sacrifice in midrange consumption will not take effect (Strotz, 1955). As a result, a bias in favor of the long and short runs may in practice yield behavior that is only oriented to the short run.

This discussion presupposes a concave value function, which—although not explicitly assumed in assumptions V1–V3—is certainly true for the function in Figure 5.4. In the loss domain, however, our working assumption is that the value function is convex, at least initially, which means that the most attractive plan for intertemporal loss allocation consists of concentrating the loss at a single point in time. The (negative) value of the loss, if allowed to accumulate at the market rate to time t, equals: $\phi(t)v(Ie^{rt})$, which means that it will pay to delay payment whenever, $\phi'(t)v(Ie^{rt}) + rIe^{rt}\phi(t)v'(Ie^{rt}) > 0$, or, after rearranging, whenever:

$$r < \frac{-\phi'(t)/\phi(t)}{\epsilon_v(Ie^{rt})}. \tag{24}$$

The product on the right is decreasing in t, because $-\phi'/\phi$ equals $\beta/(1 + \alpha t)$ by assumption D1, and $\epsilon_v(Ie^{rt})$ is increasing by assumption V3. Hence, there is a unique point in time—possibly at one or the other endpoint of the interval—at which the loss is absorbed with smallest perceived cost.

Other Predictions

Our model has several implications for the behavior of key economic variables during business cycles. First, it predicts that psychological factors will amplify the tendency for businesses to cut back on investment during periods of lower than anticipated profits. In high-profit periods, the investment project is viewed in terms of equivalent variation, as a choice between two gains: Take the excess profit now, or take greater profits from investment later. But in periods of low or negative returns, an identical investment opportunity would be viewed in terms of compensating variation, that is, as incurring a current loss in exchance for a future gain, which, as shown in the previous section, will induce a higher subjective discount rate. There may, of course, be good economic reasons for reducing investments during economic downturns; what the model suggests is that psychological factors additionally and independently contribute to the reduction.

For consumers too, an economic downturn should cause an increase in impatience and a consequent decrease in saving. Consumers are likely to frame drops in disposable income, or negative departures from expected gains, as losses, so that saving from income will be viewed in terms of compensating variation: a further loss in the present for a gain in the future.[4] Saving out of an expanding income or out of bonus income is more likely to be viewed in terms of compensating variation, including lower discounting and greater saving. Consistent with this prediction, there is evidence that the marginal propensity to save income from bonuses is higher than that from normal income (Ishikawa and Ueda, 1984).

Our model is also possibly relevant to the so-called disposition effect in real estate (Case and Shiller, 1989) and financial markets (Ferris, Haugen, and Makhija, 1988; Shefrin and Statman, 1985). This effect refers to the fact that people tend to hold on to losing stocks and to real estate that has dropped in value, which depresses trading volume during market downturns. In such situations people have a choice between taking an immediate loss (by selling) or holding on to the asset with the potential of further loss or potential gain. Because the value function is convex in the loss domain, further losses are less than proportionately painful, while gains yield marginally increasing returns. The incentives are thus stacked in favor of holding on to the asset. The incentives are reversed on the gain side, motivating people to sell quickly assets that have gained in value.

In general, the market level implications of the model depend critically on the presence or absence of arbitrage opportunities that exist in a particular economic domain. Arbitrage opportunities are exten-

---

[4]The low rates of savings and negative real rates of interest in the 1970s (Mishkin, 1981), may reflect the shortfall from expectations induced by economic stagnation following the prolonged economic boom of the 1960s. At a social level, the tax cuts of the early 1980s, which entailed a transfer of income from the future to the present, can be interpreted similarly.

sive in some markets, such as those for fixed rate financial assets where leveraged short sales are possible. In other markets, for example, labor markets, arbitrage opportunities are virtually nonexistent. We would expect to see the effects of subjective time discounting manifested more clearly in the latter markets, in the specific case through labor contracts that offer large initial wage increases.

In financial markets, the effects of scale and sign, produced by the curvature of the value function, will presumably be arbitraged away. If a particular market were to offer high interest rates on small investments, reflecting the magnitude effect, investors would simply borrow large sums and then invest them in small packages, driving down the rate on small investments.

Hyperbolic discounting is less easily arbitraged, even in financial markets. If most people demanded lower rates of return for long investment periods than for short ones, the yield curve could be downward sloping with no opportunities for arbitrage. Those who discounted the future at a constant rate would tend to invest in short-term securities, and might even short the long-term securities, but they could not do so without risk. Without denying that many purely economic factors influence the yield curve, our model suggests that psychological biases will independently exert pressure toward downward sloping.[5]

Concluding Remarks

The discounted utility model has played a dominant role in economic analyses of intertemporal choice. Although economists have experimented with alternative formulations, these efforts have typically responded to a single limitation of DU (e.g., increasing consumption postretirement) rather than to a more comprehensive critique. DU's basic assumptions and implications have, for the most part, not been questioned. This chapter presents an integrated critique of DU, enumerating a series of intertemporal choice anomalies that run counter to the predictions of DU.

Perhaps most important, sensitivity to time delay is not well expressed by compound discounting. A given absolute delay looms larger if it occurs earlier rather than later; people are relatively insensi-

---

[5] Our analysis may help to explain Fama's (1984) finding that, contrary to the liquidity preference hypothesis, the yield curve tends to drop, on average, past a certain point.

tive to changes in timing for consumption objects that are already substantially delayed. Second, the marginal utility of consumption at different points in time depends not on absolute levels of consumption, but on consumption relative to some standard or point of reference. Generally, the status quo serves as reference point; people conserve on cognitive effort by evaluating new consumption alternatives in isolation, rather than integrating them with existing plans.

Our model by no means incorporates all important psychological factors that influence intertemporal choice. For example, like any model with nonconstant discounting, it yields time inconsistent behavior or "myopia," as Strotz (1955) called it. However, it cannot explain the high levels of conflict that such myopic behavior often evokes. Intertemporal choice often seems to involve an internal struggle for self-command (Schelling, 1984). At the very moment of succumbing to the impulse to consume, individuals often recognize at a cognitive level that they are making a decision that is contrary to their long-term self-interest. Mathematical models of choice do not shed much light on such patterns of cognition and behavior (but see Ainslie, 1985).

Such episodes of internal conflict are not entirely random. Certain types of situations, such as when a person comes into direct sensory contact with a choice object, seem to elicit especially high rates of time discounting while others do not. People exhibit high rates of discounting when driven by appetites such as hunger, thirst, or sexual desire. While not incompatible with the present model, these phenomena are not predicted by it.

Finally, our model does not incorporate preference interactions between periods, despite the fact that our own recent empirical research has shown such interactions to be pervasive when people choose between sequences of outcomes. Preference interactions are revealed through a strong dislike of deteriorating outcome sequences, and through a liking for evenly spreading consumption over time (Loewenstein and Prelec, 1991). A taste for steady improvement seems to capture the preferences of most subjects, when sequences are being considered. Generally, the present model is more applicable to short-range decisions involving simple outcomes rather than long-term planning of consumption. No simple theory, however, can hope to reflect all motives that influence a particular decision. We have attempted to demonstrate that a theory with only two scaling functions can explain much of the observed deviation in preference from the normative discounted utility model.

We thank Wayne Ferson, Brian Gibbs, Jerry Green, Richard Herrnstein, Robin Hogarth, Mark Machina, Howard Rachlin, and, especially, Colin Camerer and Joshua Klayman for useful suggestions. The assistance of Eric Wanner, the Russell Sage Foundation, the Alfred P. Sloan Foundation, the IBM Faculty Research Fund at the University of Chicago Graduate School of Business, and the Research Division of the Harvard Business School is also gratefully acknowledged. This article originally appeared in *Quarterly Journal of Economics* and is reprinted with permission.

References

Aczel, J. *Lectures on Functional Equations and Their Applications*. New York: Academic Press, 1966.

Ainslie, G. "Specious Reward: A Behavioral Theory of Impulsiveness and Impulse Control." *Psychological Bulletin* 82 (1975): 463–509.

———. "Beyond Microeconomics. Conflict Among Interests in a Multiple Self as a Determinant of Value." In J. Elster (ed.). *The Multiple Self*. Cambridge, UK: Cambridge University Press, 1985.

Bazerman, M. "The Relevance of Kahneman and Tversky's Concept of Framing to Organizational Behavior." *Journal of Management* 10 (1984): 333–343.

Benzion, U., A. Rapoport, and J. Yagil. "Discount Rates Inferred from Decisions: An Experimental Study." *Management Science* 35 (March 1989): 270–284.

Case, K.E., and R.J. Shiller. "The Efficiency of the Market for Single Family Homes." *American Economic Review* 79 (March 1989): 125–137.

Chung, S.H., and R.J. Herrnstein. "Choice and Delay of Reinforcement." *Journal of the Experimental Analysis of Behavior* 10 (1967): 67–74.

Debreu, G. "Topological Methods in Cardinal Utility in Theory." In K.J. Arrow, S. Karlin, and P. Suppes (eds.). *Mathematical Methods in the Social Sciences*. Stanford, CA: Stanford University Press, 1959, pp. 16–26.

Duesenberry, J. *Income, Saving, and the Theory of Consumer Behavior*. Cambridge, MA: Harvard University Press, 1949.

Fama, E.F. "Term Premiums in Bond Returns." *Journal of Financial Economics* 13 (1984): 529–546.

Ferris, S.P., R.A. Haugen, and A.K. Makhija. "Predicting Contemporary Volume with Historic Volume at Different Price Levels; Evidence Supporting the Disposition Effect." *Journal of Finance* 43 (July 1988): 677–697.

Ferson, W.E., and G.M. Constantinides. "Habit Formation and Durability in Aggregate Consumption: Empirical Tests." Paper presented to the American Finance Association meeting, December 1988.

Fishburn, P.C., and A. Rubinstein. "Time Preference." *International Economic Review* 23 (1982): 677–694.

Gately, D. "Individual Discount Rates and the Purchase and Utilization of Energy-Using Durables: Comment." *Bell Journal of Economics* 11 (1980): 373–374.

Harvey, C.M. "Value Functions for Infinite-Period Planning." *Management Science* 32 (1986): 1123–1139.

Hausman, J. "Individual Discount Rates and the Purchase and Utilization of Energy-Using Durables." *Bell Journal of Economics* 10 (1979): 33–54.

Herrnstein, R.J. "Self-Control as Response Strength." In C.M. Bradshaw, E. Szabadi, and C.F. Lowe (eds.). *Quantification of Steady-State Operant Behavior.* Amsterdam: Elsevier/North-Holland, 1981.

Holcomb, J.H., and P.S. Nelson. "An Experimental Investigation of Individual Time Preference." Unpublished working paper, 1989.

Horowitz, J.K. "Discounting Money Payoffs: An Experimental Analysis." Working paper, Department of Agricultural and Resource Economics, University of Maryland, 1988.

Hotz, V.J., F.E. Kydland, and G.L. Sedlacek. "Intertemporal Preferences and Labor Supply." *Econometrica* 56 (1988): 335–360.

Ishikawa, T., and K. Ueda. "The Bonus Payment System and Japanese Personal Savings." In M. Aoki (ed.). *The Economic Analysis of the Japanese Firm.* Amsterdam: North Holland, 1984.

Kahneman, D., and A. Tversky. "Prospect Theory: An Analysis of Decision Under Risk." *Econometrica* 47 (1979): 363–391.

Koopmans, T.C. "Stationary Ordinal Utility and Impatience." *Econometrica* 28 (1960): 287–309.

Landsberger, M. "Consumer Discount Rate and the Horizon: New Evidence." *Journal of Political Economy* 79 (1971): 1346–1359.

Loewenstein, G. "Anticipation and the Valuation of Delayed Consumption." *Economic Journal* 97 (1987): 666–684.

———. "Frames of Mind in Intertemporal Choice." *Management Science* 34 (1988a): 200–214.

———. "Reference Points in Intertemporal Choice." Working Paper, Center for Decision Research, University of Chicago, 1988b.

———. "The Weighting of Waiting: Response Mode Effects in Intertemporal Choice." Working Paper, Center for Decision Research, University of Chicago, 1988.

———, and D. Prelec. "Preferences over Outcome Sequences." *American Economic Review, Papers, and Proceedings* 81 (1991): 247–352.

———, and N. Sicherman. "Do Workers Prefer Increasing Wage Profiles?" *Journal of Labor Economics* (1991): 67–84.

Markowitz, H. "The Utility of Wealth." *Journal of Political Economy* 60 (1952): 151–158.

Mazur, J.E. "An Adjustment Procedure for Studying Delayed Reinforcement." Chap. 2 in M.L. Commons, J.E. Mazur, J.A. Nevins, and H. Rachlin (eds.). *Quantitative Analysis of Behavior: The Effect of Delay and Intervening Events on Reinforcement Value.* Hillsdale, NJ: Erlbaum, 1987.

Mishkin, F.S. "The Real Interest Rate: An Empirical Investigation." *Carnegie-Rochester Conference Series on Public Policy* 15 (1981): 151–200.

Moore, M.J., and W.K. Viscusi. "Discounting Environmental Health Risks: New Evidence and Policy Implications." Paper presented to joint session of American Economic Association, December 1988.

Pollak, R.A. "Habit Formation and Dynamic Demand Functions." *Journal of Political Economy* 78 (1970): 745–763.

Prelec, D. "Decreasing Impatience: Definition and Consequences." Harvard Business School Working Paper, 1989.

———, and G. Loewenstein. "Decision Making Over Time and Under Uncertainty: A Common Approach." *Management Science* 37 (1991): 770–786.

Schelling, T. "Self-Command in Practice, in Policy, and in a Theory of Rational Choice." *American Economic Review* 74 (1984): 1–11.

Shefrin, H.M., and M. Statman, "Explaining Investor Preference for Cash Dividends." *Journal of Financial Economics* 13 (1984): 253–282.

———, and M. Statman. "The Disposition to Sell Winners too Early and Ride Losers too Long: Theory and Evidence." *Journal of Finance* 40 (1985): 777–792.

Strotz, R.H. "Myopia and Inconsistency in Dynamic Utility Maximization." *Review of Economic Studies* 23 (1955): 165–180.

Thaler, R. "Toward a Positive Theory of Consumer Choice." *Journal of Economic Behavior and Organization* 1 (1980): 39–60.

———. "Some Empirical Evidence on Dynamic Inconsistency." *Economics Letters* 8 (1981): 201–207.

Tversky, A., and D. Kahneman. "Reference Theory of Choice and Exchange." Unpublished working paper, 1990.

Weber, M., and C.F. Camerer. "Recent Developments in Modeling Preferences Under Risk." *OR Spectrum* 9 (1988): 129–151.

Yaari, M.E. "On the Consumer's Lifetime Allocation Process." *International Economic Review* 5 (1964): 304–317.

· 6 ·

Delay of Gratification in Children

WALTER MISCHEL, YUICHI SHODA,
AND MONICA L. RODRIGUEZ

To function effectively, individuals must voluntarily postpone immediate gratification and persist in goal-directed behavior for the sake of later outcomes. The present research program analyzed the nature of this type of future-oriented self-control and the psychological processes that underlie it. Enduring individual differences in self-control were found as early as the preschool years. Those 4-year-old children who delayed gratification longer in certain laboratory situations developed into more cognitively and socially competent adolescents, achieving higher scholastic performance and coping better with frustration and stress. Experiments in the same research program also identified specific cognitive and attentional processes that allow effective self-regulation early in the course of development. The experimental results, in turn, specified the particular types of preschool delay situations diagnostic for predicting aspects of cognitive and social competence later in life.

For almost a century the infant has been characterized as impulse-driven, pressing for tension reduction, unable to delay gratification, oblivious to reason and reality, and ruled entirely by a pleasure principle that demands immediate satisfaction (Freud, 1959).

From Walter Mischel, Yuichi Shoda, and Monica L. Rodriguez, "Delay of Gratification in Children," in *Science* vol. 244, May 26, 1989: 933–938. Copyright © 1989 by the Association for the Advancement of Science. Reprinted by permission.

147

The challenge has been to clarify how individuals, while remaining capable of great impulsivity, also become able to control actions for the sake of temporally distant consequences and goals, managing at least sometimes to forgo more immediate gratifications to take account of anticipated outcomes. The nature of this future-oriented self-control, which develops over time and then coexists with more impetuous behaviors, has intrigued students of development, who have made it central in theories of socialization and in the very definition of the "self" (Harter, 1983). Such goal-directed, self-imposed delay of gratification is widely presumed to be important in the prevention of serious developmental and mental health problems, including those directly associated with lack of resilience, conduct disorders, low social responsibility, and a variety of addictive and antisocial behaviors (Bandura, 1986; Bandura and Mischel, 1965; Mischel, 1966, 1968, 1986; Rutter, 1987; Stumphauzer, 1972).

To explain how people manage to exercise self-control, concepts like *willpower* or *ego strength* are readily invoked, although these terms provide little more than labels for the phenomena to which they point. Some people adhere to difficult diets, or give up cigarettes after years of smoking them addictively, or continue to work and wait for distant goals even when tempted sorely to quit, whereas others fail in such attempts to better regulate themselves in spite of affirming the same initial intentions. Yet the same person who exhibits self-control in one situation may fail to do so in another, even when it appears to be highly similar (Mischel, 1968). The research program reviewed here addresses the nature of these individual differences, the psychological processes that underlie them, and the conditions in which they may be predictable.

Overview

We review findings on an essential feature of self-regulation: postponing immediately available gratification in order to attain delayed but more valued outcomes. Studies in which 4-year-old children attempt this type of future-oriented self-control reveal that in some laboratory situations individual differences in delay behavior significantly predict patterns of competence and coping assessed more than a decade later (Mischel, Shoda, and Peake, 1988). Experiments in the same laboratory situations have identified specific cognitive and attentional processes that allow the young child to sustain goal-directed delay of gratification even under difficult, frustrating conditions (Mischel, 1974).

We begin with a summary of major individual differences associated with this type of self-regulation early in life, and the long-term developmental outcomes that they predict. Then we examine the specific processes that seem to underlie effective self-imposed delay of gratification in young children, as revealed by the experimental studies. These results, in turn, pointed to the types of preschool delay situations diagnostic for predicting aspects of cognitive and social competence in adolescence. Finally, we consider the development of the child's understanding of self-control and the concurrent links found among components of self-regulation in children with behavioral problems.

Measuring Self-Control: From Choice to Execution

Two complementary methods were used to investigate delay of gratification in the research program reviewed here. Initially, preferences for delayed, more valuable versus immediate but less valuable outcomes were studied as choice decisions. In this approach, individuals choose under realistic conditions among outcomes that vary in value and in the expected duration of time before they become available. Sets of such choices were given to people from a wide range of sociocultural backgrounds, family structure, and economic circumstances (Graves, 1967; Klineberg, 1968; Melikian, 1959; Mischel, 1966). As expected, these choices are affected predictably by the anticipated delay time and the subjective value of the alternatives. For example, preferences for delayed rewards decrease when the required time for their attainment increases and increase with the expectation that the delayed outcomes will occur (Mischel and Metzner 1962; Mischel and Staub, 1965). The choice to delay (1) increases with the values of the delayed rewards relative to the immediate ones; (2) increases with the subject's age; and (3) is susceptible to a variety of social influences, including the choice behavior and attitudes that other people display (Bandura and Mischel, 1965; Mischel, 1966, 1974; Mischel and Metzner, 1962). Choices to delay were related significantly to a number of personal characteristics assessed at about the same time. For example, children who tend to prefer delayed rewards also tend to be more intelligent (Mischel and Metzner, 1962), more likely to resist temptation (Mischel and Gilligan, 1964), to have greater social responsibility (Mischel, 1961; Stumphauzer, 1972), and higher achievement strivings (Mischel, 1961, p. 543). The obtained concurrent associations are extensive, indicating that such preferences reflect a meaningful dimension of individual differences, and point to some of the many determinants and correlates of decisions to delay.[1]

As efforts at self-reform so often attest, however, decisions to forgo immediate gratification for the sake of later consequences (e.g., by dieting) are readily forgotten or strategically revised when one experiences the frustation of actually having to execute them. Because intentions to practice self-control frequently dissolve in the face of more immediate temptations, it is also necessary to go beyond the study of initial decisions to delay gratification and to examine how young children become able to sustain delay of gratification as they actually try to wait for the outcomes they want. For this purpose, a second method was devised and used to test preschool children in the Stanford University community (Mischel and Ebbesen, 1970; Mischel, Ebbesen, and Zeiss, 1972).

In this method, the experimenter begins by showing the child some toys, explaining they will play with them later (so that ending the delay leads to uniform positive consequences). Next, the experimenter teaches a game in which he or she has to leave the room and comes back immediately when the child summons by ringing a bell. Each child then is shown a pair of treats (such as snacks, small toys, or tokens) that differ in value, established through pretesting to be desirable and of age-appropriate interest (e.g., one marshmallow vs.

---

[1] Researchers in other areas, beyond the scope of the present article, have pursued somewhat parallel problems in self-control. In one direction, a large operant conditioning literature has investigated self control in lower organisms by using analogous situations to those in the present article. Typically, a pigeon in a Skinner box has to choose among alternatives varying in the amount and delay of the reinforcer. This research indicates that organisms sharply discount future rewards as a function of the temporal distance from the time of choice. [G.W. Ainslie, *Psychol. Bull.* 82 (1975): 463; A.W. Logue, *Brain Behav. Sci.* 4 (1988): 665; A.W. Logue, M.L. Rodriguez, T.E. Pena-Correal, and B. Mauro, *J. Exper. Anal. Behav.* 41 (1984): 53; H. Rachlin and L. Green, *ibid.* 17 (1972): 15; H. Rachlin, A.W. Logue, J. Gibbon, M. Frankel, *Psychol, Rev.* 93 (1986): 33; M.L. Rodriguez and A.W. Logue, *J. Exp. Psychol. Anim. Behav. Proc.* 14 (1988): 105]. Preference for a small, immediate reward, over a larger, more delayed one, reverts as the time between choice and delay of rewards increases (Rachlin and Green, above; Logue, Rodriguez, Pena-Correal, Mauro, above). Moreover, by using analogs to the self-imposed delay of gratification situation described in this article, parallel results also were reported with pigeons [J. Grosch and A. Neuringer, *J. Exp. Anal. Behav.* 35 (1981): 3. In a second direction, economists have studied how delayed outcomes affect economic decisions and savings behavior of humans, again with interesting parallels to the research reported here [I. Fisher, *The Theory of Interest,* Macmillan, London, 1930; H.M. Shefrin, and R.H. Thaler, *Econ. Inq.* 26 (1988): 609].

two; two small cookies vs. five pretzels). The children are told that to attain the one they prefer they have to wait until the experimenter returns but that they are free to end the waiting period whenever they signal; if they do, however, they will get the less preferred object and forgo the other one. The items in the pair are selected to be sufficiently close in value to create a conflict situation for young children between the temptation to stop the delay and the desire to persist for the preferred outcome when the latter requires delay. After children understand the contingency, they are left on their own during the delay period while their behavior is observed unobtrusively, and the duration of their delay is recorded until they terminate or the experimenter returns (typically after 15 minutes). With this method, "self-imposed delay of gratification" was investigated both as a psychological process in experiments that varied relevant features in the delay situation and as a personal characteristic in studies that examined the relation between children's delay behavior and their social and cognitive competencies.

A recent follow-up study of a sample of these children found that those who had waited longer in this situation at 4 years of age were described more than 10 years later by their parents as adolescents who were more academically and socially competent than their peers and more able to cope with frustration and resist temptation. At statistically significant levels, parents saw these children as more verbally fluent and able to express ideas; they used and responded to reason, were attentive and able to concentrate, to plan, and to think ahead, and were competent and skillful. Likewise they were perceived as able to cope and deal with stress more maturely and seemed more self-assured (Mischel, Shoda, and Peake, 1988, p. 687).[2] In some variations of this laboratory situation, seconds of delay time in preschool also were significantly related to their Scholastic Aptitude Test (SAT) scores when they applied to college (Shoda, Mischel, and Peake, 1990). The demonstration of these enduring individual differences in the course of development, as well as the significance attributed to purposeful self-imposed delay of gratification theoretically, underline the need to understand and specify the psychological processes that allow the young child to execute this type of self-regulation in the pursuit of desired outcomes.

[2]Studies following children's development over many years, using other measures of self-control requiring different types of delay of gratification, also found evidence of enduring psychological qualities [D.C. Funder, J.H. Block, and J. Block, *J. Pers. Soc. Psychol.* 44 (1983): 1198]. The particular qualities, however, depend on the specific type of delay behaviors sampled [see Table 5 in Mischel, Shoda, and Peake (1985) for comparisons of long-term correlates obtained].

Effects of Attention to the Rewards

Theoretical analyses of the delay process have assumed for almost a century that the individual's attention during the delay period is especially important in the development of the ability to delay gratification (Freud, 1959; James, 1890). William James, noting a relation between attention and self-control as early as 1890, contended that attention is the crux of self-control. Beginning with Freud, it has been proposed that attention to the delayed gratifications in thought, mental representation, or anticipation provides the mechanism that allows the young child to bridge the temporal delay required for their attainment. When children become able to represent the anticipated gratifications mentally, it was reasoned, they become able to delay for them by focusing on these thoughts or fantasies, thereby inhibiting impulsive actions. Some learning theorists also have speculated that the cognitive representation of rewards allows some sort of anticipatory or symbolic covert reinforcement that helps sustain effort and goal-directed behavior while external reinforcement is delayed (Mischel, 1974).

In spite of the fact that rewards were given paramount importance in psychological attempts to explain the determinants of behavior, their role in the delay process had remained mostly speculative because of the difficulty of objectively studying thoughts about rewards, particularly in young children. To study how their thinking about the rewards affects self-imposed delay, preschool children in the Stanford University community were assessed in several variations of the self-imposed delay situation described earlier. If thinking about the rewards facilitates delay, then children who are exposed to the rewards or encouraged to think about them should wait longer. The first study varied systematically whether or not the rewards were available for attention while the children were waiting (Mischel and Ebbesen, 1970). For example, in one condition, they waited with both the immediate (less preferred) and the delayed (more preferred) rewards facing them, exposed. In a second condition, both rewards were also present but obscured from sight (covered), and in two other conditions, either the delayed reward only or the immediately available reward was exposed during the delay period. The results were the opposite of those the investigators predicted: Attention to the rewards consistently and substantially decreased delay time instead of increasing it. Preschool children waited an average of more than 11 minutes when no rewards were exposed, but they waited less than 6 minutes on average when any of the rewards were exposed during delay.

To test the effects of thinking about the rewards more directly, in a second study, different types of thoughts were suggested to orient the children's attention with regard to the rewards (Mischel, Ebbesen, and Zeiss, 1972). The results showed that when preschoolers were cued to think about the rewards when waiting, delay time was short, regardless of whether the objects were exposed or covered (Figure 6.1). When distracting ("fun") thoughts were suggested, children waited for more than 10 minutes, whether or not the rewards were exposed. On the other hand, when no thoughts were suggested, delay time was greatly reduced by reward exposure, confirming the earlier findings. Distracting thoughts counteracted the strong effects of exposure to the actual rewards, allowing children to wait about as long as they did when the rewards were covered and no thoughts were suggested. In contrast, when the rewards were covered, and the children were cued to think about them, the delay time was as short as when the rewards were exposed and no distractions were suggested.[3,4] Thus, the original prediction and attention and thought directed to the reward objects would enhance voluntary delay was consistently undermined.

Observation of children's spontaneous behavior during the delay process also suggested that those who were most effective in sustaining delay seemed to avoid looking at the rewards deliberately, for example, covering their eyes with their hands and resting their heads on their arms. Many children generated their own diversions: They talked quietly to themselves, sang, created games with their hands and feet, and even tried to go to sleep during the waiting time. Their attempts to delay gratification seemed to be facilitated by external conditions or by self-directed efforts to reduce their frustration during the delay period by selectively directing their attention and thoughts away from the rewards (Mischel, 1974). However, it also seemed unlikely that sheer suppression or distraction from the frustration caused by the situation is the only determinant of this type of self-control. Indeed, when certain types of thoughts are focused on the rewards they can facilitate self-control substantially, even more than distraction does, as the next set of experiments found.

---

[3] When the rewards were exposed, children cued to think about fun did not differ significantly from those who faced the covered rewards with no thoughts suggested or who were cued to think about fun. Delay time also was not significantly different for children waiting with the rewards exposed when no thoughts were suggested and those cued to think about the rewards.

[4] When children waited in a similar self-imposed delay situation, they also estimated the delay to be longer when the reward was present physically, supporting the interpretation that attention to the rewards in this situation increases frustration [D.T. Miller and R. Karniol, *J. Pers. Soc. Psychol.* 34 (1976): 310].

Figure 6.1. Average delay time shown by 52 Stanford preschoolers when different types of thoughts were suggested (●, fun thoughts; ■, thoughts about the rewards; ○, no thoughts suggested) and the rewards were exposed or covered [based on Figure 4 in Mischel and Zeiss, 1972].

From Distraction to Abstraction

The results so far show that exposure to the actual rewards or cues to think about them undermine delay, but the studies did not consider directly the possible effects of images or symbolic representations of rewards. Yet it may be these latter types of representation—the images of the outcomes, rather than the rewards themselves—that mediate the young child's ability to sustain delay of gratification (Freud, 1959; Mischel and Moore, 1973). To explore this possibility, the effects of exposure to realistic images of the rewards were examined by replicating the experiments on the effects of reward exposure with slide-presented images of the rewards. It was found that although exposure to the actual rewards during the delay period makes waiting difficult for young children, exposure to images of the rewards had the opposite effect, making it easier. Children who saw images of the rewards they were waiting for (shown life-size on slides) delayed twice as long as those who viewed slides of comparable control objects that were not the rewards for which they were waiting, or who saw blank slides (Mischel and Moore, 1973). Thus, different modes of presenting rewards (i.e., real vs. symbolic) may either hinder or enhance self-control.

To test more directly the effects of the cognitive representations of rewards on delay behavior, preschool children were taught to transform "in their heads" the stimuli present during delay (real rewards or pictures of them) by turning real rewards into pictures and pictures into real rewards in their imagination (Moore, Mischel, and Zeiss, 1976, p. 419). How the children represented the rewards cognitively was a much more potent determinant of their delay behavior than the actual reward stimulus that they were facing. For example, children facing pictures of the rewards delayed almost 18 minutes, but they waited less than 6 minutes when they pretended that the real rewards, rather than the pictures, were in front of them. Likewise, even when facing the real rewards, they waited almost 18 minutes when they imagined the rewards as if they were pictures.

This pattern of results may reflect two different aspects of reinforcing (rewarding) stimuli that, in turn, may have completely different effects on self-control behavior. Consistent with earlier work (Berlyne, 1960), we hypothesized that stimuli can be represented both in an arousing (consummatory) and in an abstract (nonconsummatory) informative manner. In an arousing representation, the focus is on the motivating, "hot" qualities of the stimulus that tend to elicit completion of the action sequence associated with it, such as eating a food or playing with a toy. In an abstract representation, the focus is on the more informative, "cool," symbolic aspect of the stimulus, for example, as in a cue or reminder of the contingency or reason for delaying the action sequence associated with it (Mischel and Baker, 1975).

Specifically, it was suggested to one group of children that they could focus their thoughts on the arousing qualities of the rewards (such as the pretzel's crunchy, salty taste), and to another group of children that they could focus on the reward's abstract qualities and associations (by thinking about pretzel sticks, for example, as long, thin brown logs). Two other groups were given the same type of suggestions as to how they could think while waiting, but directed at comparable control objects that were not the rewards (Figure 6.2). When encouraged to focus on the abstract qualities of the rewards, children waited an average of more than 13 minutes, but they waited less than 5 minutes when the same type of thoughts were directed at the comparable objects that were not the rewards, suggesting that the abstract representation of the actual reward objects provides more than just distraction.

The longest mean delay time (almost 17 minutes) occurred when the suggested thoughts were also about control objects but with regard to their arousing qualities (e.g., children waiting for marshmal-

Figure 6.2. Delay time as a function of objects on which thoughts were focused (rewards versus comparable control objects) and type of cognitive representation in thoughts [arousing (■) versus abstract (○)]. All 48 Stanford preschool children were facing the exposed rewards [data are from Table 1 in Mischel and Baker, 1975].

lows who had been cued to think about the salty, crunchy taste of pretzels). Thus, while hot ideation about the rewards made delay difficult, such ideation directed at comparable objects that are not the rewards for which one is waiting may provide very good distraction. The results support the view that attention to the rewards may have either a facilitating or an interfering effect on the duration of delay, depending on whether the focus is arousing or abstract.

The experimental results, taken collectively, help specify how young children can become able to sustain self-imposed delay gratification for substantial periods. Delay is difficult for the preschooler when the rewards are exposed, unless distractions are provided or self-generated. Suggestions to think about the rewards, or attention to them, can facilitate or interfere with delay, depending on whether the rewards are represented in ways that lead to a focus on their arousing or abstract features. An abstract focus on the rewards can help self-imposed delay even more than comparable distractions; an arousing focus makes delay exceedingly difficult. How the child represents the rewards cognitively in this regard, rather than whether they are exposed physically or as images, crucially influences the duration of delay.

Preschool Delay Conditions for Predicting Long-Term Developmental Outcomes

On the basis of the experimental research reviewed so far, it also becomes possible to specify the types of preschool delay conditions in which the child's behavior will be more likely to predict relevant long-term developmental outcomes. The significant links noted earlier between delay of gratification at age 4 years and adolescent competence did not take account of the particular delay conditions. When the rewards are exposed, delay becomes highly frustrative for preschoolers, so that to sustain their goal-directed waiting they must use effective strategies, for example, by distracting themselves or by representing the rewards cognitively in an abstract, "cool" way. When preschoolers are not given strategies for sustaining delay, but the rewards are exposed, they must generate and execute such strategies on their own to delay, and therefore, their behavior should reveal more clearly individual differences in this type of competence. To the degree that this ability is stable and has enduring consequences for adaptation, we expected that preschool delay time when the rewards are exposed and no strategies are suggested would be diagnostic for predicting relevant developmental outcomes. In contrast, when the rewards are obscured, delay behavior was not expected to reflect children's ability to generate effective self-control strategies because that situation does not require the use of such strategies.

These expectations were supported in another follow-up study of the Stanford preschool children, in which we increased the sample of respondents so that the role of conditions could be analyzed in relation to long-term outcomes (Shoda, Mischel, and Peake, 1990). To obtain a more objective measure of cognitive academic competencies and school-related achievements in adolescence, we also included Scholastic Aptitude Test (SAT) scores. In conditions in which the rewards were exposed and no strategies were supplied, those children who delayed longer as preschoolers were rated in adolescence by their parents as significantly more attentive and able to concentrate, competent, planful, and intelligent. They also were seen as more able to pursue goals and to delay gratification, better in self-control, more able to resist temptation, to tolerate frustration, and to cope maturely with stress. Beyond parental ratings, in the same conditions SAT scores were available for 35 children, and both their verbal and quantitative SAT scores were significantly related to seconds of preschool delay time. The linear regression slope predicting SAT verbal scores from seconds of preschool delay time was .10 with a standard error of .04; for predicting SAT quantitative scores, the slope was .13 with a standard error of .03. The correlations were .42 for SAT verbal scores and .57 for SAT quantitative scores. In contrast, individual differences in delay behavior when the rewards were obscured did not reliably predict either parental ratings or SAT performance.

The significant correlations between preschool delay time and adolescent outcomes, spanning more than a decade, were relatively large compared to the typically low or negligible associations found when single measures of social behavior are used to predict other behaviors, especially over a long developmental period (Mischel, 1968). On the other hand, although the obtained significant associations are at a level that rivals many found between performances on intelligence tests repeated over this age span (Bloom, 1964; Honzik, Macfarlane, and Allen, 1948), most of the variance still remains unexplained. The small size of the SAT sample dictates special caution in these comparisons and underlines the need for replications, especially with other populations and at different ages.

As previously noted, preschool delay time in the diagnostic condition was significantly related not only to academic abilities of the sort assessed by the SAT but also to other indices of competence. Even after statistically controlling for SAT scores, preschoolers who had delayed longer were later rated by parents as more able to cope with a number of social and personal problems, suggesting that the relation between preschool delay time and later parental judgments is not completely attributable to school-related competencies as measured by the SAT.

The causal links and mediating mechanisms underlying these long-term associations necessarily remain speculative, allowing many different interpretations. For example, an early family environment in which self-imposed delay is encouraged and modeled also may nurture other types of behavior that facilitate the acquisition of social and cognitive skills, study habits, or attitudes that may be associated with obtaining higher scores on the SAT and more positive ratings by parents. It also seems reasonable, however, that children will have a distinct advantage beginning early in life if they use effective self-regulatory strategies to reduce frustration in situations in which self-imposed delay is required to attain desired goals. By using these strategies to make self-control less frustrating, these children can more easily persist in their efforts, becoming increasingly competent as they develop.

Of course, the self-regulatory strategies that have been described are not the only ones useful for sustaining goal-directed delay and effort. The particular strategies required depend on the type of delay situation, for example, self-imposed versus externally imposed delay (see footnote 4). During the delay process, children may use a variety of strategies, including self-instructions, rehearsal of the specific contingencies for goal attainment while avoiding an arousing focus on the rewards themselves, and self-monitoring of progress (Mischel, 1974). Related research in variations of the delay of gratification situation with young children showed the value for self-control of specific, carefully rehearsed, and elaborated plans for inhibiting temptations to terminate goal-directed efforts (Mischel and Patterson, 1978). Such plans are used spontaneously, in varying degree, even by preschool children. Similar self-regulatory strategies have been identified in research on the acquisition of cognitive skills for mastery of other tasks requiring self-control, like reading (Brown, Bransford, Ferrara, and Campione, 1983; Brown and DeLoache, 1978) and impulse inhibition (Meichenbaum and Goodman, 1971). It is also plausible that the specific competencies necessary for effective self-regulation are a component of a larger ability or set of abilities involving both cognitive and social knowledge and skills. Whereas self-regulatory competencies in the pursuit of goals are not even considered as a factor in traditional conceptions and tests of intelligence (Sternberg and Detterman, 1986), they are directly relevant to more recent attempts to devise a theory of social intelligence that integrates findings from cognitive, social, and developmental psychology to thoroughly reconstruct the analysis of intelligent behavior (Cantor and Kihlstrom, 1987).

The Development of Knowledge about Effective Self-Regulatory Strategies

In the course of development, children show increasing understanding and awareness of the strategies that facilitate various kinds of self-control. In a sample of middle-class children in the Stanford community, from preschool through grade six, the children's knowledge of the strategies that might help during the delay process were assessed (Mischel and Mischel, 1983). The overall results indicate that 4-year-olds often prefer the least effective strategies for self-imposed delay, thereby inadvertently making self-control exceedingly difficult for themselves. For example, they significantly prefer to expose the rewards during the delay period and to think about them (e.g., "because it makes me feel good"), thus defeating their own effort to wait. Within a year, most children understand and choose more effective strategies. They soon prefer to obscure the temptations and consistently reject arousing thoughts about them as a strategy for self-control. At that age many begin to recognize the problem of increased temptation produced by thinking about the arousing attributes of the rewards and try to self-distract ("just sing a song"). They also start to see the value of self-instructions, focusing on the contingency and reiterating it ("I'll wait, so I can get the two marshmallows instead of one" or "I'll say, 'do not ring the bell' . . . If you ring the bell and the teacher comes in, I'll just get that one"). The self-control rule that does not seem to become available until some time between the third and sixth grades requires recognition of the value of abstract rather than arousing thoughts, suggesting possible links between the development of this type of understanding and the child's achieving operational thought in the Piagetian sense (Piaget and Inhelder, 1966).

Extensions to Older Children at Risk

The research described so far specified some of the strategies that facilitate delay experimentally and summarized the development of children's growing knowledge and understanding of those strategies. However, the links between children's knowledge of effective strategies, their spontaneous use of such strategies when attempting to control themselves in the pursuit of delayed goals, and their success in sustaining delay remained unexamined. The delay process in older children with behavior problems, such as aggressiveness, conduct disorders, or hyperactivity, has been surprisingly unstudied, although these are the very individuals for whom effective attention deployment and sustained delay of gratification are assumed to be especially difficult (Ross and Ross, 1982). So far, research on delay of gratification has concentrated on preschool children without known developmental risks. Therefore, a recent study extended the delay paradigm to a population of older children, described as having a variety of social adjustment difficulties, such as aggressiveness and withdrawal (Rodriguez, Mischel, and Shoda, 1989).

In this sample, ages 6–12 years, assessed in a summer residential treatment facility, children's knowledge of self-control processes was significantly correlated with duration of their self-imposed delay. For example, those who knew that an abstract rather than an arousing representation would make waiting easier also delayed longer. Similarly, the children's spontaneous attention deployment during the delay period was significantly related to their actual delay time: As the delay increased, those who were able to sustain self-control spent a higher proportion of the time distracting themselves from the frustrative situation than did those who terminated earlier. Even when controlling statistically for the effects of verbal intelligence, the relations among knowledge of self-control, spontaneous use of effective delay strategies, and duration of delay remained significant. In addition, those individuals who scored higher on these indices of self-control in the delay situation, especially when the rewards were exposed, also were rated as significantly less aggressive throughout the summer (Rodriguez, Shoda, Mischel, and Wright, 1989). The overall findings obtained with older children at risk indicate that the cognitive attentional strategies that allow effective delay of gratification, as identified in the earlier experiments, also seem to be used spontaneously by individuals who delay longer.

Summary

Taken collectively, the results from the research programs we reviewed specify some of the cognitive processes that underlie this type of delay of gratification early in life. Whether or not attention to the rewards, or distraction from them, is the better strategy for sustaining self-control depends on how the rewards are represented cognitively. A focus on their arousing features makes self-control exceedingly difficult; a focus on their more abstract, informative features has the opposite effects. Moreover, the type of cognitive representation generated can overcome, and reverse, the effects of exposure to the rewards themselves.

Significant links were found between self-control behavior as measured in this paradigm and relevant social and cognitive outcomes years later. The experimental research allowed identification of the conditions in which these long-term relations were most clearly visible. The child's spontaneous understanding of effective self-regulatory strategies also was found to develop in a clear age-related sequence. Finally, delay of gratification in the same paradigm with older children at risk showed the expected concurrent relations to knowledge of effective self-control strategies and spontaneous attention deployment while trying to exercise self-control. An unanswered question now is whether or not teaching delay of gratification skills and strategies of the sort identified to those who lack them, early in life, would in fact reduce later developmental risks such as school failure. Postponing gratification sometimes may be an unwise choice, but unless individuals have the competencies necessary to sustain delay when they want to do so, the choice itself is lost.

•

Although more reviewers than can be thanked here provided constructive criticism on earlier drafts, we are especially grateful to J. Hochberg and H. Zukier, who were exceptionally generous with their time and commentary.

References

Bandura, A. *Social Foundations of Thought and Action: A Social-Cognitive Theory.* Englewood Cliffs, NJ: Prentice-Hall, 1986.

Bandura, A. and W. Mischel. "Modification of Self-imposed Delay of Reward Through Exposure to Live and Symbolic Models." *Journal of Personality and Social Psychology* 2 (1965): 698–703.

Berlyne, D. *Conflict, Arousal and Curiosity.* New York: McGraw-Hill, 1960.

Bloom, B.S. *Stability and Change in Human Characteristics.* New York: Wiley, 1964.

Brown, A.L., J.D. Bransford, R.A. Ferrara, and J.C. Campione, in P.H. Mussen (ed.). *Handbook of Child Psychology,* vol. 3. New York: Wiley, 1983, pp. 77–166.

Brown, A.L., and J.S. Deloache, in R.S. Seigler (ed.). *Children's Thinking: What Develops?* Hillsdale, NJ: Erlbaum, 1978, pp. 3–25.

Cantor, N., and J.F. Kihlstrom. *Personality and Social Intelligence.* Englewood Cliffs, NJ: Prentice-Hall, 1987.

Freud, S. *Collected Papers,* vol. 4. New York: Basic Books, 1959, pp. 13–21.

Graves, T. "Psychological Acculturation in a Tri-ethnic Community." *Southwestern Journal of Anthropology* 23 (1967): 337–350.

Harter, S., in P.H. Mussen (ed.). *Handbook of Child Psychology,* vol. 4. New York: Wiley, 1983, pp. 275–385.

Honzik, M.P., J.W. Macfarlane, and L. Allen. "The Stability of Mental Test Performance Between Two and Eighteen Years." *Journal of Experimental Education* 17 (1948): 309–324.

James, W. *Principles of Psychology.* New York: Holt, 1890.

Klineberg, S.L. "Future Time Perspective and the Preference for Delayed Reward." *Journal of Personality and Social Psychology* 8 (1968): 253.

Meichenbaum, D.H., and J. Goodman. "Training Impulsive Children to Talk to Themselves: A Means of Developing Self-control." *Journal of Abnormal Psychology* 77 (1971): 115.

Melikian, L. "Preference and Delayed Reinforcement: An Experimental Study Among Palestinian Arab Refugee Children." *Journal of Social Psychology* 50 (1959): 81–86.

Mischel, H.N., and W. Mischel. "Development of Children's Knowledge of Self-control Strategies." *Child Development* 54 (1983): 603.

Mischel, W. *Personality and Assessment*. New York: Wiley, 1968.

———. "Processes in Delay Gratification," in L. Berkowitz (ed.). *Advances in Experimental Social Psychology*, vol. 7. New York: Academic Press, 1974, pp. 249–292.

———. *Introduction to Personality: A New Look*, 4th ed. New York: Holt, Rinehart & Winston, 1986.

———. "Preference for Delayed Reinforcement and Social Responsibility." *Journal of Abnormal and Social Psychology* 69 (1961): 1.

———. "Delay of Gratification, Need for Achievement, and Acquiescence in Another Culture." *Journal of Abnormal and Social Psychology* 69 (1961): 543.

———. "Theory and Research on the Antecedents of Self-imposed Delay of Reward," in B.A. Maher (ed.). *Progress in Experimental Research*, vol. 3. San Diego, CA: Academic Press, 1966, pp. 85–132.

———, and N. Baker. "Cognitive Appraisals and Transformations in Delay Behavior." *Journal of Personality and Social Psychology* 31 (1975): 254.

———, and E.B. Ebbesen. "Attention in Delay of Gratification." *Journal of Personality and Social Psychology* 16 (1970): 329.

———, E.B. Ebbesen, and A.R. Zeiss. "Cognitive and Attentional Mechanisms in Delay of Gratification." *Journal of Personality and Social Psychology* 21 (1972): 204.

———, and C. Gilligan. "Delay of Gratification, Motivation for the Prohibited Gratification, and Responses to Temptation." *Journal of Abnormal and Social Psychology* 69 (1964): 411.

———, and R. Metzner. "Preference for Delayed Reward as a Function of Age, Intelligence, and Length of Delay Interval." *Journal of Abnormal and Social Psychology* 64 (1962): 425–431.

———, and B. Moore. "Effects of Attention to Symbolically Presented Rewards on Self-control." *Journal of Personality and Social Psychology* 28 (1973): 172–179.

———, and C.J. Patterson. "Effective Plans for Self-control in Children," in W.A. Collins (ed.). *Minnesota Symposia on Child Psychology*, vol. 11. Hillsdale, NJ: Erlbaum, 1978, pp. 199–230.

———, Y. Shoda, and P.K. Peake. "The Nature of Adolescent Competencies Predicted by Preschool Delay of Gratification." *Journal of Personality and Social Psychology* 54 (1988): 687.

———, and E. Staub. "The Effects of Expectancy on Waiting and Working for Larger Rewards." *Journal of Personality and Social Psychology* 2 (1965): 625.

Moore, B., W. Mischel, and A. Zeiss. *Journal of Personality and Social Psychology* 34 (1976): 419.

Piaget, J., and B. Inhelder. *L'image mentale chez l'enfant*. Paris: Presses Universitaires de France, 1966.

Rodriguez, M.L., W. Mischel, and Y. Shoda. "Cognitive Person Variables in the Delay of Gratification of Older Children at Risk." *Journal of Personality and Social Psychology* 57 (1989): 358.

―――, Y. Shoda, W. Mischel, and J. Wright, "Delay of Gratification and Children's Social Behavior in Natural Settings," paper presented at the Eastern Sociological Association, Boston, March 1989.

Ross, D.M., and S.A. Ross. *Hyperactivity: Current Issues, Research and Theory.* New York: Wiley, 1982.

Rutter, M. "Psychosocial Resilience and Protective Mechanisms." *American Journal of Orthopsychiatry* 57 (1987): 316.

Shoda, Y., W. Mischel, and P.K. Peake. *Developmental Psychology* 26 (1990): 978.

Sternberg, R.J. and D.K. Detterman (eds.). *What Is Intelligence? Contemporary Viewpoints.* Norwood, NJ: Ablex, 1986.

Stumphauzer, J.S. "Increased Delay of Gratification in Young Prison Inmates Through Imitation of High-Delay Peer Models." *Journal of Personality and Social Psychology* 21 (1972): 10–17.

PART THREE

·

Self-Control

· 7 ·

Self-Command:
A New Discipline

T.C. SCHELLING

IN A cocaine addiction center in Denver, patients are offered an opportunity to submit to extortion. They may write a self-incriminating letter, preferably a letter confessing their drug addiction, deposit the letter with the clinic, and submit to a randomized schedule of laboratory tests. If the laboratory finds evidence of cocaine use, the clinic sends the letter to the addressee. An example is a physician who addresses a letter to the State Board of Medical Examiners confessing that he has administered cocaine to himself in violation of the laws of Colorado and requests that his license to practice be revoked. Faced with the prospect of losing career, livelihood, and social standing, the physician has a powerful incentive to stay clean.

The clinic's procedure is exceptional in its explicitness and formality and in the drastic quality of the self-imposed deterrent threat, but it epitomizes a problem that is almost universal in its incidence, and it exemplifies a tactic that is not uncommon in coping with the problem. The problem is to make oneself behave as one has resolved to behave, especially in moments of crisis or whenever the resolve may lapse, and the tactic is to structure incentives so that even if the original motivation for behaving as resolved should fade or be rationalized away, there remains a forbidding consequence of misbehavior to provide the necessary discipline. Familiar and less drastic examples

167

are announcing ostentatiously to friends and workmates that one has quit smoking, so that visible relapse will bring embarrassment and shame, or joining a coalition to lose weight in which the members who fail to reach target must publicly acknowledge defeat by paying token, or perhaps substantial, financial penalties to their partners.

Most of us are continually engaged in efforts at self-management. There are things we hope to do that we are not sure we shall do and things we hope not to do that we are fearful we may do, and we seek ways to make our future behavior conform with what we now perceive to be our true or genuine or legitimate or long-range interest. Staying off cocaine is a deadly serious problem for only a few among us; staying off cigarettes has been a problem for nearly a hundred million of us in this country, of whom half have succeeded so far. Less life-threatening but more common and familiar is how to arrange that one will get out of bed when the alarm goes off in the morning.

The cocaine-clinic procedure nicely exhibits a characteristic of self-management tactics that helps to fit the subject of self-management within the broader topic of managing behavior generally, whether one's own behavior or the behavior of somebody else. The ways that one may try to assure that one will indeed get out of bed when the alarm goes off are for the most part the same as the ways that one would try to arrange that one's roommate will get out of bed when the alarm goes off. For the cocaine addict, we can conceive of two alternative coercive procedures in addition to the voluntary self-coercion that is offered the patient in Denver. Suppose the physician in our example, the one who wrote the self-incriminating confession, has a receptionist or secretary who has become privy to his cocaine habit and writes a letter to the State Board of Medical Examiners detailing the illicit use of cocaine by the physician and providing or promising evidence, and shows this letter of incrimination to the physician and says that the letter will be sent unless the physician ceases use of cocaine. We can even imagine the employee demanding that the physician submit to laboratory tests on some appropriate schedule.

This is done, we may suppose, and as the physician may appreciate, entirely for the benefit of the physician. The idea is that the physician has a problem that he or she cannot solve, and the loyal employee is so concerned as to threaten exposure "disloyally." It is the same tactic, and it can be offered by the clinic for voluntary acceptance, or it can be imposed for the physician's own good against the wishes of the physician by an employee who thinks it is in the best interest of the physician. It is the same technique whether used to constrain one's own behavior or the behavior of someone else.

We can generalize the tactic even further. Imagine that the employee writes this letter to the State Board of Medical Examiners and shows a copy to the physician proposing that the letter will be sent unless the physician doubles the employee's salary. This is simple blackmail for profit. But in the earlier case, it was still blackmail—blackmail for the benefit of the physician, imposed by the "loyal" and concerned employee. One can blackmail a person for the benefit of the blackmailer, or blackmail a person for the victim's own benefit. The cocaine-clinic procedure can be construed as an opportunity for self-blackmail in one's own long-term interest.

I have gone through this somewhat detailed analysis of the extraordinary procedure of the Denver clinic mainly to show that such an extraordinary procedure, although dramatic and exceptional, epitomizes a common phenomenon, that of efforts at self-management. And it illustrates that what may be done to coerce or otherwise to constrain and manage one's own behavior is not altogether different from the ways that we deal with the behavior of others. And this last point is important, because there may be available a substantial body of knowledge about striking bargains and otherwise influencing the behavior of others that can be assimilated to this problem of managing oneself. If we know something about military discipline, about disciplining employees, about negotiating with neighbors and business associates, even about controlling the behavior of children, it may be that the subject of self-management can draw on what is already known about influencing the behavior of others. Of course, it may work both ways: If we knew a lot about the way to manage our own behavior, we might be able to transfer that knowledge to managing the behavior of others. But there has been extensive attention to bargaining, managing, disciplining the behavior of others, compared with managing oneself, so that the main transfer of knowledge is likely to be from the coping with other's behavior to the coping with one's own.

Actually, there has been some philosophical interest in recent years in this issue of how to conceptualize the conflict between immediate self-interest and some kind of longer-term, more genuine or more durable or more legitimate self-interest, as epitomized by the smoker or the drinker or the drug addict or the sexually undisciplined in coping with relapse. The story of Ulysses and the Sirens is the classical instance. But temptation, whether addictive or sexual or elicited by the classical song of the Sirens, is only one dimension of the problem of self-management. Let me survey a wider area in which people may need to think about commanding and constraining their own future behavior.

Less poignant than cocaine addiction or sexual arousal or nicotine dependency but nevertheless universally familiar is the problem of drowsiness. Getting out of bed in the morning is a mundane but not trivial problem. Staying awake is, similarly, not a trivial problem; for some people it may be beyond control, for others it is a problem with self-control. Actually, even behavior *while* asleep is a problem that concerns some of us. I have in mind not the dramatic case of the somnambulist but rather the person who may scratch a wound or assume a posture that his or her orthopedist does not recommend. To illustrate again that what one does to govern one's own behavior is not so different from what one does to govern the behavior of somebody else, I can point out that if one is afraid that a child will scratch chicken pox lesions while asleep, one may put mittens on the child, and if an adult has chicken pox, the adult may similarly pull mittens onto his or her own hands.

Then there is behavior while depressed. Pregnant women about to deliver may be advised of the possibility of postpartum depression, a period lasting a day or several days during which the woman may have the blues and do things she will later regret. (If she gave up smoking for the duration of the pregnancy, this may be the time when she will relapse.) People who undergo severe surgery often suffer several days of postsurgical depression, and while there may not be much mischief they can do while still in the hospital, there are things they may say and possibly some decisions they *can* make, that they will wish to forestall if they are appropriately warned in advance. Cardiac patients who are sternly advised never to smoke again may be incapable of following that advice because of postsurgical depression.

Then there is rage. And there are pain and panic and temper. People who lose their tempers are advised to count to ten before saying or doing anything drastic. People who know intellectually that the worst thing to do when confronting a wild beast is to turn their back to the beast and run may turn and run, and may need disciplining devices to prevent that impetuous behavior. People who know that when the car skids in snow the worst thing they can do is slam on the brakes may need special practice or technological protection against the impetuous urge to do exactly what one should not do when the car skids.

Phobias are an important self-management problem. Some people find difficulty in making themselves perform naturally in the presence of an abyss. Many people cannot cope with needles, although closing one's eyes or simply not looking is a technique regularly taken advantage of. I once spoke to a friend who was going to become commander of an army airborne division. I asked him whether he had ever jumped, and he had not. I asked him whether he would have to jump, and he said yes. I asked him whether he had any apprehension about being able to propel himself out of the aircraft, and he smiled and said that he understood that the army had a man who would take care of that. I have often wondered whether, if I badly wanted to initiate a skydiving hobby, I would ever be able to make that first jump.

I saw a movie 40 years ago about Scottish fishermen, in which a fisherman got his thumb caught by the shell of a huge clam, a monster that could not be dragged on shore or forced to release its grip. The tide was rising, and the fisherman would drown unless he could extricate his thumb. When the water reached his throat, he drew a knife with his other hand and carved away the trapped thumb. I have often wondered whether, if my life depended on it, I could use a knife to carve away my own thumb to release myself from such a trap. The conclusion I usually reach is that yes, I could, once the water rose above my nostrils, but by then I wouldn't have time to complete the job.

Then there is simple fear. Phobias are unreasonable fears, but there is genuine fear that one may need to overcome. Let me quote the first paragraph of the first chapter of my favorite book on baseball: "Fear."

That's the paragraph. The second paragraph says, "Fear is the fundamental factor in hitting, and hitting the ball with the bat is the fundamental act of baseball." Similar to fear is nervousness. I saw a movie in which Robert Donat during World War II disassembled unexploded bombs in London. He wore a headset into which he described everything he did, so that if he suddenly disintegrated there would be a record of what he had been doing. He used his fingers very gently to unscrew the fuse at the tip of the bomb. According to the movie, the physical feat of disassembling the fuse was not difficult. The problem was trembling. Anybody could disassemble a dummy bomb; in practice on a dummy, nobody's fingers trembled. Robert Donat represented the person whose fingers didn't tremble when he sat astride a real bomb with his fingers on the fuse. Most of us cannot control our nervousness and trembling, just as many teenagers cannot control their giggling. Whether this should be called the control of voluntary or of involuntary behavior is not easy to answer, but giggling teenagers may learn that to avoid *involuntary* giggling, they can avoid *voluntarily* looking at each other, and best of all not to be in the same room after a giggling attack has commenced.

Then there is captivation. We can be captivated by television and know that we should turn it off because we have more important things to do but sit spellbound. I have often wished that hotels, perhaps for a $5 fee, would disconnect my room television before I arrive. But there is also captivation by reverie and fantasy and even puzzles that one works on. There is the book that one idly reads while flying home on an airplane, the flying time being "time out" when one is allowed to waste time reading some mystery novel, but if one hasn't finished it upon landing, one may be unable to discard it before wasting another couple of hours finishing the damn book.

Then there is insomnia. Insomnia may be a specific instance of a more generic problem of one's mind engaging in wayward behavior. There are bad thoughts that come to mind that we cannot exclude from our minds. There is worrying about pain to come in the dentist's office, there is pain and guilt and shame from things we have done that we cannot exclude from our minds. There are things we cannot exclude from imagination. There are people who know perfectly well that flying is safer than driving but who cannot prevent thoughts of fiery crashes but can perfectly well ignore the possibility of automobile disaster. I love Japanese raw fish, sashimi. I recently read that there is a rare occurrence of a live worm in raw fish, a worm that is not destroyed either by the chewing or the digestion of the fish. There are two such worms, one of which is very serious because it can do harm in the intenstine; the other is less serious but uglier, and it can be regurgitated and come out of one's mouth. I know the odds on this happening, and there is absolutely no reason to think that suffering such trauma at a Japanese restaurant is more likely than dying in an automobile crash on the way to the restaurant. But I cannot keep myself from thinking about that dreadful worm, and I shall probably never again eat sashimi.

Finally, we come to the phenomenon with which I began this talk, namely, addiction, appetite, temptation. But even in this context, "addiction" is not unique. The problem of the cocaine addict on the verge of relapse in the throes of a craving, may not be altogether different from the situation of a person who is suffering extreme thirst and advised not to drink water. Consider the man with a stomach wound who must under no circumstances drink water for 36 hours. He understands that if he drinks water, he will die. He would rather live than relieve the discomfort of thirst. But if there is visibly available a glass of water, he is likely to drink it and die. I think we should not deduce that he preferred instant relief to long life. I think we should deduce that this central nervous system was programmed, through millions of years of biological evolution, to relieve extreme thirst. As the hours went by, and his thirst increased, his mind's capacity to think about the consequences of drinking the water steadily diminished, and his mind's preoccupation with the need to quench his thirst increased. He didn't "decide" that he would rather drink than live; he was under the control of a brain that knew that thirst could kill and didn't know that drinking could.

Consider the case of George, who quit cigarettes 7 weeks ago and is becoming encouraged that he has finally kicked the habit, who plays cards at his club, has more drinks than usual, and begins to think that maybe he could have a cigarette or two without completely relapsing. Having announced to his club friends that he quit cigarettes, he doesn't dare light up in their presence, but he thinks he will go out on the sidewalk and enjoy the lovely fragrance of a richly aromatic cigarette. He excuses himself, goes downstairs to the cigarette machine and buys a pack, strolls out the door onto the sidewalk, opens the pack and puts a cigarette in his mouth, lights a match, and is hit on the head. He wakes up several minutes later, minus his wallet containing $300 and a driver's license and several credit cards, suffers a headache, walks home because he has no cab fare, and wakes up none the worse except for having lost his wallet.

Somebody asks him how he enjoyed his evening. He responds that it was the luckiest evening of his life. He almost smoked a cigarette. He was ready for relapse. He had the cigarettes, had one in his mouth; he lit the match, and some beloved thug hit him on the head, interrupted his smoke, and took his wallet. All he lost was $300 and some credit cards and a driver's license. He was rescued from losing the 7 weeks he had invested in not smoking. It only cost him $300 to be saved.

Let me turn now to some of the things that people do to cope with these ubiquitous problems of self-management. And let me point out again that most of these things that people do to cope with their own self-management are things, or are like things, that they would do to cope with somebody else's. I've already mentioned putting mittens on to prevent scratching, whether it is one's own scratching or one's child's.

One tactic is to relinquish control. Give your car keys to the host, and tell him or her not to give them back unless you are sober when you leave. Another is commitment. If you can, make the decision now in a way that you cannot rescind when you relapse. I know a corporate dining room that has the rule that everyone must phone in his or her lunch order at 9:30 in the morning, and at lunch will be served only what was ordered at 9:30. The idea is that at 9:30 in the morning, after a decent breakfast, long before lunch appetite takes over, people will order frugally and prudently. Then at lunch, they can have only what they ordered when their appetite was at a nadir. I suppose the system works because the collective-decision process by which this scheme is kept in place is submitted for referendum at 9:30 in the morning and not at 12 noon.

Then there is removing the offending or tempting substance. Don't keep the food or the liquor or the guns at home. I have mentioned my interest in having the hotel disconnect the TV. Most people who try to quit smoking dispose of their pipes or their cigarettes, and people who wish to eat fewer calories or less fat may try to keep none of the offending foods in the kitchen.

Disabling is another technique. There are people who know that they are binge shoppers, who leave their credit cards at home when they go window shopping.

And there is incarceration. There are people who have succeeded in doing what they always intended to do but never did until they were snowbound for a day at an airport. The Hungarian dissident Georg Lukacs was visited by George Steiner, who admired the works of Lukacs on the bookshelf. Lukacs was amused and said, "You want to know how to get work done? House arrest!"

Then there is the deliberate rigging of penalties. I mentioned the cocaine-clinic self-blackmail scheme. But there are people who individually pledge to send $100 to the political party they most despise if they ever smoke a cigarette. How does this work? It isn't altogether clear, but at least the smoke-quitter has an answer to the question, "What harm could smoking one little cigarette do?"

The remarkable thing is that he or she can believe that the penalty will indeed be exacted tomorrow. And having to send a check for $100 to the party one despises is a very explicit and immediate incentive that cannot be rationalized away.

Then there are delays. It is remarkable how effective delays can be. People who try to get off cigarettes or cocaine may be able to impose on themselves delay procedures according to which they can decide, at anytime they wish, to resume consumption but only after 4 hours or 8 hours or 24. The possibility of resuming consumption may make it less frightening to declare emancipation, and the delay often seems to block relapse. Even that Denver clinic allowed people to break out of the compact by submitting a notarized declaration of withdrawal from the arrangement. There was a 2-week delay. Anybody who submitted his or her request for withdrawal could retrieve the incriminating letter after 2 weeks. But if during the 2 weeks' interim, the withdrawal was rescinded, then it would require another

2 weeks' notice. Many of the patients had invoked the withdrawal procedure, none had gone 2 weeks without revoking the revocation.

Precursors are important. Many people who quit smoking relapse when they have been drinking alcohol. If they can easily quit drinking but only with difficulty quit smoking, quitting drinking is a useful way to reduce the likelihood of cigarette relapse.

Those are some of the tactics that may or may not work. A related issue is what kinds of rules or behavior specifications may be conducive to success. Some of the characteristics of rules that are conducive to success in self-management are familiar from the study of rules about governing the behavior of others. For example, rules seem to work better if they are unambiguous, if they are discrete, if they make clear what is and what is not a violation. But then there are precautionary rules, rules intended to stay away from danger. For children, "don't go in the water" is better than "don't wade in too deep"; what is too deep is ambiguous, but what is in the water is not. Don't drink alcohol is discrete and unambiguous; don't drink too much is not. Zero is especially attractive, and while one cannot control calories by adopting the zero-calory regime, it may be easier to quit alcohol or tobacco with a zero resolution.

Ceremonies and contracts seem to make a difference. Books on controlling one's behavior recommend formal written contracts. There are two features of a contract that are interesting. One is that a written contract may cover details that, if left unspecified, are opportunities for relapse. If one has resolved not to drink alcohol, the contract may specify those exceptions that would be irresistible but that would shake one's confidence. If the contract specifies that at the wedding reception one may drink two glasses of champagne, one may do so without loss of confidence in the original contract. The second advantage of the contract is simply ceremonial; the contract is a formal document, and one may well feel that violating a contract is different from changing one's mind about what one had resolved to do.

Self-imposed rules have to deal with exceptions, like the glass of champagne at somebody's wedding, and with violations. It may help to have specific penalties for violations; otherwise, there may be no way to procure one's way back into good standing. Consuming excessive calories may be punitively compensated by, say, a two-to-one ratio for doing without calories during the week after one has consumed excessively. Having won one's entry back into good graces may mean that in the event of relapsed behavior, one can resume the regime rather than have to start over again altogether.

This is not a complete dissertation on the subject of self-management, but an introduction. The subject is one that receives remarkably little attention outside the clinical literature and not much within that literature. I wish I could attract more attention to the subject, especially because the literature on bargaining and management that is oriented toward bargaining with and managing others proves to be largely applicable to bargaining with oneself and managing oneself.

The subject has wide appeal because almost none among us is without some problem of the kind that I have addressed in this essay in self-management.

· 8 ·

Self-Control

George Ainslie and Nick Haslam

7|8|9c

Chapter 3 presents evidence that a person does not "have" a preference, in the sense of a disposition to choose that is stable unless acted upon. Viewed over even short periods of time, he is a population of successive preferences. We argue in that chapter that successively dominant rewards cannot be weighed against each other, but give rise to *interests*, sets of behaviors to obtain these rewards. The conflict he experiences at a given moment is among incompatible interests, each based upon a reward that is preferred at some times and that, thus, has some likelihood of occurring. Interests can be described as short- or long- or even midrange, depending on the relative delays of the rewards on which they are based; longer-range implies greater absolute size of reward, because a reward that is both more delayed and no larger than its competitor will never be preferred, and, thus, never give rise to an interest.

We argue in this chapter that these interests relate to one another strategically. That is, the dominant interest at a given moment makes choices so as to forestall other interests that might undermine its plans, and allows for the possibility that interests dominant at other times may do the same toward it. This situation is responsible for the familiar properties of impulsiveness and self-control, which is a matter of forestalling anticipated temporary preferences for inferior goods. Of the four possible means of doing this—using extrapsychic devices, controlling one's attention, using the momentum attached to emotions, and making personal rules—the last is the most complex and has the most far-reaching consequences for the process of choice. In effect it establishes the same relationship among some sets of successive motivational states as there is among players of a repeated game of prisoner's dilemma, thereby transforming the nature of choice: It changes the competition of impulse and control from a sequential to a simultaneous one; it requires a subjective estimation of the risks of discerning failure to cooperate with one's own future motivational states, which may overshadow the estimation of reward magnitudes; and it makes some choices more important as precedents than as events in their own right, thereby variously generating the experiences of free will and compulsion. In this way, a seemingly multiple self can arise through the strict maximization of discounted expected reward.

The Necessity of Commitment

If the future is intrinsically discounted at a constant rate, the resulting exponential curves offer no mechanism for learning delay of gratification. Even where their steepness has created sharp overvaluation of an earlier reward relative to a later one, these curves predict that the rewards will be valued in the same proportion at a distance as up close. Hyperbolic curves, on the other hand, predict the same original overvaluation of imminent reward but also suggest that an individual can compensate for it by indirect means in order to attain his long-range goals. The most obvious method is for him to commit his motivation or behavior before his preference changes toward an inferior good.

Commitment devices involving both modification of future motives and physical limitations of future behavior have been described in the literature, usually under the title of *impulse control*. This term is sometimes used too broadly for our purposes. By *impulses,* people sometimes mean behaviors that are merely spontaneous, that is, motivated by a whim. Sometimes (e.g., Barratt and Patton, 1983) they use it for quasi-delinquent behaviors, the symptoms of *dyscontrol* that used to be called *choleric* (Schalling, Erdman, and Asberg, 1983), behaviors that might or might not be preferred only temporarily. However, much of the literature on impulsiveness is applicable to people's attempts to forestall their own temporarily powerful motives.

An economist, Strotz (1956), was the first modern author to specifically postulate an expectable change of preference:

> An individual is imagined to choose a plan of consumption for a future period of time so as to maximize the utility of the plan as evaluated at the present moment. . . . If he is free to reconsider his plan at later dates, will he abide by it or disobey it—*even though his original expectations of future desires and means of consumption are verified?* Our present answer is that the optimal plan of the present moment is generally one which will not be obeyed, or that the individual's future behavior will be inconsistent with his optimal plan. If this inconsistency is not recognized, our subject will typically be a "spendthrift". . . . If the inconsistency is recognized, the rational individual will do one of two things. He may "precommit" his future behavior by precluding future options so that it will conform to his present desire as to what it should be. Or, alternatively, he may modify his chosen plan to take account of future disobedience, realizing that the possibility of disobedience imposes a further constraint . . . on the set of plans which are attainable. (p. 166)

These two responses are not actually alternatives. The rational individual should make no plans that are unlikely to be realized, and should enlarge the category of realizable plans by commitment. The individual's commitment devices include irrevocable contracts, compulsory savings plans, telling friends to "Kick me if I don't. . . ." and so on.

A sociologist, H.S. Becker (1960), seems to have come independently to a similar device. He spoke of a commitment as a making of "side bets," irreversibly arranging to forfeit something valuable, especially social standing, if the given decision were not maintained: "Decisions not supported by such side bets will lack staying power, crumpling in the face of opposition or fading away to be replaced by other essentially meaningless decisions until a commitment based on side bets stabilizes behavior."

Freud's concept of defenses against impulses had much in common with the notion of commitment skills, but his view of consciousness and behavior as alternative outlets of the psychic apparatus led him to confound two distinct motives for defense: Defenses can avoid either unpleasant perceptions and emotions, or impulses and "instincts." If a person cultivates a benign, magnanimous nature in order to avoid beating up his little brother, he is said to be defending himself against impulses. If he cultivates this attitude in order to resemble Christ and, thus, avoid perceiving himself as powerless, this is also called a defense mechanism, even though its purpose is not impulse control. Modern psychoanalytic therapists often acknowledge the usefulness of defense mechanisms of the former kind, that is, defenses against impulses; many behavior therapists have gone further, actively striving to build such skills (reviewed in Ainslie, 1986a).

Four Methods of Precommitment

Much of what little empirical research has been done on impulse-controlling devices has been organized according to the psychoanalytic list of defense mechanisms (elaborated most fully in Sjoback, 1973) and, thus, has necessarily confounded impulse control with self-deception. These studies have shown that individuals' self-reports about their personality traits do cluster into patterns like those described by analytic writers (Gleser and Ihilevich, 1969; Lazare, Klerman, and Armor, 1966, 1968) but have not explored the specific role of these traits in impulse control, much less how this role might be performed.

By contrast, clinical reports and other descriptions of self-control give a rich selection of self-control methods. Critical examination of these descriptions shows that all of them rely on one or more of four basic tactics for influencing future motivational states to accommodate the present one: extrapsychic mechanisms, control of attention, preparation of emotion, and personal rules. Note that these tactics work both ways: There are circumstances under which each can also serve a shorter-range interest against a longer-range one.

Extrapsychic Mechanisms

Devices of the extrapsychic kind involve arranging for either physical or social action upon the person's future motivational state. These have been recommended since ancient times, not only in the literary example of Ulysses and the Sirens, but also in the physician Galen's (1963) advice to the person trying to control his passions: This person should find someone who will "disclose his every action which is wrong . . . none of us can succeed unless he has someone to point out his every error" (p. 44). They are widely proposed in behavior therapy manuals (Stuart and Davis, 1972; Thoreson and Mahoney, 1974). A person who is trying to avoid overeating, for instance, has been variously advised to take a drug that suppresses appetite, to keep fattening foods out of the house, or even to have his jaws wired together. If he can enlist the cooperation of a friend, he might ask the friend to exert pressure on him when he seems about to overeat, deposit money with the friend that is to be given away whenever he overeats, or simply make a public statement of intent to lose weight so that he will look foolish if he does not.

Psychodynamic writers have described how a person may act up in order to attract the attention of someone in authority, who will then guard him and prevent the occurrence of more serious impulsive behavior. This maneuver has been called *asking for controls*.

In situations where a temporary preference arises regularly, even pigeons will sometimes learn a committing operant, and they will perform it regularly once it is learned (Ainslie, 1974; Deluty, Whitehouse, Mellitz, and Hineline, 1983; Hayes, Kapust, Leonard, and Rosenfarb, 1981; Rachlin and Green, 1972). Thus, at least one device to forestall changes of preference can be learned in the absence of "higher" mental functions, entirely on the basis of the differential effect of the larger reward before the smaller reward becomes dominant.

Control of Attention

Repression, which Freud (1914, p. 16) at one time held to be the cornerstone of all defensive processes, is said to operate by keeping attention away from thoughts that might lead to impulses:

> A repressed instinctual impulse can be activated (newly cathected) from two directions: from within, through reinforcement from its internal sources of excitation, and from without, through the perception of an object that it desires. The hysterical "anticathexis" is mainly directed outwards, against dangerous perceptions. It takes the form of a special kind of vigilance which, by means of restrictions of the ego, causes situations to be avoided that would entail such perceptions, or if they do occur, manages to withdraw the subject's attention from them. (Freud, 1926, p. 158)

Repression can be seen in terms of simple information processing. When deciding whether to pursue a given activity, a person does not call up all his knowledge of it at once, but begins with a capsule with which he has previously summarized this knowledge (Shiffrin and Schneider, 1977). He is apt to evaluate options for further information processing according to the likely payoffs for these options, perhaps arrayed in what has been called a *sentry matrix* (Bruner, Goodnow, and Austin, 1956, p. 75). If he has categorized his knowledge of the activity according to its impulsiveness, and the capsule he recalls first tells him that the activity is indeed impulsive, he will know that further review risks revealing it to be imminently available. He may thus be motivated to stop the review at that point.

Such avoidance of further information represents the act of repression. Of course, if he estimates the risk of discovering its availability to be high already, that very estimate may have changed his preference in favor of further review, and the repression will have failed. Furthermore, if the capsule contains information that further review is apt to be unpleasant (using what Williams, Watts, Macleod, and Mathews [1988, p. 171] call *affective salience*), the individual may decide in his short-range interest not to pursue it further. He will then be using repression for its other defensive purpose, maintaining short-range comfort. Whatever its purpose, if the person were able to report a decision to avoid further information, it would be called *suppression* rather than repression, a distinction that is not important for this discussion.

The disadvantage of attention control as a defense against impulses is that it may hinder the gathering of useful information, possibly leading to serious gaps in the person's orientation to reality. In this spirit, Freud believed that all repression was pathological, and particularly apt to lead to *hysterical* symptoms (Breuer and Freud, 1895).

Preparation of Emotion

Freud initially included in his concept of repression the disconnection of thoughts from feelings (1895), a distinct process he later named isolation of affect: A person pays attention to experiences that would be expected to cause emotionality, but reports feeling no emotion (1926). This may be understood as an example of commitment if we notice the effect that an emotion has on subsequent motivation. It is commonly recognized that basic emotions such as anger, sexual arousal, and fear are, up to a point, vicious circles. After the emotion has gotten under way, there is a lower threshold for further emotional activity of the same kind, until some satiation point has been reached. If a person expects an emotion to make an otherwise unpreferred reward temporarily dominant, he may commit not to choose the reward through early inhibition of that emotion.

A concrete example of this strategy is the advice that used to be given to teenagers in dating manuals on how to avoid sexual intercourse by avoiding foreplay. Avoidance of the emotion usually produced by foreplay would be expected to have the same result. Although there has been little research on voluntary control of the emotional process, Lazarus (1975a,b) has described credible examples from everyday life. The discovery that people can learn extensive voluntary control of vegetative functions like blood pressure, organ perfusion, and brain waves (Kimmel, 1974; Schwartz, 1975) tends to confirm the practicality of voluntarily controlling emotions. Early inhibition of emotions is probably a powerful means of commitment, although this device costs whatever reward is dependent on that emotion for its consumption. For instance, the person who controlled his sexual temptations by the early avoidance of sexual affects might run the risk of losing his capacity for sexual enjoyment.

A person can also decrease the attractiveness of a particular activity by cultivating a contradictory emotion. For instance, when a person enters a situation that he expects to provoke unwanted tender feelings, he might forestall these feelings by summoning rage at the earliest opportunity. Conversely, if he is worried about rage, he might cultivate tender feelings. Examples of this device have been discussed under the name of reversal of affect (A. Freud, 1966; Freud, 1914).

Reversal seems to represent a special case of general strategy: finding activities that reduce one's appetite for, or increase one's appetite for the alternative to, a particular reward. This general strategy has been called reaction formation (A. Freud, 1966; Freud, 1926). Russell (1978) points out that this strategy need not be unconscious, but may be pursued deliberately.

Where a long-range interest cannot forestall a shorter-range interest just by cultivating a nonimpulsive alternative, it may nevertheless be able to prevail by finding a still more briefly preferred activity that is incompatible with the target activity. Examples from ordinary life are common enough. A person may have a long-range interest in asserting himself in a relationship where he is being bullied, but always shrink from doing it when the opportunity is present. To actually act in his long-term self-interest, he may need to find a short-term interest such as getting drunk, an activity he might not ordinarily indulge in, in order to "get his courage up." Without the help of the long-range interest, a midrange interest in preserving a certain social role might forestall the urge to get drunk. This midrange interest might in turn undermine the person's long-range interest in rising above this role in order to stop the bullying.

The disadvantage of the emotion-control tactic seems to be that the activities that forestall a particular temporary preference may not happen to be otherwise productive in the long run, and they may thrive to the point that they represent nuisances in their own right. Obsessional thoughts seem to be an example of this. There is also the potential that short-range interests will look for long-range ones to protect them. When Elster's (1989) cream cake eater says, "I wish I was less vain," the eater becomes suspicious of this lofty goal: "But do I think that only when I wish to eat cake?" (p. 37 note). In any case, the need to maintain a close balance of emotions might greatly reduce the person's reward-getting efficiency.

The distinction between controls on attention and on emotion is sometimes hard to make. Information processing is part of any mental activity; the cultivation or inhibition of an emotion is apt to be experienced as "getting one's mind" on or off that emotion. Whether the person's intent is to restrict the processing of information or to prepare an emotional climate may sometimes be just a matter of emphasis. In studies of delay of gratification performed by Mischel and his coworkers, for instance, it can be difficult to separate the two processes. Although some children devised "self-distraction" techniques to avoid succumbing to a temptation (Mischel and Ebbeson, 1970), further research suggested that the crucial ingredient in delaying consumption was to think about the food rewards in nonconsummatory, even deliberately disgusting ways, or to think about the task of delaying itself, so as not to stimulate their appetites (Mischel and Moore, 1980; Mischel and Mischel, 1983). Successful delayers in these experiments seem to have been modulating their affect more than blocking information about the imminent availability of the rewards.

Personal Rules

Only a few of the many defense mechanisms that have been described in psychoanalytic literature seem to be simple commitment devices: asking for controls, repression, denial, isolation of affect, reversal of affect, and reaction formation. Furthermore, simple commitment does not seem to account for the kind of impulse control we call will power, which allows a person to resist impulses while both attracted by them and able to pursue them. Such a power is well known in common experience, but it has never been precisely characterized by behavioral science.

Galen, for instance, who was quoted earlier on the value of getting other people to help control one's passions, also proposed an internal technique: The person should consider for each daily task whether it is better to be the slave of passion or to go by reason. That is, a person should classify every behavior into one of two accounts, passionate or reasonable (1963). Galen implied that a decrease in the passionate behaviors would follow as a matter of course, but he gave few clues as to what he thought the mechanism would be. He did say it was harder for people who are out of practice: "A man who has for a long time habitually fallen into error finds it difficult to remove the defilement of the passions from his soul." Galen also implied that a little backsliding would be disproportionately damaging: "He must not relax his vigilance for a single hour" (1963, p. 45).

This short list of properties had not changed much by the time of the Victorian psychologists, who were the last group to subject the will to serious analysis. Sully (1884) did say a little more about the formation of mental accounts:

> When the child begins to view each individual action in its bearing on some portion of his lasting welfare, his actions become united and consolidated into what we call conduct. Impulse as isolated prompting for this or that particular enjoyment becomes transformed into comprehensive aim and rational motive. Or to express the change otherwise, action becomes pervaded and regulated by principle. The child consciously or unconsciously begins to refer to a general precept or maxim of action, as "maintain health," "seek knowledge," "be good," and so forth. Particular actions are thus united under a common rule, they are viewed as members of a class of actions subserving one comprehensive end. In this way the will attains a measure of unity. (p. 631)

He reaffirms Galen's point about the cumulative effect of choices: "Every repetition of this kind of action . . . tends to fix conduct in this particular direction" (1884, p. 663). His contemporary Bain (1886) noted the disproportionate damage done by backsliding: "It is necessary, above all things, never to lose a battle. Every gain on the wrong side undoes the effect of many conquests on the right" (p. 440).

The gist of these descriptions was that the person defined a category of similar choices, such that each had an effect on those still to come. The motive to shore up subsequent choices in the category might be substantially greater than the motive to control an individual impulse for its own sake. The great virtue of will power was that it left perception and emotion undistorted. As William James (1890) said, "both alternatives are steadily held in view, and in the very act of murdering the vanquished possibility the chooser realizes how much in that instant he is making himself lose" (p. 534).

Derivation of Personal Rules from Discount Functions

It is possible to deduce a mechanism for will power from the existence of deeply concave discount curves like those described in Chapter 3, if we assume only that curves from multiple rewards combine in an additive fashion. Little research has been done on the summed effect at a single moment of a series of rewards separated by intervals of time. Some kind of summation clearly occurs, even in pigeons. Mazur (1986) has recently shown that the value to pigeons of up to three rewards delayed by up to 30 seconds is the exact sum of their individual values discounted for delay. Because this simple summation is also the most parsimonious mechanism for the combination of reward effects, we will assume it to be valid while we await confirmational data.

If an individual must make a series of choices between rewards of amount A_i and, later, larger rewards of amount A'_i (i.e., all $A'_i > A_i$ and all $T'_i > T_i$), each choice will be described simply by the matching law unless the choices are linked. If, for instance, the whole series of choices must be made in the same direction and all at once, then the choice will be governed by the summed values of the rewards on each side. If one uses Mazur's general formulation of the matching law (see Chapter 3), the crucial time at which preference between the two whole series of rewards changes will be represented by the t when the value V' of the series of larger rewards equals the value V of the series of smaller ones, called $t_{indifference}$:

$$\frac{V}{V'} = \frac{\Sigma A_i / (Z + \Gamma (T_i - t_{indifference}))}{\Sigma A'_i / (Z + \Gamma (T'_i - t_{indifference}))} = 1$$

where Z and Γ are empirical constants that seem not to range far from 1.0. If the choice is made before $t_{indifference}$, it will favor the series of larger, later rewards, and if it is made after $t_{indifference}$, it will favor the series of smaller, earlier ones.

This would be a trivial application of the matching law to the case of multiple rewards except for an important phenomenon: $t_{indifference}$ between the series of larger (primed) rewards to the series of smaller (nonprimed) ones will move closer to the moment when the first smaller reward is available as the series is made longer (Ainslie, 1986b). The period of temporary preference for the smaller reward will be reduced or eliminated. With appropriate mathematical transformations, this finding holds equally for a stream of continuous reward as for discrete, monetary rewards.

The practical effect of choosing a whole series of rewards at once

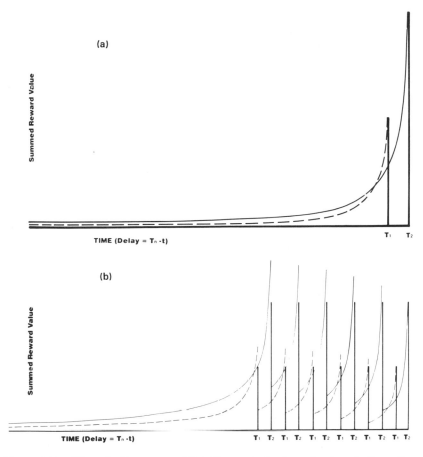

Figure 8.1.   Hyperbolic curves of the discounted value of pairs of alternative rewards, calculated according to formula 2 in Chapter 3 and summed: one pair (Figure 8.1a) and six pairs (Figure 8.1b).

is thus to increase the individual's tendency to choose the larger rewards (Figure 8.1). He could approach much closer to the smaller, earlier rewards, and therefore be more flexible in his behavior, without forming temporary preferences for them. This predicted phenomenon obviously might be relevant to the problem of human impulse control.

But how can a person arrange to choose whole series of rewards at once? In fact he does not have to physically commit himself. The values of the alternative series of rewards cannot depend on whether he will actually get them, an event that has not yet occurred, but only on his expectation of getting them. If we assume a person is familiar with the outcomes of his choices, the main element of uncertainty will be the direction of his own future choices. In situations where temporary preferences are likely, he is apt to be genuinely ignorant of what his own future choices will be. His best information is knowledge of his past behavior under similar circumstances, with the most recent examples probably being the most informative. Furthermore, if he has chosen the poorer reward often enough that he knows self-control will be an issue, but not so often as to give up hope that he may choose the richer rewards, his current choice is likely to be what swings expectation one way or the other: If he makes an impulsive choice, he will have little reason to believe he will not go on doing so. If he controls his impulse, there is evidence that he may continue to do so.

Take, for example, the predicament of a person on a weight-reducing diet who has been offered a piece of candy. The person knows that the calories in one piece of candy will not make any noticeable difference in weight, and yet he is apt to feel that he should not eat the candy. What would it cost him? Common experience tells us: his expectation of sticking to the diet. He will face many chances to eat forbidden foods, and if he sees himself eating this one, it will not seem likely to him that he will refuse the others. If he succumbs to the temptation to eat the candy, it will cost him not only its small caloric burden but also the expectation of getting whatever benefits he had hoped for from the diet. And yet the very knowledge that he is in this predicament may make him refuse the candy where otherwise he would accept it.

This amplification of impulse control can be expected to occur to some extent whenever a person perceives a series of confrontations with impulses as similar to each other. He will not necessarily notice the process itself or develop any way of describing it. He might develop an extensive practical understanding of it by trial and error but have only tangential theories about how it works. However, insofar as he has become aware of this phenomenon, he will be able to induce it where it has not occurred spontaneously, by arbitrarily defining a category of gratification-delaying behaviors that will thereafter prevail or not as a set (Ainslie, 1975).

This means of commitment is an example of side betting, because it works by putting additional reward at stake in each individual choice. Schelling (1960) and Becker (1960) have described side betting as a way people sometimes commit themselves to a course of action by arranging to forfeit things of value—money, reputation, freedom—if they do not make a particular choice in a specified direction. For instance, a person may commit himself not to tell lies by cultivating a reputation as a truthful person, which would be lost if he were caught lying. In the examples of Schelling and Becker, however, the side bets are held by other people, who exact the penalty if the person does not behave as he said he would. Public side bets like those are a case of an extrapsychic commitment device. In the interdependent series of behaviors described earlier, no one need hold the bet; if he perceives himself not to have waited for a large reward, he will automatically pay the forfeit, and at once, by losing the expectation that he will wait for similar rewards in the future. The dieter who has, in effect, bet himself that he will not eat candy, pays for a lapse by a fall in his own expectations.

Thus, a person can bind his behavior by a private side bet, which does not depend on the cooperation of any other person. It has the same properties as the promise one businessperson makes another where the value to each of their sustained cooperation is greater than what is at stake in the situation at hand, a promise that has been called a *self-enforcing contract* (Klein and Leffler, 1981; Macaulay, 1963). In effect, a private side bet is a self-enforcing contract that the person makes with his own future motivational states.

Personal rules are the most flexible and accessible commitment devices. They are not without grave side effects, however, as will become apparent.

Personal Rules and Intrapersonal Bargaining

The temporary preference phenomenon creates a relationship among an individual's successive motivational states that can be described as limited warfare (Schelling, 1960): Successive motivational states have some interests in common, and others that are peculiar to them. The interests in common are identical with the person's long-range interest. The peculiar ones are short-range interests in whatever rewards happen to be imminently available. At any given time, the alcoholic wants to drink less in the aggregate—he does not want to be an alcoholic—but may currently want to drink a great deal. The alcoholic's long-range interest, common to all his successive motivational states, is to be generally sober; this interest is challenged and often overwhelmed by a succession of short-range interests in getting drunk just once.

Each person has, in Winston's phrase (1980), a "stock of human capital"—in sobriety, health, good will, reputation, and many other goods besides money. He is called upon daily to decide whether or not to cash in some of it for immediate consumption. Each day he has much the same interest in preserving his capital for the future, but he is also drawn to plans that consume a disproportionate share of it in the present. His successive motivational states may either cooperate with one another in their mutual long-range interest or abandon this interest for the sake of each one's short-range interest. His long-range interest is apt to prevail only if he believes he can generally preserve this interest from one time to the next, that is, if at each decision he expects future motivational states to cooperate with his long-range plan. An effective personal rule is one that specifies a common interest in such a way that the person never prefers to abandon it. A person may want to lose weight as quickly as possible, but if an 1,800-calorie diet will sometimes make a person so hungry that he will change his mind, he had better adopt a 2,400-calorie one instead.

Making personal rules is obviously a learnable skill, similar to the skills required of a lawyer or a negotiator. Indeed, recently described principles of interpersonal negotiation closely fit the interaction of impulses and impulse controls (Schelling, 1960; Shefrin and Thaler, 1978; Taylor, 1975). The most important aspect of the relationship among those processes is the fact that they must operate together over a long and repetitive lifetime, so that current decisions may be more important as precedents for future decisions than as events in their own right. The need of the long-range interest to draw a line against impulses is like the interest of the negotiator who must face an opponent not just once but repeatedly, a position that Schelling (1960) defines well: "To persuade the other that one cannot afford to concede, one says in effect, 'If I concede to you here, you would revise your estimate of me in our negotiations; to protect my reputation with you I must stand firm' " (p. 30).

This logic does not change if it is the self, not the other, who must be convinced. By similar logic, players in experimental bargaining games like the prisoner's dilemma are motivated to choose the cooperative solution if this choice will be seen as a precedent for future games, but they often choose the noncooperative solution if it will not (Taylor, 1975; Telser, 1980). Theories of bargaining and games may let us make explicit much of the logic of impulse control, which, like bargaining itself, has long been left to intuition.

To put the analogy another way, the relationship of successive motivational states is similar to that of larger entities, such as countries at war, which may preserve some common interests (e.g., fair treatment of prisoners, avoidance of poison gas warfare) only if each expects the other to cooperate in those areas. The paradigm of this relationship is the prisoner's dilemma. Because following suit is both the most obvious strategy and the most successful one in prisoner's dilemmas (Axelrod, 1984), it is reasonable for each side to expect the other to follow it knowing only that the other's payoffs are in a prisoner's dilemma pattern (i.e., "both defect" being worth substantially less, and "only self defects" substantially more, than "both cooperate").

Notice that in the game with repeated moves, the two players do not have to make their decisions simultaneously for the prisoner's dilemma to arise. Each country will base its decision about using gas, for example, on the other's known moves; the existence of a simultaneous, as yet unknown move, will not affect the rationale for choice. Thus, the choices made by a legislature that is dominated alternatively by conflicing interests are also apt to follow a true prisoner's dilemma pattern: One party may want to build arms and the other to disarm, but neither wants to waste money. When each is in power, it must choose between cooperation—a middle level of armament—and defections, a series of which would mean alternately building and scrapping expensive weapons systems.

But this is the pattern of payoffs faced by successive motivational states within the individual. Say that a person at midnight faces the choice of staying up for about 2 more hours and having fun before finally giving in to fatigue, but feeling tired at work the next day versus giving up the present fun and expecting to feel rested at work. He values the imminent fun at 60 units per hour (a gradual decrease with fatigue will not be computed for simplicity) and expects to lose 60 units per hour of comfort from when he gets up at 7 A.M. until leaving work at 5 P.M. At midnight the value of staying up will be:

$$V_{up} = \Sigma_{i=0.5 \to 1.5} i = 0.5 \to 1.5 \, 60/1 + i = 64$$

and the differential value of feeling rested at work will be:

$$V_{bed} = \Sigma_{i=7.5 \to 16.5} 60/1 + i = 49$$

Given only this one choice, he will stay up and suffer the next day. However, if he will face this choice nightly, he may perceive current choice as a precedent for future nights as well (Figure 8.2). If we assume he believes that he will go to bed on time on subsequent nights if he does tonight, and not otherwise, the values of his alternatives are:

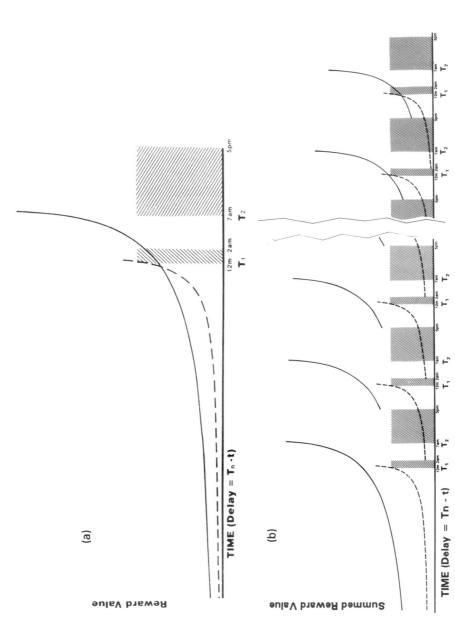

Figure 8.2. Hyperbolic curves of the discounted value of staying up for two hours at midnight versus going to bed and feeling rested until the end of the next workday, calculated as in Figure 8.1 ($Z = 1$ hour): one pair (Figure 8.2a) and ten pairs (Figure 8.2b).

192

$$V_{up} = (\Sigma_{i=0.5\to1.5}60/(1 + i)) +$$
$$(\Sigma_{i=24.5\to25.5}60/(1 + i)) + (\Sigma_{i=48.5\to49.5}60/(1 + i))$$
$$+ \ldots\ldots + (\Sigma_{i=216.5\to217.5}60/(1 + i)) = 78$$

for staying up on the next 10 nights versus

$$V_{bed} (\Sigma_{i=7.5\to16.5}60/(1 + i)) +$$
$$(\Sigma_{i=31.5\to40.5}60/(1 + i))$$
$$+ \ldots\ldots + (\Sigma_{i=223.5\to232.5}60/(1 + i)) = 105$$

for going to bed early on the next ten nights. He will go to bed, *if* he expects to be motivated also to follow suit on the subsequent nights.

Considering separately the present values of the alternatives in his first choice (64 vs. 49) and the present values of two subsequent series of nine choices all in one direction (14 for always staying up vs. 56 for always going to bed), his incentives form a prisoner's dilemma matrix (Table 8.1). From his present point of view, going to bed on time both today and in the future is worth 105, and staying up both today and in the future is worth 78. However, if he can stay up today and still expect to go to bed on time in the future, that is worth 120. Conversely, if he goes to bed today but fails to go to bed in the future, that is worth only 63. The latter two outcomes respectively represent successful defection and being the victim of successful defection. The nature of the matrix does not change if we consider a series of 99 future choices, which are worth 25 for staying up versus 110 for going to bed, almost the one-to-five ratio of the "objective" rewards.

The person's best move at present will thus depend on how he forecasts future perceptions. He must ask two questions: In the future will he see this choice as having been a precedent for his bedtimes?

Table 8.1   Present Value of Present and Future Choices

		Future	
		Stay Up	To Bed
Now	Stay Up	64 + 14 = 78	64 + 56 = 120
	To Bed	49 + 14 = 63	49 + 56 = 105

If so, will the aggregate expected value of going to bed on time usually be enough to motivate this behavior? If he stays up tonight and sees it as a precedent, he should expect to go on staying up. If he goes to bed now and sees it as a precedent, it will increase his likelihood of doing so in the future. But if this likelihood is still low, he will have wasted the effort. If he stays up or goes to bed but sees it as an exceptional case, he will not have changed his prior expectations. Insofar as he sees his current choice as a precedent, he will be motivated by the prisoner's dilemma incentive structure.

In summary, the will is created by the perception of impulse-related choices as precedents for similar choices in the future. This perception generates the same pattern of incentives that operate in a repeated prisoner's dilemma game. Personal rules are promises to cooperate with the individual's own subsequent motivational states in such a game. They are self-enforcing insofar as the expected value of cooperation exceeds that of defection at the times when the choices are made. This difference in value can also be regarded as the stake of a private side bet that the person "makes" to commit his future behavior. It is this stake that gives the will its force.

The Properties of Personal Rules

To be cost-effective, a personal rule must be drawn with three characteristics: (1) The series of rewards to be waited for must be long enough and valuable enough so that it will be preferred over each impulsive alternative. (2) Each member of the series and its impulsive alternatives must be readily identifiable, without ambiguity. (3) The features that exclude a choice from the series must either occur independently of the person's behavior or have such a high intrinsic cost that he would not be motivated to bring them about just for the sake of evading the rule.

These three requirements are illustrated by the common problem of trying to lose weight: (1) To succeed, a person must expect enough cumulative reward from weighing less to motivate each of the many acts of abstinence that will be necessary. (2) The person must also have clear guidelines that identify which food choices are permissible. In the absence of clear boundaries between impulsive and adaptive eating behaviors, it will be hard for him to know when he has violated his rule. Mark Twain told of limiting himself to one cigar a day for the sake of his health. He shopped for bigger and bigger cigars, until he finally had each made "to such proportions that I could have used it as a crutch" (1899). Doubtless it is the absence of a simple cue distinguishing adaptive eating from overeating that makes people turn to the cumbersome legalism of formal diets. (3) Finally, it would be evident folly for a person to eat only what he puts on his plate or only what he buys. W.C. Fields' temperance lecturer was clearly on a slippery slope when he permitted himself a swig of alcohol-based snake bite remedy, "which I always keep handy. Only, however, after being bitten by a snake . . . which I also keep handy."

These requirements—adequate size, adequate clarity, and criteria that do not depend on the person's own behavior—are all that should be necessary for the success of personal rules made in advance and maintained without modification. However, in a changing environment, a person is apt to find that he has committed himself to forego an unexpectedly large amount of reward. The chance to reap more reward while avoiding damage to his rule will motivate him to redefine it. However, because it is usually possible to formulate loopholes that will grant an exception in the case at hand, the indiscriminate redefinition of rules may prove fatal to them. If a person is going to redefine his rule in such a way that he retains his expectation of acting prudently, the occasion he uses must not only be rare but must also stand out in some way from other possible occasions that are not rare enough. Interests based on smaller, earlier rewards find countless ways to say, "just this once"; the long-term interests must defend themselves by arguing, "This, too, is a matter of principle." Ultimately the decision between the two depends on the person's guess about whether a particular exception will in fact lower his expectation of generally adhering to his rule.

The availability of boundaries that cannot be moved just a little bit is vitally important to the long-term interest. Activities like smoking and drinking have such a line in an obvious place, that is, between any indulgence and no indulgence; but people who eat too much or spend too much money cannot completely give up these activities, and so must find some way to make a single diet, or budget, stand out from all the others to which they are apt to retreat under pressure. Lawyers call such a unique boundary a *bright line*. The concept expresses why countries blessed with unique boundaries like a mountain range or a river without large tributaries have fewer wars than countries just set out on a plain.

Whether interests, or nations, must depend on a bright line to maintain cooperation in a limited war situation, or can use less prominent lines to gain more flexibility, depends on factors like their history and skill in that situation and the amounts at stake. For instance, war between great powers may have been prevented since World

War II by the widespread belief that even skilled policymaking could not restrict it to conventional weapons. Thus, their very history of failing to avert the escalation of wars, added to the new threat of nuclear destruction, may have deterred them from venturing beyond the bright line between some war and no war at all. Similarly, alcoholics find that they cannot engage in "controlled drinking"—following somewhat arbitrary rules to stop after two drinks, or three, or when they feel high, or when their spouses say they have had enough—and are advised by Alcoholics Anonymous to regard themselves as "helpless against alcohol."

Frank (1988) has recently pointed out that a morality higher than the simple prudence that requires one not to risk getting caught may still be consistent with strict self-interest (pp. 71–95). The logic is exactly that of Alcoholics Anonymous: Because of the tendency to overvalue present gratification of one's own particular vices, a person who tries to indulge them in a controlled way according to rules for prudence will often find loopholes that lead him beyond prudence into behavior for which he will be caught and blamed. The person who draws a line farther from his impulses—who, for instance, resolves to be virtuous for the sake of virtue—has the same improved chance of avoiding impulses as the alcoholic who perceives himself to be helpless against alcohol. This may be the only person who succeeds enough at being prudent to keep a reputation for virtue. Unless he sincerely renounces the relevant vice, he may be like the "dry drunk" who is just waiting for a loophole. This incidentally reinforces Elster's (1981) astute observation that there may be states—like contentment, dignity, and perhaps even sleep—that cannot be achieved by direct effort. The direct approach to them tempts the person into those shortsighted behaviors like hedonism, pomposity, and "trying to sleep" that undermine the original goals.

Behavioral Research on the Perception of Precedents

Controlled experiments on personal rules are intrinsically difficult to conduct, because service as an experimental subject is an extraordinary circumstance that can represent a loophole in anyone's rules. However, it may be possible to study the cognitions involved in judging what behaviors may set precedents. Insofar as a person is in a relationship of limited warfare with his own expected motivational states, we hypothesize that the process of judging internal precedents will be much the same as that of judging precedents in interpersonal bargaining. If human subjects are repeatedly offered alternative outcomes that simulate the motives predicted by matching law discount curves, these alternatives should pose to these players the same strategic problems that people face in intertemporal choices. It should make no difference whether the successive players are successive motivational states of the same person or different people who move successively. Each player has a whole person's resources at his disposal, as does each successive motivational state within an individual. Although individuals can doubtless keep secrets from each other more effectively than can successive motivational states, this difference should not be crucial to the conduct of the game: As long as past behavior is the best predictor of future behavior, it will not matter much whether each choice maker's intentions and stratagems are secret or not. Individuals also seem to differ from groups in being able to form intentions, but that is the very process to be studied—the intention as a solution to the problem of conflicting interests. Our hypothesis is that forming intentions follows the same logic as making tacit agreements in an interpersonal, limited-war situation.

Pairs of human subjects use computer terminals to play a prisoner's dilemma game with an outcome matrix similar to the nightly bedtime problem described earlier, although with values of 100 and 80 for defection versus cooperation, instead of 64 and 49 (Ainslie, Lyke, and Freeman, forthcoming). No attempt is made to use actual delays to generate the differential incentives. The object is not to study the effect of delay, but a matrix of the reward values that hyperbolic discounting would typically produce. The subjects choose between distributions of points that are all exchangeable for money at the end of a session. They are given a scheduled but unpredictable number of turns choosing between two distributions of points to be added to their and their partner's scores: On most turns, the choice is between 80 points for both ("cooperation") versus 100 points for the player and none for his partner ("defection"). At these baseline values, players have usually cooperated, but defections are not uncommon. After five consecutive baseline cooperations, the self-only option for one subject on one turn is made higher, anywhere from 120 to 400 points (a "lure"). His partner is offered a lure subsequently, but only after there have been several more cooperations. Subjects are allowed to communicate with each other only by their choices on their computer terminals.

In an experiment already completed, it was hypothesized that subjects would interpret a partner's defection to a lure differently depending on whether the lure was high or low—just as a personal lapse in the face of exceptional temptation does less damage to one's future self-control than a lapse under ordinary circumstances. According to this hypothesis, defection to a relatively low lure in the prisoner's dilemma game would be seen as sign of low willingness to cooperate, often leading the subject to defect on his next (baseline) turn; defection to a high lure would be more apt to be seen as an exception to the tacit agreement to cooperate and, thus, not a cause for retaliation. Lures were observed to produce defections on about half of the turns where they were offered, and the subsequent move by the other player confirmed the hypothesis 71 percent of the time (Ainslie, Lyke, and Freeman, forthcoming). This primitive experiment shows the feasibility of studying human cognitions about personal rules and their loopholes by a repeated prisoner's dilemma analogy.

Transformation of the Nature of Choice

Three consequences of personal rules are particularly important: Personal rules turn the sequential preference pattern described by simple hyperbolic discount curves into the kind of conflict people more often experience, where the prudent and impulsive incentives exert pressure simultaneously. Second, rules tend to change the evaluation of events from a weighing of amounts of reward to a prediction of risks, viz., the risk that an impulsive choice will set a precedent. Third, the magnification of small choices through their importance as precedents gives them a self-confirming property that often overshadows the influence of the incentives that are literally at stake. This positive feedback effect can produce either a sense of being compelled by forces beyond the person's control or, near the balance point of the choice, the experience of free will.

The Simultaneity of Impulses and Controls

In principle, personal rules make it possible for a person never to prefer a small early alternative at the expense of the series of larger later ones. He may be able to keep temptations close at hand without succumbing to them. However, although he may always prefer a series of larger later rewards to the small, early one at hand, he must even more strongly prefer to have both. The danger is no longer one of the poorer reward coming so close that he will suddenly choose it, but of finding a credible distinction between this choice and the other members of the series that form the stake of his private side bet. Proximity is still a contributor to temptation, of course; however, the deciding factor is no longer whether a prior commitment is too weak but whether a tentative loophole currently looks to the person like he could get away with it. The person will not experience this situation as the exotic voyage past the Sirens, but as a simultaneous struggle between two ways of perceiving a choice. His rules have enabled him to live in close proximity to his temptations, but while this proximity exists the struggle will be continuous rather than episodic.

The Formation of "Lapse Districts"

The perception of precedents transforms a diffuse array of choices into a single, highly charged dichotomy, which results in more consistent behavior toward temptation. The major side effect of such perceptions is that when a lapse occurs, the person is apt to fear that he will lose the ability to control impulses. He might call this fear anxiety, guilt, or foreboding, and unless he is conscious of his internal bargaining process in some way that makes sense to him, he will be apt to say that the fear is unaccountable, that he "knows" there is nothing to be afraid of. Another perception might be that his self-esteem or self-respect is in danger. The actual danger is to his expectation of following the rule, and it is proportional to the degree he has staked this expectation on that choice. Insofar as he has lost the expectation, he is apt to abandon part or all of the rule (see Marlatt and Gordon, 1980). That is, the person might hope to preserve part of his personal rule structure by abandoning the most vulnerable rules, thus accepting some impulsive behavior in return for a greater likelihood of following narrower, perhaps more fundamental, rules.

In regressing to a less ambitious rule, the person abandons an area of functioning to the sway of his short-term interest. For example, a person who normally resists thoughts of danger while driving, or self-conscious feelings while talking in public, or the urge for a cigarette while under social pressure, may have his will "broken" by conspicuous failure in one of these endeavors. Subsequently the person will have less expectation of control to stake against his urges. However, he might preserve this expectation in some areas by distinguishing the area of loss from his urges generally. That is, if the person can interpret the lapse not as a sign that "my will is weak" but that "I can't resist cigarettes," he can save credibility against other impulses at the cost of virtually abandoning the task on which defeat occurred. He is apt to experience a loss of control of these urges when driving, talking in public, or facing smoking peers. Such a situation will form a large, stable loophole, a circumscribed lacuna in the person's impulse controls, which may even be experienced as an automatism or irresistible urge. He will "automatically" panic in traffic, freeze while speaking, or reach for a cigarette. Such a labeling process has been described by "attribution theory" (e.g., Peterson and Seligman, 1984), but as a simple deductive error rather than a compromise between strong motives. Abandonment of a sector of choice making to one's impulses creates a strongly motivated tendency to lapse that is unlikely to change through mere logic.

In such a lacuna, it will be hard for a person's long-term interest to retrieve its credibility, because the self-confirming property of personal rules works both ways. Once the person has identified a feature that has accompanied past failures, it will be used by the relevant short-range interest to argue that "once more won't make any difference" and by the long-range interest to avoid making losing investments. He will have abandoned a sector of choice making to his impulses and will subsequently experience great difficulty in reclaiming it. Again the situation has an analog in social groups: Disreputable activities that have been too strongly motivated to outlaw completely become encapsulated in what used to be called *segregated vice districts*, areas where by tacit or even explicit agreement, the relevant laws are not enforced. The purpose, of course, is to preserve the "good" neighborhoods from vice. Within the person, sectors of choice making that have been abandoned to limit failures of will form *lapse districts*.

Contrary to one's instinct, the best strategy to restore a broken rule is to make small resolutions, as in the "one day at a time" of Alcoholics Anonymous, so that a cumulation of actual choices in the right direction can gradually rebuild the kitty of the bet. Even so, the area will long be suspect and be written off at the least sign of backsliding.

The periodic accumulation and loss of the kitty for one circumscribed bet is the basis of binging. For instance, if temporarily abstinent alcoholic subjects are led to believe that they have taken a drink of alcohol, they report a marked increase in craving, whether or not they have actually had any alcohol (Engel and Williams, 1972; Maisto, Lauerman, and Adesso, 1977). Loss of control after the first drink is universally reported at the beginning of binges (Evenson, Altman, Sletton, and Knowles, 1973). Likewise, binge eating has been observed to result from a combination of dieting and the person's belief (whether accurate or not) that he has just consumed a too-large caloric load, an event that "triggers overeating by ruining the diet temporarily" (Polivy and Herman, 1985). The person who is suspicious of his self-control ability in such an area will repeatedly build up some credibility in the area but hesitate to add his expectation of self-control in other areas to the stake, thus leaving the behavior in question prone to crises of confidence and consequent "losses of control." Without periodic recoveries of some self-control, a lapse district takes the form of a stable symptom.

Distortion of the Internal Marketplace

The second side effect of using rules is a shift in the person's concern from evaluating the magnitude of rewards to judging their membership in categories. That is, for individual decisions that are perceived as precedents for much larger categories of decision, it matters less how profitable the immediate choice promises to be than how likely the person is to see it as a lapse. Of course, the ultimate determinant of choice is still the total discounted reward that is expected on each side. But the loss from disobeying a personal rule is hard to estimate, just as it is hard to know how the failure of a particular business will affect the stock market. In the wake of a loss, the person might conceive it as unique and not predictive of further lapses. Alternatively, the person might see himself as having broken a narrow rule, say a diet, thus reducing his expectation of getting the benefits of that rule but not boding ill for his behavior toward other rules. However, he might see the lapse as predictive of lapses against similar rules, or even of lapses generally, and thereby suffer a much greater fall in expected reward.

The interface between the process of weighing rewards and the process of estimating the danger from lapses is always an uneasy one. It resembles the interface between regulated and free-market sectors of an economy. Goods that are priced by regulation distort the prices of related goods as well as the reliability of supply, and they cause rebounds once controls are removed (Mitchell, 1978, Chapters 2 and 10). They generate a black market operated by interests willing to put a cash value on the risk of legal action against them. Similarly for the individual, it is not hard to decide which of two foods to eat or which of two friends to visit if these are only matters of taste. The only problem in that case occurs when the person expects them to be about equally rewarding and has to decide arbitrarily. If, however, eating one food violates a personal rule, or if he has resolved to see, or not see, one of the friends, the situation is different. Now the person is weighing simple reward against a duty, still an economic process but one complicated by the need for self-prediction. He must estimate the likelihood that consuming the simple reward will make him lose the expectation of getting a series of rewards.

Utilitarian theories have depicted choice makers as analog computers, weighing the value of alternative rewards against each other and reaching a quantitative solution. However, because of the deeply bowed shape of the discount curve, which leads to temporary preference and a consequent need for personal rules, the more important tasks facing people are digital ones: constructing sets of categorical requirements that permit some kinds of weighing and not others. A simple weighing of preferences would leave the person open to temporary changes of preference. On the other hand, a decision-making process that does not respond to weights, only categories, will have difficulty distinguishing trivial incentives from vital ones. The cost of this kind of impulse control is reduced efficiency at foraging: If one sticks to a rigid schedule, he cannot take advantage of big opportunities offered by the environment if they also represent any kind of small lapse. He is apt to become "penny-wise and pound-foolish," a widespread trait that has heretofore lacked a behavioral explanation. Likewise, in a situation where one can always do a little more work, or be a little more careful, or show a little more concern, the person will be a prisoner of a rule that requires completeness. The only remedy will be to hedge on his rules, and to do this without impairing them takes skill.

The Self-Referential Nature of Choice

The third consequence of using rules is a sensation that some choices are free or unfree. The choices that get called free are those not dictated by any definable motive, whether it comes from the environment or from internal pressures like desires or passions. Apparently, they must involve some subtlety of the self. Once a train of causality is seen to determine a choice reliably, that choice is called unfree. Thus, freedom has seemed to suffer from a paradox of definition, in that as soon as an author specifies the steps by which he imagines choice to proceed, he takes choice out of the self and thereby renders it unfree. Accordingly, Hollis (1983) complains that conventional economic rationality reduces the person to a calculating machine: "Preference is automatically transmitted into outcome so as to solve the maximising problem. The agent is simply a throughput" (p. 250).

Explanations of the experience of free will that do not violate strict determinism have focused on the unpredictability of free choices. Because the most conspicuous feature of choices that feel free is the sensation that one "might have" done something else (James, 1884/ 1967), any situation that renders prediction imponderable may suffice to make choices in that situation feel free. Because the task of maximizing external rewards can often be solved by a formula that makes choice predictable, freedom must imply the presence of some kind of buffering against the control of external contingencies.

This would be the case for a self-referential choice. For instance, Hollis (1983) points out that choices often lead not only to their expected consequences but also to changes in the person's valuation of those consequences. In choosing, the choice maker is transformed, so that one is "always shaping his identity by his choices" (p. 158). Choice is then no less determinate, but much less predictable, than simple choice among goods.

However, changes in one's preferences are apt to occur relatively slowly, a fact that would seem to allow for predictability in the short run. By contrast, the self-prediction that is basic to the use of personal rules can shift with each new bit of evidence about one's disposition and, thus, seems a more likely source of the sensation of freedom: The perception of choices as precedents creates the kind of prisoner's dilemma payoff matrix in Table 8.1. The relative values in such a table fall into one of two rough zones: balanced, so that small changes in the prospects for future cooperation swing the decision between cooperation and defection (e.g., where the person's ability to get to bed on time hinges on morale and affects it in turn); and unbalanced, so that changes in decision look unlikely (the person always gets to bed early, or has given up on ever doing so). In the balanced zone, an assumption about the direction of the current choice will be a major factor in estimating future outcomes. But this estimate in turn affects the probability that the current choice will be in that direction. Thus, the decision process is recursive—not tautological but continuously fed back like the output of a transistor to its own input. Where the relevant future choices are relatively momentous, this feedback process may play a bigger role in one's decision than any given incentive, external or internal.

Such a process is not subtle conceptually, but it eludes any calculation based only on the contingencies of reward and buffers the person's decision against coercion by these contingencies. Thus, it may generate the experience of exercising free will. Furthermore, such an explanation allows us to characterize free choices better than saying that they are too close to predict. After all, many behaviors are quite predictable in practice and are still experienced as free. What becomes crucial is the person's belief that a given choice depends on this self-prediction process, in whatever terms he has found to describe his experience of that process. If a preference is subject to change through such "reflection," it is identified as free even though it never actually changes.

The Origin of Compulsions

Conversely, unbalanced decision matrices are only driven further out of balance by the self-prediction process. If the person knows of no way of defining precedents and no manipulation of self-attention that would change his expected line of choice, he is apt to feel unfree, despite, or rather because of, the fact that his behavior is strongly motivated.

Two kinds of coercive motivational forces have been described by philosophers and theologians since antiquity: a capricious, seemingly irrational one that is commonly called an *impulse*, and a relentless, highly consistent one that is often called a *compulsion*. For example, Aristotle described not only passions that could overcome people suddenly, but also dispositions, forces that develop through consistent choice (habit) in one direction and subsequently impel further choice in that direction (Kenny, 1963). Similarly, Kant depicted an egolike part of the will, the *wilkur*, which can let itself be led on one side by impulses and on the other by personal maxims for conduct (the content of the *wille*; Kant, 1960). He said that choice in either direction creates a disposition that impels further choice in that direction. The religious philosopher, Paul Ricoeur (1971), has said that freedom of will is encroached upon not only by sin but by moral law, through the "juridization of action" by which "a scrupulous person encloses himself in an inextricable labyrinth of commandments" (p. 11).

From the perspective of the matching law, the subjectively unfree choices of single imminent rewards known as impulses are the ordinary state of nature. Compulsions, on the other hand, seem to result from overcommitment by personal rules. A person with little skill at formulating rules or with unusually strong impulses is apt to compensate for those defects by increasing the number of behaviors that he classifies as covered by each private side bet, or by connecting each bet with some or all other bets. Either way of making his choices more independent will increase the differential reward for turning down each temptation, but at the expense of making his behavior more rigid: Increasing his tendency to classify behaviors as impulsive or not will give his experience a dry, rational, lawyerlike quality, because he will choose actions less and less for their intrinsic value, and more according to whether they meet the terms of a bet. Increasing the interdependency of bets will give every choice a cataclysmic, life-or-death quality, because the person would incur an enormous fall in expectations if he perceived himself to have violated any personal rule. The person will come to feel that he acts at great peril, and begin to examine each choice with such care as to render himself utterly indecisive. Such a pattern of imprisonment by a comprehensive set of rules is characteristic of the compulsive personality.

Every author who has dealt with the two apparent forces impinging on the will has agreed that coercion by the "lower," or impulsive, principle should be minimized. However, the desirability of coercion by powerful personal rules has been in dispute. Before the last century, there seems to have been general agreement that safety lay on the side of lawfulness. However, modern man has been warned by a number of writers that his sense of will may decrease rather than increase if he binds himself too extensively to rules. The existentialists have provided the most comprehensive analysis of this danger; their greatest goods, such as authenticity and living in the present (Ellenberger, 1958), are clearly threatened by a perception that gives one's current choice more importance as a precedent than as something in itself. However, authors from other schools have also warned that, under some circumstances, personal rules can become prisons (reviewed in Ainslie, 1992, Chapter 6).

It is unlikely that such self-imposed prisons serve the person's longest range interest. He must, of course, expect his rule to serve a longer-range interest against a shorter-range one; it is only this property that gives a rule its self-enforcing power. However, a rule can serve a midrange interest against both shorter- and longer-range interests. Many familiar rules serve midrange interests. Rules like "don't tolerate weakness," "never buy at retail," or "avenge every insult" keep the person from taking the course of least resistance in common situations, but may create traits like rigidity, miserliness, or vengefulness that undermine the person's own perceived longest range interest. Rules are particularly apt to serve interests in the sell out range, where they produce tangible, reliable gains at the expense of the person's subtler values. They will be maintained by the person's inability to deal with his perceived spontaneous behavior without the rule—weak, lazy, cowardly, etc.

Summary

We must conclude that self-control, the prevention of one's shorter-range interests from undermining his longest range ones, is far from a simple matter. Short-range interests are not aberrant phenomena but a basic consequence of the elementary valuation process. Thus, they cannot be "cured" by any means, or controlled just by insight into what one's longest range interests are. The four possible means of committing oneself to pass by impulses each has serious limitations. Personal rules, while probably the most powerful of these means, also have the most far-reaching side effects, and may often serve impulses in the sell out range of duration. Self-control that is experienced as freely willed, which the person owns as his, is that which somehow escapes coercion by both immediate reward and the logic of precedent.

The interaction of successive motivational states can be studied by some of the same means used to study limited warfare and other interpersonal bargaining situations—broadly speaking, by the tools of economics. Some further attempts to analyze this interaction are described by Ainslie (1992).

References

Ainslie, G. "Impulse Control in Pigeons." *Journal of the Experimental Analysis of Behavior* 21 (1974): 485–489.

———. "Specious Reward: A Behavioral Theory of Impulsiveness and Impulse Control." *Psychological Bulletin* 82 (1975): 463–496.

———. "Manipulation: History and Theory." in M.P. Nichols and T.J. Paolino, Jr. (eds.). *Basic Techniques in Psychodynamic Psychotherapy*, New York: Gardner Press, 1986a.

———. "Beyond Microeconomics: Conflict Among Interests in a Multiple Self as a Determinant of Value." in J. Elster (ed.), *The Multiple Self*, Cambridge: University Press, 1986b.

———. *Picoeconomics: The Strategic Interaction of Successive Motivational States within the Person*. Cambridge, U.K.: Cambridge University Press, 1992.

————, J. Lyke, and R. Freeman. "An Experimental Model of Intertemporal Conflict." in N.N. Commons, J. Mazur, J. Nevin, and H. Rachlin (eds.). *Quantitative Analyses of Behavior*, vol. 9: Behavioral Economics, forthcoming.

Axelrod, R.M. *The Evolution of Cooperation*, New York: Basic Books, 1984.

Bain, A. *The Emotions and the Will*. New York: Appleton, 1886.

Barratt, E.S., and J.H. Patton. "Impulsivity: Cognitive, Behavioral, and Psychophysiological Correlates." in M. Zuckerman (ed.). *Biological Bases of Sensation Seeking, Impulsivity, and Anxiety*, Hillsdale, NJ: Lawrence Erlbaum, 1983.

Becker, H.S. "Notes on the Concept of Commitment." *American Journal of Sociology* 66 (1960): 32–40.

Breuer, J., and S. Freud. *Studies on Hysteria* (1895), in J. Strachey and A. Freud (eds.). *The Standard Edition of the Complete Psychological Works of Sigmund Freud*, vol. 2. London: Hogarth Press, 1956.

Bruner, J.S., J.J. Goodnow, and G.A. Austin. *A Study of Thinking*. New York: Wiley, 1956.

Deluty, M.Z., W.G. Whitehouse, M. Mellitz, and P.N. Hineline. "Self-control and Commitment Involving Aversive Events." *Behavior Analysis Letters* 3 (1983): 213–219.

Ellenberger, H.F. "A Clinical Introduction to Psychiatric Phenomenology and Existential Analysis." in R. May, E. Angel, and H. Ellenberger (eds.). *Existence: A New Division in Psychiatry and Psychology*. New York: Basic Books, 1983, pp. 92–124.

Elster, J. "States that are essentially By-products. *Social Science Information* 20 (1981): 431–73. Reprinted in Elster, J. *Sour Grapes: Studies in the Subversion of Rationality*, Cambridge, UK: Cambridge University Press, 1983, pp. 43–108.

————. *Nuts and Bolts for the Social Sciences*. Cambridge, UK: Cambridge University Press, 1989.

Engel, K., and T. Williams. "Effect of an Ounce of Vodka on Alcoholics' Desire for Alcohol." *Quarterly Journal of Studies on Alcohol* 33 (1972): 1099–1105.

Evenson, R., H. Altman, J. Sletton, and R. Knowles. "Factors in the Description and Grouping of Alcoholics." *American Journal of Psychiatry* 130 (1973): 49–54.

Frank, R.H. *Passions Within Reason*. New York: W.W. Norton and Company, 1988.

Freud, A. *The Ego and the Mechanisms of Defense*. New York: International Universities Press, 1966.

Freud, S. *The Complete Psychological Works of Sigmund Freud*, Vol. 1. (J. Strachey and A. Freud, eds.). London: Hogarth (1895), 1956.

————. Ibid., Vol. 14, 1914.

————. Ibid., Vol. 20, 1926.

Galen (Harkins, P.W., trans.). *Galen on the Passions and Error of the Soul*. Columbus, OH: Ohio State University Press, 1963.

Gleser, G., and D. Ihilevich. "An Objective Instrument for Measuring Defense Mechanisms." *Journal of Consulting and Clinical Psychology* 33 (1969) 51–60.

Hayes, S.C., J. Kapust, S.R. Leonard, and I. Rosenfarb. "Escape from Freedom: Choosing not to Choose in Pigeons." *Journal of the Experimental Analysis of Behavior* 36 (1981): 1–7.

Hollis, M. "Rational Preferences." *The Philosophical Forum* 14 (1983): 246–262.

James, W. "The Dilemma of Determinism." in J. McDermott (ed.). *The Writings of William James*, Chicago: University of Chicago, 1884/1967.

———. *Principles of Psychology*. New York: Holt, 1890.

Kant, I. *Religion Within the Limits of Reason Alone* (T. Green and H. Hucken, trans.). New York: Harper and Row, 1960.

Kenny, A. *Action, Emotion, and Will*. London: Humanities Press, 1963.

Kimmel, H. "Instrumental Conditioning of Autonomically Mediated Responses in Human Beings." *American Psychologist* 29 (1974): 325–335.

Klein, B., and K.B. Leffler. "The Role of Market Forces in Assuring Contractual Performance." *Journal of Political Economy* 89 (1981): 615–640.

Lazare, A., G. Klerman, and D. Armor. "Oral, Obsessive, and Hysterical Personality Patterns: An Investigation of Psychoanalytical Concepts by Means of Factor Analysis." *Archives of General Psychiatry* 14 (1965): 624–630.

———, ———, and ———. "Oral, Obsessive, and Hysterical Personality Patterns: Replication of Factor Analysis in an Independent Sample." *Journal of Psychiatric Research* 7 (1968): 275–290.

Lazarus, R. "A Cognitively Oriented Psychologist Looks at Biofeedback." *American Psychologist* 30 (1975a): 553–561.

———. "The Self Regulation of Emotion. in L. Levi (ed.). *Emotions, Their Parameters and Measurement*, New York: Raven, 1975b.

Macaulay, S. "Non-contractual Relations in Business: A Preliminary Study." *American Sociological Review* 28 (1963): 55–67.

Maisto, S., R. Lauerman, and V. Adesso. "A Comparison of Two Experimental Studies of the Role of Cognitive Factors in Alcoholics' Drinking." *Journal of Studies on Alcohol* 38 (1977): 145–149.

Marlatt, G.A., and J.R. Gordon. "Determinants of Relapse: Implications for the Maintenance of Behavior Change." in P.O. Davidson and S.M. Davidson (eds.). *Behavioral Medicine: Changing Health Lifestyles*. Elmsford, NY: Pergamon, 1980, pp. 410–452.

Mazur, J.E. "Choice Between Single and Multiple Delayed Reinforcers." *Journal of the Experimental Analysis of Behavior* 46 (1986): 67–77.

Mischel, W., and E. Ebbeson. "Attention in Delay of Gratification." *Journal of Personality and Social Psychology* 16 (1970): 329–337.

———, and B. Moore. "The Role of Ideation in Voluntary Delay for Symbolically-presented Rewards." *Cognitive Therapy and Research* 4 (1980): 211–221.

Mischel, H.N., and W. Mischel. "The Development of Children's Knowledge of Self-control Strategies." *Child Development* 54 (1983): 603–619.

Mitchell, J. *Price Determination and Prices Policy*. London, Allen & Unwin, 1978.

Peterson, C., and M.E.P. Seligman. "Causal Explanations as a Risk Factor for Depression: Theory and Evidence." *Psychological Review* 91 (1984): 347–374.

Polivy, J., and C.P. Herman. "Dieting and Binging: A Causal Analysis." *American Psychologist* 40 (1985): 193–201.

Rachlin, H., and L. Green. "Commitment, Choice and Self-Control." *Journal of the Experimental Analysis of Behavior* 17 (1972): 15–22.

Ricoeur, P. "Guilt, Ethics, and Religion." in J. Meta (ed.). *Moral Evil Under Challenge.* New York: Herder and Herder, 1971.

Russell, J.M. "Saying, Feeling, and Self-deception." *Behaviorism* 6 (1978): 27–43.

Schalling, D., G. Erdman, and M. Asberg. "Impulsive Cognitive Style and Inability to Tolerate Boredom: Psychobiological Studies of Temperamental Vulnerability." in M. Zuckerman (ed.). *Biological Bases of Sensation Seeking, Impulsivity and Anxiety.* Hillsdale, NJ: Lawrence Erlbaum, 1983.

Schelling, T.C. *The Strategy of Conflict.* Cambridge, MA: Harvard University Press, 1960.

Schwartz, G. "Biofeedback, Self-regulation and the Patterning of Physiological Processes." *Scientific American* 63 (1975): 314–324.

Shefrin, H., and R. Thaler. *An Economic Theory of Self-Control,* Stanford, CA: National Bureau of Economic Research (Working Paper No. 208) (PC), 1978.

Shiffrin, R.M., and W. Schneider. "Controlled and Automatic Human Information Processing: II Perceptual Learning, Automatic Attending, and a General Theory." *Psychological Review* 84 (1977): 127–190.

Sjoback, H. *The Psychoanalytic Theory of Defensive Processes.* London: Wiley, 1973.

Strotz, R.H. "Myopia and Inconsistency in Dynamic Utility Maximization." *Review of Economic Studies* 23 (1956): 166–180.

Stuart, R., and B. Davis. *Slim Chance in a Fat World.* Champaign, IL: Research Press, 1972.

Sully, J. *Outlines of Psychology.* New York: Appleton, 1884.

Taylor, M. *Anarchy and Cooperation.* London: Wiley, 1975.

Telser, L.G. "A Theory of Self-enforcing Agreements." *Journal of Business* 53 (1980): 27–45.

Thoreson, C., and M. Mahoney. *Behavioral Self-Control.* New York: Holt, Rinehart and Winston, 1974.

Twain, M. "Following the Equator." in *The Complete Works of Mark Twain,* vol. 13. New York: Harper and Brothers, 1899, pp. 9–10.

Williams, J.M.G., F. Watts, C. MacLeod, and A. Mathews. *Cognitive Psychology and Emotional Disorders.* New York: Wiley, 1988.

Winston, G.C. "Addiction and Backsliding: A Theory of Compulsive Consumption." *Journal of Economic Behavior and Organization* 1 (1980): 295–324.

PART FOUR

·

Internalities

· 9 ·

Utility from Memory and Anticipation

JON ELSTER AND GEORGE LOEWENSTEIN

ALTHOUGH not a central focus of economics, the idea that people derive pleasure and pain from other people's experiences is widely accepted by economists. Duesenberry's "relative income hypothesis,"[1] Leibenstein's "bandwagon, snob and Veblen effects,"[2] Robert Frank's work on the market for status,[3] and Roth's research on social comparison in experimental games[4] attest to the wide range of economic implications that stem from such second-order effects. What is less well recognized, although perhaps equally consequential for economics, is the idea that we derive utility not only from contemplating others' experiences, but also from contemplating our own at other times. As Bentham recognized early on,[5] much of the pleasure and pain we experience in daily life arises not from direct experi-

---

[1] J. Duesenberry. *Income, Saving, and the Theory of Consumer Behavior*. Cambridge, MA: Harvard University Press, 1952.

[2] *Beyond Economic Man: A New Foundation for Microeconomics*, Cambridge, MA: Harvard University Press, 1976.

[3] *Choosing the Right Pond*. New York: Oxford University Press, 1985.

[4] For a recent summary, see A. Roth, *Bargaining Experiments*, forthcoming in *Handbook of Experimental Economics*, 1991.

[5] Bentham included the pleasures and pains of memory, imagination, and expectation in his short list of sources of utility and disutility. See pp. 34–35, *The Principles of Morals and Legislation*. New York: Macmillan (1789), 1948.

ence—that is, "consumption"—but from contemplation of our own past or future or from a comparison of the present against the past or future. The fact that experiences are carried forward in time through memory enables them to affect welfare at later times. Similarly, an experience that is foreseen before it actually occurs can, through anticipation, affect welfare at earlier times. We refer to the effect on current utility of contemplating the past as a *backward effect*, and the effect of contemplating the future as a *forward effect*.

The impact of memory and anticipation on current utility lead to a type of triple counting of experience. A single event can influence utility first through anticipation, then through direct experience, and finally through memory. But the manner in which memory and anticipation influence current utility are qualitatively different.

Unlike the future, the past cannot be altered, so that its effect on the present is largely determined by prior decisions. Our current selves[6] are largely at the mercy of past selves, although we have some limited capacity to direct our thoughts toward or away from the past, and even to represent the past as we wish. But, if past selves have endowed us with an overly rich or lean stock of memories, there are limits to our capacity to cognitively amend them without lapsing into autism.[7] Our relationship to past selves is like that toward other people who care about us, but whose behavior we cannot influence. At the same time, however, our current self plays the role of past for future selves, so that, caring about how our present will be presented as memory to future selves, we may take actions in the present to alter the memories that the future has to draw upon.

Anticipation of the future has its own unique characteristics. Unlike the past, we *can* exert at least a weak influence on the future. Moreover, the future is inherently uncertain, so we have greater freedom to imagine it as we wish than is the case with memory. Our future selves are like children away at college. We can only minimally

---

[6]References here and later to successive selves do not imply a commitment to a weak concept of personal identity, as advocated for instance by D. Parfit, *Reasons and Persons*, Oxford University Press, 1984. We use the phrase merely as convenient shorthand for a person's experience at different times.

[7]As G.L.S. Shackle wrote, "We have to distinguish between pure or free imagination, unfettered fantasy, on the one hand, and on the other, that kind of constrained imagination which we call expectation. There are, of course, pleasures to be had from mere daydreaming, but they are of a different sort from those of expectations" [Amsterdam: North Holland (1958): 41]. The degree to which we are able to delude ourselves is discussed in Elster's *Sour Grapes*, Cambridge: Cambridge University Press, 1983, and more specifically our ability to misrepresent our pasts to ourselves, is discussed in Cottle and Kleinberg, *The Present of Things Future*, New York: Free Press, 1974.

influence their behavior and can gain only a fuzzy and distorted image of their experiences; often that is all we desire.

We now proceed as follows. In the first section, we propose a general framework for the study of utility that arises from contemplation of the past and future. In the second section, we focus specifically on the effect of contemplating the past on current utility, drawing on Tversky's distinction between contrast effects and endowment effects.[8] In the third section, we discuss forward-looking effects generated by anticipation, drawing on Loewenstein's earlier work on "savoring" and "dread."[9] We conclude, in the final section, by considering the impact of these effects on time discounting.

The Structure of the Emotions[10]

What we shall call the *primary emotions* arise in our immediate encounters with the external world. Paradigm situations that arouse (positive) primary emotions include pleasing sights, sounds, and tastes; sexual stimulation; play and work that allow the use and development of one's powers and abilities; and social recognition and social approval. Negative emotions are, by and large, mirror images of the positive ones. These primary emotions have several properties. First, they derive from my experiences, not from those of other people. Second, they relate to my current experiences, not to my past or future ones. Third, they arise from my actual experiences, not from those I may have or could have had. These experiences, that are here, now, and mine, we call primary experiences. All other experiences we refer to as nonprimary. Many nonprimary experiences are, have been, or will be someone's primary experiences; however, this is not always the case. For example, counterfactual or subjunctive experiences ("If only I could fly. . . ." may not ever, in fact, be experienced by anyone.

We call some emotions primary not because they necessarily form

---

[8] See notably, A. Tversky and D. Griffin, "Endowment and Contrast Effects in Judgments of Well-Being," forthcoming in R. Zeckhauser (ed.), *Strategic Reflections on Human Behavior: Essays in Honor of Thomas C. Schelling*. The distinction was first aired by Tversky in the early 1980s. Later, we show that it was already present, in a more general form, in the work of Hume.

[9] G. Loewenstein, "Anticipation and the Valuation of Delayed Consumption," *Economic Journal* 97 (1987): 667–684; see also, for some related ideas, J. Elster, "Weakness of Will and the Free-Rider Problem," *Economics and Philosophy* 1 (1985): 231–265.

[10] This section draws on J. Elster, "Sadder but Wiser? Rationality and the Emotions," *Social Science Information* 24 (1985): 375–406.

the most important sources of satisfaction or unhappiness. Parents sometimes derive more happiness from their children's pleasure than from anything they do or experience themselves. Some people are most happy when daydreaming or when reading novels. Rather, these emotions are primary in the purely logical sense of being pre-supposed by the higher-order emotions. When we have a daydream of being in state X, that state is almost never defined as one in which we are daydreaming about state Y; rather, it is defined as a state in which we do enjoyable things or enjoyable things happen to us. We can imagine a world in which all emotions were primary ones, but not a world in which there were emotional states without any primary emotions.

Nonprimary experiences enter into emotional life in two ways. On the one hand, we can derive utility from the past or future almost as if the secondary experiences were occurring in the present. Through memory, I may relive a positive or negative experience from my past.[11] Similarly, through anticipatory savoring, it is possible to de-rive utility from a future event even before it occurs. We shall refer to these as the backward and forward *consumption effect*. The con-sumption effect can also be applied to altruistic contemplation of other persons' experiences. I suffer when I see my child suffer, and likewise I derive pleasure from her pleasure.

The consumption effect has two defining properties. First, the emotion evoked by contemplation of the nonprimary experience tends to be of the same hedonic sign, and to vary directly in intensity, with the emotion that the experience evokes when and by whom it is experienced directly. Second, the impact of the nonprimary experi-ence does not depend critically on one's current, primary, experi-ences. For example, to a first approximation, the pleasure we derive from our children's experience does not depend qualitatively on our own level of well-being.

On the other hand, higher-order experiences can change the con-text of primary experiences, providing new contrasts and conditions that make them more or less gratifying. We refer to this second im-pact of nonprimary experience on utility as the *contrast effect*.[12] When emerging from an illness, I enjoy my health more than I did before I fell ill. Contemplating other people's misery, I can better appreciate

---

[11]Cp. T.C. Schelling, "We consume past events that we can bring up from mem-ory," in *Choice and Consequence*, Cambridge, MA: Harvard University Press, 1984, p. 344.

[12]As noted earlier, this term was coined by Tversky for the special case of temporal externalities. (His term for the consumption effect in this case was the *endowment effect*.)

my own well-being. My past experiences shape the upper and lower limits of my range of comparisons, which in turn influence the pleasure I get from any given event.[13] The experiences of other people can extend the range if we can say to ourselves, plausibly, "there but for the grace of God," or more generally, "it could have been me." Such counterfactual ideas can also arise without being attached to other, actual persons. Their impact depends on their plausibility and vividness.[14]

The identifying features of the contrast effect are first, a negative relationship between the emotional quality of the nonprimary experience and the emotion it evokes. The more perfect was the past, the more deficient appears the present; the grander our neighbor's house, the more inadequate seems our own. Second, the effect is interactive; we do not consume the nonprimary experiences directly; instead, they alter the satisfaction or dissatisfaction that we derive from our primary experiences. The same past or future experience can have a very different impact on utility via the contrast effect, depending on the nature of one's current situation.

There are second-order effects that do not neatly fit this dual classification. When we take pleasure in the well-deserved suffering of evil individuals,[15] the experience is due neither to the consumption effect (because the hedonic signs are opposed) nor to the contrast effect (because the experience is independent of our own current welfare). A similar comment applies to the pleasure we occasionally derive from our own past misery if we feel it was deserved. Often we derive pleasure from recalling events that were at the time miserable (e.g., an arduous mountain ascent), and not only because they cast the present in a more favorable light. Just as common are situations that are painful to recall even though they were pleasurable at the time.[16] Moreover, the relationship between nonprimary consumption and the present emotions it evokes is often complex. For example, we may applaud our office colleague's raise if our salary is superior, but

[13] See A. Parducci, "The Relativism of Absolute Judgments," *Scientific American* (December 1968): 84–90, and "Value Judgments: Toward a Relational Theory of Happiness," in J.R. Eiser (ed.), *Attitudinal Judgment*, New York: Springer-Verlag, 1984, pp. 3–21.

[14] For the laws of plausibility, see D. Kahneman and A. Tversky, "The Simulation Heuristic," in D. Kahneman, P. Slovic, and A. Tversky (eds.), *Judgment under Uncertainty*, Cambridge, UK: Cambridge University Press, 1982, pp. 201–208.

[15] Indeed, according to Just-World theory (M.J. Lerner, *The Belief in a Just World*, New York: Plenum, 1980), we tend to infer from the fact that people suffer that they must have done something to deserve it. Indirectly, then, the mere spectacle of suffering may provide the satisfaction of seeing justice done.

[16] This is particularly true when our tastes change, or our sense of propriety.

lament (at least inwardly) the raise if it elevates the colleague's salary past the critical threshold defined by our own. Such a pattern suggests a transition from a dominant consumption effect to a dominant contrast effect that occurs at the point of equality.[17]

To our knowledge, the first writer to identify the dual effects of nonprimary experiences was Hume:

> In general we may observe that in all kinds of comparison an object makes us always receive from another, to which it is compared, a sensation contrary to what arises from itself in its direct and immediate survey. A small object makes a greater one appear still greater. A great object makes a little one appear less. Deformity of itself produces uneasiness; but makes us receive new pleasure by its contrast with a beautiful object, whose beauty is augmented by it; as on the other hand, beauty, which of itself produces pleasure, makes us receive a new pain by contrast with any thing ugly, whose deformity it augments. The case, therefore, must be the same with happiness and misery. The direct survey of another's pleasure naturally gives us pleasure, and therefore produces pain when compared with our own. *His pain, consider'd in itself, is painful to us, but augments the idea of our own happiness and gives us pleasure.*[18]

Hume may also have been the first to recognize the close analogy between interpersonal and intrapersonal (intertemporal) relationships:

> Nor will it appear strange, that we may feel a reverse sensation from the happiness and misery of others; since we find the same comparison may give us a kind of malice against ourselves, and make us rejoice for our pains, and grieve for our pleasures. Thus the prospect of past pain is agreeable, when we are satisfied with our present condition; as on the other hand our past pleasures give us uneasiness, when we enjoy nothing at present equal to them. The comparison being the same, as when we reflect on the sentiments of others, must be attended with the same effects.[19]

---

[17] In a wide range of situations, people dislike any type of inequality between themselves and others; but they feel much more strongly about discrepancies that give the other party more than those that give them more. See G. Loewenstein, L. Thompson, and M. Bazerman. "Decision Making in Interpersonal Contexts," *Journal of Personality and Social Psychology* 57 (1989): 426–441.

[18] David Hume, *A Treatise on Human Nature*, Selby Bigge (ed.), Oxford, UK: Oxford University Press, 1960, pp. 375–376. The phrase we have italicized shows that Hume was clearly aware of the dual effect phenomenon.

[19] Hume, op. cit.

Aside from our own past and future experiences and those of other people, there are other nonprimary experiences that also operate via the consumption and contrast effects. Subjective and counterfactual experiences have a dual effect in the same way as do past and future experiences and those of other persons. They can serve both as a source of direct emotional arousal and as a reference point that shapes our reaction to primary experiences.

Consider first the subjunctive emotions, "If I were to. . . ," where the dots could indicate getting a promotion, winning the state lottery, or receiving the Nobel prize for chemistry or some other desirable event that is largely independent of any action one could now take to bring it about. (It may, however, depend on actions one has undertaken in the past.) On the one hand, imagining the event occurring is inherently pleasant. On the other hand, by changing the reference point, it provides an unpleasant reminder of the current and less attractive situation.[20]

Counterfactual emotions, characteristically expressed in the phrase "If only. . . ," are directed toward states that could have obtained, but did not; they encompass near disasters as well as near successes. Whereas subjunctive emotions turn on events outside the actor's control, counterfactual emotions can be directed both to what the actor could have done and to events that might have come about. The train of thought set in motion by the idea "If only I had asked her to marry me" differs from that of "If only she had agreed to marry me." The former is more poignant, both because it involves a less extensive rearrangement of the world and, hence, is more plausible, and because it tends to induce self-blame[21] that reinforces the negative feelings created by the contrast.

In sum, the consumption effect preserves the hedonic sign of the nonprimary experience: It is pleasant when arising out of a pleasant experience, painful when created by a painful one. In the the contrast effect, the hedonic sign is reversed. When both effects operate, both

---

[20] Tversky and Griffin, op. cit., take the relevant contrast effect in such cases to be the disappointment suffered if the hoped-for event does not materialize, whereas we define it as a negative evaluation of one's current situation induced by the thought of a future, better state of affairs. Similarly they define the endowment effect in such cases as a good or bad feeling created by the lingering memory of past hopes or dreads, whereas we define the analogous consumption effect directly in terms of those hopes or dreads themselves. The memory of an anticipation, like the anticipation of regret, is a tertiary rather than a secondary emotion.

[21] See D.T. Miller and W. Turnbull, "The Counterfactual Fallacy: Confusing what Might Have Been with What Ought to Have Been," *Social Justice Research* 4 (1990): 1–16.

pleasure and pain will be provided. In general, the net effect is inde-
terminate, but with regard to specific types of experiences, we may
be able to determine whether the consumption effect or the contrast
effect dominates. Also, the strength of these effects may vary across
individuals. People differ a great deal in the extent to which they
enjoy reliving old love affairs, dread going to the dentist, suffer from
the sufferings of their children, or compare themselves to other people. Thus, while it is possible to adduce some general principles concerning the impact of the two effects in different situations, it is impossible in any specific situation to predict how a particular person
will be affected by secondary emotions.

The Role of the Past

The issue of the net utility effect of past experiences preoccupied
poets well before it came to the attention of psychologists. A famous
verse by Tennyson could be read as asserting the dominance of the
consumption effect: " 'Tis better to have loved and lost than never
to have loved at all."[22] Conversely, the following line from Donne
may be understood as asserting the superior strength of the contrast
effect: " 'Tis better to be foul than to have been fair." Donne may
plausibly be taken as saying that the sum of the two positive effects
of beauty—the direct benefits of being beautiful and the consumption
effect of having been beautiful—is smaller than the loss of utility
caused by the contrast effect. A fortiori, then, the consumption effect
taken by itself must be smaller than the contrast effect. A similar
reading of Tennyson would interpret him as saying that the sum of
the direct effect and the consumption effect of being in love exceeds
the loss of utility caused by the contrast effect, from which nothing
follows about the relationship between the contrast effect and the
consumption effect taken by itself.

   In this section we consider a variety of ways in which past experiences shape current welfare. In addition to the contrast effect and
the consumption effect, we discuss the idea of learned discrimination, Stigler and Becker's idea of "consumption capital," Solomon's
opponent-process theory, and Scitovsky's theory of pleasure and
comfort.

   The consumption effect and the contrast effect operate through
consciousness. The moment an experience is forgotten, it is no longer

---

[22] An alternative interpretation is that the sum of primary pleasure from love experienced over time outweighs the primary pain experienced from the loss of that love.

a direct source of pleasure or pain. Similarly, the contrast effect requires, for its operation, that the past event remain present in consciousness to serve as a reference point for evaluating primary experiences. Presence in consciousness is only a necessary condition, however, for an event to be a reference point for current experiences. It must also be similar to them in some relevant respect: A superlatively good meal in a French restaurant may devalue later, more ordinary meals in French restaurants, but need have no impact on meals in Chinese restaurants.[23] Hence, framing and conscious or unconscious psychic manipulation come into play. To maximize happiness, "One should find ways to treat the positive experiences of the past as different from the present (to avoid a sense of letdown). By the same token, one should compare present conditions to worse conditions in the past (to enjoy the benefits of a positive contrast)."[24]

The memory of a good experience is a good memory. Yet, equally good experiences need not generate equally good memories. I may be indifferent now between spending $15 on a bottle of good wine or on a movie, but get much more pleasure out of the memory of the movie than of the memory of the wine. Often, the act of seeing a movie is not merely perceived as getting 90 minutes worth of entertainment but also as adding to one's stock of movie experiences.

In addition to the consumption effect of memory, there is a "learning effect" by which the movie enhances the pleasure of seeing and remembering later movies or raises my general level of sophistication. This second effect is different from the consumption effect in that it need not be mediated by consciousness. I may remember nothing of a movie I saw 15 years ago, and in fact may not even recall having seen it, and yet it may have had a substantial and lasting impact on my ability to appreciate movies.

Or consider again the superlative French restaurant. When I have a meal later at a mediocre French restaurant, the contrast effect taken by itself reduces my happiness. The impact of the earlier meal could also, however, be mediated by its contribution to my capacity for discrimination—a capacity I may retain after the meal itself is forgotten. That improved capacity can enhance my enjoyment of later meals or reduce it. If a superlative meal is followed by a very poor one, the latter is devalued not only through the contrast effect, but also through a learning effect. It is only as a result of having a taste of the real thing that I fully understand how bad the poor imitation is. If it is followed by a meal that, while not superlative, is quite well

[23] Tversky and Griffin, op. cit.
[24] Ibid.

prepared, the learning effect may actually make me enjoy it more, whereas the contrast effect, as before, detracts from my enjoyment.[25]

The contrast effect is also related to, yet different from, a number of other mechanisms. The "opponent-process theory," for instance, suggests that positive experiences tend to generate negative ones and vice versa.[26] According to the opponent process theory, a physiological equilibrating mechanism within the body acts to neutralize pain and pleasure. When the source of pain or pleasure is terminated, the opponent process continues to operate for some period, creating the opposite hedonic experience. Thus, upon being told that she does not have the breast cancer she feared, a woman does not return to her normal emotional state but instead experiences intense euphoria. Conversely, interruption of a pleasurable sexual experience creates acute irritation, and it takes some time before one returns to an emotionally neutral state.

While superficially similar to the contrast effect, the opponent-process is a quite different phenomenon. The contrast effect results from the impact of a previous experience on a later, independently generated one. A superlative meal can devalue a later meal. The opponent-process effect arises when one experience generates another of the opposite hedonic sign. A superlative meal can leave a mild depression in its wake.[27] Also, the opponent-process effect is not mediated by conscious memory. It has been demonstrated in dogs no less than in human subjects, and there are indications that the opponent-process mechanism is subject to framing. The two effects differ, moreover, in that the opponent-process effect requires real stimuli: Memory is neither necessary nor sufficient. Thus, the following comment on the contrast effect would not apply to the opponent-process effect: "The ideal lower end-point might be a strong electric shock, unbearable but quickly over. The shock would

[25] Such learning has been described as building up "consumption capital" (see G. Stigler and G. Becker, "De gustibus non est disputandum," *American-Economic Review* 67 (1977): 76–90), but this approach is too coarse-grained to be very useful. We need to understand not only why exposure to good music allows us to enjoy it more, but also why it causes us to hear music we used to like as painful rather than pleasant. If we are unavoidably exposed to a good deal of bad music, the net effect of the "consumption capital" may in fact be negative.

[26] See, notably, R.L. Solomon and J. Corbit, "An Opponent-Process Theory of Motivation," *Psychological Review* 81 (1974): 119–145, and R.L. Solomon, "The Opponent-Process Theory of Acquired Motivation: The Costs of Pleasure and the Benefits of Pain," *American Psychologist* 35 (1980): 691–712.

[27] Solomon mentions (ibid., p. 694), as a perceptual analogy to the opponent-process effect, the fact that when a red light is turned off, an aftereffect of green is created. For the contrast effect, the analogy would rather be that a strongly red patch seen at an earlier time causes a patch of medium redness later to be seen as pink.

have to be readministered occasionally, whenever it dropped from the context or whenever its memory ceased to be dreadful."[28]

Another idea that bears a family resemblance to the contrast effect and the opponent-process effect can be traced back at least to Leibniz. Against Locke, Leibniz insisted that pain ("uneasiness") is not the opposite of pleasure, but that discomfort and small pains are integral to pleasure: "Je trouve que l'inquiétude est essentielle à la félicité des créatures, laquelle ne consiste jamais dans une parfaite possession qui les rendrait insensibles et comme stupides, mais dans un progrès continuel et non interrompu vers de plus grands biens."[29] Pleasure is produced by the continual overcoming of the pain and discomfort attached to unsatisfied desires. More recently, Scitovsky has argued that "pleasure is the feeling associated with the relief of discomfort."[30] Although he refers to this principle at the Law of Hedonic Contrast, it differs from the contrast effect as we have defined it. Scitovsky sees pleasure as being produced by the cessation of pain, rather than being enhanced by the memory of pain or the observation of the pain of others. Also, he does not allow for the possibility that outstanding pleasures today may ruin later experiences by providing an unattainable benchmark.[31] The Leibniz-Scitovsky effect is similar to the opponent-process effect,[32] but the two frameworks are conceptually quite different. For instance, there is nothing in the opponent-process theory that corresponds to Scitovsky's idea that there is an optimal, that is, pleasure-maximizing, degree of novelty.

The Role of the Future

The importance of anticipation as a source of pleasure and pain has long been recognized by economists[33] and has been documented in

[28] Parducci, "Value Judgments," p. 16.

[29] G.W. Leibniz, *Philosophische Schriften*, Gerhard Leipzig (ed.), 1875–1890, vol. V, p. 175; see also p. 152.

[30] T. Scitovsky, *The Joyless Economy*, London: Oxford University Press, 1976, p. 62.

[31] Kahneman and Varey, "Notes on the Psychology of Utility," in J. Elster and J. Roemer (eds.), *Interpersonal Comparisons of Wellbeing*, Cambridge, UK: Cambridge University Press, 1991, pp. 127–163.

[32] Scitovsky, *The Joyless Economy*, p. 129 ff. cites the opponent-process theory as closely related to his own.

[33] Jevons saw anticipation as the single most important source of utility, at least for the elite: "There is little doubt that, in minds of much intelligence and foresight, the greatest force of feeling and motive is what arises from the anticipation of the future" (1871, p. 40). Other prominent economists such as Marshall and Pareto also commented on the importance of anticipation as a source of utility; their views are discussed in the first chapter of this book.

diverse social science research. One study that followed the health records of men during 2 years when two factories were scheduled to close found that "the period of anticipation of unemployment was associated with the greatest reported illness" rather than the period of actual unemployment.[34] Another study, in which college students ranked the days of the week, observed that Sunday was ranked below Friday, even though classes were held on Friday. Apparently Sunday was marred by anticipation of the approaching week of classes.[35]

Like memory, anticipated experiences affect current utility through the consumption and contrast effects. Through the consumption effect we are able to, in effect, consume events before they occur through anticipation. As the philosopher Bain stated, "every actual delight casts before it a corresponding ideal." We define *savoring* as the process of deriving positive utility from anticipation of desirable events,[36] and *dread* as the emotional impact of contemplating future negative experiences. Savoring and dread act as multipliers of experience, causing individuals to experience the hedonic impact of future events repeatedly before they actually occur; as Shakespeare's Julius Caesar states, "cowards die many times before their deaths."

Although the exact determinants of savoring and dread are uncertain, some basic principles can be elucidated. As Jevons observed, the intensity of savoring or dread varies directly with the emotional intensity of the anticipated event. Also, savoring and dread become more intense as the event approaches in time:

> An event which is to happen a year hence affects us on the average about as much one day as another; but an event of importance, which is to take place three days hence, will probably affect us on each of the intervening days more acutely than the last."[37]

The same properties also apply to memory.[38]

---

[34] S.V. Kasl, S. Gore, and S. Cobb, "The Experience of Losing a Job: Reported Changes in Health, Symptoms and Illness Behavior," *Psychosomatic Medicine* 37 (1975): 105–122.

[35] Saturday was the most preferred and Monday the least. M.L. Farber, "Time Perspective and Feeling Tone: A Study in the Perception of the Days," *Journal of Psychology* 35 (1953): 253–257.

[36] This term was suggested by Robert Abelson.

[37] P. 41, *Theory of Political Economy*, 1871.

[38] See, for example, G. Ekman and U. Lundberg, "Emotional Reaction to Past and Future Events as a Function of Temporal Distance," *Acta Psychologica* 835 (1971): 430–441.

But, even after allowing for the intensity of future feeling and time delay, future events differ in their capacity to evoke savoring and dread, and there are fluctuations over time in an individual's propensity to experience either emotion. First, it is difficult to savor an event in the future that does not appeal to us in the present. Contemplating a future dinner when we have just overeaten is repulsive, no matter how hungry we will be, and no matter how delicious the dinner will be when it is experienced. Savoring seems to depend mainly on the utility that we would *currently* derive from an anticipated event, rather than the utility that we expect to derive at the time. One reason why luxuries may be such a consistent source of anticipatory pleasure is that the taste for luxuries does not depend very much on transient appetites.

The question of whether we use our current or future tastes to evaluate delayed experiences also has a close analog in the interpersonal domain. Deriving pleasure or pain from another person's experiences, we can base our own feelings either on our own preferences or those of the other person. In the latter case—when we derive pleasure from how they feel—it is like basing savoring on our own future preferences. For example, we might enjoy knowing our daughter is happy at college, without considering the reasons for her happiness. Alternatively, we might apply our own tastes to her experiences, deriving pleasure if her happiness stems from success in school, but pain if her happiness results from a newfound discovery of the pleasures of hallucinogens.

Anticipated experiences also affect current well-being via the contrast effect, by serving as a point of comparison against which current consumption is measured. When the future is expected to be superior to the present, the comparison leads to a denigration of the present. Many social commentators have noted the frustration-engendering effect of expectations of improvement. Tocqueville commented that "evils which are patiently endured when they seem inevitable become intolerable once the idea of escape from them is suggested,"[39] while Gurr in his classic *Why Men Rebel* includes "the promise of new opportunities" among the antecedents of discontentment and rebellion.[40] Like the superior attainments of other people, expectations of personal improvement in the future can become a source of relative deprivation. According to the relative deprivation literature, moreover, people tend to choose as objects of comparison others who

[39] P. 214, *The Old Regime and The French Revolution*, J. Bonner (trans.), New York: Harper and Bros., 1856.
[40] P. 14, *Why Men Rebel*, Princeton, NJ: Princeton University Press, 1970.

are similar to themselves. Who could be more similar than our own future selves?

Strangely, however, the contrast effect is completely eclipsed by the consumption effect when current consumption is higher than future consumption. Rarely does one derive satisfaction from comparing the opulence of the present to the poverty of the future. Perhaps any pleasurable contrast effect is squelched by recognition that opulence of the present will eventually form a negative contrast for the future. A similar distaste for downward comparison is observed in research on social comparison; people derive considerable pain when relevant others receive more, but little pleasure from comparing themselves to others who are disadvantaged.[41]

The consumption and contrast effects associated with anticipation are not mutually exclusive. One can derive pleasure from anticipating a scheduled date, but also experience frustration by comparing current loneliness against the bright prospect of companionship. Which effect dominates—that is, whether the scheduled date enhances or detracts from current utility—depends on the relevance of future experiences as a yardstick against which to compare the present, and on how vividly the future can be imagined.[42] Luxury goods such as fancy restaurant dinners or vacations provide considerable anticipatory pleasure without inducing a strong contrast effect because they tend to be vivid, but they are not relevant as referents for the present. Perhaps for the same reason, people do not direct their envy toward the superrich.[43]

When future improvements are expected to be prolonged, the contrast effect will be especially strong. The promise of a job following graduation, the termination of a long and boring journey, or release from prison[44] are all situations in which frustration is often intense

[41] See Messick and Sentis, "Estimating Social and Nonsocial Utility Functions from Ordinal Data," *European Journal of Social Psychology* 15 (1989): 389–399; Loewenstein, Thompson, and Bazerman, op. cit.

[42] For a discussion of this issue, see D. Kahneman and D.T. Miller, "Norm Theory: Comparing Reality to its Alternatives," *Psychological Review* 93 (1986): 136–153.

[43] For discussion of this point see L. Festinger, "Social Comparison Theory," *Human Relations* 7 (1954): 117–140; L. Wheeler, "Motivation as a Determinant of Upward Comparison," *Journal of Experimental Social Psychology* Supplement 1 (1966): 27–31; and, more recently, J. Elster, "Envy in Social Life," working paper.

[44] Kurt Lewin claimed that prison breakouts tend to occur toward the end of prison sentences. If true, an obvious explanation would be that as the end of the sentence draws near, the contrast between current incarceration and impending freedom makes the former intolerable. In informal research on this question, the second author found a relatively flat distribution, even for long sentences. This is itself rather paradoxical, because it would appear to make sense to break out toward the beginning of a long

as one approaches relief. Grinker and Speigel found that airmen in World War II adopted an attitude of fatalistic and bitter resignation that protected against anxiety. But "the protection . . . often breaks down when the individual comes to the end of his combat tour. . . . During the last few missions, hope of survival again becomes realistic, and at that point concern for his own fate again returns to the individual. Once he begins to hope and to care, he may suddenly develop intense anxiety."[45] The expectation of prolonged improvement in the future seems to engender dissatisfaction with one's current state, although this dissatisfaction is tempered by pleasure derived from savoring the future. Those who would discourage revolution might be advised either to quell expectations or, if that strategy is impractical, to make the expected improvements as vivid and, hence, savorable as possible.

Anticipation is similar to memory in that the consumption and contrast effects are operative. But there is a crucial difference between the backward and forward effects. Memory has as its object events that have already occurred, which are thus certainties. Anticipation focuses on events in the future that are by this fact inherently uncertain. The likelihood that the anticipated event will actually occur is an important determinant of the intensity of savoring and dread.

Stotland, in his book, *The Psychology of Hope,*[46] includes as a basic proposition: "The higher an organism's perceived probability of attaining a goal and the greater the importance of that goal, the greater will be the positive affect experienced by the organism." But the relationship between affect and probability is likely to be more complex.

At very low probability levels, below a threshold of conceivability, savoring and dread will be nil. Beyond this threshold, we would expect a sudden jump and then low marginal sensitivity over a wide range of probabilities beyond that point. Savoring and dread arise from mental imaging of delayed experiences, and it is difficult to incorporate probability into a mental image. One's image of a terrible car crash remains equally vivid if its probability of occurring is 10 percent or 50 percent; the delights of imagining a weekend date do not depend on the probability that one will be stood up. Of course,

---

sentence. (Despite movie depictions of dramatic escapes, most breakouts occur from medium- or low-security institutions in which breaking out is a relatively simple matter.) Perhaps more interesting, and also consistent with the contrast effect, was the observation on the part of several wardens that breakouts often tend to occur following an unsuccessful bid for parole.

[45] From Stotland, *The Psychology of Hope,* San Francisco: Jossey Bass, 1969, p. 35.

[46] Ibid.

one may spend more time imagining an event that is more likely to occur, but the opposite is also possible. A date that is certain requires little prior attention, but one that is uncertain requires fall-back planning, which is likely to maintain the focus of attention on the date itself.

The insensitivity of anticipatory emotions to probability can explain simultaneous purchase of lottery tickets and insurance. As lottery managers and marketers understand, people who buy lottery tickets are not simply purchasing a probability of getting rich, but are "buying a dream."[47] If the pleasurableness of the dream depends little on the probability of winning, then it is efficient to buy a cheap ticket, which offers a very small chance of winning a very large amount of money, along with a large dose of savoring. Consistent with the notion that people are more focused on prize values than on probabilities, mass media advertisements for lottery tickets are approximately four times as likely to include information about payoffs than they are to include information on odds of winning.[48] Similarly, by purchasing insurance against low probability events, one can buy "peace of mind" at low cost—protection from dread that is out of proportion to the actual probability of the event occurring.

As the probability of the anticipated event rises still further, a curious reversal often occurs. Beyond a certain point, events are reframed; a 90 percent chance of a date with a love object becomes reframed as a 10 percent chance of being stood up. A 90 percent chance that one's cancer is malignant is transformed into a 10 percent chance of escape. Thus, paradoxically, people may experience anxiety when waiting for highly probable desirable events, and hope when waiting for highly probable undesirable events.

Time Discounting

The notion that utility depends on memory and anticipation has numerous implications for behavior. These are of two types: implications for the timing and sequencing of experiences, and implications

[47]From M. Landau, *A Manual on Lotteries*, Ramat Gan, Israel: Masada Publishing, 1968. "In spite of the great unlikelihood of winning the desirable sum of money, an individual may still be willing to pay a relatively high price for a lottery ticket because of the satisfaction he is deriving from the thrill of anticipation and the illusion that he may succeed and become wealthy" (p. 36).

[48]C.T. Clotfelter and P.J. Cook, *Selling Hope: State Lotteries in America*, Cambridge, MA: Harvard University Press, 1989.

for the types of experiences selected at any one point in time. For example, the backward consumption effect should cause people to shift pleasurable experiences forward in time (to the present), so they can be enjoyed later through recollection, and it also should cause a shift toward pleasurable experiences that are more memorable.

There is a crucial difference between the implications of the backward and forward effects. When memory influences behavior via the consumption or contrast effect, one changes current behavior to alter the memories of future selves. The behavior is in the present and its impact on utility is in the future. When anticipation influences behavior, typically one modifies plans for the future or takes actions in the present that will affect the future in order to alter experiences anticipated by the present self. The behavior is in the future, and its impact on utility is in the present. Thus, the positioning of actor and beneficiary are reversed for memory and anticipation.

The implications of backward effects—those mediated by memory—depend on whether the consumption or contrast effect dominates. If the consumption effect dominates, then consuming more in the present contributes to future well-being.[49] There is a type of "trickle down" from present to future that can justify immediate indulgence. Suppose that at $t = 1$, one knows that in the ordinary course of events a certain pleasurable event will take place at $t = 3$, but that one has the option of (costlessly) moving it forward or backward 1 unit of time. A person who derives much utility from consuming the past might choose to move it up to $t = 2$ so as to lengthen the period of pleasurable recollection. Consumption early in life provides a stock of memories that can be drawn upon for the duration of life; concentrating consumption early in life is efficient because it gives one ample time to "amortize" the investment in memories. The hyperrationalist might conjecture that the high level of risk taking and experience seeking of adolescents reflects an optimal early investment in memories.

The consumption effect also has implications for atemporal choice. Given two options, one might choose the option with smaller immediate utility if the expected stream of memory-utilities is sufficiently much greater. If people derive disproportionate pleasure from peak

---

[49] The contrast effect, as we said, is subject to framing. Although the problem of frame selection is poorly understood, one hypothesis is that people choose the frame that will make them best off. For obvious reasons, though, such choices can hardly be made consciously. Unconscious mechanisms are certainly conceivable, but existing evidence does not support the "hedonic framing" hypothesis. See R. Thaler and E. Johnson, "Gambling with the House Money and Trying to Break Even: The Effects of Prior Outcomes on Risky Choice," *Management Science* 36 (1990): 643–660.

experiences—for example, if one excellent dinner is recalled more pleasurably than two mediocre dinners—then one might opt for the former, even if the latter were more gratifying in the short run.

To what extent do people internalize (take account of) the backward consumption effect when making current consumption decisions? On the one hand, people do seem to invest in memories. Phrases like "we'll remember this for the rest of our lives" ease the massive expenditures associated with huge weddings and expensive cruises, and help the participants to enjoy them rather than to focus on their shrunken savings. However, whether this is evidence of the consumption effect influencing behavior, or actually ex-post rationalization, is questionable. Similar rationalizations follow decisions that were obviously bad—for example, "well, it may have been crazy to go down into the canyon in midsummer, but it's an experience we won't forget." If individuals ignore or underweight backward effects in planning current consumption, as some have argued,[50] then we have the intrapersonal equivalent of an interpersonal externality—a situation in which one self ignores the impact of his or her actions on future selves. Herrnstein, Loewenstein, Prelec, and Vaughan[51] refer to situations in which people ignore the indirect consequences of their own behavior for themselves as "internalities."

Whether deliberate memory creation is even possible, is questionable. Many of the good things in life are characterized by surprise, spontaneity, serendipity, and lack of planning. Hence, the idea of novelty seeking for the purpose of memory creation borders on the paradoxical or self-defeating, as in the "be spontaneous!" paradox. To act in the present for the sake of (among other things) future memory streams could easily undermine the spontaneity and value of the immediate experience and devalue the stream of memories flowing from it. Reliving old loves can be wonderful, but memory investment by itself hardly justifies engaging in a love affair. People who go on vacation constantly on the lookout for the opportunity to take photographs that will remind them later of what a wonderful

---

[50] Richard Thaler (personal communication) argues that people do not adequately take account of the backward consumption effect and thus invest insufficiently in memorable experiences. From a myopic perspective, two pleasant restaurant dinners might be valued equally with one spectacular dinner; but the one spectacular dinner is much more likely to be remembered. Thaler's argument is similar to Scitovsky's notion that we tend to opt for comfort instead of pleasure, even though in the long run, pleasure provides greater satisfaction than comfort.

[51] "Utility Maximization and Melioration: Internalities in Individual Choice," working paper, Department of Social and Decision Sciences, Carnegie-Mellon University, 1990.

time they had, may not have much of a wonderful time.[52] Sometimes, to live in the future imperfect is not to live at all.

The backward contrast effect has the opposite consequence for behavior. If the contrast effect alone were operative, we would want to hold back on pleasure in the present to create a low referent against which the future will be evaluated. We speak of children who are "spoiled," suggesting that too many possessions or too much attention at an early age can spoil a person's later life. As Parducci commented, "If the best can come only rarely, it is better not to include it in the range of experience."[53]

The backward contrast effect should induce a preference for sequences of experiences that improve over time. In such sequences the present is superior to almost any summary (e.g., mean, maximum) of the past. This prediction has received considerable empirical support. Survey respondents report that they would prefer wage profiles that increase yearly over flat or declining profiles of equal undiscounted value.[54] Others, asked to choose between different orderings of three weekend dinners, one crummy, one mediocre, and one fancy, overwhelmingly prefer to eat the crummy one first and the fancy one last.[55]

To summarize, if an experience is positive, we would like it to carry forward via the consumption effect rather than the contrast effect so as to enhance future well-being. If unpleasant, we should attempt to carry it forward via the contrast effect. We should engage in enjoyable behaviors that are memorable, but that do not create a standard against which future experiences are judged. And we should expose ourselves to painful experiences to lower our standards, as long as the memory of those experiences (the consumption effect) is not too painful.

When one turns to anticipation, the implications for behavior are more straightforward. If, as we have claimed earlier, the consumption effect swamps the contrast effect when the future is inferior to

[52]For a further discussion of these problems, see Chapter II of J. Elster, *Sour Grapes*, Cambridge, UK: Cambridge University Press, 1983.

[53]Parducci, op. cit. p. 90.

[54]This research is reported in G. Loewenstein and N. Sicherman, "Do Workers Prefer Increasing Wage Profiles?" *Journal of Labor Economics* 9 (January 1991): 67–84. See, also, Chapter 15 from this volume, and C.K. Hsee and R.P. Abelson, "Velocity Relation: Satisfaction as a Function of the First Derivative of Outcome Over Time," *Journal of Personality and Social Psychology* 60 (1991): 341–347.

[55]For a discussion of preferences for outcome sequences, see Loewenstein and Prelec, "Negative Time Preference," *American Economic Review* 81 (1991): 347–352 and "Preference Over Outcome Sequences," *Psychological Review*, 1992 (forthcoming).

the present, then there is a strong incentive to build improvement over time into one's plans. The preference for sequences that improve over time, discussed earlier, may be so robust because it is overdetermined. In Proust's *Swann's Way*, the narrator's desire to defer a goodnight kiss illustrates the two motives for deferral: "So much did I love that goodnight kiss that I reached the stage of hoping it would come as late as possible, so as to prolong the time of respite during which Mamma would not have appeared." On the one hand, the narrator wants to be able to look forward to the goodnight kiss (a forward consumption effect). On the other hand, he doesn't want to be in a position in which the kiss has already occurred (a backward contrast effect).

The dominance of the consumption effect when the future is inferior to the present suggests that people will take measures to prevent such a state of affairs from arising. The so-called equity puzzle in finance—the almost pathological levels of risk aversion evident in the high return paid on risky stocks relative to safe bonds—may reflect a strong aversion to investments that would permit the future to be worse than the present.

Whether forward effects actually contribute to a preference for improvement, or rather to a desire for constancy over time, depends on the relative strength of the consumption and contrast effects. If the consumption effect dominates, people should prefer sequences that improve over time; if the contrast effect dominates, they should prefer constant sequences of utility. Once again, which effect dominates depends on the characteristics of the individual and on the nature of the experience. Again, for luxury goods or goods experienced over a short duration, the consumption effect should dominate the contrast effect. Consistent with this intuition, most respondents to a survey on timing decisions reported that they would prefer to defer a kiss from the movie star of their choice, at least by a few days, and would get a nonlethal electric shock over with immediately, if given the option.[56] Both of these choices are inconsistent with time discounting and can be explained by the operation of a forward consumption effect.

The many possible configurations of backward and forward consumption and contrast effects, when combined with even mundane exponential time preference, can lead to a wide range of overall patterns of discounting. For example, strong backward consumption effects could augment the preference for the present leading to disproportionate discounting of short delays. As Strotz and Ainslie have

[56] See Loewenstein, op. cit., 1987.

demonstrated, such a discount function produces choice reversals characterized by impatience in the present with intentions of future farsightedness. But a more likely scenario is a choice reversal of a dramatically different "miserly" type that would result if backward contrast and forward consumption effects were dominant.[57] Such a pattern would give rise to a choice reversal in which a person, instead of indulging him- or herself, plans to consume an item in the near future, but repeatedly defers when the scheduled time for consumption arrives. Consider a simple example, involving only memory and anticipation. A person is planning how to distribute 1 unit of a consumption good over four time periods. The person's pure time preferences lead him or her to attach equal weight to each of the future periods. We assume for simplicity that his or her utility from current consumption is proportional to the amount consumed. The mental externalities are defined as follows: Current utility of one utile in the last period is $\frac{1}{3}$, whereas the current utility of one utile in the next period is $\frac{1}{2}$. It is then easy to show the following. At the beginning of period 1, the person plans to concentrate all his or her consumption in period 3. In period 2 this remains the preferred plan, but when period 3 comes, the person wants to concentrate it entirely in period 4. Misers and children who store away their Halloween candy until it goes stale exemplify such a pattern.

As a consequence of the hedonic effects discussed earlier, pure time preferences cannot immediately be read off observed behavior. A person who saves little for the future may do so despite a low rate of time discounting due to very strong backward externalities. Conversely, a person who saves much may have a high rate of time discounting, but very strong forward externalities. An analogous distinction arises in interpersonal contexts. A person may take account of the welfare of others on impersonal utilitarian grounds, or because he derives pleasure from their pleasure; *sympathy* is sometimes defined as the former, *empathy* as the latter.

And just as in the interpersonal case it is seemingly impossible to determine the relative importance of sympathy and empathy, the same is true in the intertemporal case. Perhaps there is no such thing as intertemporal sympathy. As Jevons seemed to believe, perhaps the only reason we defer consumption is because we derive immediate pleasure from savoring it. Or maybe "pure" discounting is effectively

---

[57] Prelec and Loewenstein, "Decision-Making Over Time and Under Uncertainty: A Common Approach," *Management Science*, 37 (1991): 770–786, argue that the backward contrast and forward endowment effects are likely to dominate the backward endowment and forward contrast effects in most situations.

zero, as Ramsey advocated. Maybe if it weren't for the forward contrast effect that makes us, in effect, envy our future selves, we would not discount future satisfactions at all.

The reality is undoubtedly complex. People differ in the extent to which they derive utility from memory and anticipation and in the degree to which they compare the present to the past and future. A person can be myopic for a number of reasons: because the backward consumption effects dominate contrast effects, or forward contrast effects dominate consumption effects. Alternatively, myopia can arise if a person attaches little weight to his or her welfare in later periods, independently of any pleasure or pain derived from contemplating the past or future. Just as understanding interpersonal interactions requires an appreciation of utility interdependencies between persons, our understanding of time preference can be enhanced by an appreciation of the complex interdependencies between selves at different points in time.

· 10 ·

Melioration

RICHARD J. HERRNSTEIN AND DRAZEN PRELEC

ECONOMIC theory assumes that people's choices are efficient, in the sense that they can be interpreted as flowing from constrained maximization of a well-defined objective function. However, a growing body of evidence from both human and animal choice experiments points to systematic departures from optimal choice, departures that typically do not diminish with prolonged exposure to the experimental situation. A common finding is that instead of equalizing the marginal returns per unit investment (e.g., in choice frequency, time, or money), subjects settle into stable choice patterns at which average returns are equalized.

We present a theory (*melioration*) that formalizes this pseudomaximizing search for higher average values. The choices predicted by melioration are reasonably efficient in some situations, markedly inefficient in others. An experiment is described in which the majority of subjects were induced to meliorate, even though this choice pattern *minimized* the rate of money earnings from the experiment. On a more speculative level, a variety of apparent suboptimalities in consumer behavior, such as underinvestment in skills and pathological addiction, may also be understood as consequences of a meliorating strategy.

Introduction

In modern expositions of the theory of rational choice, the notion of what constitutes an object of choice is kept deliberately vague, in order not to restrict unduly the range of possible problems to which the theory will be applied later on. A recent advanced textbook on consumer behavior (Deaton and Muellbauer, 1980), for example, initially defines the objects of choice as "individual purchases of commodities" (p. 269), but this concrete definition yields quickly to the more abstract notion of a commodity "bundle" (p. 269), which, however, is rarely obtained through an individual purchase. Implicit in this exchangeability of terms is the supposition that in applying the theory it does not matter whether,

   (A) The "choice" corresponds to an actual decision, made at a specific point in time.

or

   (B) The "choice" is an aggregate of many smaller decisions, distributed over a period of time.

In this chapter, we develop a theory of individual choice for which the distinction between choices of type A and type B is critical, and which implies that choices of type B may be reliably and predictably suboptimal, in light of the person's own preferences. If true, this would imply that preferences as revealed in the marketplace may be a distortion of the true underlying preferences whenever the measured economic variables are aggregates of a stream of smaller decisions; the extent, and direction, of the distortion is then something that the theory will need to explain.

Our theory draws support from two sources. First, over the last 25 years, experimental psychologists have accumulated much data about repeated choice, indicating that for both human and animal subjects, the long-run distribution of choices between alternatives conforms in many cases to a rule that optimizes return only under special circumstances. At the same time, this rule has a deceptive appearance of rationality, so that it is easy to mistake it for a form of dynamic or "hill-climbing" optimization.

The second source of support is somewhat more speculative. Let us consider some typical examples of type B, or *distributed* choices, as we will hereafter call them:[1]

- expenditure rate on various nondurables
- frequency of athletic exercise
- rate of work, in free-lance type occupations
- allocation of leisure time
- rate of savings (or dissavings)
- expenditures on lottery tickets, and other forms of gambling

It is relevant that when people express dissatisfaction about their choices, the dissatisfaction is clustered much more around distributed choices than those in category A. For example, complaints that one is working too hard (or not hard enough), exercising too little (or too much), wasting time, overeating, overspending, and so on, are commonplace. Many of these anomalously suboptimal patterns of behavior have already been noticed by economic theorists, and have stimulated a burgeoning literature on models of "self-control" (Ainslie, 1975, 1982, 1986; Elster, 1984; Schelling, 1980; Thaler and Shefrin, 1981; Winston, 1980).

The next two sections of the chapter spell out the basic theory we are proposing, including a simple formal account, in the third section, in which the relationship with traditional consumer theory is emphasized. The fourth section applies the theory to "pathological" consumption patterns, and shows that one should find a general underinvestment in those activities that exhibit increasing average returns to rate of consumption, and an overinvestment in activities that have an addiction-like interaction between value and rate. The final section interprets the theory as essentially describing an "externality" internal to the choices of a single individual, and it contrasts the theory with other approaches to suboptimal choice.

Melioration: Basic Concepts

Figure 10.1 plots the familiar diminishing marginal utility schedules, for two commodities (if one assumes that utility is additively separable in two commodities). A rational person purchases additional units

[1]The boundary between type A and type B choices will vary across individuals. For example, for some people the savings rate is determined by a deliberate, perhaps automatically enforced policy, while for others it is the unintentional byproduct of their expenditure rate.

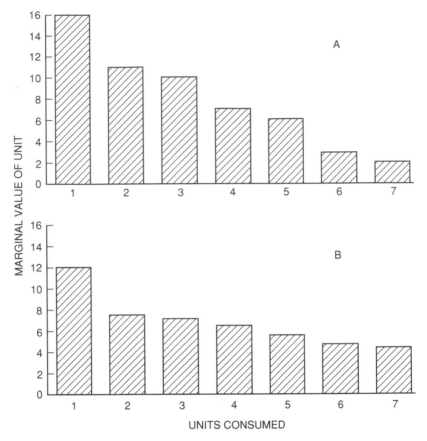

Figure 10.1. Marginal tradeoffs in a nondistributed context: Diminishing marginal value of a unit of commodity A (upper panel) or B (lower panel), as a function of the total number of units purchased. If one assumes equal prices per unit, an optimal allocation of income across the two commodities can be achieved by starting with the higher valued first unit (A, in this case) and then continuing with the highest of the remaining units, until budgeted income is exhausted.

of either commodity until income is exhausted, at which point the marginal utility of one extra unit is the same for both commodities. While such graphs rarely appear in modern expositions of utility theory, the robust intuitions that they embody are probably still with us.

For certain choice situations, this model seems appropriate. Giving the house a fresh coat of paint or, say, buying a new series for a stamp collection—in such decisions the marginal benefit is clearly imaginable, as a contrast between the "before" and "after," that is, the house with or without the paint, the collection improved or not, and so on. In such situations, only a perverse individual would choose the action with a lower marginal benefit.

But for another class of decisions, alluded to in the Introduction, the correct marginal quantities are not as apparent. In Figure 10.2, the horizontal axis is a time line, along which are plotted individual choices between two items or activities (A and B), perhaps a choice between two types of restaurant, or forms of entertainment, etc. The vertical axis represents satisfaction experienced as a result of each individual choice. Before point t^0, there is a predominance of A choices, as indicated by the number of solid bars; after t^0, the person shifts to more B choices, and fewer A choices. As a result of the change, the satisfaction received from subsequent choices of B decreases (on average), while that received from an A choice increases.

Does the shift in the relative frequency of A and B choices repre-

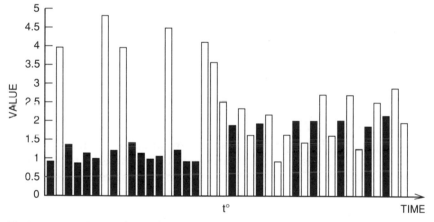

Figure 10.2. Marginal tradeoffs in a distributed context: A sequence of choices of alternatives A and B. The height of the individual bars represents satisfaction derived from a single choice of A (black bars) or B (white bars). For the first twenty choices (prior to t^0), the distribution of choices was 80–20 percent, in favor of A; for the last twenty choices, the distribution shifted to 65–35 percent, in favor of B. The actual heights of the bars were generated by the following computation: At each choice occasion, the program calculated the value of the current choice distribution, (x_A, x_B) $(x_A + x_B = 1)$, by averaging the last seven choices (with an A choice interpreted as a "1" and a B choice as a "0"). The averaging rule generally placed more weight on the more recent of the seven choices. The vertical bar heights for an A or B choice were then given by two linear equations (illustrated in Figure 10.3): $v_A = 2.5 - 2x_A$; $v_B = 5 - 5x_B$. Thus, both alternatives exhibit a reduction in satisfaction per choice as choice frequency increases.

sent an improvement by the criterion of overall satisfaction? It is hard
to tell, from the information supplied in Figure 10.2. To answer that
question, one would have to calculate the satisfaction obtained on
average per single choice (of A or B), before and after t^0. Such an
average would lie somewhere between the satisfaction obtained from
A and B—specifically, it would be a weighted average of the two
quantities, with the weights corresponding to the relative fractions
of A and B choices.

Our central conjecture is that in such circumstances, people will
typically *not* calculate the overall utility level associated with a particular distribution of choices; the rule that they will use, instead, can
be described by means of the following two principles:

(I) *Value accounting:* Keep track of the average satisfaction (or *value*)
received per unit invested on each alternative (where the unit of
account might be a single-choice occasion, a time interval, or a
money unit).

(II) *Melioration:* Shift behavior (choice, time, money) to alternatives that
provide a higher per unit return, as calculated in I.

If this process continues, we will in the long run observe a stable
distribution of choices such that the accounted values (see Thaler,
1980, for an early consideration of value accounting) of both alternatives are equal, or, as the other possibility, that only one alternative
is chosen (i.e., that choice has stabilized at a corner solution).

The contrast between this equilibrium, and the optimal long-run
distribution of choice, can be clearly seen by plotting the relationship
between value and choice rate for the two alternatives, as is done in
Figure 10.3. The x axis represents a budget interval—the combined
rate of choosing both alternatives, presumed to be constant here; the
distance from a point on the axis to the left corner is the choice rate
on alternative A, while the distance to the right corner is the choice
rate on alternative B. The solid and unfilled squares are the accounted
or estimated average values for choosing A or B, if a person is choosing the two alternatives at rates indicated by the point on the x axis;
the value of each alternative decreases as it is chosen more often, in
keeping with the standard assumption of diminishing returns. If one
refers again to Figure 10.2, the choice rates and the values attached
to A and B before and after t^0 correspond to .8 and .35 on the x
axis in Figure 10.3, respectively (see captions for further details). The
remaining curve (solid diamonds) is a weighted average of the other
two curves, with the weights being proportional to the relative frac-

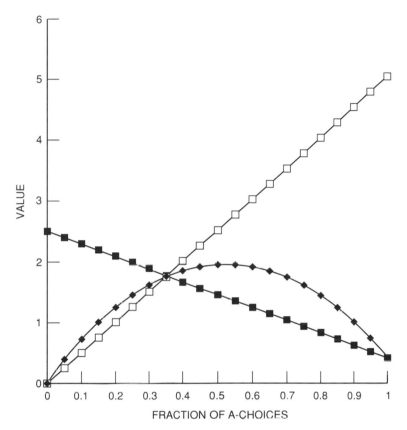

Figure 10.3. Value functions for alternatives A and B, plotted as a function of relative choice rate on alternative A. Solid squares trace the value of A, v_A = 2.5 − $2x_A$, open squares the value of B, v_B = 5 − $5x_B$ = $5x_A$ (because: x_B = 1 − x_A). The average value obtained per single choice is then a quadratic in x_A (shown by the diamond-shaped points):

$$x_A v_A + x_B v_B = x_A(2.5 - 2x_A) + (1 - x_A)5x_A.$$
$$= 7.5x_A - 7x_A^2.$$

tions of A and B choices. This curve represents *the average value obtained from a single choice, given the choice proportions on the horizontal axis*; it is, therefore, the "objective function" that a rational agent would wish to maximize.

The intersection of the two value curves, at .35 allocation to A, identifies the choice rates at which we would expect a person to stabilize, if he or she is following the rule described by principles I and II above. The choice rates at .35 are not optimal, and the person would suffer a modest loss in overall value or utility relative to the maximum that the situation makes potentially available.

Implicit in the model, then, are some assumptions about how a person collects, interprets, and uses information about satisfaction (utility) derived from alternative sources. Expressed in ordinary language, the model assumes that people are primarily able to assess how much they like specific activities or objects—whether they like a good book more than TV, sports more than classical music, Chinese or Italian food, etc. What they have difficulty with, however, is in assessing the relative standing of entire distributions of activities or objects—whether a 20–80 percent mix of reading and TV is preferred to a 50–50 percent mix, for example. The source of the difficulty is that pairs of distributions are not concurrently available for comparison, unlike the objects or activities over which the distributions are defined.

Melioration: An Experiment and a Formal Definition

The theory that we propose was originally conceived in order to explain findings in experiments on human and animal choice behavior. A recent experiment by Herrnstein, Prelec, and Vaughan (1986) provides an illustration of meliorating behavior leading to a suboptimal allocation. In the experiment, human subjects were instructed to complete a series of binary choices as quickly as possible. Every choice response yielded the same, fixed monetary reward, with probability 1.0. Each choice was followed by a pause, which lasted anywhere from 2 to 8 seconds, prior to the next opportunity to make a choice. The duration of the pause depended on the current choice, as well as on previous choices, in a manner that will be explained later. The subjects were not told of the relationship between choice and pause-duration; they were, however, given 100 practice trials, during which they could try to figure out "how the program works." Overall speed during the subsequent 10 minutes determined the pay for the experiment (which ranged from $3.50 to $6.50).

The pause that followed a choice of either alternative depended, in fact, on the distribution of choices over the previous ten trials (including the current trial). Specifically, alternative 1 exhibited *increasing* marginal cost, in that pause duration increased from a minimum of 2 seconds to a maximum of 6 seconds, in linear proportion to the number of 1-choices among the previous ten (see Figure 10.4). Alternative 2, on the other hand, exhibited *decreasing* marginal cost,

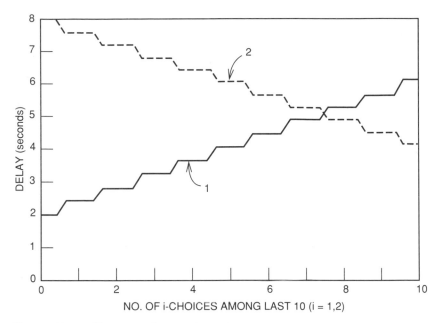

Figure 10.4.   Human subjects chose between two alternatives providing equal money rewards with probability 1.0. The time delay from one choice trial to the next was always 2 seconds shorter following a choice of alternative 1 than it was following a choice of alternative 2, but the delays were also an increasing linear function of the proportion of 1 choices in the preceding ten trials. The solid line shows the delays following a choice of 1 as a function of the proportion of 1-choices in the preceding ten trials; the dashed line shows the delays following a choice of 2 as a function of the proportion of 2-choices in the preceding ten trials (adapted from Herrnstein, Prelec, and Vaughan, 1986).

in that the pause duration decreased, from a maximum of 8 seconds to a minimum of 4 seconds, again in linear proportion to the number of 2-choices among the previous ten. For any mixture of prior choices, the pause after a 1-choice was 2 seconds shorter than that after a 2-choice. The optimal strategy, given perfect information about the structure of the problem, is nevertheless to choose the second alternative exclusively, thereby enduring a pause of 4 seconds each time.[2] The majority of our subjects, however, preferred alternative 1 (see Figure 10.5), with some individuals stabilizing virtually at exclusive

---

[2]We ignore here the "endgame" problem, which would make a few 1-choices at the end of the experiment advantageous. In fact, the subjects showed no evidence of having been influenced by the endgame contingency.

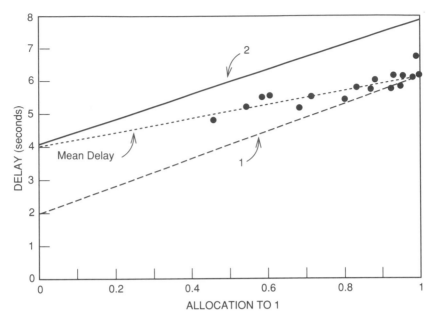

Figure 10.5. Showing the procedure represented in Figure 10.4, with the delays following choices as functions of the proportion of 1-choices in the preceding ten trials, and also the mean delay at each allocation. The seventeen filled points are for subjects who worked on the procedure for a single session, as described in the text (adapted from Herrnstein, Prelec, and Vaughan, 1986).

preference for it, which is the worst of all possible strategies, yielding a 6-second delay.

An intuitive explanation of this result can be constructed along the following lines. For any strategy that is entertained as a provisional "solution" to the problem, the 1-choice components of that strategy will produce pauses that are 2 seconds shorter, on average, than pauses that follow 2-choices. This differential in delay creates an impression that an even better strategy could be found, by increasing 1-choices at the expense of 2-choices. Melioration thus impels the subject toward 1-choices. Any such substitution, however, will increase *both* pauses, while keeping the 2-second differential intact. The only point that is immune to such incremental "improvements" is at exclusive preference for alternative 1, which as we have already noted, is the least successful strategy.

As with all laboratory experiments, we may wonder about how

hard the subjects are trying, and about how well the experiment elicits the strategies and decision processes used in natural settings. But, while little money was at stake, two other motivating factors amplified the financial incentives. First, delays—even of a few seconds—are quite annoying, independently of the economic value of time (any PC user will appreciate this). Second, the "puzzle" aspect of the experiment presents a challenge that is presumably satisfying to solve.

As for the general relevance of the finding, the procedure can readily be seen as a laboratory simplification of real-life economic situations. The decision maker's past choices interact with the reward structure. In natural settings, too, reward structures may be affected by economies of scale, by depletions of the reward resource, by time-dependent changes in the external environment and in motivational states, and the like, all of which, in turn, may be affected by past behavior. Choices of restaurant, entertainment, product brands, minor investments, or expenses (e.g., clothing, decorative jewelry, repairs to an automobile or television set) are typically made without proper regard to the way they may, in turn, affect the reward structure by having been chosen, but only in regard to their relative values when the choice is made.

The feedback relationship between choice and reward can be stimulated in the laboratory to any degree of complexity. The decision maker often confronts, in nature or laboratory, a "black box," as far as the feedback relation is concerned. The uncertainty he faces is of a particular sort: His behavior is driven by the environment, but the environment is, in turn, driven by his behavior. He has neither inside knowledge nor any more intuition about the black box than is provided from the different vantage points of the few choice allocations than are actually experienced.

The experimental setup is considerably simpler than the real world in many respects. First, there is a large number of trials (200 or more) with immediate feedback (differences of a second or so are easily detectable over these ranges of pause-duration), during which the underlying relation between behavior and its consequences is held constant. Second, unlike the real world, in the experiment there are no distractions from other unrelated problems, that would require simultaneous attention.

The results of this experiment, and those of many other comparable ones (cited later), prompted the following formal definition of the conditions that a choice distribution should satisfy, in order for it to be a possible end result of a meliorating process, as described in principles I (i.e., value accounting) and II (i.e., melioration). As stated in the Introduction, our intended area of application is to the class of individual decision problems in which the economically significant decision variable is in fact an aggregate of many temporally distinct choices, each of which has a small impact on the value of the aggregate variable. The basic variables, denoted by x_i, are the rates at which definable and repeatable economic actions, indexed by $i = 1, \ldots, n$, are taken over an observation interval. The total rate at which choices are made is constrained to a constant value, which is the combined or overall choice rate, k:

$$\Sigma_i x_i = k. \tag{1}$$

A complete *choice distribution* is the vector of individual rates, $\mathbf{x} = (\mathbf{x_1}, \ldots, \mathbf{x_n})$.

Value Accounting

As in standard economic analysis, we start by positing a global utility function, $U(x)$, that represents the individual's true welfare if his or her choice rates are stabilized at x. While it can be said that the individual is aware of $U(x)$ in the sense that he or she *experiences* the current value of $U(x)$, it is not assumed that the individual knows which x is optimal or, indeed, which of two distributions x and x' has higher utility. Instead, we assume that choice is driven by a complement of (continuous and differentiable) *value accounting functions* (or value functions, for short), $v_i(x)$, one for each alternative, which indicate how much value or satisfaction is perceived to be obtained (on average) from a single choice of type i, when the rates of choice are given by x. Most important, the value functions must account for all utility obtained, in the following sense:

$$U(x) = \Sigma_i x_i v_i(x). \tag{2}$$

Like the original utility function, $U(x)$, the value functions represent how tastes are determined by consumption; in addition to that, however, they also reflect the manner in which a person interprets the hedonic information that his or her body and imagination provide. The analogy with an accounting system is quite apt here, because an accounting system also decomposes a single dimension of value (overall profit) into the per-unit profitability of individual products (which then have to exhaust total profit, or loss, as in principle

II).[3] It follows that two individuals might share the same "tastes," in the sense of having the same—perhaps biologically determined—utility function $U(x)$, but might interpret these tastes differently, by adopting a different value accounting scheme. In that case, their choices (and "revealed preferences") would, of course, not coincide, in our theory. This extra measure of theoretical flexibility is an important aspect of our theory, because it allows us to explain apparent suboptimality in consumer choice as reflecting the accounting scheme or other specific biases or illusions in value-attribution.[4]

Melioration as an Externality

Given freedom to redistribute choice, a person will favor higher-valued activities at the expense of the lower-valued ones, in accordance with the meliorating principle given in II. The process of redistribution will then stop (if it stops at all) at a distribution where either *one* alternative absorbs all choice, or at a distribution where all surviving alternatives have equal value. In the experimental literature, this distribution is referred to as *matching*, inasmuch as all active alternatives yield equal returns per unit of behavior invested.[5] At a

[3]Faulhaber and Baumol (1988, p. 592) have observed that the influence of marginal analysis on business and government decision making has been minimal. Elsewhere, Baumol (1977) has listed several reasons why firms conduct their calculations in terms of average rather than marginal quantities, reasons that are relevant to our model of individual choice, as well. Perhaps the most important of these is the fact that average quantities can be obtained on the basis of information about the firm's current operating levels, while marginal quantities, intrinsically, "represent answers to hypothetical questions" (Baumol, 1977, pp. 34–35).

[4]This chapter does not deal explicitly with the way the melioration principle can make contact with some of the paradoxes of choice arising in particular accounting schemes, or what is also called the "framing" problem (e.g., Thaler, 1980; Tversky and Kahneman, 1981), but see Herrnstein and Mazur (1987) and Rachlin, Logue, Gibbon, and Frankel (1986) for examples.

[5]Several hundred experiments have confirmed the matching relation. A review of the empirical literature would be out of place here, so we instead quote the conclusion of such a review, from the *Stevens' Handbook of Experimental Psychology:* "The generality of the matching relation has been confirmed by a large number of different experiments. Such studies have shown matching, at least to a first approximation, with different species (pigeons, humans, monkeys, rats), different responses (keypecking, lever pressing, eye movements, verbal responses), and different reinforcers (food, brain stimulation, money, cocaine, verbal approval). Apparently, the matching relation is a general law of choice" (Williams, 1988, p. 178).

In the notation that has become standard for experimental psychology, matching would be expressed as:

$$\frac{B_1}{B_1 + B_2} = \frac{R_1}{R_1 + R_2}$$

minimum, then, the *distributions* that survive the meliorating process will have the following property (Herrnstein, 1970, Prelec, 1982):

> *Definition 1:* x^0 is a *matching* distribution if and only if all sampled alternatives enjoy equal value:

$$x_i^0 \text{ and } x_j^0 > 0 \text{ implies } v_i(x^0) = v_j(x^0).$$

These correspond to "first-order" conditions for equilibrium. Before we define supplementary "second-order" stability conditions, it may be useful to pause and compare Definition 1 with the first order conditions for an optimum. Noting that the utility function is a sum, $\Sigma_i x_i v_i(x)$, we can write out the marginal utilities (U_i) as:

$$U_i = v_i + \Sigma_j x_j v_{ij}(x), \tag{3}$$

where $v_{ij}(x)$ is the partial derivative of $v_i(x)$ with respect to x_j. The first order conditions for an interior optimum require equality of marginal utilities for the two alternatives. Comparing this with the equal value condition stated in Definition 1, we see that the meliorating individual maximizes utility, but with the second term in Equation (3) lopped off. Formally, the meliorating person ignores the cross effects of his or her choices; in that sense, the person is victim to an *externality*, but one that is internal to his or her own choices, in that he or she

---

where B_i and R_i respectively refer to the rates of responding and of reward collected on a pair of alternatives, $i = 1,2$. The rates are calculated as simply the number of events (responses, or rewards) over the duration of the experimental session. The equation implies also that $R_1/B_1 = R_2/B_2$, or that the same fraction of responses are rewarded on both schedules. It is in this latter sense that matching behavior equalizes the average benefit per response across the two alternatives.

Note that the matching relation here differs from "probability matching" (Bitterman, 1965; Simon, 1957), according to which agents distribute their behavior so that the relative proportion of choices matches the relative proportion of reward *probabilities*. That is, instead of the earlier equation for matching, probability matching would be stated as:

$$\frac{B_1}{B_1 + B_2} = \frac{(R_1/B_1)}{(R_1/B_1) + (R_2/B_2)},$$

because the ratio, R_i/B_i, is the probability of reward per single response. Herrnstein (1970) discusses some of the formal differences between the two principles of choice. Probability matching failed to be substantiated as a general principle of choice and will receive no further treatment here (but see Herrnstein, 1970; Herrnstein and Loveland, 1975).

does not take into account how a change in the choice rate will affect the values of the sampled alternatives.[6]

Stability

Matching distributions always do exist (exclusive preference for *any* alternative is, trivially, such a point). Among these, however, there will be some that are unstable, in the sense that a small—perhaps unintentional—increase in the choice rate for a particular alternative will cause that alternative to increase in value relative to the others, thus initiating a further increase in its choice rate. When there are only two alternatives, it is not difficult to decide which distributions are stable. Returning to Figure 10.3, we see that a small displacement from x^0 to the right, indicating more A choices, leads to reduction in the value of alternative A relative to that of alternative B, which will push choices back toward the equilibrium point. With two alternatives, then, the stable matching distributions are just those for which the v_1 curve intersects the v_2 curve from above (Herrnstein and Vaughan, 1980). Appendix A discusses stability for three or more alternatives.

The stability requirement in Definition 2, which is for the general case of n alternatives (see Appendix A), states that a brief period of experimentation with the new distribution will cause the alternatives that make up y to appear collectively worse, relative to the average value obtained from all sources.

> *Definition 2:* A distribution x^0 is a *stable matching equilibrium* (SME), if there exists a sufficiently small $\epsilon > 0$, such that for any other distribu-

---

[6]In brief, prices are introduced into the model by modifying the accounting assumptions so that the value of an alternative is understood to mean *value per money unit.* Melioration is then defined as the redistribution of purchases toward items that offer greater than average value per dollar. Letting p_i denote the price of alternative i, and $z_i \equiv p_i x_i$, the rate of expenditure on i, we define a new set of value functions (w_i) in terms of expenditure rather than choice rates:

$$w_i(z_1, \ldots, z_n) \equiv p_i^{-1} v_i(p_1^{-1} z_1, \ldots, p_n^{-1} z_n).$$

A stable matching equilibrium, defined with respect to the z_i, and satisfying the expenditure constraint, $\Sigma_i z_i = \Sigma_i p_i x_i$ = Income, is a set of expenditure rates such that the value obtained per dollar (i.e., the w_i value) is the same for all items that are purchased with positive frequency. The actual purchase rates can then be obtained from the expenditure rates by dividing each z_i by its own price.

tion y, and $y^\epsilon \equiv (1 - \epsilon)x^0 + \epsilon\, y$,

$$\Sigma\, y_i v_i(y^\epsilon) < \Sigma\, ((1 - \epsilon)x_i^0 + \epsilon\, y_i)v_i(y^\epsilon). \tag{4}$$

or, equivalently,

$$\Sigma\, y_i v_i(y^\epsilon) < \Sigma\, x_i^0 v_i(y^\epsilon)).$$

For example, if the disturbance of the SME is created by simple substitution of choices of alternative i at the expense of alternative j (that keeps the choice rates on all remaining alternatives constant), then the stability criterion in Equation (4) implies that the value of alternative i will initially dip below the value of alternative j. More complex choice perturbations are briefly discussed in Appendix A.

Although stable matching points are not necessarily optimal, they do exhibit a limited consistency with maximum-seeking behavior (proof for Property 2 in Appendix B; neither property is true for unstable matching points):

> Property 1: If the values are (distinct) constants, independent of choice rate, then the unique SME will be at the optimum, that is, the corner corresponding to the highest valued alternative.

> Property 2: If the value function for one alternative is replaced by a function that is slightly lower at all choice rates, then the choice rate on that alternative at the new interior SME will decrease.

As a result of these two properties, much of the behavior of a meliorating person will appear rational on the surface. When values do not change with consumption, the meliorator will eventually settle down at the best alternative (Property 1). Even if values are dependent on consumption, the person will "correctly" adjust consumption in response to a uniform improvement or deterioration in the quality of an alternative (Property 2). A more entertaining television program will fetch a larger audience; likewise, the information that cigarettes are harmful will cause people to reduce their smoking rate, on average, and so on. Anyone predisposed to believe in the rational choice model will find numerous such examples of consumer rationality to support his or her intuitions. However, these examples generally do not discriminate between optimization and weaker forms of reward-seeking behavior, such as melioration (a point originally made by Becker, 1962, in a different context).

Pathologies of Distributed Choice

Although the meliorating process has a flavor of rationality to it, the meliorating consumer will not invariably hone in on the optimal distribution, and, as we saw in the experiment discussed in the third section, may in some cases, settle at the worst possible distribution. Can we find similar examples of poor, yet stable, choice distributions *outside* the laboratory?

In our culture, we are frequently warned that certain patterns of consumption may diminish personal welfare. We agree about extreme examples, such as drug addiction, perhaps because of the clear testimony of former victims. But such obviously disastrous consumption patterns are surrounded by a penumbra of less clear cases. Television, for example, has been labeled addictive by some, as have gambling, shopping, athletic exercise, personal relationships, and even plain work (Becker and Murphy, 1988). If we broaden our concept of consumption to cover choice of lifestyle, or character, we would find a host of new examples of tenacious yet unsatisfying patterns of behavior, ranging from the traditional seven deadly sins (lust, wrath, avarice, pride, envy, sloth, gluttony), to those that modern psychiatry recognizes as personality defects (Ainslie, 1982).

The common element to all these phenomena is that they are instances of distributed choice, as we have defined the term. A person does not normally make a once-and-for-all decision to become an exercise junkie, a miser, a glutton, a profligate, or a gambler; rather, he or she slips into the pattern through a myriad of innocent, or almost innocent choices, each of which carries little weight. The person may, indeed, be the last one to recognize "how far he or she has slipped" and may take corrective action only when prompted by others.

In its most egregious form, the slippery slope of distributed choice leads to addiction, which is to say, a devastating level of overindulgence in some commodity or activity. To the extent that economic theory has addressed the problem of addictions, it has done so in essentially two ways. One approach, initiated by Stigler and Becker (1977) and further developed by Becker and Murphy (1988), builds a taste-changing mechanism into a global, multiperiod consumption function, so that the marginal substitutibilities among various commodities change as a function of consumption history. The demand functions that result from a once-and-for-all maximization of the intertemporal utility function will exhibit changes over time (in demand elasticities, e.g.) that mimic "harmful" and "beneficial" forms of addiction. Because tastes are fathered by a global utility function, each consumer, no matter what his or her consumption pattern, is still at a personal optimum, according to this theory, and would presumably benefit from a reduction in price, or increased general availability, of *any* commodity or substance, no matter how lethal by ordinary standards.

The second (but earlier) approach, associated ith the work of Pollack (1970) and von Weizsacker (1971), among others, assumes that the taste-change process (also called *habit formation*) is essentially opaque to the consumer. In von Weizsacker's two-period model, for example, a consumer myopically maximizes current-period preferences, which are themselves conditioned by consumption in the previous period. What is problematic about this work is that it draws a sharp separation between a type of taste change to which the person adjusts optimally, namely, the taste change that is embodied within the one-period preference-structure, and a second type of taste change, *across* periods, which the consumer ignores completely. It is not made clear in the theory why the process of taste change encountered in addiction should be treated differently from the ordinary taste change that occurs when, for example, one eats fish too many days in a row.

The meliorating theory of distributed choice, developed here, models choice as generically suboptimal whenever tastes (i.e., values, in our terminology) are affected by rate of consumption. What distinguishes more or less nonproblematic choices, such as allocating the food budget, from clearly problematic ones, like addictions, is not that the typical individual has a technique for maximizing the former, which he or she fails to apply to the latter, but, rather, that the value functions for the first category produce a matching point that is relatively efficient (in terms of maximizing utility), while those for the second category do not.

A particular class of inefficiencies in earning reward flow from an elementary property of meliorating equilibria, stated here. The proof is given in Appendix C.

Property 3: If the value of an alternative (or distribution) is increased by choosing it more often than called for by an interior SME, then choosing that alternative (or distribution) more often will also increase total utility.

Figure 10.6 illustrates this result for the two alternative case. Moving away from the equilibrium in the direction of more 1-choices will increase the value of 1. Because the equilibrium is stable, then this change in v_1 will have to be accompanied by an even greater positive

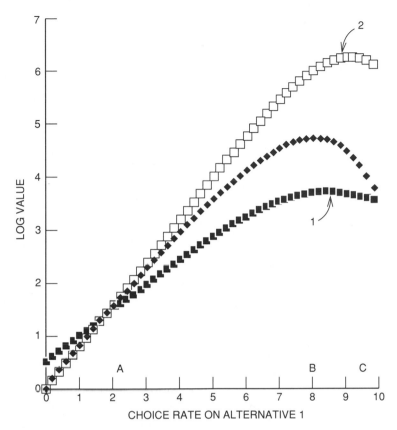

Figure 10.6. A hypothetical set of reward contingencies for two alternatives, showing value per unit of allocation for alternative 1 (filled squares) and alternative 2 (open squares), as functions of allocation to alternative 1. Average returns at each allocation are given by the diamond symbols. Over most of the range of allocations, 1 earns increasing returns with consumption, while 2 earns decreasing returns with consumption. The letter A indicates the stable matching point; B, the maximally rewarding allocation; C, an unstable matching point. Notice also that if the value of the second alternative is uniformly reduced (which would be represented by a downward shift in the entire value function for the second alternative), the stable matching point would slide to the right and *upward*, indicating an improvement in overall utility.

change in v_2, so that behavior is pushed back to equilibrium. Because both alternatives increase in value, total utility must increase with increased allocation to 1.

There are two possible interpretations of this result.

Case I: If alternative 1 represents an activity whose value intrinsically depends on its own rate of choice, and the value is increasing with rate (so that $v_i(x) = v_i(x_i)$, $v_i' > 0$), then the condition of inefficiency stated earlier is satisfied, and the activity is underconsumed at a stable meliorating equilibrium. This type of value function would be characteristic of skilled activities (such as music or sports) that provide greater satisfaction if maintained at higher rates.

Case II: The second interpretation of Figure 10.6 is that alternative 1 does indeed have the usual property of diminishing marginal value with consumption, but that this effect is swamped by a negative impact of alternative 2 on the value of 1. Consuming the second alternative, in other words, destroys the satisfaction produced by engaging in alternatives complementary to it. This seems to correspond to our understanding of harmful addiction, as a process in which consumption of the addictive substance casts a shadow over other pleasures. (A more complete account of addiction in the melioration framework is presented in Chapter 13, this volume.) Students of opiate addiction often observe, for example, that addicts lose their appetite for food, making simple malnutrition one of the primary health risks for addicts. In other words, as the consumption level for v_2 (e.g., heroin) rises, the value of v_1 (e.g., food) declines. Or, as another example, the habitual heavy use of alcohol erodes the gratifications to be had from family, work, and even ordinary physical pleasures as one's health deteriorates.

The sharply diminishing value of v_2 with its own consumption is likewise consistent with the phenomenology of addictive substances. For the usual addictive substance, high rates of consumption typically lead to the development of "tolerance," which is to say, a shrinking hedonic harvest from a given quantity of the commodity. Solomon and Corbit's (1974) opponent-process theory of acquired motivation describes how the positive pleasures at a low rate of consumption are transformed into the avoidance of the agony of withdrawal at high rates. The remaining pleasures are then minimal.

At the SME point (i.e., A) in Figure 10.6, the value of the addictive alternative has itself almost evaporated, that is, it has been reduced to the value level of the complementary activity. In the case of overeating, for example, this state describes a person who eats at a more or less continuous rate, not allowing true hunger to develop. As long as food is readily available, such a person would not experience eating as especially pleasurable (a finding that has some support in the research literature on obesity; see Schachter, 1971).

An interesting aspect of the configuration in Figure 10.6 is that a reduction in the v_2 curve, which may be interpreted as the effect of some nonfinancial penalty, hindrance, or a substitution of an inferior commodity for the original alternative 2 (like methadone for heroin, e.g.), would slide the SME to the right and improve individual welfare.[7]

The common element to both Cases I and II is an underconsumption of the first alternative; the difference is that in Case I, the suboptimality is accounted for by a peculiarity of that same alternative, namely, its increasing returns to consumption, while in Case II, the culprit is alternative 2, because it destroys the value of the complementary activity. Using the terminology of Stigler and Becker, we would say that meliorating persons generally underinvest in beneficial addictions, for which training and exposure build up "enjoyment capital" and overinvest in harmful addictions, for which enjoyment capital depletes rapidly.[8]

Time discounting is often invoked as an explanation of this same pattern of over- and underinvestment: A person with a sufficiently high discount rate would simply not care about acquiring the skills necessary to enjoy the so-called beneficial addictions, nor would he or she worry about the future penalties of harmful addiction. Unusually sharp time preference may be a contributing factor to addiction, but it is conceptually distinct from the melioration process per se. We elaborate with Case II; a comparable story may be told for Case I.

The psychological remoteness of the cost of a single drug-consumption episode is compounded by two separate factors. First, the cost of an increased tolerance level is delayed in time compared to the "benefit," which may be instantaneous; second, the impact of that single episode on the tolerance level is small, and probably diffi-

[7]The effect of a *financial* penalty, such as a tax, is ambiguous, because of the income effect (which would manifest itself through a reduction in the length of the x axis in Figure 10.6).

[8]Stigler and Becker's choice of "beneficial" and "harmful" as labels is quite revealing, given that their theory does not allow for any suboptimality in consumption patterns. Melioration theory explains why the errors people make in executing an optimal plan cumulate in different directions for so-called beneficial and harmful addictions. Maximization theory, which allows no systematic errors, does not.

cult to imagine even if one was perfectly informed. The former is the time-discounting perspective on addiction; the latter is the perspective peculiar to distributed choices. The total cost of the episode, one should remember, is the aggregate, appropriately discounted, future reduction in pleasure caused by the incremental shift in tolerance. Even in the absence of time discounting, we claim, people would still be vulnerable to addiction if they were unable to correctly assess and compute such costs.

Although important, discounting does not seem to be a sufficient explanation of addiction, which seems, to us, often to be more a process of invidious slippage than a cool decision adventitiously supported by a high discount rate. Educational materials designed to discourage addiction typically do not work on altering time preference, but on persuading people to think of addiction in an all-or-nothing decision. We are warned that we cannot maintain a reasonable or moderate rate of consumption, that it is a case of all or nothing at all. The task of the educator is, in short, to get the person to act as if the choice is a one-time event, rather than distributed. We will not discuss here how, within the melioration framework, it is possible to avoid or escape from addiction, beyond noting that the issues are discussed elsewhere (Herrnstein, 1990; Prelec and Herrnstein, 1991; Herrnstein, 1990, Chapter 13, this volume).

The model depicted in Figure 10.6 is a minimal theory of pathological choice; it yields a final common path for behavior. The value functions may have the shape they have in Figure 10.6 for many reasons. Exogenous or endogenous chemical agents may alter reward centers in the brain in a particular way, one may learn how to enjoy ("acquire a taste for") a certain class of rewards, different rewards may have different time horizons associated with them, and so on. But if, for whatever reason, the resulting structure conforms to that outlined here, the result is a pathology of choice.

Concluding Remarks

The notion that human behavior falls short of the ideal is accepted by us all at the level of common sense. For this reason, too, we all have certain favored explanations about the most prevalent causes of inefficient or dramatically suboptimal behavior—intuitions that sometimes give rise to full-blown theories. In this concluding section of the chapter, we would like to clarify the relation of our approach to some other approaches to suboptimal choice behavior.

Satisficing

According to the satisficing concept (Simon, 1955, 1956), economic agents fail to maximize utility perfectly but do maximize "well enough," as defined by their own levels of aspiration. Within our theory, agents may sometimes maximize, but, in other circumstances, their choices may be suboptimal, far worse than any conceivable level they may originally aspire to. For any given accounting scheme, the melioration principle contains within itself a specification of which circumstances produce maximization and which do not. One could say that the critical difference between melioration and satisficing is that melioration decribes an endogenously changing aspiration level, which is the mean value obtained from all sources at a choice point, while satisficing assumes an aspiration level that is externally set, typically by a larger institutional context.

Excessive Discounting ("Myopia")

The behavior of a person with a high discount rate would in some respects resemble that of a meliorizer, in that he or she would on each occasion choose the alternative that offered the highest value. Such a person, however, should shift the optimal allocation as the time scale over which the choices are made was systematically reduced. Our theory, in contrast, makes explicit reference to time only insofar as it distinguishes between distributed choice and nondistributed choice (see first section). Given that choice is distributed, it makes the same prediction irrespective of whether the choices are made once a week, or once every few minutes.[9]

Ignorance or Incomplete Learning

A person who believes mistakenly that values remain constant, independent of choice rate, would behave exactly like a meliorizer. However, this does not imply that melioration is necessarily produced by the assumption of constancy. It is possible that a person is aware of the relationship between choice rates and values, but that he or she

[9]Certainly, the results of Herrnstein, Prelec, and Vaughan described earlier cannot be attributed to time discounting in the range of times involved in, say, overeating or undersaving, as the entire experiment for a subject did not last much more than 20 minutes, and the impacts of choices within the procedure were deferred for time periods less than a minute.

sees no reason to doubt that a meliorationlike process is nevertheless an efficient behavioral choice rule. When people are asked to imagine choosing among alternatives whose values interact in a particular way with choice rate, and they have been told what this interaction is, their answers typically display the same kinds of suboptimalities that are observed in experimental simulations of these situations (see examples in Herrnstein, 1990; Herrnstein and Mazur, 1987).

Taste Change

The change in values in response to changes in choice rate can often be thought of as a matter of taste formation. Inasmuch as this change is a key element in the present account of suboptimality, it may seem that we are proposing just another version of a taste formation theory, in which ad hoc assumptions about taste have been tailored to substantiate a theory. In the standard utility-maximization theory, changes in the marginal rates of substitution, embodied in indifference curves, constitute an implicit theory of taste formation in response to consumption levels. Indeed, any theory that includes a concept of subjective utility or value must infer the subjective entity, which is in principle not directly observable, from some observable aspect of behavior. The difference between the present theory and the standard one is, not in the fact that it postulates taste changes, but in the hypothesis it uses to connect subjective utility or value to behavior (Prelec, 1983). The present theory employs the hypothesis of melioration, rather than maximization. It is this difference, rather than the particular suppositions about taste changes, that sets the theories apart.

The notion of melioration echoes ideas at other levels of analysis (Vaughan and Herrnstein, 1987). At a more inclusive level, consider an n person, noncooperative game (Schelling, 1978). We expect each player to adopt the strategy most favorable to him or her, which, because of various externalities, may not be the optimal distribution of strategies for the players as a group. At a lower level of analysis, evolutionary biologists have been alerted to the importance of "frequency-dependent selection," the recognition that the selective fitness of a gene may depend on its proportion in a population. Genes in competition are, in other words, subject to the effects of externalities. As a result, the equilibrium points for genetic competition may not coincide with the optimum for the species as a whole (e.g., Dawkins, 1976).

What is new here is the suggestion that the familiar notion of externalities producing nonoptimal equilibria applies to the analysis of individual human (or animal) behavior. One could say that the difference between maximization and melioration is that melioration contains a weaker concept of personal identity than maximization. Within the melioration framework, the alternative behaviors are in competition with each other, vying for the organism's investment of time, effort, etc. Beyond the dynamics of this competition itself, no one is in charge. Within the maximization framework, the alternatives are, in principle, so perfectly articulated with each other that they lose their individuality. Only the utility of the whole choice bundle matters, rather than the utility attached to its constituents, as in the melioration framework.

It would be possible to develop theories that are more explicit about the dynamic learning process that brings the subject to an equilibrium near the matching distribution;[10] we have not attempted to do so here, for three reasons. One, we do not know much about how equilibria are reached, and, in fact, the process of entertaining and rejecting different distributions that people go through may be quite disorderly, and may vary a great deal from one person to another. Two, our primary goal here has been to fashion an explanation for choice that refers to the same variables as the standard choice model does, and that has approximately the same degree of complexity and rigor. Finally, whether the correct principle of equilibrium is maximization or melioration (or some other), a full account of behavior must, in time, include a theory of learning. It seems economical to us to decide first on which equilibrium we would like to explain in our learning theory, and then try to do so, rather than vice versa.

•

The authors are grateful to Jerry Green, Ronald Heiner, Vijay Krishna, George Loewenstein, Howard Rachlin, Richard Thaler, William Vaughan, Jr., and Richard Zeckhauser for valuable discussion of the ideas presented here. The concept of melioration itself was initially formulated in collaboration with Vaughan (see Herrnstein and Vaughan, 1980), and some of the most striking experimental substantiations of it are in his experiments (e.g., Vaughan, 1981). We owe thanks, too, to the Russell Sage Foundation for providing us with support and an environment conducive to developing these ideas.

[10] For example, the results of Taylor and Jonker (1978) on population dynamics in evolutionary games could be adapted easily to our problem.

References

Ainsle, G. "Specious Reward: A Behavioral Theory of Impulsiveness and Impulse Control." *Psychological Bulletin* 82 (1975): 463–509.

———. "A Behavioral Economic Approach to the Defense Mechanisms: Freud's Energy Theory Revisited." *Social Science Information* 21 (1982): 735–779.

———. "Beyond Microeconomics: Conflict Among Interests in a Multiple Self as a Determinant of Value." In J. Elster (ed.). *The Multiple Self.* Cambridge, UK: Cambridge University Press, 1986.

Baumol, W.J. *Economic Theory and Operations Analysis.* Englewood Cliffs, NJ: Prentice-Hall, 1977.

Becker, G.S. "Irrational Behavior and Economic Theory." *Journal of Political Economy* 70 (1962): 1–13.

———, and K. M. Murphy. "A Theory of Rational Addiction." *Journal of Political Economy* 96 (1988): 675–700.

Bitterman, M.E. "Phyletic Differences in Learning." *American Psychologist* 20 (1965): 396–410.

Dawkins, R. *The Selfish Gene.* Oxford, UK: Oxford University Press, 1976.

Deaton, A., and J. Muellbauer. *Economics and Consumer Behavior.* Cambridge, UK: Cambridge University Press, 1980.

Elster, J. *Ulysses and the Sirens.* Cambridge, UK: Cambridge University Press, 1984.

Faulhaber, G.R., and W.J. Baumol. "Economists and Innovators: Practical Products of Theoretical Research. *Journal of Economic Literature* 26 (1988): 577–600.

Herrnstein, R.J. "On the Law of Effect." *Journal of the Experimental Analysis of Behavior* 13 (1970): 243–266.

———. "Rational Choice Theory: Necessary but Not Sufficient. *American Psychologist* 45 (1990): 356–367.

———, and J.E. Mazur. Making up our Minds: A New Model of Economic Behavior. *The Sciences* November/December (1987): 40–47.

———, D. Prelec, and W. Vaughan, Jr. "An Intra-personal Prisoners' Dilemma." Paper presented at the IX Symposium on Quantitative Analysis of Behavior: Behavioral Economics, Harvard University, 1986.

———, and W. Vaughan, Jr. "Melioration and Behavioral Allocation." In J.E.R. Staddon (ed.). *Limits to Action: The Allocation of Individual Behavior* New York: Academic Press, 1980, pp. 143–176.

Pollack, R.A. "Habit Formation and Dynamic Demand Functions." *Journal of Political Economy* 78 (1970): 745–763.

Prelec, D. "Matching, Maximizing, and the Hyperbolic Reinforcement Feedback Function." *Psychological Review* 89 (1982): 189–230.

———. "The Empirical Claims of Maximization Theory: A Reply to Rachlin, and to Kagel, Battalio, and Green." *Psychological Review* 90 (1983): 385–389.

———, and R.J. Herrnstein. "Preferences or Principles, Alternative Guidelines for Choice." in R.J. Zeckhauser (ed.). *Strategy and Choice*, Cambridge, MA: 1991, pp. 319–340.

Rachlin, H., A.W. Logue, J. Gibbon, and M. Frankel. "Cognition and Behavior in Studies of Choice." *Psychological Review* 93 (1986): 33–45.

Schachter, S. "Some Extraordinary Facts about Obese Humans and Rats." *American Psychologist* 26 (1971): 129–144.

Schelling, T.C. *Micromotives and Macrobehavior.* New York: Norton, 1978.

———. "The Intimate Contest for Self-Command." *The Public Interest* No. 60 (Summer 1980): 94–118.

Simon, H.A. "A Behavioral Model of Rational Choice." *Quarterly Journal of Economics* 59 (1955): 99–118.

———. "Rational Choice and the Structure of the Environment." *Psychological Review* 63 (1956): 129–138.

———. *Models of Man: Social and Rational; Mathematical Essays on Rational Human Behavior.* New York: Wiley, 1957.

Solomon, R.L. and J.D. Corbit. "An Opponent-Process Theory of Motivation: I. Temporal Dynamics of Affect. *Psychological Review* 81 (1974): 119–145.

Stigler, G., and G. Becker. "De gustibus non est disputandum." *American Economic Review* 67 (1977): 76–90.

Taylor, P.D., and L.B. Jonker. "Evolutionarily Stable Strategies and Game Dynamics." *Mathematical Bioscience* 40 (1978): 145–156.

Thaler, R. "Toward a Positive Theory of Consumer Choice." *Journal of Economic Behavior and Organization* 1 (1980): 39–60.

———, and H.M. Shefrin. "An Economic Theory of Self-Control." *Journal of Political Economy* 89 (1981): 392–410.

Tversky, A., and D. Kahneman. "The Framing of Decisions and the Psychology of Choice." *Science* 211 (1981): 453–458.

Vaughan, W., Jr. "Melioration, Matching, and Maximization." *Journal of the Experimental Analysis of Behavior* 36 (1981): 141–149.

———, and R.J. Herrnstein. "Stability, Melioration, and Natural Selection." In L. Green and J.H. Kagel (eds.). *Advances in Behavioral Economics,* vol. 1, Norwood, NJ: Ablex, 1987, pp. 185–215.

Weizsacker, C.C. von. "Notes on Endogenous Change of Tastes." *Journal of Economic Theory* 3 (1971): 345–372.

Williams, B.A. "Reinforcement, Choice, and Response Strength." In R. C. Atkinson, R.J. Herrnstein, G. Lindzey, and R.D. Luce (eds.). *Stevens' Handbook of Experimental Psychology,* vol. 2 New York: Wiley, 1988, pp. 167–244.

Winston, G.C. "Addiction and Backsliding." *Journal of Economic Behavior and Organization* 1 (1980): 295–324.

Appendix A

Stability with Three or More Alternatives

Let us define the value of an entire alternative choice rate distribution y (alternative, i.e., to the current actual distribution x) as

$$v(y,x) = \Sigma_i(y_i/k)v_i(x), \qquad (A1)$$

which is a weighted average of values v_i, with the weights being proportional to the fraction of choices (y_i/k) allocated to alternative i in the new distribution. If the direction of disturbance consists of an increase in the rate of just one alternative, say the first one, then $y = (k,0, \ldots, 0)$, and $v(y,x) = v_1(x)$. Observe, also, that $v(x,x)$, being the average value obtained per single choice from all sources, is the objective function that a rational individual should maximize (i.e., it is proportional to $U(x) = kv(x,x)$).

Our definition of stability is perhaps less complex than it appears initially. Suppose, to set up a concrete example, that the alternatives in the choices set are whether to (1) watch TV, (2) go for a stroll, or (3) read a book, each day after dinner, and that 1 month is a sufficient time period for the values of the three activities to stabilize ($k = 30$). The current equilibrium distribution is $x^0 = (10,10,10)$, indicating that the person divides evenings equally among the three possibilities. Now, suppose that the person decides to replace TV entirely by reading (so that the alternative distribution is $y = (0,10,20)$). After 6 days of this regimen, the relevant choice distribution, over the 1-month window, has shifted to something like $y^\epsilon = (8,10,12)$ ($\epsilon = .2$), at which point the experiment will be judged unsuccessful (by Definition 2) if and only if $v(y_1 y^\epsilon) < v(y^\epsilon, y^\epsilon)$. After expanding in terms of v_1, v_2, and v_3 [from Equation (A1)], we see that this will be true if:

$$.33v_2 + .67v_3 < .8(.33v_1 + .33v_2 + .33v_3) + .2(.33v_2 + .67v_3),$$

or $.33v_3 < .33v_1$, which is to say,

$$v_1(8,10,12) > v_3(8,10,12),$$

that is, if TV starts to look more enjoyable than reading at the slightly shifted distribution $(8,10,12)$.

What would the stability test be if the person embarked upon a reduction in TV, while keeping the other two activities in constant proportion? In that case, $y = (0,15,15)$, and $y^\epsilon = (8, 11,11)$, for $\epsilon = .2$. After some algebra, Equation 4 (see page 250) reduces to the condition:

$$v_1(8,11,11) > .5(v_2(8,11,11) + v_3(8,11,11)),$$

or that TV has greater value than the average of the other two activities.

Appendix B

Proof of Property 2

Let x^0 be the original SME, and suppose that the value of alternative 1 is diminished, from $v_1(x)$ to $v_1^*(x) = v_1(x) - \delta(x)$, where $\delta(x)$ is a small but strictly positive quantity. If one assumes that the values of the other alternatives are not changed, $(v_i^*(x) = v_i(x), i \geq 2)$, a new SME will appear at the slightly shifted position, y^ϵ. Evaluating $v(y^\epsilon, y^\epsilon)$ at that point,

$$v(y^\epsilon, y^\epsilon) = v^*(y^\epsilon, y^\epsilon) + \delta(x)y_1^\epsilon \qquad \text{(by definition of } v^*)$$

$$= v^*(x^0, y^\epsilon) + \delta(x)y_1^\epsilon \qquad \text{(because: } v_i^*(y^\epsilon) = v_j^*(y^\epsilon), \text{ all } i, j)$$

$$= (v(x^0, y^\epsilon) - \delta(x)x_1^0) + \delta(x)y_1^\epsilon \text{ (by definition of } v^*)$$

$$= v(x^0, y^\epsilon) + \delta(x)(y_1^\epsilon - x_1^0).$$

Consequently,

$$\delta(x)(y_1^\epsilon - x_1^0) = v(y^\epsilon, y^\epsilon) - v(x^0, y^\epsilon).$$

Because x^0 is a stable equilibrium, $v(x^0, y^\epsilon) > v(y^\epsilon, y^\epsilon)$, for y^ϵ sufficiently close to x^0 [Equations (4) and (A1)], which implies then that the reduction in the value of 1 has caused the choice rate on 1 to go down $(y_1^\epsilon - x_1^0 < 0)$.

Appendix C

Proof of Property 3

Let x^0 denote the original SME point, y the new distribution, and y^ϵ a small reallocation of choice, to $(1 - \epsilon)x^0 + \epsilon y$. Then,

$$U(y^\epsilon) = kv(y^\epsilon, y^\epsilon)$$

$$> kv(y, y^\epsilon) \quad \text{[by stability, Equation (5)]}$$

$$> kv(y, x^0) \quad \text{(because the value of } y \text{ is presumed to increase as it is chosen more often, at } y^\epsilon)$$

$$= kv(x^0, x^0) \quad \text{(because } x^0 \text{ is an interior SME, } v_i(x^0) = v_j(x^0), \text{ all } i, j)$$

$$= U(x^0).$$

· 11 ·

The Role of Moral Sentiments in the Theory of Intertemporal Choice

ROBERT H. FRANK

T HE standard neoclassical theory of intertemporal choice begins with the assumption that people are rational, which means that they act as if trying to maximize a discounted flow of utility. At least two types of rationality are distinguished according to the types of motives people hold (see Parfit, 1984). Under the "present-aim" standard, persons are rational if they are efficient in the pursuit of whatever aims they happen to hold at the moment of action. No attempt is made, under this standard, to assess the rationality of the aims themselves. The competing concept of rationality is called the *self-interest* standard. It assumes at the outset that people's motives are egoistic. Motives like altruism, fidelity to principle, a desire for justice, and the like are simply not considered under the self-interest standard.

In textbook accounts of rational choice, economists generally embrace the present-aim standard. Tastes are given exogenously, we say, and there is no logical basis for questioning them. In Bentham's words, a taste for poetry is no less valid than a taste for pushpins.

The difficulty with the present-aim standard is what George Stigler might call the "crankcase oil" problem. If we see a person drink the used crankcase oil from a car, and he or she then writhes in agony and dies, we can assert that the person must have *really* liked crankcase oil. (Why else would the person have drunk it?) Virtually any behavior, no matter how bizarre, can be "explained" after the fact by simply assuming a taste for it. Thus, the chief attraction of the present-aim model turns out also to be its biggest liability. Because it allows us to explain everything, we end up explaining nothing.

With this difficulty in mind, most economists assume some version of the self-interest standard of rationality in their actual research.[1] This approach has generated many powerful insights into human behavior. It explains, for example, why divorce rates are higher in states with liberal welfare benefits; why car pools form in the wake of increases in gasoline prices; why the members of "service" organizations are more likely to be real estate salespersons, dentists, chiropractors, insurance agents, and others with something to sell than to be postal employees or airline pilots; and so on.

Yet apparent contradictions abound. Travelers on interstate highways leave tips for waitresses they will never see again. Participants in bloody family feuds seek revenge even at ruinous cost to themselves. People walk away from profitable transactions whose terms they believe to be "unfair." The British spend vast sums to defend the desolate Falklands, even though they have little empire left against which to deter future aggression. In these and countless other ways, people do not seem to be maximizing utility functions of the egoistic sort.

In this essay, I will argue that egoistic persons perform poorly relative to less egoistic persons in a variety of important circumstances involving intertemporal choice.[2] More specifically, I will argue that moral sentiments enable people to solve two types of time-inconsistency problems. First, they help people make advantageous commitments in cases, such as one-shot prisoner's dilemmas, where mere threats or promises would not be credible. And second, they help people avoid the temptation to break commitments that are in their material interests to keep, such as those people make in repeated prisoner's dilemmas. To forestall any possible misunderstanding, I stress at the outset that it is not my claim that moral sentiments evolved exclusively for their capacity to solve time-inconsistency problems.

---

[1] Economists and other rational choice theorists who have taken a broader view of the utility function include Gauthier (1985), Schelling (1978), Akerlof (1983), Hirshleifer (1984), Sen (1977, 1985), Arrow (1975), Leibenstein (1976), Scitovsky (1976), Harsanyi (1980), Phelps (1975), Collard (1978), Rubin and Paul (1979), and Smith (1759).

[2] The material in this essay is drawn from my 1988 book.

Moral Sentiments as Commitment Devices

Nonegoistic motives can be accounted for within the framework of economic models if we view tastes not as ends in themselves but as means for attaining other material objectives (Frank, 1987, 1988). The role of nonegoistic motives derives from the fact that we face important problems that cannot be solved by purely selfish actors. The common feature of these problems is that they require us to make commitments to behave in ways that may later prove contrary to our interests.

Schelling (1960) provides a vivid illustration of this class of problems. He describes a kidnapper who suddenly gets cold feet. He wants to set his victim free, but is afraid he will go to the police. In return for his freedom, the victim gladly promises not to do so. The problem, however, is that both realize it will no longer be in the victim's interest to keep this promise once he is free. And so the kidnapper reluctantly concludes that he must kill him.

Schelling suggests the following way out of the dilemma: "If the victim has committed an act whose disclosure could lead to blackmail, he may confess it; if not, he might commit one in the presence of his captor, to create a bond that will ensure his silence" (1960, pp. 43, 44). The blackmailable act serves here as a *commitment device,* something that provides the victim with an incentive to keep his promise. Keeping it will still be unpleasant for him once he is freed, but clearly less so than not being able to make a credible promise in the first place.

In everyday economic and social interaction, we repeatedly encounter commitment problems like the one confronting Schelling's kidnapper and victim. My claim is that specific emotions act as commitment devices that help resolve these dilemmas.

Consider a person who threatens to retaliate against anyone who harms him. For his threat to deter, others must believe he will carry it out. But if others know that the costs of retaliation are prohibitive, they will realize the threat is empty. Unless, of course, they believe they are dealing with someone who simply *likes* to retaliate. Such a person may strike back even when it is not in his material interests to do so. But if he is known in advance to have that preference, he is not likely to be tested by aggression in the first place.

Similarly, a person who is known to "dislike" an unfair bargain can credibly threaten to walk away from one, even when it is in her narrow interest to accept it. By virtue of being known to have this preference, she becomes a more effective negotiator.

Consider, too, the person who "feels bad" when he cheats. These feelings can accomplish for him what a rational assessment of self-interest cannot—namely, they can cause him to behave honestly even when he knows he could get away with cheating. And if others realize he feels this way, they will seek him as a partner in ventures that require trust.

Being known to experience certain emotions enables us to make commitments that would otherwise not be credible. The clear irony here is that this ability, which springs from a *failure* to pursue self-interest, confers genuine advantages. Granted, following through on these commitments will always involve avoidable losses—not cheating when there is a chance to, retaliating at great cost even after the damage is done, and so on. The problem, however, is that being unable to make credible commitments will often be even more costly. Confronted with the commitment problem, an opportunistic person fares poorly.

By themselves, nonegoistic emotions are not sufficient to solve the commitment problem. Granted, strong feelings of guilt *are* enough to prevent a person from cheating. And the satisfying feeling someone gets from having done the right thing is, in a very real sense, its own reward. But the challenge—for economists, biologists, philosophers, and others concerned with human motivation—is to explain how such sentiments might have survived in the material world. We can't eat moral sentiments. Given that these sentiments often cause people to incur substantial avoidable costs, they must also confer some sort of compensating advantage in order to have persisted.

The potential gain from being honest is to cooperate with others who are also honest. In order for the noncheater to benefit in material terms, others must thus be able to recognize her as such, and she, in turn, must be able to recognize other noncheaters. The impulse to seek revenge is likewise counterproductive unless others have some way of anticipating that one has it. The person in whom this sentiment resides unrecognized will fail to deter potential predators. And if one is going to be victimized anyway, it is better *not* to desire revenge. For similar reasons, a sense of justice and the capacity to love will not yield material payoffs unless they can be somehow communicated clearly to others.

A strategically important emotion can be communicated credibly only if it is accompanied by a signal that is at least partially insulated from direct control. Many observable physical symptoms of emotional arousal satisfy this requirement. Posture, the rate of respiration, the pitch and timbre of the voice, perspiration, facial muscle tone and expression, movement of the eyes, and a host of other

	X COOPERATE	DEFECT
COOPERATE	4 for each	0 for Y 6 for X
Y		
DEFECT	6 for Y 0 for X	2 for each

Figure 11.1. Monetary payoffs in a joint venture.

readily observable physical symptoms vary systematically with a person's affective condition. In most people, at least some of these symptoms are almost completely insulated from voluntary control (see Ekman, 1985). A blush may reveal a lie and cause much embarrassment in the moment, but in circumstances that require trust, there can be great advantage in being known to be a blusher.

Illustration: The Cheating Problem

The role of nonegoistic motives as commitment devices can be seen more clearly with the help of an example of a simple ecology in which egoists are pitted against nonegoists in a struggle to survive. The commitment problem they face is the classic prisoner's dilemma.[3] The specific version of it is a joint venture, the monetary payoffs from which are given by the entries in Figure 11.1. These payoffs depend on the particular combination of strategies chosen by the participants. Note that X gets a higher payoff by defecting, no matter what Y does, and the same is true for Y. If X believes Y will behave in a self-interested way, he will predict that Y will defect. And if only to protect himself, he will likely feel compelled to defect as well. When both defect, each gets only a 2-unit payoff. The frustration, as in all dilemmas of this sort, is that both could have easily done much better. Had they cooperated, each would have gotten a 4-unit payoff.

Now suppose we have not just Y and X but a large population. Pairs of people again form joint ventures, and the relationship be-

---

[3]I should stress here that the prisoner's dilemma is but one specific form taken by the problems of cooperation and coordination that arise in economic and social interaction.

tween behavior and payoffs for the members of each pair is again as given in Figure 11.1. Suppose further that everyone in the population is of one of two types—cooperator or defector. A cooperator is someone who, possibly through intensive cultural conditioning, has developed a genetically endowed capacity to experience a moral sentiment that predisposes him to cooperate. A defector is someone who either lacks this capacity or has failed to develop it.

In this scheme, cooperators are hardcore altruists in the sense that they refrain from cheating even when there is no possibility of being detected. Viewed in the narrow context of the choice at hand, this behavior is clearly contrary to their material interests. Defectors, by contrast, are pure opportunists. They always make whatever choice will maximize their personal payoff. The task here is to determine what will happen when people from these two groups are thrown into a survival struggle against one another.

For concreteness, suppose that sympathy is the emotion that motivates cooperation, and that there is an observable symptom present in people who experience this emotion (perhaps a "sympathetic manner"). Defectors lack this observable symptom; or, more generally, they may try to mimic it, but fail to get it exactly right.

If the two types could be distinguished with certainty at a glance, defectors would be doomed. Cooperators would simply interact with one another, thus earning a higher payoff than the defectors. But suppose it requires effort to inspect the symptom of cooperation. For concreteness, suppose inspection costs 1 unit. For people who pay this cost, the veil is lifted: Cooperators and defectors can be distinguished with 100 percent accuracy. For those who don't pay the 1-unit cost of scrutiny, the two types are perfectly indistinguishable.

Now consider the problem facing a cooperator who faces the payoffs given in Figure 11.1 and is trying to decide whether to pay the cost of scrutiny. If she pays it, she can be assured of interacting with another cooperator, and will thus get a payoff of $4 - 1 = 3$ units. If she does not, her payoff is uncertain. Cooperators and defectors will look exactly alike to her, and she must take her chances. If she happens to interact with another cooperator, she will get 4 units. But if she interacts with a defector, she will get zero. Whether it makes sense to pay the 1-unit cost of scrutiny thus depends on the likelihood of these two outcomes.

If r_c denotes the share of the population composed of cooperators, the expected payoff to a cooperator when cooperators do not pay the cost of scrutiny is given by

$$E_c = 4r_c + 0(1 - r_c) = 4r_c. \tag{1}$$

Against this payoff, the cooperator weighs the certain payoff of 3 units she would get if she paid the cost of scrutiny. The resultant decision rule is to pay the cost of scrutiny whenever $3 > 4r_c$, or whenever $r_c > 3/4$.

With this rule in mind, we can now say something about how the population will evolve over time. When the population share of cooperators is below 75 percent, cooperators will all pay the cost of scrutiny and get a payoff of 3 units by cooperating with one another. It will not be in the interests of defectors to bear this cost, because the keen-eyed cooperators would not interact with them anyway. The defectors are left to interact with one another, and get a payoff of only 2 units. The population growth rule is that higher relative payoffs result in a growing population share. Thus, if we start with a population share of cooperators less than 75 percent, the cooperators will get a higher average payoff, which means that their share of the population will grow.

In populations that consist of more than 75 percent cooperators, the tables are turned. Now it no longer makes sense to pay the cost of scrutiny. Cooperators and defectors will thus interact at random, which means that defectors will have a higher average payoff. This difference in payoffs, in turn, will cause the population share of cooperators to shrink.

For the values assumed in this example, the average payoff schedules for the two groups are plotted in Figure 11.2. As noted, the

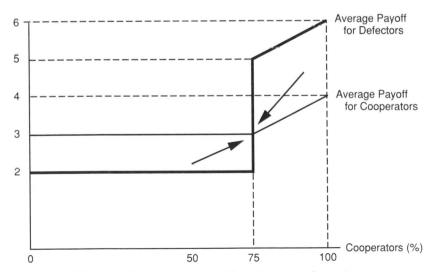

Figure 11.2. Average payoffs with costs of scrutiny.

cooperators' schedule lies above the defectors' for shares smaller than 75 percent, but below it for larger shares. The sharp discontinuity in the defectors' schedule reflects the fact that, to the left of 75 percent, all cooperators pay to scrutinize while, to the right of 75 percent none of them does. Once the population share of cooperators passes 75 percent, defectors suddenly gain access to their victims. The population growth rule makes it clear that the population in this example will stabilize at 75 percent cooperators.

Now, there is obviously nothing magic about this 75 percent figure. Had the cost of scrutiny been higher than 1 unit, for example, the population share of cooperators would have been smaller. A reduction in the payoff when cooperators pair with one another would have a similar effect on the equilibrium population shares. The point of the example is that when there are costs of scrutiny, there will be pressures that pull the population toward some stable mix of cooperators and defectors. Once the population settles at this mix, members of both groups have the same average payoff and, therefore, are equally likely to survive. There is an ecological niche, in other words, for both groups. This result stands in stark contrast to the traditional sociobiological result that only opportunism can survive.

A Constraint on the Present-Aim Standard

The view of tastes as means rather than ends helps constrain the open-ended nature of the present-aim standard of rationality. The difficulty, recall, is that the current description of that standard allows it to explain too much. The functional view of preferences suggests that the repertoire of tastes be expanded beyond the simple egoistic tastes assumed in the self-interest model, but only upon showing that the holding of a specific taste is advantageous (or at least not fatally disadvantageous) in a material sense.

Moral Sentiments as Self-Control Devices

In the preceding sections, I have argued that moral sentiments help people solve one-shot prisoner's dilemmas and other forms of the commitment problem. In this section, I will argue that the same sentiments also help solve another important, but very different, problem of economic interaction, namely, the repeated prisoner's dilemma.

As the name suggests, a repeated prisoner's dilemma occurs when the same people confront one another repeatedly in a prisoner's dilemma game. As before, the dominant strategy for any single play of the game is to defect. A higher payoff is achieved by defecting, no matter what the other player does. Again as before, however, the players each do better when both cooperate than when both defect.

Several authors have noted a method whereby pure egoists are able to solve the repeated prisoner's dilemma. I will first describe this method and then argue that it suffers from a serious implementation problem, one that moral sentiments help to solve.

Rapoport and Chammah (1965) noted that if the prisoner's dilemma game is to be played many times, a cooperator has the opportunity to retaliate if his partner defects. Once it becomes apparent that defection invites retaliation, they argue, both parties usually settle into a pattern of mutual cooperation. Rapoport and Chammah dubbed the strategy of rewarding cooperation and retaliating against defection "TIT-FOR-TAT."

Robert Axelrod (1984) investigated how the TIT-FOR-TAT strategy performed against a broad range of ingenious counterstrategies. TIT-FOR-TAT is defined formally as "cooperate on the first move, then on each successive move do whatever the other player did on the previous move." It is a "nice" strategy, in the sense that it shows an initial inclination to cooperate. But it is a tough-minded strategy as well, in that it promptly punishes defections from the other side. If each of two players play TIT-FOR-TAT, the result is perfect cooperation in every play of the game. A pair of TIT FOR TAT players thus receives the largest possible aggregate payoff.

Axelrod examined hypothetical populations of players in which not only TIT-FOR-TAT but also numerous other strategies were represented. He performed computer simulations to discover the conditions that favor the emergence of cooperation. He discovered that TIT-FOR-TAT performed extremely well against a host of cynical strategies that had been designed for the specific purpose of defeating it.

In Axelrod's scheme, the emergence of cooperation requires a reasonably stable set of players, each of whom can remember what other players have done in previous interactions. It also requires that players have a significant stake in what happens in the future, for it is only the fear of retaliation that keeps people from defecting. When these conditions are met, cooperators can identify one another and discriminate against defectors.[4] The higher payoffs inherent in suc-

---

[4]Strictly speaking, the emergence of cooperation in Axelrod's scheme also requires that the players not know exactly how many times they will interact with one another. If, for example, they knew they would interact exactly 100 times, each player would know that on the 100th, or last, interaction, the self-interested strategy would be to

cessful cooperation then cause cooperators to comprise a growing share of the population.

As described by Axelrod and Rapoport and Chammah, playing TIT-FOR-TAT does not require moral sentiments. On the contrary, it is egoism in the strictest sense—enlightened egoism, to be sure, but self-interested behavior all the same.

The sociobiologist Robert Trivers (1971) has developed a very similar theory of behavior in repeated prisoner's dilemmas, which he calls the theory of *reciprocal altruism*. That moral sentiments play a role in his theory is clear when he writes, "Selection may favor distrusting those who perform altruistic acts without the emotional basis of generosity or guilt because the altruistic tendencies of such individuals may be less reliable in the future" (pp. 50–51). He mentions parallel roles for other mediating emotions such as "moralistic aggression," friendship, and sympathy.

But Trivers never spells out how moral sentiments benefit individuals confronted with repeated prisoner's dilemmas. As both Trivers and Axelrod emphasize, each individual has a purely selfish motive for cooperating here, namely, that failure to do so will provoke retaliation. But Axelrod also stresses that this motive, *by itself*, is sufficient to assure maximum benefits.

Persons with some *additional* motive will tend to fare worse because they will sometimes cooperate when it is not in their material interests to do so. A person who wants to avoid guilt, for example, will sometimes cooperate even in a one-shot prisoner's dilemma—the person may pay her bills even when it looks like her creditor is about to go out of business. TIT-FOR-TAT, by contrast, does not even apply in this case, where the optimal strategy is simply to defect.

A person who experiences sympathy may be excessively reluctant to retaliate. In Axelrod's terms, the latter tendency is characteristic of people who play "TIT-FOR-TWO-TATS"—the strategy of retaliating only against partners who defect twice in succession. In all of the environments Axelrod studied, TIT-FOR-TAT performed considerably better than TIT-FOR-TWO-TATS.

Trivers argues that moralistic aggression may be useful because it

---

defect, because there will be no way for anyone to retaliate. But that means the there can be no effective threat of retaliation on the 99th interaction either, which in turn means that it will be best to defect then too. Because the same argument applies step by step to every interaction, the TIT-FOR-TAT solution unravels. Kreps, Milgrom, Roberts, and Wilson (1982) argue that cooperative play may nonetheless be rational in these circumstances if there is some probability that others will irrationally follow the TIT-FOR-TAT strategy.

motivates us to punish people who refuse to return a favor. But again, TIT-FOR-TAT does this as well and, as Axelrod emphasizes, in precisely the desired contexts and to precisely the desired degree. Someone motivated by moralistic aggression, by contrast, may waste energy trying to punish someone with whom he knows he will never interact again. This is often a good thing from society's point of view, of course, but any individual would do better by leaving costly aggression to others. Another difficulty with moralistic aggression is that people motivated by it may retaliate excessively against ongoing trading partners. ("Friends are even killed over apparently trivial disputes" [Trivers, 1985, p. 388]) In Axelrod's terms, moralistic aggression is thus akin to "TWO-TITS-FOR-A-TAT," another of the many strategies defeated by TIT-FOR-TAT.

If TIT-FOR-TAT required people to make complex computations, then mediating emotions might prove useful as rules of thumb. If they motivated maximizing behavior sufficiently often, and if they saved a lot of computational time and energy, they might perform better, on the average, than TIT-FOR-TAT. But in view of TIT-FOR-TAT's exceedingly simple nature, such a role hardly appears plausible. Even the most slow-witted persons can easily meet the computational demands imposed by this strategy.

Where the behaviors favored by Trivers's mediating emotions are different from those dictated by TIT-FOR-TAT, the latter will serve better. And where the two mechanisms lead to the same behaviors, the mediating emotions are redundant. Although the Trivers and Axelrod accounts of cooperation in repeated prisoner's dilemmas are very similar, Axelrod's thus appears more parsimonious.[5]

The gaps in Trivers's argument notwithstanding, it is possible to construct a coherent theory of the role of moral sentiments in helping solve repeated prisoner's dilemmas. Such a theory begins with the observation that, in addition to their powers of reason, people have their appetites to contend with. As every dieter knows, it is one thing to calculate a rational plan for meeting caloric requirements, but quite another to implement it. As with decisions about food consumption, the difficulty confronting the TIT-FOR-TAT player is that rational calculations play only an indirect role in motivation. A self-interested person sees the payoff from defecting on the current round of play, and the associated good feelings create an impulse to do so. Competing with this impulse, however, is an opposing one that arises from

---

[5]Of course, Trivers originally proposed his model of reciprocal altruism more than a decade before the appearance of Axelrod's book. Even in his most recent writings (1985), however, he continues to stress the importance of mediating emotions.

rational assessment of the consequences of defection for future rounds of play. If the costs of future retaliation are sufficiently high, rational calculation will say that defecting on the current round is not worth it. But this calculation does no more than summon a second set of feelings that compete with the impulse to defect. It is by no means certain that these competing impulses will yield a prudent choice.

On the contrary, experimental psychology provides compelling evidence for the existence of a tendency for immediate rewards to appear misleadingly attractive. The relevant evidence comes from experiments involving both humans and animals.[6] These experiments show that not only does the size of a material reward or punishment matter, but so too does its timing.

Consider, for example, the pair of choices depicted in Figure 11.3. In situation A, subjects are asked to choose today between the following two rewards: (1) $100 to be received 28 days from now, or (2) $120 to be received 31 days from now. Here, most people respond in what seems like a rational manner by picking the second reward. (This response seems rational because there are no reasonably safe investments that yield 20 percent interest in 3 days. The second reward, in other words, is simply worth more than the first.)

In situation B, subjects are asked to choose between a different pair of rewards: (1') $100 today, or (2') $120 3 days from now. The dollar amounts are the same as before, and the rewards are again 3 days apart. This time, however, most subjects choose the first reward. The inconsistency is that, for any interest rate for which reward (2) is more valuable than reward (1), reward (2') must also be more valuable than reward (1'). And yet people choose differently in the two situations. In psychiatrist George Ainslie's (1975) terminology, the earlier payoff is said to be "specious" with respect to the later one.

The behavioral psychologist's explanation for the inconsistency goes roughly as follows: With respect to the first pair of alternatives, the psychological reward mechanism regards each payoff as temporally remote. Something 28 days away seems virtually as far off as something 31 days away. Neither reward is compelling by virtue of its immediacy, and the choice between them can therefore be made dispassionately. One can't get immediate gratification anyway, so why not settle for the more valuable reward? In the second pair of alternatives, however, the immediacy of the first reward is, for many

---

[6] For a discussion and references to this literature, see Herrnstein, Loewenstein, Prelec, and Vaughan (1991).

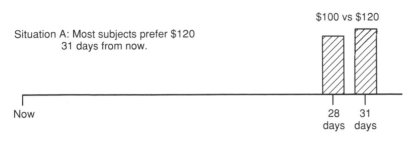

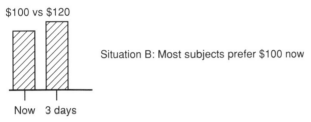

Figure 11.3.   The primacy of immediate reward.

subjects, just too vivid to ignore. It floods their consciousness and overwhelms their judgment.

Psychologists discuss time-inconsistent choices in terms of Richard Herrnstein's "matching law," one of whose properties is that the attractiveness of a reward is approximately inversely proportional to its delay.[7] In this context, the term *delay* means the amount of time that will elapse before the reward is received. The matching law implies heavy discounting of distant future rewards, and accords near primacy to those that occur immediately. (The name of the law derives from its other main prediction, which is that individuals will divide their efforts between competing activities in such a way that their rewards are equally attractive, that is, so the rewards "match" one another.)

In Figure 11.4, the attractiveness-versus-delay feature of the matching law is illustrated for a reward that will be received on January 31. The attractiveness of the reward roughly doubles each time

[7]Chung and Herrnstein (1967), Baum and Rachlin (1969), Herrnstein (1970), Ainslie and Haendel (1983), Solnick, Kannenberg, Eckerman, and Waller (1980). See also Elster (1979) and Schelling (1980). The precise form of the attractiveness versus delay relationship used in most current work is given by $V = A/(c + tk)$, where t is delay, A is the monetary value of the payoff, V is its attractiveness, and k and c are constants. The role of the constant c is to prevent the awkward implication that the attractiveness of a reward becomes unboundedly large as delay approaches zero.

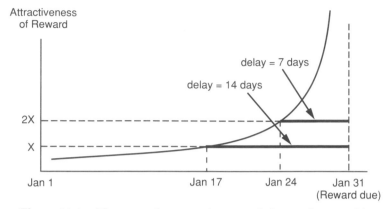

Figure 11.4. The attractiveness of a reward due on January 31.

the delay until January 31 is cut by half. Thus, for example, its attractiveness on January 24, when there is a 7-day delay, is twice that on January 17, when there is a 14-day delay.

Our concern here will be with all-or-nothing choices—such as, in Figure 11.3, the decision between the $100 and $120 rewards, or, from our earlier discussion, the decision to defect or cooperate in the current round of a repeated prisoner's dilemma. In such cases, the matching law predicts in favor of the alternative with the most attractive reward *at the moment the choice is made.*

When one is choosing between two rewards that would both be received at the same time, the outcome does not depend on when the decision is made. The larger of the two rewards will be more attractive no matter how long the delay at the moment of choice. The same cannot be said, however, when the larger of two rewards is due at a later time. For a hypothetical person, Figure 11.5 plots the attractiveness of the two rewards from the example in Figure 11.3. One curve denotes the attractiveness of a $120 reward due on January 31, the other the attractiveness of a $100 reward due on January 28.

In this example, the two attractiveness curves happen to cross on January 25. On that date, our hypothetical person would be indifferent between the two rewards. Before January 25, he would choose the larger reward. But between the 25th and the 28th, the person would pick the smaller one. Again, if one uses Ainslie's terminology, the $100 reward is *specious* with respect to the $120 reward during the interval from January 25 to January 28.

Note that the inconsistency implied by the matching law is not the result simply of the fact that we discount future rewards. There is,

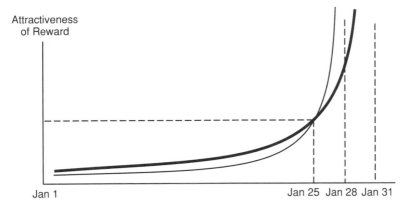

Attractiveness
of Reward

Jan 1   Jan 25 Jan 28 Jan 31

Figure 11.5.   The matching law and specious reward.

after all, nothing irrational about *that*. In an uncertain world, a bird in the hand often really *is* worth two in the bush. Inconsistencies arise because of the specific *pattern* of discounting implied by the matching law. In the exponential discounting of the rational choice model, the relative attractiveness of two rewards due at different times is the same regardless of the evaluator's temporal vantage point. Under the matching law, relative attractiveness levels depend critically on the timing of evaluation. Under exponential discounting, preference reversals of the sort we see under the matching law simply cannot arise.

The matching law, or some close variant of it, is one of the most robust regularities in experimental psychology. When a pigeon is given a chance to peck one of two buttons to choose between a morsel of food 30 seconds from now and a much larger morsel 40 seconds from now, it takes the latter. But when it chooses between the same morsel now and the larger morsel 10 seconds hence, it often picks the former. Rats behave the same way. So do cats, dogs, guinea pigs, and hogs. And so, much of the time, do humans. The matching law is apparently part of the hard wiring of most animal nervous systems.

This is not to say that material reward and delay feed mechanically into the matching law to produce a deterministic theory of human behavior.[8] On the contrary, people obviously have considerable con-

---

[8] It is clear, in any event, that a purely mechanical interpretation of the matching law leads to predictions that are contradicted by everyday experience. The matching law seems to predict, for example, that people would choose to experience pleasant events as soon as possible and to defer unpleasant ones as long as possible.

trol over the way they perceive the rewards from competing activities. So far as I know, no court of law has ever accepted a defense like, "I couldn't help stealing the money—there it was and I was under the influence of the matching law."

The matching law does not say there is anything inevitable about choosing a specious reward. Consider, for example, a person who is emotionally predisposed to regard cheating as an unpleasant act *in and of itself*, that is, someone with a conscience. Such a person will be better able than a person who lacks a conscience to resist the temptation to defect in the current round of repeated prisoner's dilemmas. If the psychological reward mechanism is constrained to emphasize rewards in the present moment, the simplest counter to a specious reward from defecting is to have a current feeling that tugs in precisely the opposite direction. Guilt is just such a feeling. And because it too coincides with the moment of choice, the matching law does not discount it relative to the competing material reward. If it is felt strongly enough, it can negate the spurious attraction of the imminent material reward.

Note that this observation does not contradict the matching law. Rather, it says that nonmaterial rewards and penalties may also matter. The matching law merely describes how the attractiveness of a reward—material or nonmaterial—tends to vary with its delay. Thus, although attractiveness tends to grow rapidly as delay approaches zero, an imminent material reward is not always irresistible. It can be effectively countered by competing rewards, even nonmaterial ones, provided they too are imminent.

Even so, the matching law makes it apparent why a merely prudent person might often find it difficult to refrain from defecting when rational analysis says defecting doesn't pay. The problem is that the material gains from defecting come right away, the penalties only later. If our psychological reward mechanism really does assign disproportionate weight to near-term rewards, a person who cares only about material rewards will defect even when it is not prudent to do so.

Loewenstein (1987) has shown, however, that most people prefer, on the one hand, to postpone intense, fleeting positive experiences (like "a kiss from your favorite movie star") and, on the other, to get unpleasant ones (like "a brief but painful electric shock") over with as quickly as possible. Loewenstein suggests that people want time to savor the prospect of the kiss and to minimize the time they spend dreading the electric shock. Once we recognize, however, that the *anticipation* of pleasure and pain often takes on much the same character as the actual experience and, thus, becomes a reinforcement in and of itself, the observed behaviors are no longer clearly in conflict with the matching law.

It is often prudent to refrain from defecting, as the TIT-FOR-TAT and reciprocal altruism theories have ably demonstrated. On such occasions, there will be advantage in being able to suppress the impulse to defect. We can thus imagine a population in which people with consciences fare better than those without. The people who lack them would defect less often if they could, but they simply have greater difficulty solving the self-control problem. People who have them, by contrast, are able to acquire good reputations and cooperate successfully with others of like disposition.

Similar reasoning will apply in the case of vengeance seeking. Often it will be prudent to exact revenge even at considerable personal cost. This will especially be true when the action helps create a reputation that will deter future acts of aggression. Perfectly rational persons with perfect self-control would always seek revenge whenever the future reputational gains outweigh the current costs of taking action.

The problem, as in the cheating example, is that the gains from a tough reputation come only in the future while the costs of vengeance seeking come now. The matching law thus again suggests an impulse-control problem. A person may realize that it pays to be tough, yet still be tempted to avoid the current costs of a tough response. Being predisposed to feel anger when wronged helps solve this impulse-control problem. As with feelings of guilt, anger helps shift the relevant future payoffs into the current moment. In cases where reputational considerations weigh in favor of action, the angry person will be more likely to behave prudently than the merely prudent person who feels no anger.

It will likewise often be prudent to refuse a favorable transaction when the terms are starkly one-sided. By so doing, one can develop a reputation for being a tough bargainer, which will mean better terms in future transactions. In this case, too, we have future gains pitted against current costs and the resulting impulse-control problem. Here, someone who feels envious when he gets less than his fair share taps into the reward mechanism in the current moment, and on that account will be more likely to behave prudently. It is easier for a person to refuse an advantageous, but unfair, proposal if accepting it would make the person feel bad.

Finally, love may also assist a person to follow a self-interested course. Future events that make it against one's interests to remain in a marriage are not the only contingencies people worry about. They also fear blundering out of a marriage that it pays to maintain. The matching law again helps explain why. A person may be tempted by the prospect of an extramarital affair, yet realize it would be better to keep the marriage intact. That the immediate rewards of the affair are specious makes them no less powerful. The gains from preserving the marriage, although more genuine, lie mostly in the future. Again, we have an impulse-control problem.

As in the other examples, competing sentiments can assist in solving it. Strong feelings of affection for one's spouse tilt the psychological rewards of fidelity toward the present. People who experience such feelings are much better equipped to deal with temptation, even if not completely immune from it. And for this reason, they are more likely to achieve their long-range objectives.

The matching law tells us that the attractiveness of a reward increases sharply as its delay approaches zero. From this it follows that people who are concerned *only* about material rewards will often defect (fail to retaliate, etc.) even when it is not rational to do so. The gains from defecting, again, come now while the costs come later.

Concluding Remarks

We have seen two ways moral sentiments might lead to better outcomes in intertemporal choice problems. In the first, moral sentiments act as commitment devices that help people solve one-shot prisoner's dilemmas and other forms of the commitment problem. The second function of moral sentiments is to help solve self-control problems that stand in the way of prudent play in repeated prisoner's dilemmas.

In the one-shot dilemma context, the problem was how to make oneself want to be *honest* when the material incentives favor cheating. In the repeated dilemma context, by contrast, the problem was to make oneself want to be *prudent* in cases where the long-term material incentives favor honesty. These two problems could hardly be more different. Solving the first seems noble, the second merely expedient. The irony is that they are solved by precisely the same moral sentiments.

References

Ainslie, George. "Specious Reward: A Behavioral Theory of Impulsiveness and Impulse Control." *Psychological Bulletin* 21 (1975): 485–489.
———, and V. Haendel. "The Motives of the Will." in E. Gottheil, A. McLennan, and K. Druley (eds.). *Etiologies of Alcoholism and Drug Addiction.* Springfield, NJ: Thomas, 1982.

Akerlof, George. "Loyalty Filters." *American Economic Review* 73 (March 1983): 54–63.

Arrow, Kenneth. "Gifts and Exchanges." in E.S. Phelps (ed.). *Altruism, Morality, and Economic Theory.* New York: Russell Sage, 1975.

Axelrod, Robert. *The Evolution of Cooperation.* New York: Basic Books, 1984.

Baum, W., and H. Rachlin. "Choice as Time Allocation." *Journal of the Experimental Analysis of Behavior* 27 (1969): 453–467.

Chung, Shin-Ho, and Richard Herrnstein. "Choice and Delay of Reinforcement." *Journal of the Experimental Analysis of Behavior* 10 (1967): 67–74.

Collard, David. *Altruism and Economy.* Oxford, UK: Martin Robertson, 1978.

Ekman, Paul. *Telling Lies.* New York: Norton, 1985.

Elster, Jon. *Ulysses and the Sirens.* Cambridge, UK: Cambridge University Press, 1979.

Frank, Robert H. "If *Homo Economicus* Could Choose His Own Utility Function, Would He Want One with a Conscience?" *American Economic Review* 77 (1987): 593–604.

———. *Passions Within Reason: The Strategic Role of the Emotions.* New York: W.W. Norton, 1988.

Gauthier, David. *Morals By Agreement.* Oxford, UK: Oxford University Press, 1985.

Harsanyi, John. "Rule Utilitarianism, Rights, Obligations, and the Theory of Rational Behavior." *Theory and Decision* 12 (1980): 115–133.

Herrnstein, Richard. "On the Law of Effect." *Journal of the Experimental Analysis of Behavior* 13 (1970): 242–266.

———, George Loewenstein, Drazen Prelec, and William Vaughan. "Utility Maximization and Melioration: Internalities in Individual Choice." Working Paper, Department of Social and Decision Sciences, Carnegie Mellon University, 1991.

Hirshleifer, Jack. "The Emotions as Guarantors of Threats and Promises." UCLA Department of Economics Working Paper, 1984.

Kreps, David M., Paul Milgrom, John Roberts, and Robert Wilson. "Rational Cooperation in Finitely Repeated Prisoner's Dilemma." *Journal of Economic Theory* 27 (1982): 245–252.

Leibenstein, Harvey. *Beyond Economic Man.* Cambridge, MA: Harvard University Press, 1976.

Loewenstein, George. "Anticipation and the Valuation of Delayed Consumption." *Economic Journal* 97 (1987): 666–684.

Parfit, Derek. *Reasons and Persons.* Oxford, UK: Clarendon Press, 1984.

Phelps, E.S. (ed). *Altruism, Morality, and Economic Theory.* New York: Russell Sage, 1975.

Rapoport, Anatol, and Albert Chammah. *Prisoner's Dilemma.* Ann Arbor, MI: University of Michigan Press, 1965.

Rubin, Paul, and Chris Paul. "An Evolutionary Model of Taste for Risk." *Economic Inquiry* 17 (1979): 585–596.

Schelling, Thomas. *The Strategy of Conflict.* Cambridge, MA: Harvard University Press, 1960.

———. "Altruism, Meanness, and Other Potentially Strategic Behaviors." *American Economic Review* 68 (1978): 229–230.

————. "The Intimate Contest for Self-Command." *The Public Interest* Summer (1980): 94–118.

Scitovsky, Tibor. *The Joyless Economy*. New York: Oxford University Press, 1976.

Sen, Amartya. "Goals, Commitment, and Identity." *Journal of Law, Economics, and Organization* 1 (1985): 341–355.

————. "Rational Fools." *Philosophy and Public Affairs* 6 (1977): 317–344.

Smith, Adam. *The Theory of Moral Sentiments*. New York: Augustus M. Kelley, (1759), 1966.

Solnick, J., C. Kannenberg, D. Eckerman, and M. Waller. "An Experimental Analysis of Impulsivity and Impulse Control in Humans." *Learning and Motivation* 11 (1980): 61–77.

Trivers, Robert. "The Evolution of Reciprocal Altruism." *Quarterly Review of Biology* 46 (1971): 35–57.

————. *Social Evolution*. Menlo Park, CA: Benjamin/Cummings, 1985.

PART FIVE

·

Applications and Extensions

· 12 ·

Mental Accounting, Saving, and Self-Control

HERSH M. SHEFRIN AND RICHARD H. THALER*

MODIGLIANI and Brumberg's life-cycle theory of saving (1954) (and the similar permanent income hypothesis by Milton Friedman [1957]) is a classic example of economic theorizing. The life-cycle (LC) model makes some simplifying assumptions in order to be able to characterize a well-defined optimization problem, which is then solved. The solution to that optimization problem provides the core of the theory.

Attempts to test the LC hypothesis have met with mixed success. As summarized by Courant, Gramlich, and Laitner (1984), "But for all its elegance and rationality, the life-cycle model has not tested out very well. . . . Nor have efforts to test the life-cycle model with cross-sectional microdata worked out very successfully" (pp. 279–280). Various alterations to the theory have been proposed to help it accommodate the data: add a bequest motive, hypothesize capital market imperfections, assume that the utility function for consumption changes over time, or specify a particular form of expectations regarding future income. These modifications often appear to be ad hoc, because different assumptions are necessary to explain each

*A previous version of this chapter was published as "The Behavioral Life-Cycle Hypothesis," *Economic Inquiry*, October 1988. It has been revised and updated for this book and incorporates material from Thaler (1990).

anomalous empirical result. In this chapter, we suggest that the data can be explained in a parsimonious manner by making modifications to the LC theory that are quite different in spirit from those cited earlier, namely, modifications aimed at making the theory more behaviorally realistic. We call our enriched model the Behavioral Life Cycle (BLC) Hypothesis.

We are aware, of course, that criticizing the realism of the assumptions of an economic theory is hardly novel. It is trite to point out that few consumers are capable of making the present value calculations implicit in the theory. This remark, while accurate, does little to help formulate a better theory. Perhaps, as Milton Friedman might argue, households save *as if* they knew how to calculate the (after-tax) annuity value of a windfall gain. Therefore, in an effort to get beyond this sort of general critique, we suggest that the LC model can be enriched by incorporating three important behavioral features that are usually missing in economic analyses. (1) *Self-control:* We recognize that self-control is costly, and that economic agents will use various devices such as pension plans and rules of thumb to deal with the difficulties of postponing a significant portion of their consumption until retirement. We also incorporate temptation into the analysis, because some situations are less conducive to saving than others. (2) *Mental accounting:* Most households act as if they used a system of mental accounts that violates the principle of fungibility. Specifically, some mental accounts, those that are considered "wealth," are less tempting than those that are considered "income." (3) *Framing:* An implication of the differential temptation of various mental accounts is that the saving rate can be affected by the way in which increments to wealth are "framed" or described. Our model predicts that income paid in the form of a lump sum bonus will be treated differently from regular income even if the bonus is completely anticipated. Building upon the research done on these topics by psychologists and other social scientists (see, e.g., Ainslie, 1975, and Mischel, 1981), we are able to make specific predictions about how actual household saving behavior will differ from the idealized LC model.

The plan of the chapter is to present first the model and to use it to derive propositions about saving behavior that can distinguish it from the standard LC hypothesis. We then present the evidence we have been able to compile from existing studies on each of the propositions.

The Model

Self-Control and Temptation: The Problem

In the *Theory of Interest* (1930) Irving Fisher bases his explanation of personal saving upon five characteristics: foresight, self-control, habits, expectation of life, and love for posterity. We concentrate here on the first three factors and the relationships among them. Foresight is important because retirement saving requires long-term planning. Self-control is necessary because immediate consumption is always an attractive alternative to retirement saving. Successfully dealing with self-control problems requires the cultivation of good habits. In presenting our model, we begin with the concept of self-control.

How does self-control differ from ordinary choice? The distinguished psychologist William James (1890/1981) says that the key attribute of self-control choices is the "feeling of effort" that is present:

> *Effort of attention is thus the essential phenomenon of will.* Every reader must know by his own experience that this is so, for every reader must have felt some fiery passion's grasp. What constitutes the difficulty for a man laboring under an unwise passion of acting as if the passion were wise? Certainly there is no physical difficulty. It is as easy physically to avoid a fight as to begin one, to pocket one's money as to squander it on one's cupidities, to walk away from as towards a coquette's door. The difficulty is mental: it is that of getting the idea of the wise action to stay before our mind at all. (p. 1167)

Incorporating the effort that is present in self-control contexts involves three elements normally excluded from economic analyses: internal conflict, temptation, and willpower. The very term *self-control* implies that the tradeoffs between immediate gratification and long-run benefits entail a conflict that is not present in a choice between a white shirt and a blue one. When one is modeling choice under such circumstances, the concept of temptation must be incorporated because of the obvious fact that some situations are more tempting than others. A model of saving that omits temptation is misspecified. The term *willpower* represents the real psychic costs of resisting temptation. The behavioral LC hypothesis modifies the standard LC model to incorporate these features. To capture formally the notion of internal conflict between the rational and emotional aspects of an individual's personality, we employ a dual preference structure. Individuals are assumed to behave *as if* they have two sets of coexisting and mutually inconsistent preferences: one concerned with the long run, and the other with the short run.[1] We refer to the former as the planner and the latter as the doer.[2] To place the preceding concepts into a formal structure, consider an individual whose lifetime extends over T periods, with the final period representing retirement. The lifetime income stream is given by $y = (y_1,...,y_T)$. For simplicity we assume a perfect capital market and zero real rate of interest. Let retirement income y_T be zero. Then lifetime wealth is defined as $LW = \Sigma_{t=1}^{T} y_t$. Let the consumption stream be denoted by $c = (c_1,...,c_T)$. The lifetime budget constraint is then $\Sigma c_t = LW$.

The conflict associated with self-control is captured by the contrasting time horizons of the planner and the doer. The doer is assumed to be pathologically myopic, concerned only with current period consumption. At date t the doer is assumed to possess a subutility function $U_t(c_t)$. We assume *diminishing marginal utility* ($U_t(\cdot)$ is concave in c_t), and also *nonsatiation* (U_t is strictly increasing in c_t). In contrast, the planner is concerned with maximizing a function of lifetime doer utilities.

Because temptation depends on immediate consumption opportunities, we define an opportunity set X_t to represent the feasible choices for consumption at date t. If free to choose from this set, the myopic doer would select the maximum feasible value of c_t (because that would maximize U_t on X_t). The planner would usually prefer a smaller c_t. Suppose the planner wants to reduce consumption by exerting willpower. We assume that if exercise of willpower does diminish c_t, there must be some psychic cost. If this were not the case, then exerting willpower would be effortless, and self-control problems such as overeating and overspending would not occur. The psychic cost of using willpower is represented by the symbol W_t. W_t may be thought of as a negative sensation (corresponding roughly to

---

[1]Several other scholars have tried to model intertemporal choice taking self-control into account. All rely on some type of two-self formulation, although the models differ in how the two selves interact. See Elster (1979), Margolis (1982), Schelling (1984), and Winston (1980).

[2]While the planner-doer framework is in the tradition of "as if" economic models, our economic theory of choice is roughly consistent with the scientific literature on brain function. This literature deals with the organizational structure of the brain and its associated division into functional subcomponents. The *prefrontal cortex* has been called the "executive of the brain" (Fuster, 1980) and has been identified as the location of rational thought and planning. The planner in our model represents the prefrontal cortex. The prefrontal cortex continually interfaces with the *limbic system*, which is responsible for the generation of emotions (Numan, 1978). The doer in our model represents the limbic system. It is well known that self-control phenomena center on the interaction between the prefrontal cortex and the limbic system (Restak, 1984).

guilt) that diminishes the positive sensations associated with U_t. Total doer utility, denoted as Z_t, is then the sum of the pleasure and the pain:

$$Z_t = U_t + W_t \tag{1}$$

The doer is assumed to exercise direct control over the consumption choice, and, being myopic, chooses c_t in order to maximize Z_t on X_t. This choice reflects the combined influence of both planner and doer. Willpower effort is effective if the maximizing values for Z_t and U_t (on X_t) are not the same.

Willpower effort can be applied in varying degrees. Therefore, we define a *willpower effort variable*, denoted θ_t, to represent the amount of willpower exerted at date t. The function $\theta_t^*(c_t, X_t)$ gives the degree θ_t of willpower effort required to induce the individual to select consumption level c_t when opportunity set X_t is being faced. The following assumptions characterize the significant features about willpower effort.

1. An increase in willpower effort is necessary to reduce consumption; that is, θ_t^* is decreasing in c_t.
2. Increased willpower effort is painful in the sense that reductions in consumption resulting from willpower are accompanied by reductions in Z_t. Specifically, $\partial Z_t / \partial \theta_t$ is negative, which together with the previous assumption implies:

$$\partial Z_t / \partial \theta_t\ \partial \theta_t^* / \partial c_t > 0 \tag{2}$$

3. Increased willpower effort is not only painful, but becomes increasingly more painful as additional willpower is applied. Specifically:

$$\partial / \partial c_t \{\partial Z_t / \partial \theta_t\ \partial \theta_t^* / \partial c_t\} < 0 \tag{3}$$

To represent the idea that the planner corresponds to the rational part of the individual's personality, we associate a neoclassical utility function $V(\cdot)$ to the planner, with the arguments of V being the subutility levels Z_1 through Z_T. Because $\partial Z_t / \partial \theta_t$ is negative, willpower costs are incorporated in the planner's choice problem.

Because willpower is costly, the planner may seek other techniques for achieving self-control. These techniques are the subject of the following section.

Rules and Mental Accounting: The Solution

One solution to the conflict between planner and doer preferences is for the planner to restrict future choices by imposing constraints that alter X_t. For example, placing funds into a pension plan that disallows withdrawals reduces disposable income and, thus, shrinks the doer's choice set. We refer to any precommitment device of the above type as a rule.[3]

Suppose that the planner were able to choose a rule that completely precommitted future consumption to a particular path. Because the doers would have no choices to make, no willpower effort would be required. In this situation, the planner would choose c to maximize V subject to the budget constraint, while leaving $\theta = 0$. Denote this optimal choice of c by c^p. The path c^p is a first-best solution to the planner's problem and corresponds precisely to the LC consumption path. Therefore, the LC hypothesis can be interpreted as a special case of the BLC model in which either willpower effort costs are zero, or a first-best rule is available to the planner. The predictions of the two models diverge because neither of these conditions is likely to be met. The person with zero willpower costs is obviously a rarity, and first-best rules are generally unavailable. While pension plans and other saving vehicles are marketed, there is a limited selection available, and they do not completely determine a consumption plan. Uncertainty about both income flows and spending needs renders such plans impractical.[4]

When the precommitment enforcement mechanism is accomplished primarily by an outside agency, as with a pension plan, we refer to the rule as being *external*. Another class of rules, *internal* rules, are self-enforced and require greater willpower effort. An example of such a rule is a self-imposed prohibition on borrowing to finance

[3]It needs to be emphasized that in our model, the planner can actually implement any budget feasible consumption plan by selecting θ appropriately. The only issue is at what cost. Precommitment offers the possibility of implementing a given consumption plan at reduced willpower cost.

[4]King (1985) has criticized our characterization of the conflict between the planner and the doer as an agency problem on the grounds that there is no information asymmetry present. This criticism is misplaced. While in standard principal–agent models of the firm, it is the information asymmetry that prevents the principal from achieving a first-best outcome, an agency problem can exist without information asymmetry if the principal has limited *control* over the agent's actions. That is the case we consider, for the reasons just described. The alternative bargaining formulation King suggests fails to capture some essential features of the problem such as the asymmetry between the strategies employed by the two parties. The planner precommits, the doer does not. The doer in our model generally does not engage in strategic behavior.

current consumption. Again, is it natural to ask whether a system of internal rules can be used to achieve a first-best (LC) outcome? The answer is no, because willpower is needed to enforce the rule. Formally, this feature is captured by assuming that the marginal utility decrease attributable to less consumption per se is less than the corresponding utility loss when willpower effort is used; that is:

$$D = \partial Z_t / \partial \theta_t \; \partial \theta_t^* / \partial c_t - \partial Z_t / \partial c_t > 0. \tag{4}$$

where $\partial Z_t / \partial c_t$ is evaluated at $\theta = 0$. The difference D can be regarded as the net marginal cost of using willpower. We make the additional assumption that willpower effort is especially costly at low consumption levels but essentially costless at high levels. In other words, D decreases with c_t and approaches zero for c_t sufficiently large.

There are limits on the type of rules that can be enforced at low willpower costs. A reading of the psychology literature on impulse control (e.g., Ainslie, 1975) suggests that effective rules must have the following characteristics: First, a habitual rule must exhibit simplicity, because complex responses seem to require conscious thinking, whereas habitual responses are subconsciously guided. Second, exceptions must be well defined and rare, again in order to avoid the need for conscious responses. Third, the rule must be dynamically stable: Habits are not easily altered. Both internal and external rules then are second-best; therefore, descriptive models of saving behavior must reflect the second-best solutions that are adopted by real savers.

While households' internal rules are idiosyncratic and context specific, there appear to be enough common elements to generate useful aggregation predictions. One of the most important elements concerns the decomposition of household wealth into a series of accounts called *mental accounts*.[5] One simple and stylized version of a mental accounting system divides wealth into three components: current spendable income (*I*), current assets (*A*), and future income (*F*). In the BLC, the marginal propensity to consume wealth is assumed to be account specific. This contrasts sharply with the traditional LC model that treats the labelling of wealth as irrelevant because wealth is regarded as completely fungible in a perfect capital market. Specifically, traditional theory postulates that the marginal propensity to consume is the same for the following four events: a $1,000 bonus received at work; a $1,000 lottery windfall; a $1,000 increase in the

---

[5]For more on mental accounting, see Thaler (1985) and Kahneman and Tversky (1984).

value of the household's home; and an inheritance, to be received with certainty in 10 years, with a present value of $1,000. In contrast, our behavioral enrichment of the LC model assumes that households code various components of wealth into different mental accounts, some of which are more "tempting" to invade than others.

As explained later, the BLC theory postulates a specific set of inequalities in connection with the marginal propensity to consume from the preceding four wealth descriptions. The direction of these inequalities is not arbitrary, and we hypothesize that they evolved as a means of helping individuals to save. The decomposition of wealth into mental accounts constitutes an example of *framing*; see Kahneman and Tversky (1984). In treating wealth as fungible, traditional LC theory makes an implicit frame invariance assumption. The BLC model assumes frame dependence.

To illustrate how the three account formulation works, consider a household that uses a pension rule that at each date deducts a fraction s of income, and prohibits access to accumulated funds before retirement. The mental account balances at data $t < T$ are as follows:

1. The current income account, $I = (1 - s)y_t$.
2. The current wealth account A (corresponding to cumulative discretionary (i.e., nonpension) savings through date $t - 1$) is:

$$\sum_{\tau=1}^{t-1} [(1 - s)y_\tau - c_\tau]$$

(5)

3. The balance in the future wealth account is the sum of future income (after pension withdrawals have been made) and pension wealth sY.

Of course, this three-account formulation is a great simplification of actual mental accounting rules. In general, a more realistic model would break up the A account into a series of subaccounts, appropriately labeled. Some households may have a children's education account, which would be treated as being similar to a future income account until the children reached college age. Also, there is some ambiguity in how households treat various changes to their wealth. Asset income, for example, is generally kept in the A account, except perhaps dividend payments, which may be treated as current income.[6] Small windfalls are likely to be coded as current income, while larger windfalls are placed into A. We assume that pension wealth is

---

[6]See Shefrin and Statman (1984).

framed as future retirement income, although some households might treat it more like current assets. Similarly, there will be variation in the way in which households treat home equity; some will treat home equity as if it were part of F (and will not take out home equity loans), others as if it were part of A. We expect differences among households in the way they treat various accounts, and the model we present here can be considered a description of the representative household.

While the mental accounting system described here may seem bizarre to economists, it is remarkably similar to the accounting systems used by most private universities. A typical private university will distinguish between money in the "current" account that can be spent immediately, and money in the endowment. From the endowment, only income (somehow defined) can be spent, while the principal must remain intact. The rules for allocation gifts to the different accounts are of interest. For example, small gifts from alumni that are part of the annual giving campaign are normally treated as "income," spendable immediately. Larger gifts and those that are received as part of a "capital campaign" are put into the endowment account. Finally, a gift that is pledged, but only payable at the time of the donor's death, is generally not acknowledged in either the income or endowment accounts, and will therefore create no increase in current spending.

Suppose next that the individual wants to save more than the maximum pension deduction rate offered to him or her, that is, the person wants to engage in what we term *discretionary* saving. Then it is necessary to use some willpower effort in order to generate the associated additional savings, avoid depleting those savings before retirement, and refrain from borrowing against future earnings. The magnitude of the associated willpower effort costs is assumed to depend inversely on the temptation to spend. Some situations are more tempting than others. Irving Fisher associated great temptation with payday, because individuals are flush with cash. In our model we assume that temptation to spend a (marginal) dollar of wealth depends on the location of that dollar in the mental accounting system, with current income being the most tempting, followed by current assets, and then future wealth.

Technically, we take the doer utility function Z_t to be parameterized by the underlying mental accounting structure.[7] Recall that mar-

---

[7]Formally, Z_t is parameterized by the choice set X_t where X_t specifies the account balances I_t, A_t, and F_t.

ginal doer utility is given by

$$\partial Z_t / \partial \theta_t \, \partial \theta_t^* / \partial c_t \tag{6}$$

and reflects the cost of willpower effort at the margin. Figure 12.1 depicts the graph of $Z_t(c_t, \theta_t^*, X_t)$ against c_t for a given mental accounting structure and account balances. It reflects the essential structure that we impose on the model. Consider the effects on Z_t due to increments in c_t. We take the first marginal unit of consumption to be financed out of the I account, with Equation (4) reflecting the marginal utility of consumption. As consumption increases, the reduction in willpower effort contributes to higher utility, but in accordance with Equation (3) at a diminishing rate. When the entire balance in the I account is consumed, no willpower effort need be applied to this account. The next marginal unit of consumption is then financed out of the A account.

We model the A account as being less tempting than the I account by assuming that as long as consumption from A is zero, the self-

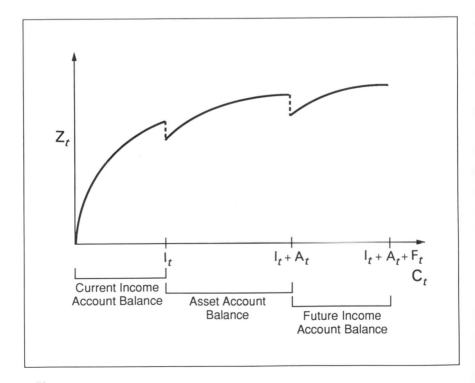

Figure 12.1

control technology requires no willpower effort in connection with this account. However, any positive consumption from A produces a fixed disutility penalty (representing an entry fee for invading the A account). Consequently, the first unit consumed from A is especially costly. Additional consumption from A results in additional utility as willpower effort is reduced. Again this occurs at a diminishing rate. Similar remarks apply when the F account is invaded.

To indicate how differential willpower effort costs for the various mental account balances can be incorporated into the model, we focus attention on the current income account, and denote its balance at the outset of date t by the symbol m_t. When one is contemplating financing consumption from the current income account, m_t measures the amount of temptation to be faced. We postulate that the greater the temptation, the greater the willpower effort required to choose any given consumption level $c_t < m_t$. Formally, we assume that at any given level of c_t, increased temptation will make the doer worse off, in the sense that:

$$\partial Z_t / \partial m_t = \partial W_t / \partial m_t + \partial W_t / \partial \theta_t \, \partial \theta_t^* / \partial m_t < 0 \qquad (7)$$

and

$$\partial / \partial m_t \{ \partial Z_t / \partial \theta_t \, \partial \theta_t^* / \partial c_t \} < 0 \qquad (8)$$

For example, consider an individual who plans to spend $1,200 of his regular monthly take-home pay of $1,500. The preceding inequalities suggests that were his take-home pay $2,000, then stopping at $1,200 would require greater willpower effort (cost). However, we also postulate that:

$$\partial^2 Z_t / \partial m_t^2 > 0 \qquad (9)$$

so that successive unit increments in the income account produce less of a negative impact. That is, given the intention to consume $1,200 out of the income account, the impact on temptation of additional take home pay of $500 (from $2,000 to $2,500) involves less additional willpower effort than the $500 increase from $1,500 to $2,000.[8]

Further details about the model and about the first-order conditions used to derive the predictions discussed later are presented in

---

[8]We make the stronger assumption that the left-hand side of Equation (8) goes to zero monotonically as m_t approaches infinity.

the appendix. In many ways, however, the key property of the model is the relaxation of the fungibility assumption of the LC model, and the introduction of the assumption that the marginal propensity to consume additions to wealth depends on the form in which this wealth is received. At a given date, the marginal propensity to consume is typically highest out of income (I), lowest out of future wealth (F), and somewhere in between for current assets (A). This implies that the BLC aggregate consumption function must incorporate at least three different income or wealth measures corresponding to the three mental accounts. That is, $C = f(I,A,F)$, where I, A, and F now stand for their aggregate counterparts. The model suggests that:

$$1 \approx \partial C/\partial I > \partial C/\partial A > \partial C/DF \approx 0 \qquad (10)$$

This set of inequalities and the other features of the model yield a series of testable predictions. It is those predictions to which we now turn.

The Differential Marginal Propensity to Consume (MPC) Hypothesis

One simple check on the validity of the differential MPC hypothesis is to ask people a few hypothetical questions. Along these lines, we conducted a small survey as a direct test of the hypothesis.[9] A group of evening MBA students at Santa Clara University (most of whom work full-time) was recruited to fill out a questionnaire. The questions are reproduced in Table 12.1. Each question asks the respondent to estimate the marginal propensity to consume a windfall with an (approximate) present value of $2,400. In question 1, the windfall comes in increments of $200 a month, and is most likely to be coded as regular income. In question 2, the windfall comes in a $2,400 lump sum, which we hypothesize is large enough to be placed in the assets account, and should thus have a lower MPC. For question 3, the windfall is not payable for 5 years, and, as it will be coded in the future income account, should yield a very low MPC. The results support the differential MPC hypothesis. The median annual MPCs for the three questions are $1,200, $785, and $0, respectively. These medians were the same for the whole sample as well as for the subset

[9] A similar study was conducted by Simon and Barnes (1971). Their results also support the differential MPC hypothesis.

Table 12.1.   Saving Questionnaire

Sample: Santa Clara University Part-Time MBA Students
($N = 122$)

For each of the following scenarios, please think about how you would actually behave. There are no right or wrong answers. Your responses are anonymous and confidential. If you are employed, please answer these questions as if the events described occurred this week. If you are a full-time student, please answer as you think you would behave if you were employed full-time. Thank you very much for your cooperation.

1. You have been given a special bonus at work. The bonus will be paid monthly over the course of a year, and will increase your *take home pay* by $200 per month for 12 months.
    By how much would you expect your monthly consumption to increase during the year? _____ dollars per month. **Median = $100 Total Consumption = $1,200**
2. You have been given a special bonus at work. It will be paid in a lump sum of $2,400 (after tax) this month.
    By how much would you expect your consumption to increase in the following month? _____ dollars per month. **Median = $400**
    By how much would you expect your monthly consumption to increase during the rest of the following year? _____ dollars per month. **Median = $35   Total Consumption = $785**
3. You have been told that a distant relative has left you a small inheritance which has an after tax value of $2,400. You will not receive the money for 5 years. During that time, the money will be invested in an interest bearing account. After the 5 years you will definitely receive the $2,400 plus interest.
    By how much would you expect your consumption to rise *this* year as a result of this gift? _____ dollars per month. **Median = $0**

of 93 subjects that reported having at least $5,000 in liquid assets, so liquidity constraints are not an issue.

While we find these intuitions of MBA students compelling, it is important to obtain evidence based on actual behavior. Courant, Gramlich, and Laitner (1986) distinguished between two types of wealth: current and future. Current wealth includes current income. They report being astonished by the difference in the estimated marginal propensities to consume from these two accounts, because no difference is expected in the LC framework. They estimated the MPC out of current assets to be very high, implying that households consume approximately 25% of their existing assets every year. They point out that this suggests a high positive subjective rate of time discount. Yet the MPC out of future wealth was found to be considerably lower, in fact suggesting a *negative* discount rate (p. 302).

In an earlier study, Holbrook and Stafford (1971) used a permanent income model that differentiates among different sources of income (labor income, capital income, transfer payments, etc.). However, the permanent income framework employed treated the timing of wealth as irrelevant (holding the present value constant). Consequently, the Holbrook–Stafford analysis did not distinguish among wealth that has been accumulated in the past, arrives as current income, or will arrive as part of future income. In our theory, we assume that different sources of income are encoded into different mental accounts. Specifically, labor income is encoded into current income (I), while capital income (with the possible exception of dividend income, see Shefrin and Statman 1984) is encoded into the A account upon arrival. Therefore, we predict that the marginal propensity to consume from capital income is less than from labor income. This is what Holbrook and Stafford found. The estimated MPC out of labor income was approximately .9, while the estimated MPC out of capital income was .7. Interestingly, the MPC out of transfer payments received by members of the household other than the head is approximately 30%, indicating that such income tends to be saved, rather than consumed (p. 16).

The first direct test of the BLC's differential MPC hypothesis (against the LC alternative) is provided by Levin (1992). Levin used the Longitudinal Retirement History Survey (RHS) to analyze the consumption behavior of individuals in their late 50s or older. He was able to study how expenditures in ten consumption categories respond to changes in current income, current assets, and future wealth. The consumption categories included groceries, vacations, dues to social organizations, entertainment, and nonvacation trips. Because home equity is the principal component of current assets, and social security benefits the principal component of future wealth for most of the households in the RHS, Levin disaggregated current assets into home equity and nonhome equity assets, and he disaggregated future wealth into social security and nonsocial security wealth. Those results described below, which pertain to social security, may be open to interpretation because of empirical issues associated with the data.

Levin found confirming evidence for the differential MPC hypothesis in most consumption categories. After one controls for household demographics (household size, marital status, state of health, etc.), the following general expenditure picture emerges. For most consumption categories except vacations, the expenditure elasticity is highest for current income, smaller for current assets other than home equity, and zero (i.e., statistically insignificant) for home equity and future wealth. In other words, individuals finance most of their consumption out of current income, and to a lesser extent from assets other than the equity in their homes. The preceding patterns vary in their strength across consumption categories. The effect is weakest for grocery expenditures, which is not very sensitive to wealth variations, but strong for entertainment. In contrast to other categories of consumption, vacations are principally financed from current assets (other than home equity). The data indicate that vacation spending increases after the spouse retires. Many households build up assets during the working portion of their lives to finance vacations during their later years.

When it comes to spending future wealth, individuals appear willing to spend a small portion on dues, charitable contributions, and vacations. Other categories are unaffected by future wealth. This reluctance to spend future wealth does not appear to change after retirement. However, retired households do appear more willing to access current assets (except home equity). Retired households treat current assets more like current income.

Evaluation

The existing evidence strongly supports the differential MPC hypothesis.

Pensions and Saving

Consider an individual who saves 10 percent of his or her yearly income for retirement. Suppose that total saving consists of 6 percent that is required to be put into a pension plan and 4 percent into "discretionary" savings. What will happen to total saving if the individual is forced to increase the pension component from 6 percent to 7 percent? If one puts aside issues of bequests, liquidity constraints, tax rates, vesting, and induced retirement, the LC prediction is that total saving will be unaffected. Discretionary saving should fall by the amount of the increase in the pension contribution, in order to preserve the choice of lifetime consumption plan c. This follows from the general assumption of fungibility. Let PS be pension saving and DS be discretionary saving. Then the LC prediction is that $dDS/dPS = -1.0$.

302 Applications and Extensions

The corresponding prediction of the BLC model is:

Prediction 1: The change in discretionary saving with respect to a change in pension saving is less (in absolute value) than 1.0 and, for the young, will approach zero.

The intuitive explanation behind this prediction is easily described. The representative household in our theory has a marginal propensity to consume from its income (I) account of nearly 1.0, but a marginal propensity to consume from its future wealth (F) account of 0. Therefore, when the pension plan transfers $1.00 from I to F, total saving rises by almost $1.00. Because expenditures are usually adjusted to be consistent with disposable income, the payroll deduction reduces the money readily available to spend. Then, once the pension contribution becomes pension wealth, it is off-limits to current consumption. The formal argument is more involved, and is summarized in the appendix.

Prediction 1 illustrates the quasi-rational or second-best nature of our model. Our representative savers are not fools. They have genuine human weaknesses that act as constraints on the planner's maximization problem. People who join Christmas clubs, for example, probably know that they are giving up interest, convenience, and liquidity in return for external enforcement of willpower. They may judge that trade sensible if the perceived alternative is to have too little money for Christmas presents. But what would be downright stupid would be to join a Christmas club and then borrow against the subsequent payout. We believe few people are that silly. Similarly for pensions, we believe that people allow themselves to think of a pension contribution as a reduction in income in order that they do not defeat its primary purpose—the provision of income for retirement.

Our model also predicts a positive relationship between wealth (income) and the magnitude of the offset, specifically:

Prediction 2: The change in discretionary saving with respect to a change in pension saving increases (in absolute value) with income or wealth.

This prediction arises because the cost of exercising willpower is taken to decline with income.[10] Willpower becomes increasingly difficult to exercise when income (and therefore consumption) dimin-

[10] See also later on nonproportionality, a closely related issue.

ishes. Within the model, the prediction can be derived from the assumption that willpower is especially costly at low consumption levels combined with inequality (8). Together these imply that the impact of a change in the account balance on the marginal utility of consumption falls as the account balance increases. Think about an individual who selects the maximum deduction rate s^* and augments his pension savings with additional discretionary saving (so that $c_t(s) < I_t$). Inequality (8) suggests that the individual will be less impacted by the last marginal increment Δs than corresponding individuals with zero or minimal discretionary saving.

Evidence

The evidence pertaining to Prediction 1 is substantial. The first work on this question was done over 20 years ago by Cagan (1965) and Katona (1965). Cagan used a sample of respondents to an extensive survey of its members conducted by the Consumers Union. Saving was defined as the family's change in net worth over the year. Saving was then broken down into discretionary saving (DS), pension saving (PS), and other contractual saving. He obtained the surprising result that membership in a pension plan *increased* other forms of saving, that is, $dDS/dPS > 0$. He attributed this result to what he called the *recognition effect*. Membership in a pension plan was thought to increase the awareness of the need to save for retirement and, thus, encourage other saving. Katona's study was much like Cagan's and obtained similar results.

Cagan's study has been criticized in the literature, especially by Munnell (1974). The most troublesome problem is one of which Cagan was aware: selectivity bias. Put simply, people with a taste for saving may be more likely to work for firms that offer a pension plan. This is discussed later. Munnell also criticized Cagan on other grounds and replicated his study using the same data. She used a different measure of saving, replaced before-tax income with after-tax income, and restricted her analysis to a subset of the observations that she thought were more reliable. She then regressed the nonpension saving rate on several variables including a pension dummy. While she did not obtain the positive coefficients found by Cagan, none of the coefficients was significantly negative.[11]

[11] Another study by Munnell (1976) finds larger offsets. However, this study has some data limitations. The amount saved via pensions is unknown, so a pension dummy must be used exclusively. More important, the results are not robust. The estimates reported for two different times differ greatly. The estimate for the latter

Two more recent articles on this issue have appeared in the *Economic Journal*. Green (1981) used two British samples, the 1953 Oxford Saving Survey and a 1969 Family Expenditure Survey. Both data sets represent an improvement over those reported earlier, because the magnitude of pension saving was available (rather than just a dummy variable for membership). However, the size of employer contributions was not available. Green used three definitions of "other saving": (1) total saving minus pension saving, (2) other long-term saving, and (3) total saving plus durable purchases minus pension saving. Each was regressed on wealth, age, and pension saving. Once again the anomalous but ubiquitous positive coefficients were obtained. Breaking up the samples into homogeneous groups based on age or income had no effect.

Green also investigated the possible selectivity bias issue raised by Munnell. Before discussing his results, consider the logic of the selectivity bias argument. Suppose the true value of dDS/dPS is -1.0. How could selectivity bias yield estimates of (essentially) zero? The mean marginal propensity to save of those without pensions must exceed the mean marginal propensity to save of those with pensions by the average level of pension contributions. This seems implausible but possible. Now consider the range of pension benefits offered by various employers. It is even more implausible to think that these match up precisely with the average savings propensities of their employees. So Green reestimated his equations restricting his sample to those families with pensions. Again, all estimates of dDS/dPS were positive.

King and Dicks-Mireaux (1982) estimated the effect of pensions on wealth as part of a larger study. They used a 1976 Canadian data set. The estimated offset to saving resulting from an additional dollar of pension wealth (evaluated at the mean values for the sample) was either $-.10$ or $-.24$, depending on the definition of wealth used.[12] While these estimates are of the "right" sign, they are clearly much smaller (in absolute value) than -1.0. King and Dicks-Mireaux also report that the magnitude of the offset increases with wealth, and

---

period implies that those having pensions reduce their other saving by an amount three times the average value of pension contributions in the United States in that year. Also, the results change dramatically when an alternative specification is used. These problems make it difficult to interpret the findings.

[12] See also Dicks-Mireaux and King (1984). Using the same data set as in their earlier article, they investigate the sensitivity of the pension and social security displacement effects to prior beliefs. They conclude that the estimates are relatively robust.

this supports our second proposition. Specifically, they state, "The estimated offset is an increasing function of wealth and at the mean values for the top decile group of the distribution of net worth the reduction in saving per additional dollar of pension wealth is estimated to be $1.00 for social security and $0.40 for private pensions" (p. 265).

The last two studies we will mention utilize the most comprehensive data sets yet analyzed. Kurz (1981) used the 1979 survey conducted by the President's Commission on Pension Policy. This data set has very good information (by survey standards) on pension wealth, including the value of employers' contributions. Kurz estimated the pension wealth offset to total wealth for three subsamples: male heads, female heads, and two-head families. The marginal effect was calculated at three different ages (30, 50, and 60) using two different measures of permanent income or wealth. He estimated the total offset to be between .39 and .47, again substantially different from the 100% predicted by the LC model.

Finally, Diamond and Hausman (1984) used the National Longitudinal Survey, done between 1966 and 1976. Their estimates are not directly comparable to the others because they calculated the elasticity of the saving to permanent income ratio with respect to the pension benefits to permanent income ratio (rather than dDS/dPS). This turned out to be $-.14$, where a complete offset would again have produced an estimate of -1.0.

There is also a large related literature pertaining to the effect of social security wealth on saving. We will make no attempt to survey those studies,[13] but we do want to make one point about the debate between Barro and Feldstein. Barro has argued that individuals will not reduce their saving in response to an increase in Social Security benefits because they will want to increase their bequests to compensate their heirs for future tax increases. Whether or not this argument is plausible, notice that no similar argument applies for fully funded pensions. Even unfunded pensions have intergenerational side effects only to the extent that pensions are imperfect substitutes for other bequeathable assets. Thus, the fact that people do not offset increase in pension wealth suggests that similar findings in the Social Security arena are due to self-control reasons rather than intergenerational transfers. Thus, we feel Barro is likely to be proven empirically right, although for the wrong reasons.

---

[13] See Barro (1978) (which contains a reply by Feldstein).

Evaluation

The articles reported here used data sets spanning three decades and three countries. While the estimates of the offset vary between mildly positive (i.e., wrong sign) to nearly $-.5$, in no case is the estimated offset close to minus one. While selectivity bias could explain these results, we find that argument unconvincing, especially in light of Green's results using only pension recipients. (One could control for selectivity bias by studying the saving behavior of the continuing employees in a firm that changed pension benefits.) Other rationalizations of offsets less than unity have been made, but it is difficult to explain a zero (much less positive) offset within any neoclassical framework. We judge this particular set of results quite supportive of the BLC model.

Individual Retirement Accounts

The analysis of pensions also applies to Individual Retirement Accounts (IRAs). For several years during the 1980s, Americans could put up to $2,000 into an IRA on a tax deductible basis. The central issue is whether the money that flowed into IRAs generated "new" saving, or whether it just represented "reshuffling" of saving from other (taxable) forms to the new sheltered account. Note that this boils down to a fungibility question. As Venti and Wise (1987, p. 6) put it, "It may be tempting to think of IRAs and conventional saving accounts as equivalent assets, or goods, simply with different prices, in which case one might think of IRAs as only a price subsidy of conventional saving with a limit on the quantity that can be had at the subsidized price. . . . But, . . . the analysis indicates quite strongly that the two are not treated as equivalent by consumers." Venti and Wise use the Consumer Expenditure Survey to analyze the IRA experience, and conclude that "the vast majority of IRA saving represents new saving, not accompanied by reduction in other saving." (p. 38) They also find that most IRA contributors had not done much saving before IRAs were introduced.

Feenberg and Skinner (1989) also examine the "new" saving versus reshuffling hypothesis using a sample of tax returns. If IRAs are primarily reshuffled savings, then IRA users should have lower taxable interest income than nonusers. However, they find that within each wealth class, the IRA users had higher taxable interest income, suggesting a positive offset similar to that found in the pension studies.

Some other facts about IRA usage suggest that mental accounting and self-control factors are important. Because IRAs sheltered interest income, a rational person would purchase an IRA at the earliest possible date, so that the income would be sheltered as long as possible. This would be particularly true for someone who was just shifting assets from a taxable account to an IRA. According to the law, however, taxpayers could make tax deductible purchases for a given year up until April 15 of the following year. Summers (1986) reports that for the 1985 tax year, nearly half of the IRA purchases were made in 1986. Also, Feenberg and Skinner find that, holding everything else constant, an important predictor of whether a household will purchase an IRA is whether they would otherwise have to write a check to the Internal Revenue Service on April 15. Those who owed money were more likely to buy an IRA than those who were getting refunds. This result begs for a mental accounting interpretation. ("I would rather put $2,000 in an IRA than pay the government $800.") Feenberg and Skinner also found that wealth was a more important predictor of purchase than was income, suggesting that those households with liquid assets were more likely to buy IRAs.

If IRA purchases often come out of liquid assets, why do IRA purchases increase total saving? One reason is that money in the IRA account becomes both less liquid (it is subject to a special 10-percent tax surcharge if withdrawn before the purchaser reaches 59½ years old) and less tempting. Funds in an IRA are regarded as "off-limits" except for the most dire of emergencies. As Venti and Wise (1989, p. 11) note, "Some persons of course may consider the illiquidity of IRAs an advantage: It may help insure behavior that would not otherwise be followed. It may be a means of self-control."[14] Also, if households have a desired level of their A account, then the purchase of the IRA will only decrease the account temporarily. Similarly, those who borrow to purchase an IRA will normally pay the loan off fairly quickly (certainly before they reach retirement age) and thereby increase net saving.

Evaluation

The facts that IRAs increase saving and users often wait until the last minute to contribute both support the BLC model.

---

[14] The experience with 401-k tax-deferred retirement plans illustrates that people may value illiquidity for retirement saving. Some plans permit withdrawals for "hardships," while others do not. The Government Accounting Office reports (GAO/ PEMD-88-20FS) that participation rates and deferral rates are if anything higher in the plans that do *not* permit any withdrawals.

Housing Wealth

In the BLC model, pension wealth has a particularly low MPC because it is entered in the future income account. For home owners, housing wealth represents a similar type of situation that should be considered a separate account less tempting than the assets account. This implies Prediction 3.

> Prediction 3: The marginal propensity to consume housing wealth will be smaller than the MPC from liquid assets.

To evaluate this part of the theory, it is useful to begin with some simple facts. Krumm and Miller (1986) use the Panel Survey of Income Dynamics between 1970 and 1979 to study the effect of homeownership on other savings. They find the following pattern. Young households accumulate liquid assets in order to make a down payment on their first house purchase, then draw down those assets when they buy the home. Soon thereafter, they begin to accumulate liquid assets again. At the same time they are building up home equity by paying off their mortgage and accumulating capital gains on their home. If the wealth in their home is a good substitute for other savings, then one would expect homeowners to have less savings in other assets, holding everything else constant. However, just the opposite is true. If one compares those households in the panel who owned a house continuously from 1970 to 1979 to those who never bought a house, homeowners' nonhouse savings were $16,000 higher, *ceteris paribus*. In addition, they had $29,000 in home equity. (For a similar result, see Manchester and Poterba [1989].)

Another way of looking at the fungibility question is to estimate the MPC from housing wealth. Skinner (1989) takes this approach. He first runs a simple regression of the change in real consumption from 1976 to 1981 on the change in housing wealth for those people in his sample who owned a house and did not move. The estimated coefficient was not significantly different from zero. In more complex models, one set of regressions obtained a small but significant effect, while another set that corrected for individual differences across families suggested that shifts in house value had no effect on consumption.

Could these results be explained by Barro–Ricardo-style intergenerational transfers? If house prices go up, then people want to save more to give their kids money to buy a house. To check this, Skinner tries a housing wealth × family size interaction term, but finds that it also has no effect on consumption. Also, if Barro were right, then everyone (on average) would respond to an increase in house prices by saving more for their heirs, not just homeowners.

Housing wealth plays a key role in another LC anomaly, the saving behavior of the retired. The LC model predicts that the retired will draw down on their wealth over time, that is, dissave. Most studies of this issue do not support this prediction. Indeed, investigators using cross-sectional data have found the puzzling result that the retired actually continue to save (see, e.g., Davies [1981], Mirer, [1979] and the literature review in Bernheim [1987]). This result has been taken as strong evidence of a bequest motive. However, in a recent paper, Hurd (1987) criticized these cross-sectional studies[15] and presented new evidence from the Longitudinal Retirement History Survey. Hurd found little support for a bequest motive because the behavior of households with living children was indistinguishable from childless households. He also found that retired households do dissave. However, a question remains whether they dissave fast enough to be consistent with the LC model.

A key question in evaluating the evidence is how to treat housing wealth. Hurd found that retired households dissaved 13.9 percent of their total bequeathable (i.e., nonannuity) wealth over the period 1969–1979, and 27.3 percent of their bequeathable wealth excluding housing wealth. The former figure is clearly too low (by LC standards), while the latter figure might be considered reasonable. Hurd argued that excluding housing wealth was appropriate because of the costs of changing housing consumption levels. We are not convinced by this argument. While it is true that moving is costly, housing wealth can be reduced by borrowing. Typical retired homeowning households have no mortgage[16] and, thus, could draw down on their housing wealth using the credit market. Their failure to do so must be considered at least partially a self-imposed borrowing constraint rather than credit rationing. Indeed, "reverse mortgages"[17]

[15] The most important source of bias in the cross section, according to Hurd, is due to differential rates of survivorship. For example, the rich tend to live longer than the poor, so the older age groups have disproportionate numbers of the rich.

[16] For example, Hogarth (1986) contains information on a subsample of 770 respondents in the RHS selected as having a head of household who was working in 1969, retired in 1971, and survived through 1979. For this group, the median mortgage was zero. See also Sherman (1976), who states, "The overwhelming majority of homeowners older than 65 are without mortgage debt—apparently because they paid it off before retiring" (p. 72).

[17] With a reverse mortgage, the (usually) retired home owner uses collateral in the house to borrow money from a bank. The proceeds of the loan are typically paid to the borrower in monthly payments. When the borrower dies or decides to sell the house, the loan is repaid.

have been offered in some areas with very little consumer response. Some direct evidence that retired households voluntarily maintain the equity in their homes is provided by Venti and Wise (1989) in an article entitled "But They Don't Want to Reduce Housing Equity."

Venti and Wise study this question using the six Retirement History Surveys, from 1969 to 1979. They make use of the fact that those members of the sample who sell one house and buy another can adjust the level of their home equity at low cost, so the desired level of housing equity can be inferred from their behavior. Their behavior suggests that the mean difference between desired and actual house equity was very small, only $1,010. To put this in perspective, the desired proportion of wealth in housing equity was .53. The difference between the current and desired proportions was .0107. There was essentially no effect of age on desired housing equity. Also, whether the family had children or not had no effect on desired home equity, rendering a bequest explanation suspect. Venti and Wise conclude, "Most elderly are not liquidity constrained. And contrary to standard formulations of the life-cycle hypothesis, the typical elderly family has no desire to reduce housing equity" (p. 23).

Evaluation

The evidence strongly supports the hypothesis that housing wealth is treated as a very poor substitute for other wealth. Even the elderly appear reluctant to consume out of their "home equity" account.

Saving Adequacy

The essence of the LC hypothesis is the idea of consumption smoothing. As stated earlier, if a time-dependent utility function is allowed, then virtually any intertemporal pattern of consumption can be reconciled with the LC hypothesis, and the theory becomes irrefutable. Operationally, the theory amounts to the prediction of a smooth consumption profile, so retirement consumption should equal preretirement consumption. Alternatively put, consumption in every period should equal the annuity value of lifetime wealth. The BLC prediction is the following:

> Prediction 4: In the absence of sufficiently large Social Security and pension programs, retirement consumption will be less than preretirement consumption.

Prediction 3 is derived from the model using inequality (4), which is the formal representation of the principle that temptation induces impatience. The steeper the marginal utility of consumption function is at date t, the lower the resulting choice of c_T. If the Z_t function is the same at all dates, then the absence of entry fees into A and F (meaning the opportunity to borrow against future wealth) guarantees that the individual would choose $c_T < c_t$. Pensions and Social Security serve two functions. They reduce the temptation to spend out of income, and they protect a portion of lifetime wealth that is earmarked for retirement. Of course if mandatory pensions plus Social Security were sufficient to keep retirement consumption up to preretirement levels, then self-control problems are unlikely to be important. Thus, the size of the pension/saving offset discussed earlier becomes crucial to the interpretation of saving adequacy.

Before reviewing the evidence on this issue, it is instructive to begin with some simple facts. Nearly all retirement saving is done through some routinized program. The most important vehicles are Social Security, private pensions, home equity, and whole life insurance. The amount of discretionary saving done is qualitatively quite small. Diamond and Hausman (1984) found that half of the National Longitudinal Survey (NLS) sample of men aged 45–69 had wealth to income ratios of less than 1.6 if Social Security and pension wealth were excluded. Moreover, 30% had essentially zero nonpension wealth. Similar findings are reported by Kotlikoff, Spivak, and Summers (1982). Just the fact that so much of retirement saving is achieved through institutionalized mechanisms can be regarded as support for our framework (because the recognition of self-control problems can be viewed as the reason why people want such institutions), but the high rates of institutionalized saving also make it difficult to interpret the results.

Several authors have addressed the saving adequacy issue directly, with a wide variety of methods and data. Blinder, Gordon, and Wise (1983) used the 1971 Retirement History Survey. Their analysis can be summarized (and simplified) as follows: Let $w = W_t/W_T$ be the ratio of current wealth at age t to total lifetime wealth, where t is between age 60 and 65. Let $c = C_t/C_T$ be the ratio of the family's expected future person years of consumption at age t to the expected total when the head entered the labor market. Then the ratio $\gamma = w/c$ should be equal to unity if retirement saving is adequate. They estimated γ to be .45.

Courant, Gramlich, and Laitner (1986) used the Panel Study of Income Dynamics to analyze families' consumption profiles. They found that real consumption increases over time until retirement, then decreases. They interpret this within the LC model as implying negative subjective rates of time preference while young. Our interpretation is quite different. Consumption rises while young because real income (and thus temptation) is also rising. Consumption falls during retirement because (a) real income falls because most pension benefits are not indexed, and (b) the elderly grow to realize that their resources are inadequate and gradually adapt to a reduced standard of living.[18]

Kotlikoff, Spivak, and Summers (1982) dealt with saving adequacy directly. Using the 1969–1973 Retirement History Surveys, they calculated the ratio $RA = c_{oa}/c_{ya}$, where c_{oa} is the level annuity that can be purchased when old, given the present expected value of old age resources, and c_{ya} is the level annuity that can be purchased when young, based on the present expected value of lifetime resources. (They also calculated a similar ratio R based on simple present values without annuities.) At first glance their results seem to support the LC model. Over 90 percent of the sample had values of R or RA of at least .8; many have ratios of unity or higher. However, it turns out that nearly all the wealth the elderly possess is in Social Security, pensions, and home equity: "Slightly more than one-third of couples reported levels of net worth that represent less than 10 percent of their total future resources. In addition, 67 percent of married couples hold less than 10 percent of their future resources in liquid wealth. Of these couples, 21 percent had no liquid wealth whatsoever" (Kotlikoff, Spivak, and Summers, 1982, p. 1065).

The test of the LC model then depends crucially on the pension and Social Security offsets. If these offsets are less than complete, then the saving adequacy cannot be attributed to rational saving behavior. The authors investigated this question and concluded that "in the absence of Social Security and private pensions, consumption in old age relative to lifetime consumption would be about 40% lower for the average person" (p. 1067).

Hamermesh (1983) also addressed the saving adequacy issue, but he used a different approach from Kotlikoff, Spivak, and Summers.

---

[18] In the absence of annuities, uncertainty about the length of life can also induce consumption to fall during retirement. Yet much of wealth *is* in the form of Social Security and pension annuities. Uncertainty about the length of life can also affect the level of wealth at retirement, but the direction is ambiguous. Two risks must be weighed: the risk of dying sooner than expected (and thus having saved too much ex-post), and the risk of dying later than expected (and thus having saved too little). Our intuition suggests that most people will be more concerned with the former than the latter, and, thus Blinder, Gordon, and Wise should find $\gamma > 1$ if people are risk averse LC savers.

He analyzed the spending patterns of retired households using the Retirement History Survey linked to Social Security records for information on income. The question Hamermesh asked was whether the elderly have sufficient income to sustain the levels of consumption they maintain early in retirement. He computed the ratio of consumption to annuitized income to answer this question. He found that consumption on average is not sustainable. In 1973, 54 percent of the retired households had consumption to income ratios exceeding 1.1. Because Social Security benefits represent nearly half of retirement income in his sample, Hamermesh also computed what the consumption to income ratio would be for various assumptions about the size of the saving/Social Security offset. If the offset is 50 percent, then the average consumption to income ratio is around 1.5. If the offset is zero, then the values climb to well over 2.0. Similar results would hold for pensions that are about another 30 percent of retirement income. Finally, Hamermesh found that between 1973 and 1975, the elderly reduced their real consumption by about 5 percent per year. This is a result similar to that obtained by Courant, Gramlich, and Laitner. The elderly respond to inadequate saving by reducing real consumption.

In comparing his measure of savings adequacy with Kotlikoff, Spivak, and Summers, Hamermesh made the point that consumption follows the inverted J-shaped age-earning profiles: "It may thus be more sensible to evaluate the adequacy of Social Security [and saving generally] by comparing its ability to sustain consumption during retirement to consumption just before retirement rather than to average lifetime consumption" (p. 7). Clearly by this standard, saving is inadequate.

Evaluation

The saving adequacy issue is much more difficult to evaluate than the effect of pensions on saving. Some authors, that is, Blinder, Gordon and Wise, and Hamermesh, judge saving to be inadequate, while others, that is, Kotlikoff, Spivak and Summers, judge saving to be adequate. To the extent that saving is adequate, Social Security and pensions appear to be largely responsible. The fact that consumption seems to decline during retirement is consistent with the interpretation that saving has been inadequate, but it is also consistent with the fact that the expected age of death increases with age. Again it would be possible (in principle) to test the competing theories cleanly by studying the saving behavior of individuals who do not have access to pensions and Social Security, or for whom those institutions would be inadequate. An interesting case in point is professional athletes who earn high salaries for a short and uncertain period. We speculate that the typical 24-year-old superstar spends more than the annuity value of his expected lifetime wealth.

Nonproportionality

Wealth theories of saving are blind to levels of wealth. Consumption is smoothed, no matter what the level of permanent income happens to be. Friedman called this the proportionality principle. In contrast, our model predicts the following:

Prediction 5: The saving rate increases with permanent income.

We are not alone in rejecting the proportionality principle. In fact, our position was stated very well by Fisher (1930):

> In general, it may be said that, other things being equal, the smaller the income, the higher the preference for present over future income. . . . It is true, of course, that a permanently small income implies a keen appreciation of future wants as well as of immediate wants. . . . This result is partly rational, because of the importance of supplying present needs in order to keep up the continuity of life and the ability to cope with the future; and partly irrational, because the presence of present needs blinds one to the needs of the future. (p. 72)

Our model simply formalizes and rationalizes Fisher's intuition. In our model the marginal cost of exercising willpower is very high at low consumption levels but falls off as consumption increases. Therefore, willpower costs fall off as income (and therefore consumption) increases. To the poor, saving is a luxury.

The evidence on the proportionality issue as of 1972 was reported in the very thorough and insightful survey by Mayer (1972), who also conducted five tests of his own. We will just reproduce his conclusion: "There are many tests which disconfirm the proportionality hypothesis. What is even more persuasive, of all the many tests which have been undertaken by friends of the hypothesis, *not a single one supports it.* I therefore conclude that the proportionality hypothesis is definitely invalidated" (p. 348).

When Friedman investigated proportionality, he found that it was violated, but he argued that the observed behavior could be explained by measurement error. Those with high incomes might save more, he hypothesized, because their incomes have a large (positive) transitory component. Diamond and Hausman (1984) investigated this explanation using modern panel data. They regressed the saving to permanent income ratio on permanent income in a piecewise linear form. The results implied that for incomes less than $4,770, each extra $1,000 of permanent income raises the ratio by 3.3 percent; beyond $4,770 it rises by 5.7 percent for each extra $1,000, and beyond $12,076, it rises by 14.2 percent. The differences are all statistically significant (p. 108).

Evaluation

The evidence against the proportionality principle is very strong. While the self-control hypothesis is only one of many possible expla-nations for the observed rising saving rate, the results on the interaction between income and the pension saving offset (Prediction 2) lend some support to our self-control based explanation.

Hypersensitivity

One of the simple elegant features of the LC model is the way in which variability in income is handled. In each period (year), the consumer should consume the annuity value of his or her expected wealth. This statement applies whether or not the variability in income is deterministic or stochastic. Consumers are either implicitly or explicitly assumed to have some type of rational expectations, so permanent increases in income produce much larger responses in consumption than transitory increases because they lead to larger increases in wealth. Many factors are ruled irrelevant, for example, the timing of the income across years and within a year (as long as there are efficient capital markets) and the form of the wealth (say human capital vs. home equity).

Our model yields three propositions that are significantly in conflict with the LC hypothesis in this general area. In this section we will discuss the sensitivity of consumption to income generally. The following two sections concern the special cases of bonuses and windfalls.

Prediction 6: Holding wealth constant, consumption tracks income.

This prediction applies whether or not the variability is known (as with the age-earning profile) or unknown (as with a windfall). Formally the prediction is a consequence of the character of the planner's maximization problem. Recall that willpower effort costs are reduced by having consumption financed only out of the income account, with savings allocated directly to the asset accounts. In the first-best plan, the entire income account is consumed at each date. In a second-best setting, this feature might still hold, even though some of the fluctuations in the income stream get transmitted to the consumption stream. It is just suboptimal to invade the asset accounts in order to smooth out consumption fluctuations that are not too large.

To evaluate the hypersensitivity issue, it is instructive to compare some new evidence with some old evidence. Recall that Courant, Gramlich, and Laitner found that consumption tends to follow the same hump-shaped pattern as the age-earnings profile. They rationalize this by attributing negative rates of subjective time preference (ρ) to the young. This rationalization seems implausible on the surface and, more to the point, inconsistent with other evidence about individual discount rates. Friedman (1957) estimated ρ to be .4 (although he tended to use .33). Holbrook (1966) reestimated ρ and found it to be closer to .5 than to .33. This implies a two-year horizon in the permanent income model. Holbrook concluded:

> . . . the shorter the horizon, the better is permanent income approximated by current income. When permanent income equals current income, the only significant special assumption of the PIH remaining is that of unitary-income elasticity of consumption. Therefore, the shorter the horizon, the smaller is the distinction between the PIH and what might be called the "current income hypothesis." In this sense, the evidence may be taken to indicate that it makes little difference which hypothesis is true, nearly the same conclusions follow from both. (p. 754).

Other authors that have tried to estimate ρ in other contexts have also found rates in excess of market interest rates (e.g., Gately, 1980; Hausman, 1979; Thaler, 1981). Together these results yield an inconsistency for the wealth model. Friedman's empirical results can only be consistent with a wealth model if people have very high discount rates, while the observed consumption patterns are only consistent with wealth theories if people have negative discount rates before retirement.

Recently, the hypersensitivity issue was examined by Hall and

Table 12.2   For Real Interest Rate Per Year Equal To

		.05	.10	.20	.30
For Remaining	20 yrs	.095	.105	.170	.232
Lifetime	30 yrs	.071	.093	.167	.231

Source: Hall and Mishkin (1982).

Mishkin (1982), who derived the first truly rational expectations-based model of consumption. They separated household income into three components: a deterministic component, y_{Dt}, which rises with age until just before retirement; a stochastic component, y_{Lt}, which fluctuates as lifetime prospects change and is specified as a random walk; and a stationary stochastic component, y_{st}, which fluctuates according to transitory influences and is described by a moving average time series process.

Hall and Mishkin were particularly interested in the parameter β_t, which is the marginal propensity to consume out of transitory income, y_{st}. The model predicts that β_t should be equal to the yearly annuity value of a dollar of transitory income. Therefore, β_t is determined by the expected remaining years of life and the interest rate. Hall and Mishkin gave some illustrative values for β_t that are reproduced in Table 12.2. However, when they estimated β_t for food consumption using the Panel Study of Income Dynamics from 1969 to 1975, the estimated value for β_t turned out to be .29. This is consistent with the model only at interest rates higher than those given in Table 12.2.[19] We take this to be a reconfirmation of the earlier Friedman–Holbrook estimates of discount rates in the .33–.50 range. It is noteworthy that they obtain this result in spite of the use of food consumption as the dependent variable. Food consumption would seem to be less volatile than some other components of consumption. The high estimate for β_t surprised Hall and Mishkin, and this led them to consider whether other factors were at work. Upon closer examination, they found that 20 percent of all (food) consumption is not explained by the LC model, and in consequence hypothesized that

[19] An alternative lagged formulation yields a lower value of β_t. Recently an alternative view of these results has been offered by Deaton (1986), Campbell (1987), and Campbell and Deaton (1987). They argue that consumption is actually too smooth, rather than hypersensitive. Space limitations prevent us from discussing these interesting articles here.

it is "set to a fraction of current income instead of following the more complicated optimal rule." This led to point out that they "are unable to distinguish this symptom of inability (or unwillingness) to borrow and lend from the type of behavior characteristic of consumers who simply face high interest rates."

In our earlier article (Thaler and Shefrin, 1981), we pointed out that marginal rates of time preference greater than market rates of interest are consistent with our model if a self-imposed prohibition against borrowing (except to finance homes and other durables) is in effect. This hypothesized aversion to borrowing yields the same predicted behavior as the market-imposed credit rationing suggested by Hall and Mishkin in the passage just quoted. How then can the two hypotheses be distinguished? A data set with detailed financial information would allow the credit rationing hypothesis to be tested. First of all, capital market constraints cannot be binding for any family with significant liquid assets. Similarly, many families have equity in their homes or cash value in life insurance policies. These present easy credit sources. Finally, almost anyone with a steady job can qualify for some credit from banks and credit card companies. Any family that has not utilized these sources can be presumed to be unconstrained by the capital market. If the credit rationing hypothesis is correct, then the subset of families for whom the hypothesis can be ruled out should not display hypersensitivity. In the absence of such tests, one can only guess at the relative importance of the two hypotheses. There is some evidence that individuals have unused credit sources. For example, Warshawsky (1987) finds that many life insurance policy holders fail to take advantage of the possibility of borrowing against their insurance policy, even when the interest rate is lower than the rate at which the individual could invest. We think that it is unlikely that the average consumer is borrowed to the limit.

Evaluation

Individuals behave as if they had excessively high rates of discount. Nevertheless, much of lifetime consumption is successfully postponed. While credit markets do not permit massive borrowing against future income, we judge the hypersensitivity observed by Friedman and by Hall and Mishkin more plausibly explained by self-imposed borrowing prohibitions than by market-imposed quantity constraints.

Bonuses

Define a bonus as a fully anticipated temporary increase in income. Our model then yields the following prediction.

Prediction 7: The marginal propensity to consume bonus income is lower than the marginal propensity to consume regular income.

This prediction reflects the combination of an assumption and a principle. The assumption is that bonus income, because it arrives as a large lump sum, is allocated to the A account, not the I account. The principle discussed in the theory section is that the marginal propensity to consume out of the income account exceeds that of the asset account.

The pooling of income into a lump-sum bonus increases saving in two ways. First, by lowering regular monthly income (relative to spreading out the bonus), the temptation to spend each month is reduced. Regular monthly expenditures tend to be geared to regular monthly income. To set a higher level of monthly expenditures would require the individual either to borrow against the future bonus or draw down on the saved bonus during the year, each of which would violate typical mental accounting rules. Second, when the bonus does arrive, a considerable binge can occur and still permit an increase in the saving rate relative to normal. Also, if the binge is spent on durables, then some saving occurs in that way.

Bonuses are nice illustrations of a framing effect. In a standard economic model, a completely anticipated bonus is simply income with another name. Thus, the distribution of earnings into income and bonus would be considered irrelevant. Our model offers the potential for increased explanatory power by considering variables, such as bonuses, about which the standard theories are silent.

The only evidence we have been able to find regarding bonuses comes from Japan. In Japan, most workers receive semiannual bonuses. Ishikawa and Ueda (1984) have studied the saving behavior of the Japanese and estimate the significance of the bonuses. Using a pooled cross-sectional time series approach, they estimated the marginal propensities to consume out of regular and bonus income, respectively. Tests suggested pooling what they called normal years 1969–1973, 1977–1978, and treating the two recession–oil shock periods 1974–1976 and 1979–1980 separately. For the normal years, they could reject the hypothesis that households treat the two sources of income equivalently. The marginal propensity to consume bonus income was estimated to be .437, while the corresponding figure for nonbonus income was .685. The difference is significant. The difference holds with durable expenditures included or excluded from consumption, although as should be expected, expenditures on durables respond much more to bonus income than to other parts of income. During 1974–1976, the MPC out of bonuses jumped to over 1.0. This suggests that households used bonuses in bad years to smooth out consumption. The last period studied, 1979–1980, returns to the pattern of a lower MPC out of bonus income.

Could the low MPC out of bonus income be explained by the permanent income hypothesis if bonuses are treated as transitory income? This explanation is dubious because the bonuses are fairly well anticipated. As one Japanese observer has put it, "The trouble, however, lies in the interpretation of 'transitory' income. Although they are called bonuses, they are fully institutionalized and workers expect bonuses as an intrinsic part of their normal income. Furthermore, workers can anticipate fairly well the level of bonus payments and thus a rational worker will treat them as permanent, rather than transitory, components of his income" (Shiba, 1979, p. 207).

Nevertheless, Ishikawa and Ueda investigated this possibility directly using actual expectations data on bonus income. They used a sample of roughly 5,000 workers who were asked to estimate 6 months in advance how large their next bonus would be. Later, actual bonuses received and consumption data were also collected. The authors then tested to see whether the respondents had rational expectations and whether they responded differently to permanent and transitory components of bonus income. The results indicated that expectations were not rational (bonuses were underestimated), but the MPC out of the transitory component of bonus income was approximately the same as the MPC out of the permanent component. Both were estimated to be .46.

The authors' conclusion about their findings is the same as ours: "First, the permanent income-life cycle hypothesis does not seem to apply to Japanese worker households. . . . [and second] Households distinguish bonus earnings from the rest of their income" (p. 2).

Evaluation

The results on bonuses are probably the hardest to rationalize within the LC framework. Similar tests would be possible in the United States if a sample of workers with and without bonuses were collected. Unfortunately, most data sets do not distinguish bonus income from normal wages and salaries.

Windfalls

Predictions 5 and 6 together imply the following:

> Prediction 8: (a) For (nonnegligible) windfalls, the marginal propensity to consume is less than the marginal propensity to consume regular income but greater than the annuity value of the windfall. (b) The marginal propensity to consume out of windfall income declines as the size of the windfall increases.

The explanation of the first feature is basically identical to the argument for bonuses. The only difference is that the marginal propensity to consume from the windfall income is higher than for bonuses if the windfall is truly unexpected. This is because the individual has no opportunity to adjust his or her earlier saving in anticipation of the windfall. The explanation of the second feature is based on mental accounting. People tend to consume from income and leave perceived "wealth" alone. The larger is a windfall, the more wealthlike it becomes, and the more likely it will be included in the less tempting assets account. A corollary is that changes in perceived wealth (such as increases in the value of home equity) are saved at a greater rate than windfalls considered "income."

The best study we have found regarding actual windfalls was done by Landsberger (1966). He studied the consumption behavior of Israeli recipients of German restitution payments after World War II. What makes the study particularly useful for our purposes is that there is substantial variation in the size of the windfall within the sample. His sample of 297 was divided into five groups based on the windfall as a percent of family income. The family incomes and MPC out of total income were about the same for each group. However, as our theory predicts, the MPC out of windfall income increased sharply as the size of the windfall decreased. For the group with the largest windfalls (about 66 percent of annual income) the MPC was about 23 percent, while the group receiving the smallest windfalls (about 7 percent of annual income) had MPCs in excess of 2.0. Small windfalls were spent twice!

Evaluation

Windfalls ironically facilitate both splurges and saving. Windfalls are not treated as simple increments to wealth. Temptation matters.

Policy Implications

The theory and evidence we have presented here suggest quite novel considerations for national policies regarding personal saving. Normally, when a government wants to alter the saving rate, it concentrates on changing either the level of income or the after-tax rate of return to saving. If the desire is to increase saving, then our analysis suggests that other seemingly irrelevant changes be considered. For example:

1. A tax cut not accompanied by (complete) changes in withholding rates should increase saving more than an equivalent tax cut fully reflected in withholding. This follows because the underwithholding will yield refunds that (like bonuses) should produce high saving rates.
2. Because pensions increase saving, firms could be encouraged to offer mandatory (or even discretionary) pension plans. Requiring firms to have pension plans would have the additional benefit that future demands on the Social Security system might be reduced as the elderly begin to have substantial pension wealth.
3. Similarly, firms could be encouraged to use Japanese-style bonuses as part of their compensation scheme. This form of payment is no more costly to firms (it might even be cheaper on a present value basis) and would, according to our analysis, increase saving.

Conclusion

The LC model is clearly in the mainstream tradition of microeconomic theory. It is typical of the general approach in microeconomics, which is to use a normative-based maximizing model for descriptive purposes. The recent articles by Hall and Mishkin, and Courant, Gramlich, and Laitner are really advances in the LC tradition.

Our model is quite different in spirit. First of all, our agents have very human limitations, and they use simple rules of thumb that are, by nature, second-best. While the LC model is a special case of our model (when either a first-best rule exists or there is no self-control problem), our model was developed specifically to describe actual behavior, not to characterize rational behavior. It differs from a standard approach in three important ways.

1. It is consistent with behavior that cannot be reconciled with a single utility function.
2. It permits "irrelevant" factors (i.e., those other than age and wealth) to affect consumption. Even the form of payment can matter.
3. Actual choices can be strictly within the budget set (as in a Christmas club).

The relationship between the self-control model and the LC model is similar to the relationship between Kahneman and Tversky's (1979) prospect theory and expected utility theory. Expected utility theory is a well-established standard for rational choice under uncertainty. Its failure to describe individual behavior has led to the development of other models (such as prospect theory) that appear to do a better job at the tasks of description and prediction. The superiority of prospect theory as a predictive model, of course, in no way weakens expected utility theory's value as a prescriptive norm. Similarly, because we view the LC model as capturing the preferences of our planner, we do not wish to question its value to prescriptive economic theory. The LC model has also served an enormously useful role in providing the theory against which empirical evidence can be judged. For example, the one-to-one pension offset was a result derived from the LC model (without bequests), and the numerous studies we cite were no doubt stimulated by the opportunity to test this prediction. Saving adequacy even more directly requires an LC criterion of appropriate saving with which actual saving can be compared.

At times we have argued that the use of ad hoc assumptions, added to the theory after the anomalous empirical evidence has been brought forward, renders the LC model untestable. It is reasonable to ask whether our model is testable. We think that it is. Every one of the propositions we examined in this chapter represents a test our model might have failed. For example, if the estimated pension offsets were mostly close to −1.0 instead of mostly close to zero, we would have taken that as evidence that self-control problems are empirically unimportant. Similarly, the effects of bonuses on saving could have been negligible, implying that mental accounting has little to add.

Other tests are also possible. Our theory suggests the following additional propositions.[20]

Prediction 9: The marginal propensity to consume inheritance income will depend on the form in which the inheritance is received.

The more the inheritance resembles "income" rather than "wealth," the greater will be the MPC. Thus, the MPC will be greater for cash than for stocks, and greater for stocks than for real estate.

Prediction 10: The marginal propensity to consume dividend income is greater than the marginal propensity to consume increases in the value of stock holdings.

We have not investigated the empirical validity of these propositions. We hope others who are skeptical of our theory will do so. Nevertheless, while we think that neither our theory nor the LC theory is empty, refutation is probably not the most useful way of thinking about the task at hand. It is easy to demonstrate that any theory in social science is wrong. (We do not believe that individuals literally have planners and doers, e.g.) Negative results and counterexamples must be only a first step. We intend this chapter to be constructive rather than destructive. We hope to have shown that the consideration of self-control problems enables us to identify variables that are usually ignored in economic analyses but that have an important influence on behavior.

•

We wish to thank Franco Modigliani for providing many thoughtful comments on a previous draft of this chapter. Thaler would also like to thank the Behavioral Economics Program at the Sloan Foundation for financial support.

References

Ainslie, George. "Specious Reward: A Behavioral Theory of Impulsiveness and Impulse Control." *Psychological Bulletin* 82 (1975): 463–496.

[20] The 1988 version of this article included another "new" prediction about housing wealth. In light of the new evidence that has emerged, this prediction has been now incorporated in the chapter under "Housing Wealth."

Barro, Robert. *The Impact of Social Security on Private Saving.* Washington, DC: American Enterprise Institute, 1978.

Bernheim, B. Douglas. "Dissaving after Retirement: Testing the Pure Life Cycle Hypothesis." in Zvi Bodie, John B. Shoven, and David Wise (eds.). *Issues in Pension Economics.* Chicago: University of Chicago Press, 1987.

Blinder, Alan, Roger Hall Gordon, and Donald Wise. "Social Security, Bequests, and the Life Cycle Theory of Saving: Cross Sectional Tests." in R. Hemming and F. Modigliani (eds.). *The Determinants of National Saving and Wealth.* International Economic Association. New York: St. Martin's Press. 1983.

Cagan, Philip. *The Effect of Pension Plans on Aggregate Savings.* New York: National Bureau of Economic Research, 1965.

Campbell, John Y. "Does Saving Anticipate Declining Labor Income? An Alternative Test of the Permanent Income Hypothesis." *Econometrica.* 55 (1987): 1249–1273.

———, and Angus Deaton. "Is Consumption Too Smooth?" Mimeo, Princeton University, January 1987.

Courant, Paul, Edward Gramlich, and John Laitner. "A Dynamic Micro Estimate of the Life Cycle Model." in Henry G. Aaron and Gary Burtless (eds.). *Retirement and Economic Behavior.* Washington, DC: Brookings Institution, 1986.

Davies, James B. "Uncertain Lifetime, Consumption, and Dissaving in Retirement." *Journal of Political Economy* 89 June (1981): 561–577.

Deaton, Angus S. "Life-Cycle Models of Consumption: Is the Evidence Consistent with the Theory?" National Bureau of Economic Research Working Paper No. 1910, 1986.

Diamond, Peter, and Jerry Hausman. "Individual Retirement and Saving Behavior." *Journal of Public Economics* 23 (1984): 81–114.

Dicks-Mireaux, Louis, and Mervyn King. "Pension Wealth and Household Savings: Tests of Robustness." *Journal of Public Economics* 23 (1984): 115–139.

Elster, Jon. *Ulysses and the Sirens.* Cambridge: Cambridge University Press, 1979.

Feenberg, Jonathan, and Jonathan Skinner. "Sources of IRA Saving." in Lawrence Summers, ed. *Tax Policy and the Economy,* vol. 3, Cambridge, MA: MIT Press, 1989, pp. 25–46.

Fisher, Irving. *The Theory of Interest.* London: MacMillan, 1930.

Friedman, Milton. *A Theory of the Consumption Function.* Princeton, NJ: Princeton University Press, 1957.

Fuster, Joaquin M. *The Prefrontal Cortex.* New York: Raven Press, 1980.

Gately, Dermot. "Individual Discount Rates and the Purchase and Utilization of Energy-Using Durables: Comment." *Bell Journal of Economics* 11 (1980): 373–374.

Green, Francis. "The Effect of Occupational Pension Schemes on Saving in the United Kingdom: A Test of the Life Cycle Hypothesis." *Economic Journal* 91 (1981): 136–144.

Hall, Robert, and Fredrick Mishkin. "The Sensitivity of Consumption to

Transitory Income: Estimates from Panel Data on Households." *Econometrica* 50 (1982): 461–481.

Hamermesh, Daniel. "Consumption During Retirement: The Missing Link in the Life Cycle." *Review of Economics and Statistics* 66 (1984): 1–7.

Hausman, Jerry. "Individual Discount Rates and the Purchase and Utilization of Energy-Using Durables." *The Bell Journal of Economics* 10 (1979): 33–54.

Hogarth, Jeanne M. "Changes in Financial Resources During Retirement: A Descriptive Study." Cornell University, Department of Consumer Economics and Housing, 1986.

Holbrook, Robert. "Windfall Income and Consumption: Comment." *American Economic Review* 56 (1966): 534–540.

————, and Frank Stafford. "The Propensity to Consume Separate Types of Income: A Generalized Permanent Income Hypothesis." *Econometrica* 39 (1971): 1–21.

Hurd, Michael D. "Savings of the Elderly and Desired Bequests." *American Economic Review* 77 (1987): 298–312.

Ishikawa, Tsuneo, and Kazuo Ueda. "The Bonus Payment System and Japanese Personal Savings." in Masahiko Aoki (ed.). *The Economic Analysis of the Japanese Firm*. Amsterdam: North Holland, 1984.

James, William. *The Principles of Psychology* (2 vols.). Holt: New York, 1890.

Kahneman, Daniel, and Amos Tversky. "Choices, Values, and Frames." *The American Psychologist* 39 (1984): 341–350.

————, and ————. "Prospect Theory: An Analysis of Decision Under Risk." *Econometrica* 47 (1979): 262–291.

Katona, George. *Private Pensions and Individual Saving*. Ann Arbor: University of Michigan, 1965.

King, Mervyn A. "The Economics of Saving: A Survey of Recent Contributions." in Kenneth Arrow and S. Hankapohja (eds.). *Frontiers of Economics*. Oxford: Basil Blackwell, 1985.

————, and L.D.L. Dicks-Mireaux. "Asset Holdings and the Life Cycle." *Economic Journal* 92 (1982): 247–267.

Kotlikoff, Lawrence, Avfa Spivak, and Lawrence Summers. "The Adequacy of Savings." *American Economic Review* 72 (1982): 1056–1069.

Krumm, Ronald, and Nancy Miller. "Household Savings, Homeownership, and Tenure Duration." Working Paper, University of Chicago, Department of Public Policy, 1986.

Kurz, Mordecai. "The Life-Cycle Hypothesis and the Effects of Social Security and Private Pensions on Family Savings." Technical Report #335, Institute for Mathematical Studies in the Social Sciences, Stanford University, 1981.

Landsberger, Michael. "Windfall Income and Consumption: Comment." *American Economic Review* 56 (1966): 534–539.

Levin, Lawrence. "Testing the Behavioral Life-Cycle Hypothesis." Unpublished, Department of Economics, Santa Clara University, 1992.

Manchester, Joyce M., and James M. Poterba, "Second Mortgages and Household Saving." *Regional Science and Urban Economics* 19 (1989): 325–346.

Margolis, Howard. *Selfishness, Altruism and Rationality*. Cambridge, UK: Cambridge University Press, 1982.

Mayer, Thomas. *Permanent Income. Wealth and Consumption*. Berkeley: University of California, 1972.

Mirer, Thad W. "The Wealth-Age Relationship Among the Aged." *American Economic Review* 69 (1979): 435–443.

Mischel, Walter. "Metacognition and the Rules of Delay." in J.H. Flavell and L. Ross (eds.). *Social Cognitive Development Frontiers and Possible Futures*. New York: Cambridge University Press, 1981.

Modigliani, Franco, and Richard Brumberg. "Utility Analysis and the Consumption Function: An Interpretation of Cross-Section Data." in K.K. Kurihara (ed.). *Post Keynesian Economics*. New Brunswick, NJ: Rutgers University Press, 1954.

Munnell, Alicia. *The Effect of Social Security on Personal Saving*. Cambridge, MA: Ballinger, 1974.

———. "Private Pensions and Saving: New Evidence." *Journal of Political Economy* 84 (1976): 1013–1032.

Numan, Robert A. "Cortical-Limbic Mechanisms and Response Control: A Theoretical Review." *Physiological Psychology* 6 (1978): 445–470.

Restak, Richard. *The Brain*. New York: Bantam, 1984.

Schelling, Thomas. "Self Command in Practice, in Policy and in a Theory of Rational Choice." *American Economic Review* (May 1984): 1–11.

Shefrin, H.M., and Meir Statman. "Explaining Investor Preference for Cash Dividends." *Journal of Financial Economics* 13 (1984): 253–282.

Sherman, Sally R. "Assets at the Threshold of Retirement." in *Almost 65: Baseline Data from the Retirement History Study*. Washington, DC: Social Security Administration, 1976.

Shiba, Tsunemasa. "The Personal Savings Functions of Urban Worker Households in Japan." *Review of Economics and Statistics* (1979): 206–213.

Simon, Julian, and Carl Barnes. "The Middle-Class U.S. Consumption Function: A Hypothetical Question Study of Expected Consumption Behavior." *Oxford University Institute of Economics and Statistics Bulletin* 33 (1971): 73–80.

Skinner, Jonathan. "Housing Wealth and Aggregate Saving." *Regional Science and Urban Economics* 19 (1989): 305–324.

Summers, Lawrence. "Reply to Galper and Byce." *Tax Notes* 9 (1986): 1014–1016.

Thaler, Richard. "Some Empirical Evidence on Dynamic Inconsistency." *Economic Letters* 8 (1981): 101–107.

———. "Mental Accounting and Consumer Choice." *Marketing Science* (Summer 1985). 199–214.

———, and H.M. Shefrin. "An Economic Theory of Self-Control." *Journal of Political Economy* 89 (1981): 392–406.

———. "Anomalies: Saving, Fungibility, and Mental Accounts." *Journal of Economic Perspectives* 4 (1990): 193–205.

Venti, Steven F., and David A. Wise. "Aging, Moving, and Housing Wealth." Cambridge, MA: National Bureau of Economic Research Working Paper, 1987.

Warshawsky, Mark. "The Sensitivity Market Incentives: The Case of Policy Loans." *Quarterly Journal of Economics* 69 (1987): 286–295.

Winston, Gordon. "Addiction and Backsliding." *Journal of Economic Behavior and Organization* 1 (1980): 295–324.

Appendix

The propositions that underlie the empirical portion of the chapter follow from the optimality conditions that characterize the planner's choice of c and s. The first-order conditions associated with c concern the marginal utility to the planner from an additional unit of c_t. This is given by:

$$\partial V/\partial Z_t\, \partial Z_t/\partial \theta_t\, \partial \theta_t^* /\partial c_t - \sum_{\tau=t+1}^{T} \partial V/\partial Z_\tau \{\partial Z_\tau/\partial m_\tau + \partial Z_\tau/\partial \theta_\tau\, \partial \theta_t^* /\partial m_\tau\} \alpha_\tau(c_\tau)$$

(11)

with $\alpha_\tau c_\tau$ equal to 1 if the A account has been invaded at date t, and zero otherwise. While the first term in the above sum is the direct utility associated with c_t, the second term reflects the reduced temptation effect associated with future consumption from the A account prior to T. This marginal utility is to be compared with the marginal utility of retirement consumption.

$$\partial V/\partial Z_T\, \partial Z_T/\partial c_T$$

(12)

The optimality conditions require that when Equation (12) exceeds Equation (11), consumption at t be reduced and transferred to T through increased discretionary saving. However, if Equation (11) exceeds Equation (12), we need to consider two cases. In the first case, the account being used to finance c_t has not been drawn down to zero. Then c_t should be increased. If the financing account has been drawn down to zero, then attention needs to be paid to whether invading the next account becomes worthwhile. If not, then Equation (11) will exceed Equation (12) at the optimum. We refer to the condition (11) = (12) as the Fisher condition (equalization of marginal utilities) and (11) > (12) as the generalized Fisher condition. The second type of optimality condition is associated with the selection of the pension deduction rate s. With c given, the impact of a marginal change in s is through the temptation effect. When $c_t < I_t$, the net benefit at t from a marginal increment Δs in s is:

$$\partial V/\partial Z_t\{\partial Z_t/\partial m_t + \partial Z_t/\partial \theta_t\, \partial \theta_t^*/\partial m_t\}I_t \tag{13}$$

When c_t is financed out of the A_t account, there is also a temptation impact caused by the amount of willpower effort needed in connection with c_t. It has the same general form as Equation (13). However, this effect is small compared to the discrete effect that occurs when the increment Δs forces the invasion of the A (and/or F) account because this entails the entry penalty. Consequently, the choice of s will essentially balance off the lowered temptation costs in the I account against the additional entry penalties for invading the A (and/or F) account.

An implication of the model is that an increase in the pension saving rate will increase retirement savings. Consider the formal argument for this statement. Begin with the case in which no pension plan is available (so that the maximum deduction rate s^* is zero), and let a small pension plan be made available ($\Delta s^* > 0$). Let the household contemplate increasing its deduction rate by Δs. Consider how total saving in our model responds to the impact of the marginal increase Δs. Let $c(s)$ be the planner's optimal choice of c, given s. If the pension deduction does not cause the household to become liquidity constrained, then the LC prediction is that $c(s)$ is invariant to the choice of s. Suppose that the increment Δs does not alter the account used to finance the representative household's marginal (i.e., last) unit of consumption at any date. For instance, if at date t the individual was consuming only out of I (prior to Δs), then it will continue to do so after Δs. Recall that the increment Δs in s shifts wealth into the F account from the I account. Suppose that $c_t(s) < I_t$ so that date t consumption is financed solely from the income account. Observe that inequality (8) implies that the impact of Δs is to cause a decrease in the marginal temptation to consume at level $c_t(s)$. However, the marginal utility of retirement consumption $c_T(s)$ remains unchanged. Therefore, Δs causes the marginal utility of $c_t(s)$ to fall below its retirement counterpart, thereby leading date t consumption to be decreased in response. Consequently, unlike the LC prediction, $c(s)$ is nonconstant in s. If date t is typical, then lifetime saving c_T rises with s. We regard this as the representative case.

There are other cases to be considered as well:

1. If consumption $c_t(s) = I_t$ (and we continue to consider the case when Δs does not induce the invasion of A), then date t consumption falls simply because I_t falls with Δs.

2. When $c_t(s)$ is financed out of the A account, then the marginal temptation hypothesis applied to $I_t + A_t$ implies that c_t declines with Δs.

3. However, when the $c_t(s) = I_t$ and the individual is indifferent to invading A_t, then the increment Δs actually induces an increase in c_t as A_t gets invaded. This situation is typical for choices of s that are greater than optimal.

Under the hypothesis that the pension deduction rate begins below the optimal levels, so that Δs is considered an improvement, we predict that lifetime saving (meaning retirement consumption c_T) rises with Δs.

· 13 ·

A Theory of Addiction

RICHARD J. HERRNSTEIN AND DRAZEN PRELEC

We would often be sorry if our wishes were gratified.
Aesop

No man ever became extremely wicked all at once.
Juvenal

THE COMPLEXITY of addiction is mirrored in the many disciplines
that study it. The chemistry of addictive substances falls in the domain of *biochemistry,* tolerance and withdrawal belong to *physiology;*
various personality or hereditary predispositions, and the role of
stressful events, are jointly addressed by *psychology* and *human genet-
ics;* the relation to the poverty, community structure, and the "social
matrix" are problems of *sociology* and *political science.*

Alongside these various approaches, however, there must also be
a theory of addiction that reconciles the ostensibly self-destructive
consequences of addiction with the central *economic* assumption that
human action can be understood as the rational pursuit of self-
interest, or, if reconciliation is not possible, to examine what the
implications are for that central economic assumption. The economic
aspect of addiction provides the focus of this essay.

Addiction resolves into two separate, but related, paradoxes for
any theory that assumes behavior to be generally utility maximizing.
First, addiction is perceived to be harmful to the person who con-
sumes the substances (above and beyond its effects on family members and society). The addict's revealed preferences are inconsistent

with society's view that addiction is a losing proposition for the addict. Second, many addicts claim that they wish to change their behavior but are unable to do so. Their stated preferences are inconsistent with the preferences that they reveal through behavior. What shall we conclude about the relation between revealed preferences and utility in light of addiction?

Four Interpretations of Addiction

Economic theory can deal with addictive behavior in four distinct ways, as follows:

(1) *Addiction as disease, not choice:* A drug addict may be viewed as having lost the power to choose whether or not to indulge his habit, in which case the addict's behavior would not need to be accounted for by *any* theory of choice, including the economic theory. The historical shift from addictions as vices to addictions as diseases was a shift to this first approach. Similarly, criminal law has formalized a principle of "no choice" in some of its tests of culpability. The *irresistible impulse* rule, for example, allows someone to be acquitted of responsibility for an act if it can be proved (in the legal sense) that, because of overpowering emotion, the perpetrator lacked the power of choice when he committed it. Criminal law also excuses people when they act without conscious intent, or *mens rea*, on the grounds that choice requires consciousness.

Physiology has also been invoked as a reason for classifying certain behaviors as outside the domain of choice. Murderers have been defended on the grounds that their decision-making ability had been destroyed by eating too much refined sugar (the "Twinkie" defense) or by a brain tumor. The premenstrual syndrome has been offered as a defense for some crimes. Everyday theorizing about unacceptable or unconventional behavior often excuses it by calling it "physiological." The no-choice approach says, in effect, that the behavior in question was not controlled by its potential consequences.

Such arguments reflect a tendency to subtract the volitional component from choice in proportion to our knowledge of the physical reasons for the behavior. Obesity, for example, might become classified as an involuntary condition, upon discovery of its physiological correlates or genetic predispositions.

Whatever the merits of these considerations for determining personal responsibility, the "no-choice" approach does not clearly identify addictive behavior. First, behavior always has physiological reasons, whether or not we know what they are. Some relatively harmless rewards—for example, sweets—have a relatively well-understood physiology, while the rewards provided by some addictive behaviors, such as gambling, are obscure.[1] According to the no-choice approach, the former behavior would not involve choice, but the latter would, at least until we discover the physiological basis for gambling. Second, the drives for addictive behavior are not always intense, as they ought to be if the irresistible impulse criterion is to apply. Experiments have shown, for example, that obese people are more easily deterred from eating than people of normal weight by the presence of minor physical obstacles to the food. Schachter (1971), for example, describes experiments in which overweight people are more deterred from eating nuts by having to shell them or from eating sandwiches by having to get them from a refrigerator than nonoverweight people are.

Finally, addictive behavior is not distinguished by the absence of conscious deliberation. Acquiring illegal drugs, or purchasing a package tour for gambling at Las Vegas, requires more planning than many "normal" consumer choices, like watching television or hailing a taxi.

(2) *Addiction as rational self-medication:* The opposite view of addiction sees it as part of a rational lifestyle, which only appears unusual and self-destructive because we do not understand its environmental and constitutional context. A sophisticated example of this approach is provided by Becker and Murphy (1988), who treat addictive behavior as part of an optimal intertemporal consumption plan. Behavior is, in effect, *perfectly* controlled by its consequences. Addicts take full account of the impact of their current behavior on the future, including their future taste for the addictive substance, according to this theory. Although addicts may be unhappy by normal standards, they would be "even more unhappy if they were prevented from consuming the addictive goods" (Becker and Murphy, 1988, p. 691).

In all but name, Becker and Murphy depict addiction as a form of medication: The addictive commodity or activity is an expensive, inconvenient, *but nevertheless rational* treatment for special psychological conditions, such as depression, stress, and low self-esteem. This outlook seems, at least on the surface, to be inconsistent with addicts'

---

[1] Although recent studies (Goleman, 1989; Roy, Adinoff, Roehrich, Lamparski, Custer, Lorenz, Barbaccia, Guidotti, Costa, and Linnoila, 1988; Roy, De Long, and Linnoila, 1989; Shaffer, Stein, Gambino, and Cummings, 1989) suggest that chronic gamblers may have low levels of activity in the noradrenergic system, abnormalities in cerebrospinal fluids, and high levels of extroversion in their personality profiles.

trying to free themselves of their habit, as well as with the relative excess of young, rather than old, addicts, despite the higher long-term risks to the former. But, in any event, if this view is correct, then policies that restrict access to drugs and criminalize their purchase are misguided and cruel, because they penalize people whose personal welfare is already extremely low.

(3) *The primrose path:* Addictive behavior is sometimes viewed as a trap into which one is lured, because the latent costs of addiction are initially hidden or because the underlying behavioral process is deficient at making rational choices. This is an approach that splits the difference between the first two: It holds that addiction truly does depend on a person's choices, but that those choices can sometimes fail the test of rationality. Behavior *is* controlled by its consequences, according to this approach, but the result may be far from perfectly adaptive. Theories that attempt to make precise this view of addiction may be labeled *primrose path* theories. The key observation is that the typical addict goes down the primrose path believing that there is little danger of losing control (Goldstein and Kalant, 1990). The danger arises because the availability of certain substances or activities creates a situation in which a person's normal behavioral rules are inadequate. The semblance of rationality that our normal, that is, nonaddictive, behavior exhibits is then the consequence not of a utility maximization process, but rather of a good match between the behavioral rules and particular circumstances. When this match is not good—as with addictive goods—then the same behavioral rules produce poor results. We are, for example, following the same fundamental rules when we develop an appetite for golf as when the developing appetite is for heroin, according to this theory. The theory developed in the second section is a primrose path theory, but there could be others.

(4) *The divided self:* The final approach starts with the observation that the same person has different preferences at different times. In the morning, for example, a person may know that he does not want to eat dessert after supper and would order appropriately if the person could bind himself to do so; at supper, he or she succumbs. Or the person may awake daily, filled with resolve not to smoke, drink, dawdle at the water cooler, snarl at the children or spouse, etc., yet fail at virtually the first chance. It is not a matter of faulty knowledge, for the scene may be reenacted daily for years.

The self seems to be divided whenever preference depends on vantage point, which is often the case in addiction. The person discovers that too much eating or drinking has been a primrose path, leading ultimately to trouble, but this discovery fails to protect the person from succumbing when the "undesirable" alternative is at hand. Consequently, persons are in the paradoxical situation of knowing how to act in their own interest in the absence of occasions to do so, but failing to do so when the occasions arise. The person seems to know just how unwise it is to drink except when he passes a saloon.

In an article about the transmission of AIDS by unsafe drug use or sexual practices, *Science* magazine quotes Marshall Becker of the University of Michigan School of Public Health on the difficulty of changing this highly dangerous behavior: "We're asking people to make these crucial decisions over and over again at the exact moment when they're most vulnerable, which is to say when they're about to have sex or right when they're about to stick a needle in their arm" (Booth, 1988, p. 1237).

How individuals and societies do or do not resolve the paradox has inspired much of the recent work on the subject of self-control (Ainslie, 1986; Elster, 1986; Schelling, 1980; Thaler and Shefrin, 1981; Winston, 1980). The common element in formalized divided self models is that the individual is viewed as a collection of rational subagents, jockeying for control of behavior. Although individually the subagents are utility maximizers, the behavior of the collective can be severely suboptimal, as numerous examples from game theory demonstrate (i.e., the Prisoner's dilemma). The third section will discuss the divided self approach to addiction, and will also show its natural links to the primrose path theory presented in the second section.

The remainder of the essay attempts to characterize addiction itself, to show its relation to primrose path and divided self theories, and, in the fourth section, to draw some implications of this analysis for public policy.

A Behavioral Model of Addiction

Four Diagnostics for Addictive Behavior

As Becker and Murphy (1988) point out, the range of activities that can at one or another time be considered addictive is extremely broad: "People get addicted not only to alcohol, cocaine, and cigarettes but also to work, eating, music, television, their standard of living, other people, religion, and many other activities" (p. 675f).

Drugs, eating, television, music, a standard of living, human relationships: What do these diverse activities have in common? Some of the activities on this list would not usually be called addictions in ordinary speech, as opposed to habits, perhaps, or acquired tastes. Habits, acquired tastes, and addictions share the characteristic that they refer to activities that become more likely with repeated choice (Becker and Murphy, 1988; Leonard, 1989). But an activity is usually called an addiction only if this change seems to be a trap of some kind, locking the person into a behavior that he would avoid if he could only view it "objectively," as may well be the case with, for example, certain personal relationships and watching television.

We agree with Becker and Murphy that addictions include many activities beyond substance abuse: gambling, spending beyond one's means, compulsive buying of particular items, such as, for example, cosmetics,[2] some deviant sexual acts like exhibitionism, probably also the "type A" (hypercompetitive) personal style, excessive temper, a tendency to form self-destructive love relationships, and many others. We could perhaps include computer hacking as a new form of addiction. If it is taken as axiomatic that *all* behavior is physiologically grounded, then the everyday characterization of addictions as being "physiological" no longer makes sense. What, then, are addiction's defining features?

Although we propose here four criteria for addictions, we do not argue for a strict logical connection between the conditions listed and the use of "addiction" in ordinary language. The conditions are meant to capture most, if not all, of the denotations of the word.

(1) Addiction is normally not produced by a single action, but is rather the result of a long stream of choices.

Here, we merely note the obvious, namely, that addiction is a *habit.* A rash decision to enlist in the Foreign Legion does not constitute an addiction, no matter how long and unsatisfying the subsequent lifestyle. Addictions, in other words, are ordinarily built up from many smaller decisions; in this respect, they are closely related to what we recognize as defects in character or personality.[3] A lazy

---

[2]From the *New York Times Magazine* (Wells, 1988): "next to the club soda, Perrier and cat food in the refrigerator are 150 tubes of lipstick. There's hardly room for such clutter in the bathroom. That is crowded with 100 or so bottles of fragrance and uncounted cases of eyeshadow, blusher and other necessities. This shrine to makeup is Margot Rogoff's apartment. . . . This is the land of the cosmetics addict."

[3]One could, in principle, become addicted from a single encounter with the addictive commodity—a super-addictive drug, for example—but even here, as should become clear, many of the characteristics of addiction, especially its harmful effects, will only materialize as the addictive behavior occurs repeatedly. An issue not dealt

person, for example, is not one who *once* chose to rest rather than work, but one who is consistently predisposed to choose rest over work. We could say that he is addicted to loafing. Likewise, a hygienic person is not someone who once chose to bathe or to wear clean clothes, but someone who is predisposed to doing so repeatedly and consistently. We are likely to refer to cleanliness or idleness as addictions only if they meet at least some of the other criteria to be described, particularly the next one.

(2) Addictive behavior has significant negative intrapersonal side effects—costs that are caused by addiction but that appear in the context of other, ostensibly unrelated activities.

From the outside, it is usually clear that addictive behavior is having profound effects on the rest of the addict's life. But, for the addict, the pattern is for the psychic benefits to be directly associated with consumption of the addictive good, while the psychic costs are to be spread all around. Thus, a heavy gambler or heroin addict craves and welcomes gambling or heroin, but finds that work and family life are not as satisfying as they used to be. The negative effects of the addiction on other activities are perceived as deteriorating personal relationships or careers or the like, rather than as part and parcel of the addictive behavior—as much a part of it, say, as the pleasures of gambling or a drug "fix."

However, activities in which the primary side effect is often perceived as beneficial can also become addictive, although the addiction is then a compulsive overdoing of an otherwise worthwhile activity. With cleanliness, as with exercise or dieting, for example, the relevant benefits of greater fitness or more attractive appearance constitute a side effect, because they are absorbed as an increase in satisfaction derived from a wide range of other activities, at least initially. Beyond a certain rate of engaging in the activity, however, the side effects become negative, in that so much time is spent washing, working, or exercising that other valued activities are placed at risk. It is only at this point that the washing, exercising, or working is likely to be considered addictive.

(3) The benefits of each instance of an addictive behavior are generally more immediate than the costs.

---

with in this chapter is the relation between whether or not a given addiction is thought of as betraying a defect of character and how many episodes of indulgence it takes a typical person to become an addict (but see Prelec and Herrnstein, 1991).

Activities whose initial impact on the occasions when it occurs is negative (i.e., painful) are not usually regarded as addictive. If, for example, the pleasure-withdrawal cycle in opiate addiction is reversed, so that significant pain precedes pleasure, then opiates would most probably cease to be addictive. This time dependence, over rather short intervals of time, seems to play some role in many addictions. The exceptions seem mostly to be cases, such as exercise, dieting, and cleanliness, for which the natural tendency is underindulgence, perhaps because of the dominance of short-term costs over long-term benefits, but become addictive when they shift to overindulgence, at which point they, too, may again have short-term benefits and long-term costs, albeit over longer intervals than opiates and the like.

(4) Addictive behavior, if not at first then eventually, displays temporary preference—it is anticipated with apprehension, looked back on with regret, and engaged in nevertheless.

Economic approaches to addiction invariably focus on changes in tastes—the developing of appetites for, say, alcohol, tobacco, or cocaine. While the tastes of an addict differ significantly from the tastes of nonaddicted persons, and perhaps differ, too, from his own tastes prior to repeated encounters with the addictive substance, this can also be said about anyone who regularly indulges in commodities of which the values depend on how often they are consumed. The class of such consumers is so broad that it probably includes everyone. The tastes of skiers differ from those of the general population, as do the tastes of stamp collectors, vegetarians, philanthropists, or rodeo fans. Those who love pasta have different tastes from those who love rice. The critical question is why among all these varied "acquired tastes" that constitute the preferences of any person, only a special class would be labeled addictive.

For a behavior to be called an addiction, rather than just a personal bent or appetite, it must be *unwanted*. The person must want to stop but fail to do so, or at least an onlooker suspects that the addict lacks the ability to stop should he ever want to. Most present addicts would have refused the addictive lifestyle if it had been presented to them as a one-shot choice that locks in a specific consumption program, like a regimented vacation plan.

Although our four conditions are not hard to state informally, it is difficult to characterize them within a rational choice model. This, in itself, is a significant limitation on rational modelling. To start with, the distinction between a one-shot choice and a habit does not appear in the normative theory, because a rational agent should be able to make a once and for all decision to choose a particular rate of consumption (even when the marketplace does not offer a "subscription" that locks him into that rate). Second, it should not matter to a rational individual whether the costs or benefits of an activity accrue while the activity is in progress, or whether they spread over other activities: The concept of *side effects* has no role as such in the rational model, inasmuch as the model in principle includes all effects of behavior. Third, in order to make time dependence relevant over the relatively brief cycles of pleasure and pain that occur in addiction, one would have to assume nonnegligible discount factors for intervals of days or hours or even minutes, which would then, by the logic of compound discounting, imply a complete insensitivity to consequences more than a few days or weeks away. Finally, as noted already, the idea that a person might dread engaging in certain behavior in advance, then engage in the behavior "voluntarily," only to regret having done so afterward, is on the face of it inconsistent with rationality.

Given the difficulty of expressing the four conditions within a rational model, we will turn to an alternative set of theoretical building blocks, which have been developed in the context of psychological research on human and animal choice behavior. The remainder of this section describes these concepts, and formulates a theory of addiction based on them.

Distributed Choice and Addiction

As we have just stated, standard economic theory does not draw a distinction between consumption variables that are decided with a single action (such as a car purchase), and variables that are the aggregate consequence of a series of individual, small-scale decisions, such as becoming obese or a habitual smoker. Our central hypothesis, derived from a growing body of experimental evidence, is that in this second class of situations, choice is guided by a particular sort of limited optimization, one that is fairly efficient in some situations and markedly inefficient (suboptimal) in others.

According to this idea, called the principle of *melioration* (Herrnstein, 1982; Herrnstein and Prelec, 1991; Herrnstein and Vaughan, 1980; Prelec, 1982), a person's behavior in situations of repeated choice eventually distributes itself over alternatives in the choice set so as to equalize the returns per unit invested, in time, effort, or some other constrained dimension of behavior. Behavior at the equilibrium point, where returns per unit invested are equal, conforms to the *matching law*. We have described melioration and matching elsewhere in this book (see Chapter 10) and will not therefore repeat it except to apply it to the question of addictive behavior. For present purposes, it should suffice to identify some commodity that is at issue—alcohol, desserts, loafing, gambling, etc.—as one of two alternatives, without saying just which one it is. The other alternative we interpret as the collection of activities and commodities that are mutually exclusive and exhaustive with respect to the commodity at issue. Thus, for drinking, one value function is for drinking, the other is simply for not drinking. The two categories of consumption are thus complementary by definition. The case for viewing alcohol consumption, and, by implication, other addictive goods, as a choice of this sort has been forcefully made by Vuchinich and Tucker (1988).

In Figure 13.1, the x axis represents *distributed choice*, namely, the rate with which the behavior associated with the commodity or activity at issue is engaged in during some appropriate interval of time— say a week, a month, a year. If one assumes a fixed budget constraint, and as long as prices are constant, this rate is proportional to the

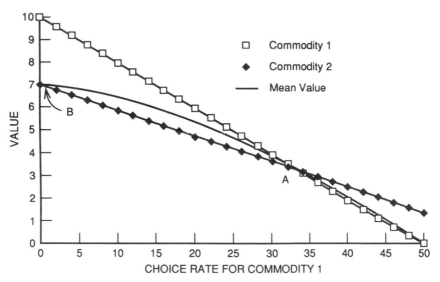

Figure 13.1.   Value as a function of allocation to alternative 1, for alternative 1 (squares) and alternative 2 (diamonds). The weighted average value over both alternatives is given by the solid curve. The matching point is at A; optimal allocation is at B.

expenditure on the item. Expenditure on everything else is proportional to the distance to the right corner of the x axis. Changes in price have been shown to produce the expected changes in consumption rates, even for the most powerfully addictive substances, such as cocaine, alcohol, and tobacco (Goldstein and Kalant, 1990).

The heights of the value functions at each allocation show the average returns at that allocation, taking into account *all* the relevant parameters affecting current value, such as drive level, past history (as embodied either in pathological physiological condition or learned valuations), reinforcement-delay, price, risk, etc. The lines through the squares and diamonds represent the value of the commodity in question and its complement at any particular long-run division of choices between them (i.e., with a pair of long-run consumption frequencies). As drawn in Figure 13.1 the value functions indicate that the taste for either commodity is a linearly diminishing function of how often commodity 1 is chosen. The solid line is a weighted average of the two individual value functions, with the weight given to each function equal to the *relative* frequency of consumption of the corresponding commodity.

The process of melioration, without further elaboration, implies that choice is guided by the heights of the two value functions at any given allocation. The equilibrium pair of consumption rates is at the point where the two value functions intersect, which is also the point where the values obtained from both alternatives exactly match the mean value obtained from both (at A in Figure 13.1). This *matching* point does not necessarily coincide with the optimal pair of choice rates, which, in this example, would require total abstinence from commodity 1 (at B).

The configuration in Figure 13.1 is representative of many settings that people perceive as being problematic. The return to each commodity depends on how much of the total behavioral investment it receives. Relatively more of commodity 1 (squares) means less return to both commodities. In the context of choices between 1 and 2, average returns to 2 (diamonds) rise with its increased consumption; those to 1 decrease sharply with its consumption.

The crossing value functions in Figure 13.1, at A, define a stable matching point (Herrnstein and Prelec, 1991 and Herrnstein and Prelec, Chapter 10, this book), in that deviations around the point are self-canceling. Matching yields much less aggregate utility than the allocation at the optimum, that is, the maximum point, B, on the average curve, where commodity 2 would be chosen exclusively, even though commodity 1 is more desirable at this allocation.

We assume that a person does not "see" the overall picture, as it is plotted in Figure 13.1, because he is psychologically embedded in it, at a certain point along the abscissa. A person who currently favors alternative 1 (e.g., at the matching point in Figure 13.1) cannot quickly test the values that would be enjoyed at the optimal distribution—or at any other distribution, for that matter. If one is in the habit of loafing, one cannot casually and instantaneously sample the fruits of long and hard labor. The interactions between consumption and taste are here modeled as a "black box," gradually shifting the value of the commodities as patterns of allocation change, and driving distributed choice toward a matching point.

It may help to think of Figure 13.1 as a representation of how a person evaluates, in reinforcement or utility terms, the two mutually exclusive and exhaustive answers, namely, "yes" and "no," to the question of consuming commodity 1 at each allocation. The question is, in principle, continuously on the table during the time interval under observation.[4]

The rate of saying yes or no intersects various of the factors affecting value. There is the obvious interaction with drive state—the average value of a slice of chocolate cake varies inversely with the rate of consumption over some range of rates. For many commodities, external availability mimics the motivational interaction. The more one visits a given berry bush, the poorer and scarcer the berries one finds.

An important class of interactions between the utility of returns and consumption rate is mediated by delay of gratification. If we say yes to cake only when it is set before us, the pleasures of eating it are likely to be forthcoming sooner than if we say yes more often, including when we are far from food, thereby initiating a chain of activities with cake at its end. It is not that we cannot initiate at any time a chain of activities with cake at the end, but that the reinforcement for doing so may be long deferred at the moment of initiation. If deferred returns are discounted, then, other things being equal, high rates of saying yes produce lower average benefits, independent of any interaction with drive or availability.[5]

[4] Later we show that certain cultural practices may be construed as ways of taking the question off the table at certain times, and thereby constraining the rate of "yesses."

[5] An equivalent formulation of this point, more obviously linked to the principle of melioration, is that a given reinforcer spread over a longer time constitutes a lower rate of reinforcement, inasmuch as reinforcement rate is given by the ratio of the absolute value of the reinforcement to the time allocated to obtaining it (Herrnstein, 1982; Herrnstein and Vaughn, 1980).

How Addictions, and Addicts, Differ

Pictures like the one in Figure 13.1 may be fairly charged with hiding more than they disclose. Their advantage is that they provide a framework for taking into account the variables that affect distributed choice for meliorators, particularly for those commodities and activities that are generally agreed to be self-destructive. We can sample only sketchily from the vast clinical literature describing the phenomenology of addictive substances, such as smoking (tobacco), drinking (e.g., caffeine, alcohol), and the many varieties of chemical abuse (psychostimulants like cocaine or amphetamine, opiates like morphine or heroin; see Irwin, 1990, for a useful classification of addictive substances), let alone the even larger literature on all sorts of repetitive, harmful behavior. The following points reflect certain general patterns that are evident in this large literature.

In what follows, it may seem that we are simply postulating functions to fit the literature, but the point is that doing so is a natural extension of melioration, rather than a contrived use of it. This is because, unlike rational choice theory, the melioration framework makes the value functions for the competing behavioral alternatives decisive in controlling choice. In a maximization framework, a person's behavior is taken as a whole.

Individual Variation   Individuals vary in their susceptibility for falling into self-destructively high or low rates of indulgence, which is to say they vary in their propensity toward a stable matching point at which the aggregate returns are significantly suboptimal. In terms of Figure 13.1, the placement and slopes of the two value functions vary from person to person. For alcohol, the indications point toward genetic dispositions toward excessive use. But individual differences need not be a matter of narrow, substance-specific susceptibilities, genetic or otherwise. Much of the clinical literature suggests that some people are launched on the (primrose) path toward addiction or other self-destructive behavior in the spirit of problem solving (e.g., Jellinek, 1960; Orford, 1985; Pattison, Sobell, and Sobell, 1977).

A person may use a psychostimulant to deal with the problem of depression (or, in some cases, obesity). Someone else may solve a shyness problem with alcohol. A youngster may find that he or she gains the admiration of peers by smoking tobacco or dope. A gambler may have been trying to solve a genuine financial problem when he fell into the bottomless pit of compulsive gambling. In short, the motivational structures relevant to addictions and other suboptimalities can extend far beyond the specific drives involved in the activities

at issue. Indeed, abusers of any given substance or activity are disproportionately likely to be abusing other substances or activities, or to
be otherwise suffering from psychiatric illness (Lesieur, 1989).

Knife Edges   The value functions for people at risk for abusing
some substance or activity may have subsidiary features that Figure
13.1 omits. It is part of the lore of certain addictions, such as that of
alcoholism, that something akin to a knife edge describes the risk of
succumbing (Koob and Bloom, 1988). Low levels of indulgence can
go on indefinitely, but, at some threshold, the pattern tips over, and
consumption seems to break free of control. Figure 13.2 is a simple
alteration of the value functions consistent with this story; drinking
(or some other comparable good) is represented by commodity 1
(squares), not drinking by commodity 2 (diamonds). The weighted
average value is given by the solid line.

Figure 13.2 postulates two stable equilibria, at A and C, and one
unstable one, B, which locates the knife edge (disregarding the two
additional unstable points at exclusive choice of either alternative).
The matching point at A would likely be encountered first, because

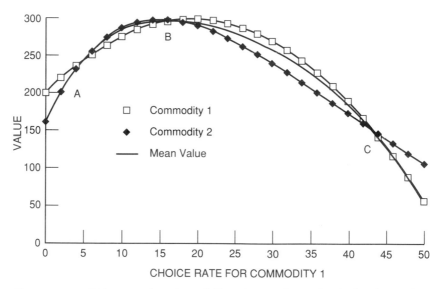

Figure 13.2.   Value as a function of allocation to alternative 1, for alternative
1 (squares) and alternative 2 (diamonds). A and C are stable matching points;
B is the "knife edge." The solid curve, the weighted average, virtually over-
laps with alternative 2 to the left of A and with alternative 1 to the right of C.

it requires only a low rate of indulgence. In this region of allocation, the person is still developing a taste for drink, or still honing whatever skills may be involved in its successful use, hence, the positive slope of the value function at this level. At the same time, using alcohol may still be solving some problem in the person's life, enhancing enjoyment of activities in addition to drink itself, hence, the positive slope of the value function for alternative 2. Thus, at and around A, the average returns from drinking and nondrinking are rising with increased use of alcohol. At this matching point, drinking would seem to be under good control.

However, should something change, either in the environment or in the person's drives, so that an ongoing pattern of allocation now falls to the right of the knife edge (i.e., B in Figure 13.2), another dynamic process takes hold. Between B and C, melioration drives allocation toward dangerously high alcohol consumption, consistent with the impression of loss of control. Increased drinking begins to cast a hedonic shadow on nondrinking as the value function for commodity 2 declines. Alcohol begins to interfere with the pleasures to be had from other activities. The person may begin to experience the "anhedonia" or "dysphoria" referred to in the literature of alcoholism. Concurrently, the value function for drinking again exceeds that for not drinking, as it did at the lowest levels of use.

At some point, the returns to drink itself start declining on the average. Average returns to 1 fall off because tolerance develops to alcohol (as to most but not all addictive substances; see Koob and Bloom, 1988). The effect of tolerance is to reduce the value gained from a unit of the substance. But even without tolerance in the familiar physiological sense, it is likely that, at higher consumption rates, longer chains of activities are involved in drinking, hence, they are lower on the delay of gratification gradient (also see footnote 5). At C, which is the stable matching point at high rates of indulgence, both drinking and not drinking have lost much of their capacities to please. Neither "yes" nor "no" works well in the vicinity of C, yet there can be a stable matching point here.

Fully Constrained Addiction   Figure 13.2 shows how certain hypothetical configurations of functions imply equilibria that are qualitatively reminiscent of the clinical literature of alcoholism and other forms of substance abuse. In Figure 13.3, the picture is adapted to the literature of gambling. Given the disposition of the value functions here, the choice distribution would not stabilize at any point between the left or right corner, where no or all discretionary finan-

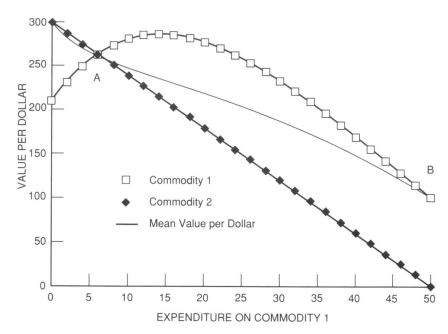

Figure 13.3.   Value as a function of allocation to alternative 1, for alternative 1 (squares) and alternative 2 (diamonds). A is an unstable matching point, a knife edge, and B is the stability point for a fully constrained addiction.

cial resources, respectively, are consumed by gambling.[6] The crossing functions, at A, are at an unstable matching point, which is to say, at a "knife edge." The right corner, B, is the point of *fully constrained addiction*, where expenditure on the addictive activity is only held in check by the sheer lack of additional resources. In hedonic terms, however, the person is still not at equilibrium.

Figure 13.3 assumes that as more financial resources are plowed into gambling (squares), the average returns from gambling will initially rise because the learning of skills or the development of tastes for the paraphernalia of gambling are rate-dependent. But at high rates of indulgence, the returns will decline if riskier bets are taken or if social disapprobation becomes part of the harvest of the activity.

Likewise, the returns from not gambling (diamonds) will also decline with increased allocation to gambling. The increasingly small

[6]To show the hypothetical value functions for a person who also has a stable matching point for low, rather than zero, levels of gambling, we need only complicate the chart slightly, borrowing the left-most end of the chart shown in Figure 13.2.

resources left to the activities other than gambling are swept up by utter necessities, enough food to live rather than to enjoy, mere shelter rather than a home to take pleasure from, and so on. Little is left for other recreational activities. Instead of vacations, gifts for one's loved ones, and so on, the shrunken complement to gambling is preempted by the need to attend to often harrowing crises in one's life, many of which are themselves the by-products of gambling. Like the alcoholic or drug addict, the compulsive gambler slides toward allocations where neither gambling nor not gambling can give much pleasure.

In constructing Figure 13.3, we charged the negative by-products of gambling against activities other than gambling, rather than to gambling itself, because this is the way people tally the consequences of their actions, according to the clinical literature. Quarrels with one's spouse, triggered by gambling, are more likely to poison domestic life than to ruin gambling. In the literature of gambling, people reform precisely when they adopt a more sophisticated approach to mental bookkeeping, and place the blame where it really belongs (see Orford, 1985; Shaffer, Stein, Gambino, and Cummings, 1989).

The distinction between constrained (as in Figure 13.3) and naturally equilibrating (as in Figure 13.2) addiction is important, yet difficult to draw precisely. Financially draining addictions, such as gambling or expensive drugs, most probably leave the addict fully constrained. Food, tobacco, or video games are good examples of unconstrained addiction, for most people, at least. Alcohol consumption could be constrained or not, depending on whether the person can still draw on a steady income.

Some addictions are constrained by sheer physical restrictions on choice rate. A baseball "addict" can only watch his team play 162 different games during the regular season; a workaholic or computer addict is constrained by the clock, as are individuals caught in a "relationship addiction."

Transitions   Other things being equal, a person who is fully constrained (Figure 13.3) should find it more difficult to break out of addiction than someone who is at an intermediate equilibrium (Figure 13.2). At or near B in Figure 13.3, not gambling would feel hedonically inferior to gambling even though virtually all resources are going into gambling. Moving leftward, toward not gambling, would require one to endure a hedonically inferior alternative for some extended period of time (until point A is reached).

The situations in Figures 13.1 or 13.2 are quite different. In Figure 13.1, a person who starts to move leftward from point A (or from point C in Figure 13.2), toward less consumption of the problematic alternative, should immediately experience an increase in satisfaction derived from *both* activities. Consequently, it may seem that only unawareness of the shape of the value functions could keep a person stuck at an intermediate, unconstrained addictive equilibrium.

But the charts have so far shown value functions only in the long run, that is to say, after each level of allocation has lasted long enough so that tastes at that point are no longer changing. Tastes interact with consumption, but the interaction may be slow, because the controlling variables for values—the basic taste changes, learning processes, social reactions to our behavior, and so on—may themselves be only slowly driven by distributed choices. For some suboptimal behavior, much, if not most, of the explanation of its tenacity probably resides in more rapid interactions with rates of consumption, the transients in the value functions as a person shifts from one allocation to another.

Goldstein and Kalant (1990) state two "special characteristics" of chemical addictants: The first is the development of tolerance, which is a decline in the hedonic yield of a given amount of the substance. Tolerance is represented in our theory as a steeply negative relation between *long-term* consumption rates and hedonic yield per unit of consumption, as shown in the earlier figures. The second characteristic is physical dependence, which leads to the *short-term* symptoms often called *withdrawal*, which we introduce at this point.

Transitory effects are especially relevant to relatively unconstrained addictions, such as smoking. The steady smoker does not experience sharp hedonic fluctuations over time, as long as cigarettes are consumed at a steady rate. The smoker, therefore, is at a point where his value functions intersect. Yet, interrupting consumption would rapidly bring on withdrawal symptoms—headaches, anxiety, tremors, and the like—which only the resumption of smoking can alleviate.

These temporary changes in value are not captured in any of the value functions considered so far. In our conceptual framework, withdrawal should appear as a shift in the value functions that is produced by a relatively brief interruption in consumption. Figure 13.4 describes a situation in which the impact of the interruption is felt as a severe reduction in the value of the nonaddictive activity. The diagram contains two value functions for this activity: The higher value function for alternative 2 (crosses) represents the satisfaction derived from nonaddictive activities *if* the consumption of the addictive substance over some relatively short-time period has exceeded a threshold level. If consumption does not meet this level, then with-

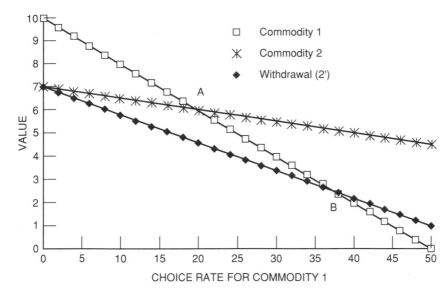

Figure 13.4. Value as a function of allocation to alternative 1, for alternative 1 (squares) and for alternative 2 if consumption of 1 is above (crosses) or below (diamonds) a threshold level. The threshold level is the level of consumption of 1 below which withdrawal symptoms appear. A is the matching point if consumption of 1 is above the threshold; B is the matching point if it is below the threshold.

drawal symptoms appear, and nonaddictive activities are evaluated according to the lower function (the *withdrawal* curve, i.e., diamonds labeled 2').

Figure 13.4 assumes, therefore, that the cost of saying no is temporarily escalated by withdrawal, hence, its net returns are down just as the person is trying to say no more often. Melioration under these conditions dictates shifting toward more of the addictive activity. The precise track of this process depends both on the time course of the short-term withdrawal symptoms and the speed with which the distributed choice process readjusts long-term tastes. In effect, the melioration process that drove the person down the primrose path to the addictive matching point is thus stacked even further against him should he try to reduce the level of indulgence.

A comparable transient influence may act on the addictive commodity itself. It has been observed that large changes in the nicotine and tar content of cigarettes may have large compensating short-term effects, but, in the long term, their effect on the consumption rates of smokers is relatively small (Gori, 1980; Russell, 1979). If smokers were regulating their habit so as to attain a preset level of nicotine or tar concentration in their bodies, as is approximately the case with certain parameters of food (e.g., calories, proteins), then it would follow that reducing nicotine (or carbon monoxide or any of the other habit-forming components of tobacco smoke) should permanently increase the number of cigarettes smoked. Instead, the long-term rate of smoking evidently sets the target levels for the habit-forming components of smoking within a broad range of consumption rates. One "gets used to" a certain physiological level of the addictant. Smoking is a self-regulating activity, but the regulatory levels are arbitrary across a range. For other "habit-forming" activities as well, a given level of indulgence sets the values of parameters around which behavior is regulated.

The opponent-process theory of motivation (Solomon and Corbit, 1974) attempts to explain this interaction between past consumption level of certain substances or activities and present motivational state by postulating homeostatic mechanisms. Substances such as nicotine, for example, induce a change in affective state. A homeostatic mechanism in the body tends to counteract that state, as part of the general tendency of the body to hold certain variables within a narrow range. If the initial affect is pleasant, the counteracting affect is unpleasant, and vice versa. The "opponent process" is affectively opposite to the original agent, but it is slower acting. As a result, after repeated exposures, it leaves the organism with a diminished initial affective reaction to the original agent, but a lingering opponent reaction.

Opponent-process theory, or something like it, handles some of the phenomena of addictions or other habit-forming commodities (Solomon, 1977; Solomon and Corbit, 1973). Rozin and his associates have suggested (Rozin, 1977; Rozin, 1982; Rozin and Fallon, 1981; Rozin and Schiller, 1980) that, for example, the taste for certain foods, such as that for chili pepper, as well as for tobacco, caffeine, and other substances, seems to conform to an opponent-process theory. The initial burning effect of chili is disagreeable, but, after one habituates to it, the lingering opponent process is pleasant, and it is the opponent process that sustains its use among habitual users. A substance that is a source of negative affect at low rates of consumption has become a source of pleasure at high rates. For substances that produce a disagreeable opponent process (known as withdrawal), such as morphine and alcohol, further indulgence in the substance itself is the antidote (as already implied by Figure 13.4 in the gap between the lines labeled 2 and 2'). Here, a high rate of consumption creates a potentially potent source of reinforcement: the avoidance of withdrawal symptoms. Whether the initial affective state is positive or negative, any attempt to decrease an established level of indulgence temporarily intensifies the desire for the substance and presumably also the reinforcement gained from consuming it.

Social and Divided Selves

The first time we let the lawn get out of hand, we may not have realized how much we will dislike the contrast between a neighbor's green grass and our green weeds. But after a few summers, we realize it all too well. Likewise, we may be warned that we are overeating, but still not know just how unpleasant it feels to catch a glimpse of our overweight selves in a mirror. Once we get there, we know. Even a meliorator, insensitive as he is to marginal returns, may know what the aggregate returns look like across a range of choice allocations.

The question is how to incorporate the effects of knowledge about the aggregate returns into the present theoretical framework. Ulysses was worldly wise enough to know the risks, ahead of time, of sailing too close to the Sirens' song and, therefore, had himself tied to the mast. Besides such individualistic solutions, the accumulated wisdom of a culture is full of warnings about the pitfalls of distributed choice. The wisdom is built into many of a culture's institutions.

Isolated and in a state of nature, we would frequently distribute choices suboptimally. The interactions between tastes and allocation are not, as a general rule, known innately, so they must be discovered by experimentation across ranges of allocations. As meliorators, however, nothing impels us to spend the time and effort looking into the black box of our taste changes. And even if we did look, we often seem to lack a natural way to keep a record of our observations. Our memories of the returns from past allocations do not usually enable us to calculate, say, just how often we should eat caviar versus hamburger in order to optimize across those alternatives. We are thus likely to ramble down the primrose path to various suboptimal equilibria, many of them far worse than overindulgence in caviar.

But in a community of meliorators, knowledge about at least some of those primrose paths would accumulate. For meliorators, it matters whether we are observing other people's behavior or just our own. Observing just our own, we are in the clutches of our own current value functions and our impoverished memories of past ones. Observing others, it would soon be noted that, as pleasing as wine may be, it can become "too much of a good thing." We would soon be saying "enough is enough," "all things in moderation," or, simply, "know thyself." Those familiar aphorisms exemplify how human culture provides meliorators like us with rules to help us cope with our suboptimalities. What follows is a sketchy attempt to classify how meliorators cope.

Social Supplementation

Society routinely exploits our sensitivity to social reinforcers. For example, we praise hard work and deplore indolence. Most people are attuned to the social reinforcers attached to their choices, and many of those reinforcers are indexed to the rates of consumption of the commodity in question. Eyebrows rise when we ask for the second, let alone third or fourth, slice of cake. Without the social supplements, many of us might work less and eat more cake than is optimal for us individually, let alone optimal for society as a whole. People who are insensitive to social reinforcers, the sociopaths, are dangerous not only to society but to themselves (Wilson and Herrnstein, 1985).

The social supplements are often keyed to circumstances—"love and marriage go together like a horse and carriage," an old song said, affirming that love (i.e., sex), like many other activities, has its proper time and place. Activities are labeled as vices, sins, evil, virtuous, etc., which is the language used to signify whether the social supplements are positive or negative and how intense they are. The concept of salvation itself is a kind of social supplement, promising benefits in the hereafter for right conduct here. When experts decide that such behaviors as gambling, excessive alcohol consumption, habitual criminality, and so on are better dealt with as "diseases" than as the "vices" they were long taken to be (Orford, 1985), an inadvertent result may be more gambling, drinking, and crime, as if a tax has been lifted from them, unless the stigma of disease is itself an incentive that fully replaces the moral incentives lost by abandoning the language of vice and virtue. By disapproving of behavior, we deter it, insofar as our disapproval has net, negative incentive value. This disregards any compensating benefits of the disease approach to bad behavior, which may be considerable.

In the framework of standard economic theory, the need for social supplements would be most readily accounted for in terms of the fundamental problem of welfare economics—that individually rational behavior may be collectively damaging. We tax the grazing of livestock on the commons and the use of other public goods, so as to avoid the "tragedy of the commons," which is to say, to deter individual freeloading. But meliorators need social supplements, too, in order to make their choices individually more nearly optimal than they would otherwise be. As Herrnstein and Prelec show (Chapter 10), the problem of externalities in welfare economics has an analogue in the allocations of individuals.

Because distributed choices often go haywire by stabilizing at the wrong rate, society invents many *rate-setting customs*. The optimal amount of alcohol consumption is probably not zero, but some relatively low level, at which one can enjoy some of its disinhibiting and analgesic effects, without wrecking the rest of one's life. For some people, the process of melioration fails to provide a stable matching point in this range of allocations, and the primrose path would lead to trouble, except for social practices that lend support to the desirable range of allocations. A daily cocktail or two before dinner, beer in 12-ounce bottles, a few holidays enlivened by drink, occasional religious observances with a taste of wine, are examples of rate-setting customs that detour the primrose path away from danger. A beer commercial on television advises us to "know when to say when."

There will still be some who, because of physiological constitution, past history, or present circumstance, succumb to excess indulgence even in the face of social protections against it. For alcohol, total prohibition remains a possibility, a potentially unstable matching point that has some hope of enduring when supported by the techniques of self-management that Ainslie and others have discussed. But for many bad habits, the "just say no" option is not feasible. We cannot say no to all eating, and it seems too harsh and costly to say no to all leisure, all sex, all unessential spending, and so on. Rate-setting practices, other than total prohibitions, therefore abound.

Here are some commonplace examples. For eating, the norm is three meals a day, and the meals themselves fall within a roughly prescribed range of sizes and nutritional contents. For people whose value functions might lead them to overeat, undereat, or otherwise malnourish themselves, the norm guides them toward a more desirable range of choices. Someone who eats six eggs and a cheeseburger for breakfast is likely to get immediate negative feedback from his dining companions; likewise for someone who eats no breakfast at all. For the "right" rate of leisure, we have the 9-to-5 working day, 5 days a week. The sabbath itself is an ancient and hallowed version of a rate-setting device for leisure, and also for religious observances. For charitable donations, tithing or other rules of giving help us maintain a level that we would like to choose but may find it difficult to attain because we meliorate. Daily clean clothes and a bath may stipulate a level of personal hygiene that people might otherwise frequently undershoot, to their own regret as well as ours.

In these, and many other, cases, the mechanism of control is the application of social incentives, pro or con, to constrain behavioral allocation beneficially, at least on average. But insofar as individuals vary, in value functions and in environmental circumstances, the social supplements are likely to be only crudely helpful in particular cases. Methods of self-management more finely tuned to the individual's own problems, therefore, need to be considered.

Buying a magazine or concert subscription is a way to transform one's own distributed choice into something closer to a once-and-for-all choice, once we realize that the distributed choices are suboptimal as we reckon our own utility. In effect, we buy a certain rate of allocation. Subscriptions often discount unit cost, but they probably need not do so in some instances. If we think we *should* go to the symphony or to the exercise clinic more often than we find we do, we may be willing to pay a premium for a package deal, as a way of buying an incentive to control our future behavior.

Divided Self

Once we buy an incentive to control our future behavior, we have begun to act as if more than one person, pulling in different directions, lives in our skin. Person A within us spends money for a subscription or some other rate-constraining device, hoping to influence the other person, B, also within us, because he knows from past experience that B may otherwise act against A's wishes. At different times, our preferences can be so inconsistent that we may entertain notions of demonic possession, loss of will, mutliple personality, and the like. Modern theorists, particularly Ainslie, Elster, Schelling, Strotz, Thaler, and Winston, have written illuminatingly about intertemporal inconsistency. The theories explaining the inconsistency vary, but the fact itself is too much a part of everyone's experience to be in serious doubt.

Only saints and liars can say they have not experienced such problems as the following: Early in the semester, we resolve to keep up with the homework assignments, but then, having failed to do so, we run out of time to catch up and fail to earn the grade we think we could have earned. It may be a surprise to discover our failure the first time, but some students go through this disappointment semester after semester; likewise resolutions to exercise more, eat less cake, save more money, read better books, watch less television, drink less beer, and so on. These are all problems of distributed choice, involving rates of consumption that violate our own assessments of utility and rationality. They are also problems that we may, in time, discover about ourselves, and we often work hard at trying to solve them. Solutions may become extreme. For example, a newspaper story (Pitt, 1988) described a man who tried to cure his drug habit by getting himself arrested and locked up in jail, where he would be treated for drug addiction while being held in a relatively drug-free environment. He broke windows in two police stations, displayed hypodermic needles and empty crack vials in another, but found "himself back on the streets each time, his pleas ignored." A judge finally helped out by persuading a private religious organization to take him into its drug rehabilitation program.

Not only have we gone down, or at least looked down, the primrose path, but we know that we must not let ourselves be guided by the current value functions. Even after the value functions have been molded by social conventions, religious teachings, and ethical principles, we may still face trouble with our choices. It is when we know our distributed choices are suboptimal that we become conscious of a process of decision making, one that is attuned to our personal irrationalities.

Ainslie (1975) has depicted the problem of conscious decision making as one involving two hyperbolically discounted delay-of-reinforcement curves. On a given occasion, we may confront a pair of alternatives, with the larger payoff more delayed than the smaller. Because time discounting is hyperbolic (rather than exponential; see Chung and Herrnstein, 1967; Mazur, 1987; Prelec, 1989), preference may switch from the later, larger reinforcement to the earlier, smaller one, as the earlier one becomes imminent. When the alternatives are both remote, the later, larger one is again preferred.

While this theory accords with both subjective experience and experimental data about time discounting, it needs to be extended to distributed choices and primrose paths, where the problem is not so much that two alternatives have temporally displaced consequences (although they may, in many cases), but that the value functions depend on levels of allocation, as illustrated in the earlier figures, and one cannot rapidly sample from other points across the range of allocations. Someone who continually watches television 12 hours a day has a hard time discovering that life would improve with a smaller ration of watching time, because the value functions for different levels of allocation are not simultaneously available for comparison. Prelec and Herrnstein (1991) have discussed some of the complexities of making choices "in the small"—for example, *a* drink versus no drink—as opposed to making them "in the large"—for example, drinking just one drink before dinner versus starting the drinking day at lunch. The former is the time discounting problem in the small; the latter is that in the large.

Addictions evidently belong to that class of behaviors for which the time discounting problem arises in the large. A person who knows he has a drinking problem, for example, is likely to want to choose a lower rate in general, but the rate he wants in the large is lower than the rate he gets by aggregating the consequences of his answers in the small. Many of the prudential rules or principles of conduct that people construct to guide their own behavior are attempts to resolve discrepancies of this form.

Conclusion: Policy Implications

It may be useful to distinguish the four approaches to addiction described in the first section by the class of policy recommendations that flow from them.

The *no-choice* approach implies a search for interventions to cure the "disease" presumably underlying the unwanted behavior. Rather than rearranging the incentives that govern choice, this approach would focus on the "root causes" of the troublesome behavior and attempt to alter them. The person should, in any case, not be held accountable for the behavior or afflicted with a sense of guilt for engaging in it, for doing so would be tantamount to trying to control behavior by incentives when incentives are, presumably, irrelevant.

The *rationality* approach implies that some people are addicts because of their endowment (where endowment includes material, constitutional, and psychological aspects). Consequently, the most efficient way to increase their welfare is to give them more money. The public policy goal for drug abusers, for example, would be to make it possible for addicts to self-medicate more easily. Disregarding the possible offsetting social welfare penalties for allowing addicts freer rein to pursue their habits, the logic of this approach argues against criminalization of addictive substances, or any other form of government action that raises prices or otherwise impedes their use (see, e.g., Becker and Murphy, 1988; Friedman, 1989; Nadelmann, 1989). It also argues against attempts to change demand by education, restrictions on the advertising of addictive substances, and the like. There should be a market for addiction insurance, that is, for insuring against the high costs of drugs, should stressful events lead to a need for drug medication. Even the restriction of substances to children violates this approach in its most thoroughgoing form. If there is an overriding social welfare argument against drug abuse even though it is individually optimal, the "rationalists" have, to our knowledge, not yet made it. The argument would take the form of showing that, even though any particular addict is making optimal choices, the utility of society as a whole is reduced by the addiction. This would not be an easy argument to make rigorously, because for every compassionately suffering loved one of an addict,[7] there may be more than one supplier of goods and paraphernalia benefiting from the addiction, along with the addict.

The *primrose path* approach suggests that society should at least provide people with more information, on the grounds that they are less likely to go down the path if they know where it is headed. A useful thought experiment in this regard is to ask whether the propensity toward addiction would be reduced by biofeedback that makes the buildup of tolerance or the imminence of physical dependence more visible. If the answer is yes, then the primrose path notion is strengthened at the expense of both of the foregoing approaches. More fanciful types of feedback might include actuarial information (vividly presented) about one's career, health, family, prospects, as a function of current behavior. Besides altering the information a person has about the long-term effects of choices, public policy could attempt to influence the value functions themselves, perhaps by applying social reinforcers to make the addictive activity less attractive in relation to its alternatives. Again, this approach splits the difference between the preceding two. It accepts the reality and significance of incentives in relation to addiction, but it does not assume that the individual can perform a rational calculation in weighing those incentives. If the first approach rejects criminalization because it is irrelevant, and the second approach rejects it because it is against the addict's self-interest, the primrose path approach may favor it for providing incentives where they could be truly helpful.

Finally, the *divided self* approach extends the analysis of the primrose path. It acknowledges that individuals can sometimes rearrange the value functions controlling their own behavior. The public policy implication is to make self-control mechanisms more accessible and more available than they evidently are now for those who succumb. Addiction, in other words, is like market failure, in that the market

---

[7] And why are they compassionately suffering, if their addicted loved one is maximizing his or her utility?

does not supply convenient self-control devices (and the legal system prohibits some of them). In the absence of external precommitment mechanisms, the individual is forced to invent personal strategies for self-control (as Ainslie and Schelling, among others, have described: see Ainslie, 1975, 1986; Schelling, 1978, 1980). Public policies could be devised to make the teaching and dissemination of self control more effective.

•

We wish to thank George Ainslie for detailed comments on an earlier draft. Thanks are also owed to the Russell Sage Foundation for support.

References

Ainslie, G. "Specious Reward: A Behavioral Theory of Impulsiveness and Impulse Control." *Psychological Bulletin* 82 (1975): 463–509.
———. "Beyond Microeconomics: Conflict Among Interests in a Multiple Self as a Determinant of Value." In J. Elster (ed.). *The Multiple Self.* Cambridge, UK: Cambridge University Press, 1986.
Becker, G.S., and K.M. Murphy. "A Theory of Rational Addiction." *Journal of Political Economy* 96 (1988): 675–700.
Booth, W. "Social Engineers Confront AIDS." *Science* 242 (1988): 1237–1238.
Chung, S.-H., and R.J. Herrnstein. "Choice and Delay of Reinforcement." *Journal of the Experimental Analysis of Behavior* 10 (1967): 67–74.
Elster, J. (ed.). *The Multiple Self.* Cambridge, UK: Cambridge University Press, 1986.
Friedman, M. "An Open Letter to Bill Bennett." *Wall Street Journal* (1989): September 7 A16.
Goldstein, A., and H. Kalant. "Drug Policy: Striking the Right Balance." *Science* 249 (1990): 1513–1521.
Goleman, D. "Biology of Brain May Hold Key for Gamblers." *New York Times* October 3 (1989): C1, C11.
Gori, G.B. "Less Hazardous Cigarettes: Theory and Practice." In G.B. Gori and F.G. Bock (eds.). *A Safe Cigarette?* Cold Spring Harbor, NY: Cold Spring Harbor Laboratory, 1980, pp. 261–279.
Herrnstein, R.J. "Melioration as Behavioral Dynamism." In M.L. Commons, R.J. Herrnstein, and H. Rachlin (eds.). *Matching and Maximizing Accounts.* Cambridge, MA: Ballinger, 1982, pp. 433–458.
———, and D. Prelec. "Melioration: A Theory of Distributed Choice." *Journal of Economic Perspectives* 5 (1991): 137–156.

————, and W. Vaughan, Jr. "Melioration and Behavioral Allocation." In J.E.R. Staddon (ed.). *Limits to Action.* New York: Academic Press, 1980, pp. 143–176.

Irwin, S. *Drugs of Abuse.* Tempe, AZ: Do It Now Foundation, 1990.

Jellinek, E.M. *The Disease Concept of Alcoholism.* New Haven, CT: College and University Press, 1960.

Koob, G.F., and F.E. Bloom. "Cellular and Molecular Mechanisms of Drug Dependence." *Science* 242 (1988): 715–723.

Leonard, D. "Market Behavior of Rational Addicts." *Journal of Economic Psychology* 10 (1989): 117–144.

Lesieur, H.R. "Current Research into Pathological Gambling and Gaps in the Literature." In H.J. Shaffer, S.A. Stein, B. Gambino, and T.N. Cummings (eds.). *Compulsive Gambling: Theory, Research, and Practice.* Lexington, MA: Lexington Books, 1989, pp. 225–248.

Mazur, J.E. "An Adjusting Procedure for Studying Delayed Reinforcement." In M.L. Commons, J.E. Mazur, J.A. Nevin, and H. Rachlin (eds.). *The Effect of Delay and of Intervening Events on Reinforcement Value.* Hillsdale, NJ: Erlbaum, 1987, pp. 55–73.

Nadelmann, E.A. "Drug Prohibition in the United States: Costs, Consequences, and Alternatives." *Science* 245 (1989): 939–947.

Orford, J. *Excessive Appetites: A Psychological View of Addictions.* Chichester, UK: Wiley and Sons, 1985.

Pattison, E.M., M.B. Sobell, and L.B. Sobell, *Emerging Concepts of Alchol Dependence.* New York: Springer, 1977.

Pitt, D.E. "Judge Hears Addict's Plea to Help Him." *New York Times* December 23 (1988): B1–B2.

Prelec, D. "Matching, Maximizing, and the Hyperbolic Reinforcement Feedback Function." *Psychological Review* 89 (1982): 189–230.

————. *Decreasing Impatience: Definition and Consequences.* Harvard Business School Working Paper 90-015, 1989.

————, and Herrnstein, R.J. "Preferences or Principles: Alternative Guidelines for Choice." In R.J. Zeckhauser (ed.). *Strategy and Choice.* Cambridge, MA: MIT Press, 1991, pp. 319–340.

Roy, A., B. Adinoff, L. Roehrich, D. Lamparski, R. Custer, V. Lorenz, M. Barbaccia, A. Guidotti, E. Costa, and M. Linnoila. "Pathological Gambling: A Psychobiological Study." *Archives of General Psychiatry* 45 (1988): 369–373.

————, J. De Long, and M. Linnoila. "Extraversion in Pathological Gamblers: Correlates with Indexes of Noradrenergic Function." *Archives of General Psychiatry* 46 (1989): 679–681.

Rozin, P. "The Significance of Learning Mechanisms in Food Selections: Some Biology, Psychology and Sociology of Science." In L.M. Barker, M.R. Best, and M. Domjan (eds.). *Learning Mechanisms in Food Selection.* Waco, TX: Baylor University Press, 1977, pp. 557–589.

————. "Human Food Selection: The Interaction of Biology, Culture and Individual Experience." In L.M. Barker (ed.). *The Psychobiology of Human Food Selection.* Bridgeport, CT: AVI, 1982, pp. 225–254.

————, and A.E. Fallon. "The Acquisition of Likes and Dislikes for Foods." In J. Solms and R.L. Hall (eds). *The Role of Food Components in Food Acceptance*. Zurich: Forster, 1981, pp. 35–48.

————, and D. Schiller. "The Nature and Acquisition of a Preference for Chili Peppers." *Motivation and Emotion* 4 (1980): 77–101.

Russell, M.A.H. "Tobacco Dependence: Is Nicotine Rewarding or Aversive?" In N.A. Krasnegor (ed.). *Cigarette Smoking as a Dependence Process*. Rockville, MD: National Institute of Drug Abuse, 1979, pp. 100–122.

Schachter, S. "Some Extraordinary Facts About Obese Humans and Rats." *American Psychologist* 26 (1971): 129–144.

Schelling, T.C. *Micromotives and Molar Behavior*. New York: Norton, 1978.

————. "The Intimate Contest for Self-Command." *The Public Interest* No. 60 (Summer 1980): 94–118.

Shaffer, H.J., S.A. Stein, B. Gambino, and T.N. Cummings. (eds.). *Compulsive Gambling: Theory, Research, and Practice*. Lexington, MA: Lexington Books, 1989.

Solomon, R.L. "An Opponent-Process Theory of Motivation: IV. The Affective Demands of Drug Addiction." In J.D. Mazer and M.E.P. Seligman (eds.). *Psychopathology: Laboratory Models*. San Francisco: W.H. Freeman, 1977.

————, and J.D. Corbit. "An Opponent-Process Theory of Motivation: II. Cigarette Addiction." *Journal of Abnormal Psychology* 81 (1973): 158–171.

————, and ————. "An Opponent-Process Theory of Motivation: I. Temporal Dynamics of Affect." *Psychological Review* 81 (1974): 119–145.

Thaler, R., and H.M. Shefrin. "An Economic Theory of Self-Control." *Journal of Political Economy* 89 (1981): 392–410.

Vuchinich, R.E., and J.A. Tucker. "Contributions from Behavioral Theories of Choice to an Analysis of Alcohol Abuse." *Journal of Abnormal Psychology* 97 (1988): 181–195.

Wells, L. "Conspicuous Consumers." *New York Times Sunday Magazine* November 20 (1988): 90.

Wilson, J.Q., and R.J. Herrnstein. *Crime and Human Nature*. New York: Simon and Schuster, 1985.

Winston, G.C. "Addiction and Backsliding." *Journal of Economic Behavior and Organization* 1 (1980): 295–324.

· 14 ·

Rational Addiction and the Effect of Price on Consumption

GARY S. BECKER, MICHAEL GROSSMAN,
AND KEVIN M. MURPHY

LEGALIZATION of such substances as marijuana, heroin, and co-caine surely will reduce the prices of these harmful addictive drugs. By the law of the downward-sloping demand function, their consumption will rise, but by how much? According to conventional wisdom, the consumption of these illegal addictive substances is not responsive to price. Limited empirical evidence from the 1970s does not support this view. Nisbet and Vakil (1972) report a price elasticity of demand for marijuana ranging from -1.0 to -1.5 in an anonymous mail questionnaire of U.C.L.A. students. Silverman and Spruill (1977) estimate the price elasticity of demand for heroin in an indirect manner from the relationship between crime and the price of heroin in a monthly time series of 41 neighborhoods in Detroit. They obtain an elasticity of $-.3$.

These empirical estimates are too unreliable to be given much weight. However, conventional wisdom is contradicted also by Becker and Murphy's (1990) theoretical model of rational addiction. Their analysis implies that addictive substances are likely to be quite responsive to price. Empirical applications of the model to the demand for such legal addictive substances as cigarettes (Becker, Grossman, and Murphy, 1990; Chaloupka, 1991) and gambling (Mobilia, 1990) support this prediction. In addition, related work on the demand for heavy consumption of alcohol by Cook and Tauchen (1982)

361

is consistent with the notion that price elasticities of addictive goods are relatively large.

In this article we summarize Becker and Murphy's model of rational addiction and the empirical evidence in support of it. We use the theory and evidence to draw highly tentative inferences concerning the effects of legalization of currently banned substances on consumption in the aggregate and for selected groups in the population.

Addictive behavior is usually assumed to involve both "reinforcement" and "tolerance." Reinforcement means that greater past consumption of addictive goods, such as drugs or cigarettes, increases the desire for present consumption. But tolerance cautions that the utility from a given amount of consumption is lower when past consumption is greater.

These aspects of addictive behavior imply several restrictions on the instantaneous utility function

$$U(t) = u[c(t), S(t), y(t)], \tag{1}$$

where $U(t)$ is utility at t, $c(t)$ is consumption of the addictive good, $y(t)$ is a nonaddictive good, and $S(t)$ is the stock of "addictive capital" that depends on past consumption of c and on life cycle events. Tolerance is defined by $\partial u / \partial S = u_s < 0$, which means that addictions are harmful in the sense that greater past consumption of addictive goods lowers current utility. Stated differently, higher $c(t)$ lowers future utility by raising values of S.

Reinforcement ($dc/dS > 0$) requires that an increase in past use raises the marginal utility of current consumption: ($\partial^2 u / \partial c \partial S = u_{cs} > 0$). This is a sufficient condition for myopic utility maximizers who do not consider the future consequences of their current behavior. But rational utility maximizers also consider the future harmful consequences of their current behavior. Reinforcement for them requires that the positive effect of an increase in $S(t)$ on the marginal utility of $c(t)$ exceeds the negative effect of higher $S(t)$ on the future harm from greater $c(t)$.

Becker and Murphy (1990, p. 680) show that a necessary and sufficient condition for reinforcement near a steady state (where $c = \delta S$) is

$$(\sigma + 2\delta)u_{cs} > -u_{ss}, \tag{2}$$

where u_{cs} and u_{ss} are local approximations near the steady state, σ is the rate of time preference, and δ is the rate of depreciation on addictive capital. Reinforcement is stronger the bigger the left-hand side is relative to the right-hand side. Clearly, $u_{cs} > 0$ is necessary if u is concave in $S(u_{ss} < 0)$, that is, if "tolerance" increases as S increases.

It is not surprising that addiction is more likely for people who discount the future heavily (a higher σ), because they pay less attention to the adverse consequences. Addiction to a good is also stronger when the effects of past consumption depreciate more rapidly (δ is larger), for then current consumption has smaller negative effects on future utility. The harmful effects of smoking, drinking, and much drug use do generally disappear within a few years after a person stops the addiction unless vital organs, such as the liver, get irreversibly damaged.

Reinforcement as summarized in Equation (2) has the important implication that the consumption of an addictive good at different times constitutes complements. Therefore, an increase in either past or expected future prices decreases current consumption. The relation between these effects of past and future prices depends on both time preference and the depreciation rate.

Figure 14.1 illustrates several implications of our approach to addiction, where $S(t)$ is measured along the horizontal axis and $c(t)$ along the vertical one. The line $c = \delta S$ gives all possible steady states where c and S are constant over time. The positively sloped curves A^1 give the relation between c and S for an addicted consumer who has a particular utility function, faces given prices of c and y, and has a given wealth. The initial stock (S^0) depends on past consumption and past life cycle experience. Both c and S grow over time when S^0 is in the interval where A^1 is above the steady-state line, and both

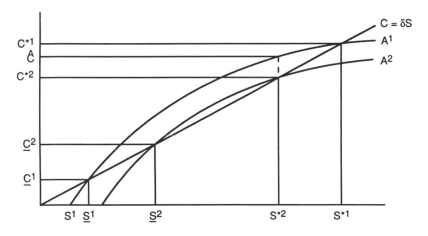

Figure 14.1

fall over time when S^0 is in the intervals where A^1 is below the steady-state line.

Figure 14.1 shows clearly why the degree of addiction is very sensitive to the initial level of addictive capital. If S^0 is below S' in Figure 14.1, a rational consumer eventually lays off the addictive good. But if S_0 is above S^1, even a rational consumer becomes addicted and ends up consuming large quantities of the addictive good.

The curve A^1 intersects the steady-state line at two points: $c^1 = \delta S^1$, and $c^{*1} = \delta S^{*1}$. Other relevant points are where $c = 0$ and $S \leq S^1$. The second point and third set of points are locally stable. If initially $c = 0$, $S \leq S^1$, and a divorce or other events raise the stock of addictive capital to a level below S^1, c may become positive, but eventually the consumer again refrains from consuming c. Similarly, if initially $c = c^{*1} = \delta S^{*1}$, c falls at first if, say, finding a good job lowers S from S^{*1} to a level $> S^1$. But c then begins to rise over time and returns toward c^{*1}. The other steady state, $c^1 = \delta S^1$, is locally and globally unstable: Even small changes in S cause cumulative movements toward $c = 0$ or $c = c^{*1}$.

Unstable steady states are an important part of the analysis of rational addictions, for they explain why the same person is sometimes heavily addicted to cigarettes, drugs, or other goods, and yet at other times lays off completely. Suppose the consumer starts out at $c^{*1} = \delta S^{*1}$, and experiences favorable events that lower his or her stock of addictive capital below S^{*1}, the unstable steady state with A^1. The consumer goes from being strongly addicted to eventually giving up c entirely. If A^1 is very steep when S is below the unstable steady state—if reinforcement is powerful in this interval—consumers would quit their addiction "cold turkey" (see the more extended analysis in Becker and Murphy, 1990).

To analyze rational addict's responses to changes in the cost of addictive goods, suppose they are at $c^{*2} = \delta S^{*2}$ along A^2, and that a fall in the price of c raises the demand curve for c from A^2 to A^1. Consumption increases at first from c^{*2} to $\hat{c}$, and then c grows further over time because $\hat{c}$ is above the steady-state line. Consumption grows toward the new stable steady state at $c^{*1} = \delta S^{*1}$. This shows that long-run responses to price changes exceed short-run responses because initial increases in consumption of addictive goods cause a subsequent growth in the stocks of addictive capital, which then stimulates further growth in consumption.

Because the degree of addiction is stronger when A is steeper, and because long-run responses to price changes are also greater when A is steeper, strong addictions do not imply weak price elasticities. Indeed, if anything, rational addicts respond more to price changes in the long run than do nonaddicts.[1] The short-run change is smaller than the long-run change because the stock of addictive capital is fixed. Even in the short run, however, rational addicts respond to the anticipated growth in future consumption, because future and current consumption of addictive goods are complements for them. But the *ratio* of short- to long-run responses does decline as the degree of addiction increases.[2]

The presence of unstable steady states for highly addictive goods means that the full effect of a price change on consumption could be much greater for these goods than the change between stable steady states given in footnote 1. Households with initial consumption capital between S^2 and S^1 in Figure 14.1 would be to the left of the unstable steady state at S^2 when price equals p^2, but they would be to the right of the unstable steady state at S^1 when price equals p^1.

---

[1]Becker and Murphy (1988) consider price effects in the context of a quadratic instantaneous utility function of the form

$$u(t) = \alpha_c c(t) + \alpha_s S(t) + \left(\tfrac{1}{2}\right)\alpha_{cc}[c(t)]^2$$
$$+ \left(\tfrac{1}{2}\right)\alpha_{ss}[S(t)]^2 + \alpha_{cs}c(t)S(t),$$

where α_c and α_{cs} are positive, and all other parameters are negative. They show [1988, Equation (18), p. 685] that the long-run change between stable steady states in response to a permanent change p_c is

$$\frac{dc^*}{dp_c} = \frac{\mu}{\alpha_{cc}B'},$$

where μ is the marginal utility of wealth, and

$$B' = 1 + \frac{\alpha_{ss} + (\sigma + 2\delta)\alpha_{cs}}{\alpha_{cc}\delta(\sigma + \delta)}$$

The term B', which ranges between 0 and 1 for an addictive good, measures the degree of addiction. Because a decrease in B' means greater addiction—$B' = 1$ indicates no addiction—the long run change in c is positively related to the strength of the addiction.

[2]One can show that a rational addict's short-run response to a permanent change in p_c equals

$$\frac{dc_s}{dp_c} = -\frac{\lambda}{\delta}\frac{dc^*}{dp_c},$$

where $-\delta < \gamma \le 0$, and λ is larger when the degree of addiction is stronger (see Becker and Murphy [1988, pp. 679–680]). Therefore, the ratio of the short- to long-term response gets smaller as the degree of addiction (measured by λ) is larger. One can also show that dc_s/dp_c itself gets larger as the degree of addiction increases.

A reduction in price from p^2 to p^1 greatly raises the long-run demand by these households because they move from low initial consumption to a stable steady state with a high level of consumption.

Temporary changes in prices of addictive goods have smaller effects on consumption than permanent changes—even when all changes are utility compensated. The reason is that the complementarity between present and future consumption is less relevant with temporary price changes, because future prices do not change.

The total cost of addictive goods to consumers equals the sum of the good's price and the money value of any future adverse effects, such as the negative effects on earnings and health of smoking, heavy drinking, or dependence on crack. Either a higher price of the good—caused perhaps by a larger tax—or a higher future cost—caused perhaps by greater information about health hazards—reduces consumption in both the short and long runs.

It is intuitively plausible that as price becomes a bigger share of total cost, long-run changes in demand induced by a given percentage change in the money price get larger *relative* to the long-run changes induced by an equal percentage change in future costs.[3] Money price tends to be relatively more important to poorer and

[3]With a quadratic utility function, the discounted value of future cost in steady states equals

$$\frac{-u_s}{\sigma+\delta}=\frac{-\alpha_s-\alpha_{ss}S-\alpha_{cs}c}{\sigma+\delta}.$$

If these costs change because of a change in α_s, the induced change in steady-state consumption would be

$$\Pi_c\frac{dc}{d\Pi_c}=\frac{dc}{d\log\Pi_c}=\frac{-\alpha_s}{\alpha_{cc}B'(\sigma+\delta)\mu}=\frac{\Pi_c}{\alpha_{cc}B'},$$

where $\Pi_c = -\alpha_s/(\sigma+\delta)\mu$. Hence, from footnote 1, the ratio of the changes in c caused by changes in $\log p_c$ and $\log \Pi_c$, respectively, is

$$\frac{dc/d\log p_c}{dc/d\log\Pi_c}=\frac{p_c}{\Pi_c}.$$

This ratio depends only on the ratio of these prices. In the text we claim that Π_c is larger for adults, and for the rich and more educated. One reason why this is so is that an increase in the addictive stock is likely to lower earnings as well as utility by reducing the time available for work. To include this effect, redefine α_s to include a component $\mu\beta w$ that gives the effect of S on earnings, where w is the hourly wage rate, and β is the negative effect of S on working time. An increase in the absolute value of β would have a larger effect on cost when w is greater.

younger consumers, partly because they generally place a smaller monetary value on health and other harmful future effects.

Poorer and younger persons also appear to discount the future more heavily (this is suggested by the theoretical analysis in Becker, 1990). It can be shown that addicts with higher discount rates respond more to changes in money prices of addictive goods, whereas addicts with lower rates of discount respond more to changes in the harmful future consequences.[4]

These implications of rational addiction can be tested with evidence on the demand for cigarettes, heavy consumption of alcohol, and gambling. Becker, Grossman, and Murphy (1990) fit models of rational addiction to cigarettes to a time series of state cross sections for the period from 1955 to 1985. We find a sizable long-run price

[4] An increase in the rate of time preference (σ) both raises the response to a change in money price (p_c) and lowers the response to a change in future costs (Π_c) if

$$\frac{-\alpha_{ss}}{\delta^2} > \frac{\alpha_{cs}}{\delta},$$

and

$$-\alpha_{cc} > \frac{\alpha_{cs}}{\delta}.$$

An increase in c between steady states where $c = \delta S$ reduces the marginal utility of c, while the increase in S raises it. The second inequality states that the direct effect exceeds the cross effect. The first inequality assumes that the increase in S has a larger effect on its marginal utility than does the increase in c. If u is concave, at least one of these inequalities must hold, for then

$$-\delta^2\alpha_{cc} - \alpha_{ss} > 2\delta\alpha_{cs}.$$

We assume that both hold.

By differentiating with respect to σ the absolute value (n) of the long-run change in c induced by a change in p_c (given in footnote 1), we get

$$\frac{\partial n}{\partial \sigma} = \frac{-[\mu(\alpha_{ss} + \delta\alpha_{cs}]}{\alpha_{cc}^2\delta\,(\sigma + \delta)^2 B'^2}.$$

This equation is positive by the assumption $-\alpha_{ss} > \delta\alpha_{cs}$. Differentiating the absolute value (m) of the long-run change in c with respect to log Π_c (given in footnote 3), we get

$$\frac{\partial m}{\partial \sigma} = \frac{(\sigma + \delta)\,\delta\,(\alpha_{cc}\delta + \alpha_{cs})\,(-\alpha_s)}{[\alpha_{cc}\delta\,(\sigma + \delta) + \alpha_{ss} + (\sigma + 2\delta)\alpha_{cs}]^2}.$$

This equation is negative by the assumption $-\alpha_{cc}\delta > \alpha_{cs}$.

elasticity of demand ranging between $-.7$ and $-.8$, while the elasticity of consumption with respect to price in the first year after a permanent price change (the short-run price elasticity) is about $-.4$. Smoking in different years appear to be complements: Cigarette consumption in any year is lower when both future prices and past prices are higher.

Chaloupka (1991) analyzes cigarette smoking over time by a panel of individuals. He finds similar short-run and long-run price elasticities to those we estimate, and that future as well as past increases in cigarette prices reduce current smoking. He also finds that smoking by the less educated responds much more to changes in cigarette prices than does smoking by the more educated; a similar result has been obtained by Townsend (1987) with British data. Lewit, Coate, and Grossman (1981) and Lewit and Coate (1982) report that youths respond more than adults to changes in cigarette prices. By contrast, the information that began to emerge in the early 1960s about the harmful long-run effects of smoking has had a much greater effect on smoking by the rich and more educated than by the poor and less educated (Farrell and Fuchs, 1982, for the United States; Townsend, 1987, for Britain).

Cook and Tauchen (1982) examine variations in death rates from cirrhosis of the liver (a standard measure of heavy alcohol use), as well as variations in per capita consumption of distilled spirits in a time series of state cross sections for the years 1962–1977. They find that state excise taxes on distilled spirits have a negative and statistically significant effect on the cirrhosis death rate. Moreover, a $1 increase in 1982 prices in a state's excise tax lowers death rates by a larger percentage than it lowers per capita consumption (10.8 percent vs. 7.2 percent).

Mobilia (1990) applies the rational addiction framework to the demand for gambling at horse racing tracks. Her data consist of a U.S. time series of racing track cross sections for the period from 1950 through 1986 (tracks over time are the units of observation). She measures consumption by the real amount bet per person attending (handle per attendant), and price by the takeout rate (the fraction of the total amount bet that is retained by the track). Her findings are similar to those in the rational addictive studies of cigarettes. The long-run price elasticity of demand for gambling equals $-.7$ and is more than twice as large as the short-run elasticity of $-.3$. Moreover, an increase in the current takeout rate lowers handle per attendant in both past and future years.

The evidence from smoking, heavy drinking, and gambling rather strongly supports our model of rational addiction. In particular, long-run price elasticities are sizable and much bigger than short-run elasticities, higher future as well as past prices reduce current consumption, lower income persons respond more to changes in prices of addictive goods than do higher income persons, whereas the latter respond more to changes in future harmful effects, and younger persons respond more to price changes than older persons. It seems reasonable to us that what holds for smoking, heavy drinking, and gambling tends to hold also for drug use, although direct evidence is not yet available, and many experts on drugs would be skeptical. Lacking the evidence, we simply indicate what to expect from various kinds of price changes if responses of drug addicts are similar to those of persons addicted to other goods.

To fix ideas, consider a large permanent reduction in the price of drugs—perhaps caused by partial or complete legalization—combined with much greater efforts to educate the population about the harm from drug use. Our analysis predicts that much lower prices could significantly expand use even in the short run, and it would surely stimulate much greater addiction in the long run. Note, however, that the elasticity of response to very large price changes would be less than that to modest changes if the elasticity is smaller at lower prices.

The effects of a fall in drug prices on demand would be countered by the education program. But because drug use by the poor would be more sensitive to the price fall than to greater information about harmful longer-run effects, drug addiction among the poor is likely to become more important relative to addiction among the middle class and the rich. For similar reasons, addiction among the young may rise more than that among other segments of the population.

A misleading impression about the reaction to permanent price changes may have been created by the effects of temporary police crackdowns on drugs, or temporary federal "wars" on drugs. Because temporary policies raise current but not future prices—they would even lower future prices if drug inventories are built up during a crackdown period—there is no complementary fall in current use from a fall in future use. Consequently, even if drug addicts are rational, a temporary "war" that greatly raised street prices of drugs may well have only a small effect on drug use, whereas a permanent "war" could have much bigger effects, even in the short run.

Clearly, we have not provided enough evidence to evaluate whether or not the use of heroin, cocaine, and other drugs should be legalized. A cost-benefit analysis of many effects is needed to decide between a regime in which drugs are legal and one in which they are not. What this chapter shows is that the permanent reduction in price caused by legalization is likely to have a substantial positive effect on use, particularly among the poor and young.

•

Our research has been supported by the Lynde and Harry Bradley Foundation through the Center for the Study of the Economy and the State, University of Chicago, and by the Hoover Institution.

References

Becker, Gary S. *Optimal Discounting of the Future*. Department of Economics, University of Chicago, 1990.

———, Michael Grossman, and Kevin M. Murphy. "An Empirical Analysis of Cigarette Addiction." National Bureau of Economic Research Working Paper No. 3322, 1990.

———, and Kevin M. Murphy. "A Theory of Rational Addiction." *Journal of Political Economy* 96 (1990): 675–700.

Chaloupka, Frank J. "Rational Addictive Behavior and Cigarette Smoking." *Journal of Political Economy* 99 (1991): 722–742.

Cook, Philip J., and George Tauchen. "The Effect of Liquor Taxes on Heavy Drinking." *Bell Journal of Economics* 13 (1982): 379–390.

Farrell, Philip, and Victor R. Fuchs. "Schooling and Health: The Cigarette Connection." *Journal of Health Economics* 1 (1982): 217–230.

Lewit, Eugene M., Douglas Coate, and Michael Grossman. "The Effects of Government Regulation on Teenage Smoking." *Journal of Law and Economics* 24 (1981): 545–569.

———, and ———. "The Potential for Using Excise Taxes to Reduce Smoking." *Journal of Health Economics* 1 (1982): 121–145.

Mobilia, Pamela. "An Economic Analysis of Addictive Behavior: The Case of Gambling." Ph.D. dissertation, City University of New York Graduate School, 1990.

Nisbet, Charles T., and Firouz Vakil. "Some Estimates of Price and Expenditure Elasticities of Demand for Marijuana Among U.C.L.A. Students." *Review of Economics and Statistics* 54 (1972): 473–475.

Silverman, Lester P., and Nancy L. Spruill. "Urban Crime and the Price of Heroin." *Journal of Urban Economics* 4 (1977): 80–103.

Townsend, Joy L. "Cigarette Tax, Economic Welfare and Social Class Patterns of Smoking." *Applied Economics* 19 (1987): 355–365.

· 15 ·

Frames of Reference and the Intertemporal Wage Profile

ROBERT H. FRANK

Iₙ THIS CHAPTER, I argue that context has important implications for intertemporal consumption allocations, and for the design of the economic institutions that help support these allocations. More specifically, I will argue that intrapersonal consumption comparisons cause the optimal intertemporal consumption profile to be upward sloping; that in occupations in which the lifetime wage profile is less steep than the optimal consumption profile, the latter requires savings during the early part of the life cycle, and dissavings during the latter part; that interpersonal consumption comparisons and simple self-control problems often make it difficult to achieve the requisite savings; and, finally, that institutions like Social Security, private pensions, and "artificially steep" wage profiles[1] have evolved to help ease this difficulty.

The Role of Context

More than two decades ago, I taught high-school mathematics and science as a Peace Corps volunteer in rural Nepal at a monthly salary

---

[1] An "artificially steep" wage profile is one in which wages rise faster than productivity.

of $40. This was not as low a figure as it may sound, for prices in Nepal were much lower than in the United States. For example, a haircut and a chiropractic neck adjustment (administered by the same person) cost only 10 cents. Even so, my consumption standard was modest. My two-room house had a thatched roof that leaked, no plumbing, and no electricity. It shook violently when the bullocks tethered outside scratched themselves along its outside walls. And for most of the year, my diet consisted of rice and potatoes.

People who have never lived under such conditions are often surprised when I say that they took only a little while to get used to. Within a few weeks they became my new standard and gradually assumed even an air of privilege, for they were noticeably better than the conditions under which most people in my village lived.

Upon my return to the United States, my immediate sensation was one of extraordinary luxury: hot showers, cold beer, red meat, stereophonic music—a cornucopia. Gradually, this feeling gave way to a mild sense of impoverishment as it became clear that my graduate student stipend placed me near the bottom of the U.S. economic totem pole. A sense of material well-being did not return until 1972, when I accepted my first teaching job at an annual salary of $13,000. Since then, steady salary increases and living in a small town with modest consumption standards have combined to sustain my sense of prosperity.

My experience is consistent with a large body of evidence showing that context affects how people evaluate their circumstances. Is a 60° November day warm? Residents of Moscow are likely to say yes, while residents of Miami will almost surely answer no. As Harry Helson's 1964 book, *Adaptation-Level Theory*, explains, the human nervous system responds less to the absolute level of any stimulus than to deviations between it and the relevant norms or reference levels encountered in local environments. Thus, for example, a sound source of given intensity may seem either loud or faint according to whether the listener lives in rural Montana or Manhattan. A person sleeping in a quiet room awakens if someone turns the television set on, and, if that same person falls asleep in a room with the television set on, he will awaken when someone turns it off. In like fashion, the psychological reward mechanism—the pleasure center in the brain—is activated not by *good* conditions but by *improving* conditions—or, more generally, by conditions that are favorable in relative terms.[2]

[2]For an illuminating discussion, see Scitovsky (1976).

Sensitivity to context is intelligible in evolutionary terms. Crudely speaking, the utility function's evolutionary role is to reward people with good feelings when they make progress toward survival and reproduction. Sensitivity to context is an important adaptation for this purpose, for in an uncertain world, local norms and conditions offer powerful guidance for behavior. To know what is attainable, it is helpful to know what others have attained, and to know what we ourselves have attained in the past.

As James Duesenberry wrote more than 40 yeas ago, two elements of context are especially important determinants of an individual's sense of well-being: the current consumption distribution for the individual's reference group, and the individual's own consumption history.[3] The relevant reference group for interpersonal consumption comparisons will generally be the people to whom one is most frequently and intensively exposed. The feelings of deprivation experienced by poor people in the United States, for example, are little diminished by the knowledge that they consume more than all but the richest citizens of many Third-World countries. Yet these same feelings fade rapidly in the face of favorable intrapersonal consumption comparisons. For instance, when a poor person receives a 20-percent salary increase, he feels happy, even though the new salary still leaves him poor relative to most of his countrymen.

The role of context can be introduced formally into economic analysis by assuming a utility function of the form

$$U_t = U[X_t, R(X_t), dX_t/dt],$$ (1)

where X_t denotes consumption at time t, $R(X_t)$ denotes rank in the relevant interpersonal consumption distribution at time t, and dX_t/dt is the time derivative of the individual's intertemporal consumption profile. Utility is assumed to be increasing in each of these three arguments for the reasons discussed. The context-free version of the utility function, by contrast, takes the simpler form $V = V(X_t)$.

For simplicity, and without loss of generality, suppose the consumer does not discount future earnings or utility. In the context-free case, the consumer's problem is then to

$$\text{Maximize}_{X_t} \quad \int_0^T V(X_t)\, dt,$$ (2)

---

[3]Duesenberry (1949).

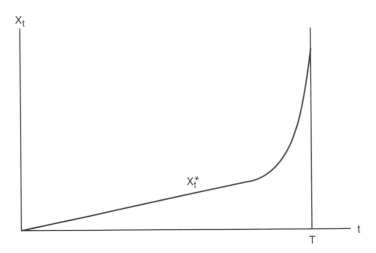

Figure 15.1.   The optimal consumption path when utility depends on both the level and rate of change of consumption. *Source:* Frank and Hutchens (1988).

subject to

$$\int_0^T X_t dt = \int_0^T W_t dt, \tag{3}$$

where X_t is the individual's lifetime consumption stream, W_t is his wage at time t, and T is the end of the planning horizon. On the standard assumption that the utility index V is concave, the optimal consumption stream is constant:

$$X_t^* = (1/T) \int_0^T W_t dt. \tag{4}$$

When context matters, the optimal consumption stream is not constant but upward sloping. Because of the presence of the dX_t/dt term in the utility index, the consumer now does best to start with relatively modest consumption and allow consumption to grow over time, as shown in Figure 15.1.[4]

The notion that utility is enhanced by a rising consumption profile is supported by election observers, who have long stressed the rate of change of consumption as a determinant of voter satisfaction. For

[4]For details, see Frank and Hutchens (1988).

example, the average performance of the U.S. economy was about the same during Ronald Reagan's first term of office as it was during Jimmy Carter's. Yet it is widely believed that a worsening economy helped defeat Carter in 1980, just as an improving economy helped reelect Reagan in 1984.

Implications for Savings

The optimal savings profile, denoted S_t^*, is the difference between the wage profile, W_t, and the optimal consumption profile, X_t^*. For the individual whose wage grows less rapidly than X_t^*, the optimal savings plan thus requires savings during the early years of the life cycle, dissavings during the later years. By contrast, if wages grow more rapidly than X_t^*, the optimal savings plan requires dissavings during the early years, and savings during the later years. Finally, if the wage and optimal consumption profiles happen to be exactly the same, optimal savings will be zero at every moment.

Individuals for whom W_t and X_t^* coincide exactly can attain their optimal consumption profiles simply by consuming all of their current income. Hardly anyone can expect to find him- or herself in this circumstance, but those who do will encounter no significant implementation problems. Those for whom W_t rises more rapidly than X_t^*—for whom optimal savings during the early years is negative—will often be unable to attain their optimal consumption profiles because of the capital market's unwillingness to finance sustained deficit spending for young workers. Our focus in what follows will be on individuals whose optimal consumption profiles require positive savings during the early years of the life cycle. Capital market constraints pose no barrier for these workers. Their lone difficulty is to execute the required savings plan, but this is often more of a problem than it may seem.

Why is it so difficult for young workers to save? In terms of the context-dependent utility index, note first that savings at any moment carries not only the direct cost of reduced consumption, but also the indirect cost of having lower current rank in the relevant consumption distribution. If current rank were unrelated to future earnings prospects, then this would be merely a transitory problem, for increased current savings will mean higher rank in future consumption distributions. Even so, many people appear to have great difficulty bearing even small current costs in return for large future benefits. Simple lack of will power may make it difficult to carry out one's savings plans.[5]

But the problem often runs much deeper than simple weakness of the will. For in many cases, current rank in the consumption distribution will affect important future monetary and nonmonetary payoffs. For example, rank in the current consumption distribution may act as a signal of ability. Spending more on one's current wardrobe enhances prospects for upward job mobility, which in turn may increase future consumption, both in absolute and in relative terms. Alternatively, saving less now enables parents to bid for a house in a better school district, which in turn will enable them to savor their children's success in later years.

The difficulty is that these payoffs are largely spurious from a social vantage point. The notion of a "good" wardrobe, for instance, is inescapably relative. When *everyone* spends more on his wardrobe, no one enhances personal prospects for upward job mobility. And no matter how much everyone bids for the houses in the best school districts, the laws of simple arithmetic guarantee that no more than 10 percent of all children can attend schools in the top decile. Because current rank in the consumption distribution has such a high payoff, however, low current savings may be optimal from the viewpoint of each individual. And yet society as a whole might strongly prefer an outcome in which all saved considerably more.[6]

Solving Implementation Problems

As noted, simple self-control problems and problems arising from concern with current consumption rankings make it difficult to execute optimal savings plans. A variety of collective actions are available to soften these difficulties.

Social Security and Employer Pensions

Elsewhere I have argued that both the Social Security system and employer pension plans help solve collective action problems with

[5]See Thaler and Shefrin (1981, 1987).
[6]Expenditures on wardrobes and houses in good school districts might reasonably be called investments rather than consumption. But regardless of how these expenditures are classified, the point remains that their social payoff is much smaller than the sum of the payoffs perceived by individuals.

respect to savings.[7] At the same time, these plans also help solve self-control problems. Strictly speaking, of course, the Social Security system is not a savings plan but a transfer from workers to retired persons. From each individual's perspective, however, it is the functional equivalent of a pension plan in the workplace. Under each system, people make contributions during their working years, then receive benefits during retirement. The effect in both cases is to shelter some income that would otherwise be available to spend in search of higher rank in the current consumption distribution, or to spend on tempting consumption items.

It is worth noting that while both Social Security and private pensions help to solve individual self-control problems with respect to savings, neither program can be justified on that basis alone. After all, people have access to a variety of other forced savings programs whereby they could solve their self-control problems individually. They can buy whole life insurance, they can save through voluntary payroll deduction plans, and so on. Not everyone suffers equally from self-control problems, and given the availability of individual programs, there is no reason to force B to participate in a group savings program in order to help solve A's self-control problem. Yet participation in both Social Security and the typical employer pension plan is mandatory. This feature is intelligible if the primary reason for the savings shortfall is the collective action problem that arises in connection with interpersonal consumption comparisons.

Rising Wage Profiles

Social Security and employer pension programs help get individuals closer to their optimal intertemporal consumption allocations by helping shift additional consumption to the final stages of the life cycle, a time when earnings are relatively low. But these programs do nothing to help achieve rising consumption profiles during the working years.

Elsewhere, Hutchens and I have argued that artificially steep wage profiles constitute an institutional device for this purpose in many occupations.[8] Our argument in support of this claim is easily summarized. We begin by observing that in many occupations wages rise considerably faster than productivity. For both commercial airline

---

[7]Frank (1985, Chapter 7).

[8]See Frank and Hutchens (1988). Loewenstein and Sicherman (1991) advance a similar claim.

pilots and intercity bus drivers, for example, productivity is roughly constant over the life cycle, even though wages rise sharply over time in both cases. The wage and productivity profiles of pilots for a leading passenger airline are compared in the top panel of Figure 15.2, whose bottom panel shows the corresponding profiles for intercity bus drivers.

Hutchens and I do not claim that the entire gap between wages and productivity is attributable to a desire for rising consumption profiles. Indeed, a variety of other explanations has been offered for why wages might rise faster than productivity in some occupations.[9] Lazear, for example, has suggested that rising wage schedules constitute an implicit bond against employee shirking and malfeasance. Spinnewyn suggests that rising wage profiles are an implicit contract motivated by employee risk aversion concerning unknown future productivity differences. But we argue that these and other explanations are collectively insufficient to account for the wage-productivity divergence we see for pilots and bus drivers.[10] Lazear's bonding explanation, for example, implies a steeper profile for passenger pilots than for cargo pilots on the grounds that malfeasance is much more costly in the former case than in the latter. Yet the wage profiles for cargo and passenger pilots are essentially the same. Risk aversion concerning future productivity differences also seems an insufficient explanation because commercial airline pilots have well-documented track records, usually as military pilots, before ever signing their first contract. We conclude that the observed profiles exist at least in part because workers desire rising consumption profiles that would be difficult to sustain through private savings.

One implication of our argument is that, holding constant the present value of total compensation, employers offering level wage profiles will recruit less effectively than their competitors who offer rising wage profiles. To test the plausibility of this claim, Hutchens and I confronted a large sample of Cornell University undergraduates with a hypothetical choice between two jobs, one with a level wage profile, another with a rising profile. They were given these instructions:

> Imagine you face a choice between two jobs, Job A and Job B, each of which lasts three years. The two jobs are identical in every respect except for the time profile of salary payments. Job A pays $30,000 each

[9]See, for example, Abraham and Farber (1987a,b), Gausch and Weiss (1980, 1982), Hutchens (1986), Lazear (1979, 1981), Mincer (1962), Oi (1962), Salop and Salop (1976), Spinnewyn (1985), and Topel (1987).
[10]See Frank and Hutchens (1988).

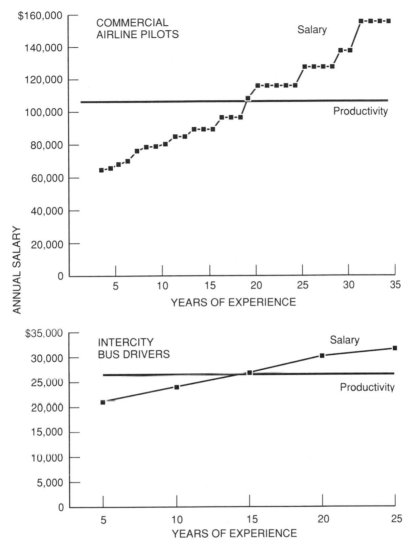

Figure 15.2. The wage profiles for commercial airline pilots (top panel) and intercity bus drivers (bottom panel). *Source:* Frank and Hutchens (1988).

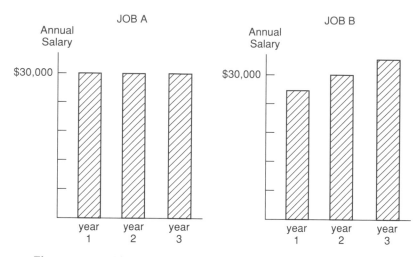

Figure 15.3. Alternative wage profiles with equal present value.

year, while Job B starts at less than $30,000, but ends up higher than $30,000. Under current market conditions, the two salary streams are equally valuable. (In technical terms, they have the same present value—that is, if each salary stream were deposited in a bank at current interest rates, at the end of the three years the salary payments plus interest would reach exactly the same totals.) Which job would you choose?

The earnings streams for the two jobs are as pictured in Figure 15.3. Of the 112 students we surveyed, 87 (78%) chose the job with the rising profile.

Many of our survey respondents were graduating seniors actively searching for their first full-time jobs. If their preferences are like those of job seekers generally, employers face substantial competitive pressure to offer jobs with upward sloping wage profiles, even in occupations in which productivity does not grow rapidly over time.

Concluding Remarks

The traditional theory of intertemporal choice begins with the assumption that the individual's goal is to maximize a utility function that is context free. Considerable evidence rejects this assumption in favor of the alternative view that utility depends strongly on both interpersonal and intrapersonal frames of reference. Because intrapersonal comparisons are important, the optimal intertemporal consumption allocation will in general be upward sloping. For workers whose productivity grows less rapidly than their respective optimal consumption streams, it is necessary to save during the early years of the life cycle and dissave during the later years. Interpersonal consumption comparisons and simple self-control problems make such savings programs difficult to implement. The Social Security system, employer pension plans, and artificially steep wage profiles may each be viewed as an institutional mechanism that helps people achieve the desired rising intertemporal consumption profile.

References

Abraham, Katherine, and Henry Farber, "Job Duration, Seniority and Earnings." *American Economic Review* 77 (1987a): 278–297.

———, and ———. "Returns to Seniority in Union and Nonunion Jobs: A New Look at the Evidence." Working Paper No. 2368, National Bureau of Economic Research, August 1978b.

Duesenberry, J. *Income, Savings, and the Theory of Consumer Behavior.* Cambridge, MA: Harvard University Press, 1949.

Frank, Robert H. *Choosing the Right Pond.* New York: Oxford University Press, 1985.

———, and Robert M. Hutchens. "Feeling Good vs. Feeling Better: A Life Cycle Theory of Wages." Cornell University Department of Economics Working Paper, 1988, *Journal of Economic Behavior and Organization,* in press.

Gausch, J. Luis, and Andrew Weiss. "An Equilibrium Analysis of Wage-Productivity Gaps." *The Review of Economic Studies* 49 (1982); 485–498.

———, and ———. "Wages as Sorting Mechanisms in Competitive Markets with Asymmetric Information: A Theory of Testing." *Review of Economic Studies* 47 (1980): 653–664.

Helson, Harry. *Adaptation-Level Theory.* New York: Harper & Row, 1964.

Hutchens, Robert M. "Delayed Payment Contracts and a Firm's Propensity to Hire Older Workers." *Journal of Labor Economics* 4 (1986): 439–457.

Lazear, Edward. "Agency, Earnings Profiles, Productivity, and Hours Restrictions." *American Economic Review* (1981): 606–620.

———. "Why Is There Mandatory Retirement?" *Journal of Political Economy* (1979): 1261–1284.

Loewenstein, George, and Nachum Sicherman. "Do Workers Prefer Increasing Wage Profiles?" *Journal of Labor Economics* 9 (1991): 67–84.

Medoff, J., and K. Abraham. "Experience, Performance, and Earnings." *Quarterly Journal of Economics* 94 (1980): 703–736.

Mincer, Jacob. "On-the-Job Training: Costs, Returns, and Some Implications." *Journal of Political Economy* 70 (Supplement 1962): 50–79.

Oi, Walter. "Labor as a Quasi-Fixed Factor." *Journal of Political Economy* (1962): 538–555.

Salop, S.C., and J. Salop. "Self-Selection and Turnover in the Labor Market." *Quarterly Journal of Economics* 90 (1976): 619–628.

Scitovsky, Tibor. *The Joyless Economy.* New York: Oxford University Press, 1976.

Spinnewyn, Frans. "Long Term Contracts and Income Redistribution." CORE Discussion Paper 8357, 1985.

Thaler, Richard, and Hal Shefrin. "An Economic Theory of Self-Control," *Journal of Political Economy* (1981): 392–406.

———, and ———. "A Self-Control Theory of Savings." *Economic Inquiry* (1987): 609–643.

Topel, Robert. "Wages Rise with Seniority," unpublished manuscript, University of Chicago, November 1987.

Index

matching law (*continued*)
and aversive process, 82; and conflicts
of preference, 68–70, 74, 77, 87;
defined, 65–67; in melioration theory,
247–250, 247n-248n, 252–254, **253;** and
moral sentiments, 277–282, 279n; and
perception of delay, 72; probability,
248n; and stability, 249–250
Mathews, A., 182
Mauro, B., 150n
maximization theory, 70; and personal
identity concept, 259
Mayer, Thomas, 314
Maynard Smith, J., 68
Mazur, J.E., 29, 66–67, 71, 98, 98n, 111,
127, 186, 247n, 258, 355
Meichenbaum, D.H., 159
Melikian, L., 149
melioration theory, 28, 235–263; and
addiction, 339–358; defined, 237–250;
vs. other theories of suboptimal
choice, 256–259; and pathologies of
distributed choice, 251–256
Mellitz, M., 181
Melzack, R., 81
memory: of anticipation, 219n; decay of,
and discount reversal, 96; investment
in, 229–231, Jost's first law of, 96, **97;**
utility from, 213–223, 224, 227,
228–234
mental accounting, 185, 293n; and addiction, 347; defined, 293–298; and
saving and self-control, 287–330
Messick, 226n
Metzner, R., 149
midrange interests, 86–87, 177, 183, 205
Milgrom, Paul, 274n
Mill, J.S., 7, 9, 60
Millar, A., 69
Miller, D.T., 153n, 219n, 226n
Miller, Nancy, 308
Mincer, Jacob, 378n
Mirer, Thad W., 309
Mischel, H.N., 159, 184
Mischel, Walter, 24–25, 24n, 27, 28, 47,
53, 53n, 59, 101, 112, 147–162, 184,
288
miser trait, 80, 233, 251
Mishkin, Fredrick, 140n, 316–318, 322
Mitchell, J., 202
Mobilia, Pamela, 361, 368

Modigliani, Franco, 287, 324
"molar maximization," 68
monetary policy, 42–43
Moore, B., 154
Moore, B.J., 23
Moore, M.J., 137
moral sentiments, 265–282
Morgenstern, O., 21
Motheral, S., 68, 70
motivation(al): -affective aspect of pain,
81–82; and close choices, 63n; conflict,
and discount function, 63, 69, 71,
73–74, 84; conflict, as intrapsychic
interests, 74–77; conflicts, as limited
warfare, 189–191, 206; effects, 4, 20n,
31; and personal rules, 178, 189–193;
and reversals of preference, 58; and
self-interest standard, 265; structure,
and addiction, 343–344
Mowrer, O.H., 111
Muellbauer, J., 236
multiple personality, 57; and self-
control, 178, 354
Munnell, Alicia, 303, 303n-304n, 304
Murphy, Kevin M., 62, 68, 251, 333,
335, 336, 356, 361–370
Murray, P., 112
myopia: and conflict or struggle, 142;
and democratic society, 49–50; vs.
melioration, 257; in political theory,
35; Tocqueville's theories and, 45–53;
and utility from memory and anticipation, 234

N

Nadelmann, E.A., 356
Najemy, J., 38n
Nalebuff, B., 39n
Narcissus trait, 80
National Longitudinal Survey (NLS), 311
Navarick, D.J., 69
Navon, D., 116
negotiations, 128
Nelson, P.S., 121
Neumann, J. von, 21
Neuringer, A., 65, 150n
Nisan, M., 53n
Nisbet, Charles T., 361
no-choice approach, 332–333, 356–357
noise relief study, 69